FAMILIES IN THE MILITARY SYSTEM

SAGE SERIES ON ARMED FORCES AND SOCIETY

INTER-UNIVERSITY SEMINAR ON ARMED FORCES AND SOCIETY

Morris Janowitz, *University of Chicago*
  Chairman and Series Editor

Charles C. Moskos, Jr., *Northwestern University*
  Associate Chairman and Series Editor

FAMILIES IN

THE MILITARY SYSTEM

PREPARED BY INTER-UNIVERSITY SEMINAR ON ARMED FORCES AND SOCIETY

Editors
Hamilton I. McCubbin
Barbara B. Dahl
Edna J. Hunter

 SAGE PUBLICATIONS   Beverly Hills / London

For information address:

SAGE PUBLICATIONS, INC.
275 South Beverly Drive
Beverly Hills, California 90212

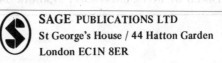

SAGE PUBLICATIONS LTD
St George's House / 44 Hatton Garden
London EC1N 8ER

Printed in the United States of America

Library of Congress Cataloging in Publication Data
Main entry under title:

Families in the military system.

(Sage series on armed forces and society)
Bibliography: p.
Includes index.
1. Soldiers—Family relationships. I. McCubbin,
Hamilton I. II. Dahl, Barbara B. III. Hunter,
Edna J.
U21.5.F35   355.1'35   75-44398
ISBN 0-8039-0667-6

FIRST PRINTING

CONTENTS

ACKNOWLEDGEMENTS

The editors are especially appreciative of the support given by their parent organization, the Naval Health Research Center, and its subsidiary, the Center for Prisoner of War Studies. Special thanks are due to CAPT E. Fisher Coil, MC, USN, Commanding Officer, Naval Health Research Center; CAPT David R. Ten Eyck, MC, USN, former Commanding Officer, Naval Health Research Center; Dr. Walter Wilkins, Scientific Director, Naval Health Research Center; and Dr. John A. Plag, Director, Center for Prisoner of War Studies. Additionally, the editors owe much to the Bureau of Medicine and Surgery, Department of the Navy, and the Office of the Surgeon General, Department of the Army; in particular, the individuals in those offices who encouraged our efforts: CDR Paul Nelson, MSC, USN, and COL Glen Williams, MSC, USA.

We also express our appreciation to our colleagues at the Center for Prisoner of War Studies who generously gave of their time to assist in the preparation of manuscripts: Ms. Susan Farish, Mr. Gary Lester, Ms. Carol Million, Ms. Beverly Ross, and Mr. Ken Ross.

Finally, we would like to express our gratitude to Ms. Fran Jackson, whose continuing efforts on behalf of the Center for Prisoner of War Studies made this volume possible; her patience and persistence in seeing that each manuscript was professionally prepared for publication helped to ease our load.

The conduct of this research and the preparation of this volume were supported by the Department of the Navy, Bureau of Medicine and Surgery, under Work Order Request Number 18-75-WR-0004, dated 1 July 1974, and by the Office of the Surgeon General, Department of the Army, under military Inter-Departmental Purchase Order Request Number 7501, dated 23 September 1974.

The opinions and assertions contained herein are the private ones of the writers and are not to be construed as official or as reflecting the views of the Department of the Navy, the Department of the Army, or the Department of the Air Force.

PREFACE

The research studies collected in this volume represent an overdue and welcome contribution to our understanding of armed forces and society. *Families in the Military System* not only advances knowledge of the military family—an important accomplishment in its own right—but also brings to the forefront a significant dimension of civil-military relations in the United States. In this sense, *Families in the Military System* is part and parcel of the new military sociology which is no longer content with an examination of military phenomena limited to active-duty personnel. And it is the holistic approach to armed forces and society which has led contemporary researchers to assess the public's evaluation of the military establishment and the uses to which it is put, to appraise reserve officer training on the college campus, to look at the impact of military spending on the national political economy, and to examine the societal implications of, earlier, the selective service system, and, currently, the all-volunteer force.

Yet the most obvious nexus of civil-military relations—the military family—has hitherto been relegated to the backwaters of social science investigation; this, despite the sheer demographic importance of the military family. In the mid-1970s, when the active-duty force seemed to be holding steady at slightly over two million persons, there were about one million wives and two million children in the military family. The salience of the military family takes added meaning in more tragic figures. It is estimated that close to 250,000 Americans suffered the loss of a close family member—husband, father, son, grandson, or brother—during the war in Vietnam. The studies assembled for this volume are broad in coverage yet rigorous in detail. They range from analyses of the military wife and adolescent to examinations of family dissolution and adjustment to retirement. It is in this context that *Families in the Military System* can be seen as redressing a major imbalance in both the sociology of the family and the sociology of the military.

The empirical findings of the research reported in this volume are best informed by a vantage which takes into account where the military family has been and where it appears to be going. Before World War II, the families of military officers were typically living encapsulated lives in a self-contained community. At the enlisted levels, the military was glaringly indifferent to family needs. In fact, excepting some senior noncoms, enlisted men were usually unmarried men who spent most of their time within the confines of the military post or adjacent sleazy districts in the model of *From Here to Eternity*. Indeed, prior to 1940 all enlisted men had to be bachelors at the time of their service entry. In World War II, millions of married men were recruited into the armed forces; except for allotment checks, however, most families of servicemen more or less fended for themselves.

Starting with the Cold War, the military began to take steps to deal with some of the practical problems faced by married personnel. Although differences in family ambience between the various services were—and still are—evident, an overarching array of on-base facilities was established or expanded to meet the needs of service families. These included medical care for dependents, on-post public schools, commissaries and post exchanges, and other commercial and recreational facilities. In the late 1960s, the services also began to institute various community and family agencies designed to increase further the range of services for family needs. With the advent of the all-volunteer force—and the concomitant elimination of the short-term draftee—the proportion of married enlisted personnel is on the increase. It is also probable that with the growing number of female service persons, the situation of the husband "dependent" will give yet another twist to the forms of the military family.

In one manner of thinking, the military's belated recognition of family needs seems to augur parallels with civilian society. From another perspective, however, we could also expect a diminishment of ties with civilian influences as family needs are increasingly met by family-service programs within the format of the armed forces. Yet countervailing trends are also evident. The erosion of military community benefits—a state of affairs not appreciated in the public at large—is a prime cause for much consternation among career military personnel and their families. At the same time, it is significant that the distinguishing features of the military family—prolonged father absence and frequent geographical mobility—are becoming more apparent in the civilian family as well. Thus, in manifold and not always consistent ways, we encounter indications of both convergence and divergence between military and civilian families.

The core reality is that *both* the family and the military are institutions in transition. *Families in the Military System* is about the intersection of two changing institutions. The Inter-University Seminar on Armed Forces and Society is pleased to present this volume in its series of publications.

Charles C. Moskos, Jr.

FOREWORD

The senior staff of the Family Studies Branch of the Center for Prisoners of War Studies has rendered an important contribution in bringing together under one cover a sample of the researches on families within the military system. The editors have drawn selectively in this initial symposium from a pool of more than 150 researches, the scope of which is treated in a most useful concluding overview chapter by the editors entitled, "Research on the Military: A Review."

The researches selected for publication in *Families in the Military System* highlight the relationships of family and the military, primarily of married careerists rather than of single draftees or short-term enlisted men who make up the large majority of wartime military personnel. My own research of the phenomenon of war separation and reunion in World War II (Hill, 1949), which is generously cited in this symposium, sampled almost entirely civilian families where the husband/father had been drafted or had enlisted in advance in order to select his branch of service. Few families in that research became a part of military communities, and virtually none would have been supportive of long-term military careers for their men. They were seen, rather, as being on temporary loan to the military with full expectations of re-entering their civilian occupations and settling back into their civilian communities after completing their military service. *Families in the Military System,* in sharp contrast, focuses on the conflicts and accommodations of the families of the professional elite who are the most integrated into the all-encompassing mission of the military system. There is at least a temporary gain in such a strategy of selection, since the New Military may be made up increasingly of married professional soldiers committed to long-term careers of twenty years or more.

The researches highlighted in this symposium illuminate the points of stress and strain between families and the military as separate systems. The military seeks to make the family instrumental to its mission of developing and maintaining an effective combat-ready body of fighting men, mobile enough to be deployed anywhere in the world when needed. Wives and children of married personnel, from the perspective of the military, should be socialized to subordinate their individual needs and desires to the "good of the service" and to minimize any family claims on the time and presence of the husband/father. The wife of a career military man might profitably pursue educational activities and perform voluntary services in the military community but should definitely not embark on an independent occupational career incompatible with her responsibilities as mother and military wife. Children should observe the rules of the military community lest the reputation of the military father be tarnished and interfere with his career. The family should be a morale builder for the military man, providing love and affection and a minimum of problems to distract him from his central task of serving the "Cause."

A hypothesis only hinted in this treatise is that without more of a quid pro quo, the families of married professional soldiers may defeat the best plans of the military system. Future research may show that, at present, the military has little understanding of the stubborn resistance that families can build up to sabotage what some might consider to be unrealistic military expectations.

Families in wartime have sacrificed and accommodated to the military out of patriotism, if the war was a "popular" war; but in peacetime and in policing type conflicts, families are more restive, assessing costs and benefits of life in the military. The research on military families reported in this treatise was conducted in just such a period of assessing the legitimacy of the military's claims on its members. What other system requires the husband/father to absent himself from his home responsibilities for indefinite periods of time at high risk to his life and health, and to relocate his family midyear from one base to another without notice? What other system subjects its personnel to what often is an involuntary retirement too late to begin a new career with any likelihood of success?

The military system would have less trouble if it could restrict membership to celibates whose only family responsibilities were filial obligations to parents. But the new military elite of careerists is very much married (93% of officers, and 80% of career enlisted men in senior grades). Completed family size of these careerists includes 3.75 children who are born and reared into adolescence coterminous with the twenty years of the professional soldier's career. There is no escaping the necessity for the military system to cope with the claims of these families on their military members for something more than their paychecks. Indeed, the military of today does recognize the family's claim on compensatory returns for dismembering the family structure so frequently and dispassionately. There are now available a host of substitutive services as well as more lenient policies of leaves and discharges for hardship reasons.

Families in the Military System samples the points of strain between families and the military with descriptive accounts of the limitations and constraints imposed on the military wife, the relative normality of adolescents growing up in military settings, the mixed effects of geographic mobility on academic and social achievements of children, and the unexpected discovery that the breakup of social networks as a consequence of residential relocation is more disruptive for the family than the prolonged absence of the father on military assignment. There are pluses as well as minuses in identity formation and personality growth from growing up in military settings, unstable and mobile though the military life might be. Children survive quite well so long as the parents' marriage appears congenial and the mother defines periodic relocation as a necessary contribution of the family to the father's advancement in his career.

Readers will be informed by this treatise not only about the realities of living within the military community and the semi-isolation of displaced military families living off the base in civilian communities, but also about several enlightening comparisons made with families in the general population. Compared with the general population, career families in the military are better educated (both wives and husbands), more traveled, more informed about services to which they are entitled, more active in voluntary organizations, and much more mobile (60% moving annually compared with 20% in the general population). Although 75 percent of families have experienced one or more prolonged periods of father absence, a smaller proportion of career officers are in the divorced status than men in the general population. A selective process may be under way that recruits and socializes families into the military, providing them with the values and the commitment to ride out the greater stresses experienced over their careers.

Social scientists will find that a number of the investigators have drawn on theories generated from research on civilians to explain and predict family behaviors in the specific setting of the military. For example, theories of anomie and alienation resulting from geographic and social mobility are examined in the military setting, where frequent relocation is common. These theories have also proved useful in explaining the rootlessness and status deprivation which families experience when the military father finds himself retired in his late forties, too early to quit work entirely, yet often too old to launch a successful second career. Socialization and modeling theories are also examined for yield in the confusing situation of prolonged military separations to explain the diffusion of gender identity in military children. This is especially clear in the special case of the more prolonged absences of prisoners of war. Indeed, the remarkable longitudinal war separation and reunion research of the Center for Prisoner of War Studies has utilized a variety of theories to organize and explain its findings on the impacts which incarceration of Vietnam prisoners of war has had on their stateside families over the years of separation. Drawing also on findings from the trauma of concentration camps in Europe and from the experiences in captivity in Korea, the CPWS researchers have sensitively drawn on my family crisis theory to account for adjustment to separation and for the course of adjustment to the return of the father and his reintegration into meaningful family roles.

The CPWS longitudinal design has permitted distinctions between short-term and long-term adjustments by children and their parents. The quality of this research would compare favorably in its methodological and theoretical sophistication with the best of contemporary research on civilian families and augurs well for future publications from the CPWS.

The overview of military family research presented in the concluding chapter suggests that most of this research has been oriented to the sensitive points of interface between the family and the military system:

1) Family Mobility (9 reports)
2) Child Adjustment and Development (19 reports)
3) Family Adjustment to Separation (38 reports)
4) Family Reunion and Reintegration (20 reports)
5) Family Adjustment to Loss and Bereavement (25 reports)
6) Families in Transition Back to Civilian Life (21 reports)
7) Services to Families Under Stress (27 reports)

These researches render the family more salient to the policy makers in the military who read them and might be termed policy-oriented research since they are heavy on family impacts of military policies or nonpolicies. But the military might also ask of family researchers what the impact of the family is on the performance of military personnel. How is the family involved in the decision to continue in a military career or to withdraw into a different and possibly less stressful environment? The researches in section 6 above. Families in Transition Back to Civilian Life, treat the issues of retirement and entering second civilian careers. But what family factors lead junior servicemen and officers to quit the military in the 3-8 year period after the services had made a substantial investment in training them? It can be hypothesized that family pressures play a big role in these career choices, even if at some earlier point a military career was seriously considered. Allied research questions of high relevance to military policy makers might include:

1) How does satisfaction with the military career of the husband and wife relate to satisfaction with marriage and parenthood in the military setting?
2) How do children and adolescents of military families cope with the antimilitary climate among their peers from civilian families and in civilian school settings?
3) What are the marriage and family problems of enlisted women making careers in the military?
4) What restrictions does the New Military place on the sex conduct of enlisted women, on fraternization across gender lines, on selection of marriage partners, and on becoming mothers? How are these restrictions related to the decision to withdraw early from military careers?

The research on the military to date, and this volume in particular, has understandably not addressed itself to several issues of theoretical concern to family investigators in more academic settings. For example, the academicians might ask of military family researchers: How do families form in the military, i.e., what is the process of marital selection to assure that the wife of a career military man fits into the system? What is the allocation of tasks and duties within the household in early marriage and after children come? How are the father's home assignments of househusbandry and child care, and his spousal responsibilities, handled during his frequent absences? What outlets are there for meeting the sex needs and companionship needs of the military wife? What styles of communication and problem-solving characterize husband-wife and father-child interactions in military families? Is there more intergenerational continuity than rejection of the military career by adolescents and young adults, as there seems to be of the paternal career in civilian families? How does satisfaction with marriage over the family life cycle among military couples compare with civilian couples? The latter appear to follow a predictable curvilinear pattern: high satisfaction in early marriage, declining over the burdened years of child rearing, and rebounding in the postparental period?

Future research on some of these issues may be stimulated by reading this volume. Perhaps such research will suggest new services and concessions for families that will make military careers of men and women more compatible with the pressing mission of their families. Perhaps the two institutions may yet learn to coexist to achieve a level of collaboration that is more rewarding than what is seen by some as the present state of antagonistic cooperation.

Reuben Hill
Regents' Professor of Family Sociology
University of Minnesota

I

THE MILITARY FAMILY

Chapter 1

A STUDY OF THE WIFE OF THE ARMY OFFICER:

HER ACADEMIC AND CAREER PREPARATIONS,

HER CURRENT EMPLOYMENT AND VOLUNTEER SERVICES

E L I Z A B E T H M. F I N L A Y S O N

This chapter explores the participation of the Army officer's wife in the areas of education, volunteer services, and employment on the premise that there are certain unique characteristics of the military environment which possibly influence and modify that participation. To begin with, it seems appropriate to define some of these characteristics of the military way of life to help one understand the climate in which the officer's wife is most apt to function. First of all, it is a mobile life. Army tours seldom exceed three years; many are considerably shorter; "home" for the army family may be a set of government quarters or a rented apartment; the community may be military or civilian; the zip code may be east or west; and, with luck, there may be an overseas tour or two. The life is likely to be beset with prolonged separations and often threatened by the possibility or the fact of hazardous duty for the officer-husband/ father.

It is a life where one identifies, it is hoped, with the military family; a life which requires continuous adaptation and "instant involvement" in a community, seemingly without geographical boundaries, which is intended to replace the grass roots of a hometown and to offer security and stability for parents and children alike. Close ties with the extended family of grandparents, aunts, uncles, and cousins are seldom possible for the highly mobile nuclear military family.

It is a life of constant change. In general, for the military man, who on each new move fills a job for which he has been preselected, there is basic job continuity in the move; however, no such path is paved for the military wife and child. Aside from the excitement and anticipation with which one generally

AUTHOR'S NOTE: This chapter is an adaptation of Finlayson, E. "A Study of the Wife of the Army Officer: Her Academic and Career Preparation, Her Current Employment and Volunteer Services," an unpublished doctoral dissertation prepared for George Washington University, 1969.

views a new assignment, it is seldom easy to move from a place that one has learned to call "home." The wife, too, is more apt to be aware of, or concerned for, the effect of the move upon the children in the family.

The life is founded on customs, traditions, and regulations—and no member of the family can completely escape them. For the officer's wife, it is a life of many roles. To her husband she is a wife. To her children she is a mother; during separations, she is both mother and father. To the Army she is a dependent, and her privileges and responsibilities are predetermined to a great extent by her husband's rank and assignment. To her civilian neighbors she represents the military, and, when on foreign soil, she is a diplomat—a representative of the United States. She is expected to balance these roles with commitment, grace, and finesse. Her identity, however, is not totally determined by the multiple roles she assumes as an army wife. Her own individuality cannot be discounted. It will determine to what extent she will accept, or rebel; to what extent army life will mean opportunity, or frustration; to what extent she will serve, or be served; to what degree she will be dependent, or independent; to what extent she will use and develop her talents and skills, or let them atrophy.

Military literature concerned with the army dependent contends that the role of the army officer's wife is not only necessary, honorable, and good, but also the epitome of womanhood; her ability to cope with the new and unexpected is unsurpassed; and, "always she complements the high calling of her husband" (Kinzer and Leach, 1966). There appears to be but one study on the army wife per se to either support or negate these claims. Also, the degree to which she suppresses her own wishes and aspirations to adopt the role of the army wife has not been fully explored.

THE REVIEW OF LITERATURE AND RELATED RESEARCH

Many of the societal changes which have taken place since World War II have resulted in a changing concept of the role of the American woman, and the army wife is not isolated from this change but shares in it. "The woman's place is in the home" is an outdated cliché. Technological advances have made obsolete many of the homemaking tasks which once consumed the time and talents of women. Women live longer today and often look for new and challenging outlets to make added years more meaningful. Those who had prepared for careers before they married often seek opportunities to utilize that preparation— through either paid employment or volunteer services. Some enter the labor force primarily for financial reasons—the constantly climbing cost of living and of sending children through college, plus a self-imposed demand for a higher standard of living. Legislation enacted during the past decade which prohibits discrimination because of age or sex have opened many doors for women which in the past, for all intents and purposes, have been closed to them.

This upward mobility of the wife in volunteer or paid positions often necessitates additional education and/or training. Women of all ages are going back to school, with new programs being geared to meet their specific educational needs. At the same time, there continues to be a need for volunteers; volunteer organizations are "big business," with thousands of woman-hours contributed yearly to serving others.

Two early historical accounts of life as an army wife, both written by officers' wives during the latter half of the nineteenth century, illustrate the significance or insignificance of the wife and family in the frontier Army (Custer, 1961; Summerhayes, 1908). Both women note in their fascinating autobiographies that, in the book of army regulations, wives are not rated except as camp followers over whom the commanding officer has complete control, with power to put them off the reservation or detain them as he chooses.

Military life, in the days of which Custer and Summerhayes wrote (the 1870s and 1880s), involved incessant changing of stations and a preoccupation with basic physical needs and preempted any time or need for added diversions; the family was considered a diversion. The volunteer helpmate was much in evidence in those early accounts. The officer's wife served as nurse, seamstress, counselor, confidante, hostess, and friend of those in need, whether they were officers, enlisted personnel, wives or children, servants, regimental animals, or personal pets! Organized volunteer services were an innovation of the future, but the foundations were laid during those early frontier days.

Until the close of World War II, there is a paucity of literature related to the army dependent. At that time, a number of publications appeared which directed themselves almost exclusively to the responsibilities and social obligations of the military. Prior to World War II a large percentage of career army officers were graduates of the service Academies. Promotions were slow in coming, but esprit de corps, inbred at the Academies, was high. At the end of World War II thousands of reserve officers were integrated into the regular Army. Their wives, who heretofore had been seen as mere adjuncts to the system during the war years, found themselves to be wives of career officers and part of a military "family." Understandably, many of these wives (as well as the wives of Academy graduates) were in need of some guidelines that would aid them in making a satisfactory and proper adjustment to army life. In spite of that need, only one such book made its appearance during the 1940s. Standing alone on the shelves of army libraries around the world, Nancy Shea's *The Army Wife* became the unofficial Bible. Many a West Point graduate reputedly presented his bride with a copy of the publication. From this rather formidable text she gleaned bits of wisdom as to what was expected of her, personally, as the wife of the military officer.

The portrayal of the Army officer's wife as one who "complements the high calling of her husband" persisted throughout the post-World War II literature. She was variously identified as the "diplomat without portfolio" . . . who "never complains when she has to move," . . . who found the "only tragedy that upsets her is separation from her husband." The wife was characterized by Shea (1954) as "an independent dependent" who, at the same time, "finds satisfaction and fulfillment in her home." Kinzer and Leach (1966) describe the military wife as one who "rears her family, generally, under conditions which would seem impossible to her civilian sisters" . . . accomplishing all "as a good soldier, whose sense of Duty, Honor and Country are those of the Army itself. In these things she will find enough of glamour, interest, satisfaction, life" (*The Officer's Guide*, 1942).

In a 1966 edition of *The Army Wife* we read, "The Army understands that if the wife is informed, and knows the score about her husband's work, she will have a positive attitude toward the Army and be a happier and more helpful wife. . . . The Army wife has definite responsibilities, and if she carries them out, she lives a full and worthwhile life, and is of real value to her husband. Her life in the Army can be happy and rewarding" (Shea, 1966).

Of all the military newspapers, magazines, and periodicals which carry an occasional article of interest to the military wife (including *U.S. Lady,* published primarily for the service wife), few carry articles that are not military-oriented; most focus primarily on military etiquette, wives' clubs activities, military pay and promotions, transfers, overseas duty, military entertainment, and distaff "personalities"—usually those who have achieved outstanding records as volunteers.

Guidebooks for the service wife published in the last decade begin to reflect the changing philosophy concerning women's role in today's world. As early as 1956 are found references to employment as acceptable, and continuing education as a commendable outside activity for the army wife—under certain circumstances. The data are not objective, but tend to suggest what may be legitimate behavior patterns for the military wife, such as going back to school (Land and Glines, 1956).

The 1966 *Officer's Guide* took an indirect approach to the need for training or education of the officer's wife. In discussing family security and the possibility of wife becoming widow, the authors pose the question, "Is the wife qualified to be self-supporting through her own efforts . . . or would she need training to resume a former vocation or undertake a new one?" (Reynolds, 1966). Nowhere in the guide was it suggested that a wife might consider updating her education or training *before* becoming a widow. Other references and guides make no mention of education for the army wife.

Although authors refer to the legitimate role of the army wife to serve as a volunteer, not as a social outlet but as an inherent responsibility, the role of the wife as a wage earner has not received as strong endorsements. In reviewing the advice and suggestions which authors present to service wives regarding employment, one sees that they are reflecting some degree of caution but also general acceptance. Aside from regulations which place limitations upon the hiring of military dependents for government employment, there is no "official" Army stand on the employed wife.

Land and Glines in 1956 questioned the traditional concept of the military wife: "Although it goes without saying that woman's first duty is to her home, it is old fashioned to assume that her place is there and nowhere else." However, these authors also pointed out the realistic covert obstacles to wives' employment: (a) employers shy away from hiring anyone who isn't going to be permanent, which is quite understandable; (b) a job may be hard to get because a wife's particular capabilities may not fit what the market—on a small base or in a small town—has to offer; and (c) the wishes of her husband's Commanding Officer must be taken into consideration.

In discussing job possibilities both on and off the military reservation, Land and Glines (1956) observed that "teachers' certificates are the next best thing to having built-in jobs; the fact that teachers are almost as much in demand as nurses means that job possibilities are excellent on base or off." Murphy and Parker (1966) also comment on the type of skills which a mobile wife would probably find of greatest value in looking for employment. With the exception of the nursing and teaching professions, they favor office and trade or service skills. To those without such skills, they recommend training or schooling and specifically refer to the possibility of finding suitable courses through the Education Center on the base.

The Officer's Guide and most of the books written for the service wife subscribe to the image of the army wife as one who *accepts* her army responsibilities and duties. Perhaps those who write of the "typical" army wife might be overlooking the basic fact that many, many *officers* are not career-minded, and both husband and wife may be more inclined to view the Army not as a *way* of life but as an *interruption* of it. The feelings of the wife of the Junior Officer cannot be ignored, for she, too, is an army wife, and she outnumbers the wives of Senior Officers two to one. An unpublished report on the career attitudes of wives of junior officers was found that was directly concerned with the officer's wife. The purpose of the study, conducted in 1963 by the Department of the Army, was "to ascertain the possible areas wherein the wife of the Junior Officer could exercise influence in her husband's choice of a career; and to isolate those areas which might by a change or reemphasis of programs cause her to become more favorable to an army career" (U.S. Army, 1963). Actually, the findings of this study indicated that only a small percentage of Junior Officers and their wives are career-minded; most view their army life as temporary.

In concluding this review of the literature, we must point out that only

Murphy and Parker (1966) approached the army wife as one who does not necessarily come to the Army fully committed to it. It is unrealistic to counsel all wives to "try and like the idea that your husband is in the Army and a public servant," and, "if you don't [like the idea] then be a good actress and pretend that you do" (Shea, 1954). To the young wife who is often inclined to feel that her husband's military service is temporary, and even unwelcome, such advice can only serve to increase any animosity which might already exist. Far better is the approach of Murphy and Parker (1966), who counsel, "but most of all, come to know yourself. For to be a successful wife, and a successful service wife, you must be yourself. . . . Be certain always that the beliefs and values which develop are truly yours, that they make of you a better person, not a weak imitation of someone else or a formless combination of other people's standards."

Affirmative action programs and the women's liberation movement are helping more women to accept the idea that a woman can attain status and self-worth independently of the status (and rank) of her husband.

RESEARCH PROCEDURES

This research is a descriptive study of the participation of wives of active-duty United States Army officers in the areas of education, volunteer services, and employment.

The population for this study is limited to the wives of the approximately 92,000 active-duty United States Army officers who, at the time of the study, were assigned to duty within the limits of the Continental United States (CONUS). A stratified random sample of eleven hundred married Army officers was selected which included 100 General officers, 500 Field Grade officers, and 500 Company Grade officers.

The eight-page questionnaire was designed with four parts, and constructed to determine the extent of education attained by the army wife, and selected factors pertaining to the current use of that education through volunteer services and employment. The concluding question of each section of the questionnaire offered the respondent an opportunity to state freely how she felt her army affiliation had influenced her participation as a student, volunteer, and worker.

The questionnaire was mailed to a total of 1000 wives. One hundred wives were eliminated from the sample because of an error in the selection or because they could not be contacted. (It should be noted that a distinguishing characteristic of the population, its mobility, resulted in considerable difficulty in making contact with many of the wives chosen for the study.) Seven hundred and fifty-three wives (75.3%) responded to the questionnaire. This total represented a 57 percent return from wives of General officers, 77 percent return from wives of Field Grade officers, and 77.6 percent return from wives of Company Grade officers (rank given on the original list provided by the Army). Promotions during the gathering of the data had had an unpredicted effect upon the actual numbers in each rank by the time the questionnaires were returned. Although the percentage of Field Grade officers' wives who answered the questionnaire was the same as the percentage of Company Grade officers' wives, there was a final count of 403 wives of Field Grade officers in the study as compared to only 292 wives of Company Grade officers.

CURRENT RESIDENCE

Nearly 40 percent of those responding to the questionnaire lived on a military post. Of the 60 percent who lived off the post in a civilian environment, nearly two-thirds lived in suburban communities. Only when the sponsor was of General rank did more families live on the post than off; even then, the difference was slight. Although military housing was sometimes dependent upon the job assignment of the husband, it was more often the availability of housing at that time that determined whether a family lived on post or off.

The population under study was highly mobile; 56 percent had been at their present residence less than a full year, with almost half of that number having moved within the preceding three months. Data from this study also showed that mobility is to some degree related to rank, with Company Grade officers rotating more often than either Field Grade or General officers. School and training programs and overseas or nonaccompanied tours are responsible for the more frequent moves of army officers, particularly those in the lower ranks (see Table 1).

EDUCATION AND CAREER PREPARATION

One of the objectives of this study was to determine the educational and career preparation of the Army officer's wife, to identify factors which the officer's wife relates as influential in her decision to seek or not to seek further education, and to identify the problems the officer's wife says she encounters as she attempts to continue her education.

TABLE 1

CURRENT RESIDENCE AND RANK OF HUSBAND

Residence	Company Grade		Field Grade		General		TOTAL	
	No.	%	No.	%	No.	%	No.	%
On post	124	43	142	35	32	55	298	40
Off post	168	57	261	65	26	45	455	60
TOTAL	292	100	403	100	58	100	753	100
Months in Residence								
3 mo. or less	108	37	90	22	11	19	209	27.7
Between 3-12 mo.	102	35	98	25	14	24	214	28.4
Over 1 year	82	28	215	53	33	57	330	43.9
TOTAL	292	100	403	100	58	100	753	100.0

Of those wives responding to this survey, 39.8 percent were college graduates and 5.4 percent had earned advanced degrees. The officers whose wives are included in this study are even more highly educated—90 percent had earned at least the baccalaureate degree. There is no significant correlation between the level of education of the wife and that of the husband, with the single exception of the wife with an advanced degree, who was usually found to be married to an officer who had at least a baccalaureate degree. Only 3 percent of the wives held a more advanced degree than did their husbands (see Table 2).

Of the 613 women, 81 percent in the study had enrolled in some type of formal educational program beyond high school. Three-fourths (74%) attended four-year institutions. One hundred and thirty-five women enrolled in institutions specializing in occupational programs—nursing, business or secretarial, technical, or trade. Thirty attended junior or community Colleges, fifteen transferring later to four-year institutions. Many who had enrolled as degree students had not completed their studies. Of all the wives included in the study, the largest number were enrolled in business school programs, many on the high school level only. Education was the most popular major field on the college level.

TABLE 2

DEGREES EARNED BY HUSBAND AND WIFE

Type of Degree	N	AD/RN*	B	2B	M	2M	Ph.D/ Ed.D	Prof	No. of Holding Husbands Degree
			No. of Wives Holding Degree						
None	57	5	13	0	1	0	0	0	76
AD or RN	1	0	1	0	1	0	0	0	3
Bachelors	204	44	145	2	8	0	2	0	405
Two Bachelors	7	2	6	0	1	0	0	0	16
Masters	69	13	55	0	11	0	0	0	148
Two Masters	6	1	3	0	1	0	0	0	11
Ph.D. or Ed.D.	8	2	3	0	5	0	0	0	18
Other Professional Degrees	21	9	21	2	9	0	0	2	64
TOTAL	373	76	247	4	37	0	2	2	741

*Associate Degree and Registered Nurse

Over 300 women had enrolled in educational programs after they married. Several wives in the study commented that their husbands' educations had influenced them in their wish to continue their own educations. Some expressed a desire to keep up with the couples with whom they socialized, others to keep up with their husbands. To those who continued their educations, many types of programs were attractive—3 women were in high school programs, 140 chose to work for college credit, 127 chose noncredit (such as continuing education) programs, and 26 chose occupational courses. Of those persons who had enrolled in credit programs, 37 pursued majors similar to those started prior to their marriage, 28 were in related areas, and 34 changed to completely new areas of study. Further examination of the data revealed that, in almost all instances where a decided change was made, the individual had a specific job goal that motivated the change. Of the 20 who elected professional training, the majority were nurses who were updating their training. Nearly one-half of the 91 who enrolled in undergraduate credit courses earned more than a semester's credit; five completed requirements for the Associate of Arts degree, and nineteen wives earned a Bachelor's degree. Over a third of the 57 enrolled in graduate programs did as well, with 23 earning one or more graduate degrees.

Over a third (36%) of these women stated that the reason they were enrolled in an educational program after they had married was for intellectual stimulation and personal growth. For 88 (77%) of the 114 wives, this was their only reason for enrolling. The rest were motivated by more utilitarian reasons, such as preparation for employment, updating skills, etc. The expressed need to be prepared for employment *in the event of the death of the husband* is one that is likely to be shared more by service wives than by wives in general. Sixty-two of the wives in this study had husbands serving in Vietnam, others knew that a hardship tour for their husbands in the not too distant future was very likely to occur. This concern was vividly expressed by one young wife of a Captain: "As an army wife there are many times when we are in complete charge of home and family so I also feel I should prepare myself for a profession in case I am thrust into the role of sole bread winner. I do not believe this attitude would be as prevalent were I a civilian [wife] though perhaps it well should be."

It was surprising that only a small number were increasing their competency for volunteer services, since several national organizations which depend heavily on volunteer personnel offer and require such training. And, as subsequent data will show, many army wives are active volunteer workers in such organizations as scouting, the American Red Cross, and Army Community Services. Over half of the wives in this study did not feel that they had completed the formal education which they needed or wanted. Others related that while they felt no need for more formal education per se, they intended to continue in programs of self-education. Almost 30% were not interested in any further education, and, of course, others were undecided. The responses would indicate that the nation-wide interest in continuing education was shared by the majority of the wives in this study.

The study further showed that the interest of this population in additional education decreased with the age of respondent. Even so, over one-third (36%) of those women in the 45 and above age group expressed a desire to continue in some kind of educational experience. This figure contrasts to the approximately two-thirds of the wives under 35 who would like more education. Educational level alone did not appear to influence the desire for additional education; over 50 percent of the wives of all educational levels indicated that they would like more education. Nationally, it has often been observed that the more highly educated, the more apt one is to participate in continuing education programs. However, the educational level of the respondent in this study seemed to be related to the reason for an interest in additional education. Those working toward meeting certification and licensing requirements, for example, were more often those wives who had previously earned degrees; the greatest percentage of wives working for a degree were those who had already earned some college credits.

Equally significant to this study were the reasons cited by those wives who had expressed an interest in additional education but who were not currently pursuing some course of study. As many as 73 persons gave some reason *directly* related to their military association for not presently being enrolled (see Table 3). This is not to imply that army life *consistently* presents obstacles to the achievement of one's goals; this inquiry was directed toward *present* enrollment, in the present location, under present circumstances. Those reasons which were "military related" were: (1) husband in Vietnam, I feel the children need me more now; (2) school is not available at present assignment (most often the comment of a student working toward a degree; one who had exhausted the number of correspondence, elective, or transfer credits allowed); and (3) recent relocation or transfer, not settled enough to look for schools, find time to study.

It would also be presumptuous to assume that all who indicated they wanted more education had any definite plan. This was especially evident in the remarks of 37 of the wives, who, in effect, said, "Interested? Yes. Motivated? No." When asked for specific *plans* for the future, as differentiated from aspirations, 388 wives did not answer, had no plans, or indicated some indecision. On the other hand, the goals of finishing one's degree requirements, of increasing employment

TABLE 3

REASONS WHY WIVES INTERESTED IN ADDITIONAL EDUCATION NOT CURRENTLY ENROLLED

Reason	Frequency
Pregnancy or young children in family	113
Family and home responsibilities	79
Reasons related to Army life: husband in VN, lack of schools in area, recent transfer, etc.	73
Expense	39
Employed	38
Own attitude: age, lack of motivation, need, goal, real interest	37
Too busy	35
Commitments outside the home	19
Family attitude, conflicts, difficulties	13
Personal health	10

potential, of meeting certification and licensing requirements, appeared to be quite real for many others. Employment preparation continues to be a primary goal in planning for the future. The oft-repeated wish to *complete* a degree requirement would indicate that there is an added incentive resulting from having "one foot in the door" which sufficiently motivates one to strive to reach a previously established or partially completed goal.

ARMY AFFILIATION AND EDUCATION

Respondents were given the opportunity to comment specifically on whether they felt their Army affiliation had influenced in any way their own participation in the activities covered in this study—education, volunteer services, employment. Typical of both the positive and the negative comments on education were the following comments:

Army life offers intellectual stimulation by the very caliber of people one must meet and communicate with. I find it necessary to keep current in all subjects, particularly those of a political, economic, and military nature.

This year's work with ACS [Army Community Service] has suddenly made me dissatisfied with myself. . . . How much more satisfying it could be if I were properly educated.

I finished my master's degree in spite of the army and four moves during my work on it. . . . It has made further education and employment virtually impossible.

It is difficult to work toward a degree due to frequent moves and residence requirements of graduate schools.

The data from this study support the claim that a sizable number of wives have a genuine interest in their own education, and, in spite of the difficulties, many wives are actively engaged in continuing their formal education. While this study focuses on the formal education and career background of the army officer's wife, a preponderance of remarks are addressed to a conviction that travel is the greatest educational opportunity afforded the army wife and family. Because the following comments are directed specifically at travel as an educational opportunity for the army wife, they are included here:

Foreign duty has stimulated a great interest in people, their customs, and history. Travel in the United States has increased my appreciation of my own heritage as well as given me a broader outlook on its people, their problems and desires. I have fewer prejudices than I had had with a small town background.

The constant change and moving give me the challenge I personally need to keep growing and learning . . . the Army has strengthened my belief that one's education never really ends.

VOLUNTEER SERVICE

The literature portrays the military wife as one who accepts without question her responsibilities as a volunteer in the civilian and/or military community in which she resides. Do the data in this survey support that claim? Is the extent of a wife's participation influenced in any way by the fact that she is a military wife, or by whether she resides on a military reservation or in a civilian community? (Data are limited to "current" volunteer participation—that of the past twelve months—thus reducing to some degree the possibility of distortion in recall.)

The data indicated that 45 percent of the wives in this survey were volunteers. Almost half of this number had volunteered in two or more activities during the year. The percentage of those persons living on military installations who worked as volunteers was greater than that of those living in civilian communities. Over half of the wives (55%) residing on the post participated in both on- and off-post activities. In contrast, only 40 percent of the wives residing in civilian communities were participating as volunteers.

The location of the post—its proximity to a neighboring city or town—did not appear to be a factor in degree of participation. The size or type of community, however, was of significance: suburbanites were more apt to volunteer than were those who lived in urban, small town, or rural areas. Those persons living on a post or in suburbia were also the ones most likely to participate in several different activities (see Table 4). The influence of on-post or off-post residence on the wife was also reflected in her choice of volunteer programs. Although only 40 percent of the wives lived on post, 60 percent of all volunteer services were provided on military installations. Of those wives living in the civilian community, nearly twice as many were working in educational and youth programs as in any other type of activity; wives and mothers living off post were more likely to volunteer to serve in some way in educational and youth programs in which their own children participated. On-post wives were particularly active in women's cultural, social, and recreational programs. Additionally, many wives living in civilian communities volunteer to serve organizations in both the army and civilian community; there appears to be personal identification with both the civilian neighborhood and the Army itself. The army wife living on post is less likely to identify with the neighboring civilian community;

TABLE 4

PLACE OF RESIDENCE, EMPLOYMENT, AND VOLUNTEER SERVICES

Residence	Employment			Volunteer Services		
	Percent Full Time	Percent Part Time	Percent Employed	Percent 1-2	Percent 3+	Total Percent
On Post						
Near City	6.2	6.2	12.4	44	11	55
Near Town	7.0	5.5	12.5	43	11	54
Off Post						
Urban	13.6	13.6	27.2	35	1	36
Suburban	9	11.7	20.7	35	9	44
Small town, rural	13.5	3.0	16.5	26	5	31
TOTAL						
On Post				44	11	55
Off Post				33	7	40
Total				37	8	45

her own elementary schoolchildren are more likely to be attending schools, Scout Clubs, etc., on the post.

There is a positive relationship between volunteer participation and the rank of the sponsor (see Table 5). Thirty percent of the Company Grade wives represented in this study indicated current volunteer activity, as did 53 percent of the Field Grade wives and 74 percent of the Generals' wives. This finding gains significance when considered in relationship to their ages, their status in the military, and their social and family responsibilities. Company Grade wives were younger; data support a logical assumption that there are more pre-schoolers in the families of younger parents. Activities and responsibilities outside the home were naturally curtailed. Comments received from the wives of General officers throw some light on the relatively larger percentage of Generals' wives who were volunteers. "A Commanding General's wife is very involved." "Volunteer service is *now* not a matter of choice but of what needs to be done on the post." "The demands made upon the wife of a senior officer cannot be ignored." Volunteer work may be seen as a responsibility commensurate with the wife's status as the General's wife.

The number of children in the family also appears to affect the wife's involvement as a volunteer. On the basis of the data obtained, the following observations are in order:

1. Those persons showing the greatest volunteer participation (59%) were the mothers who had school-age children only—no preschoolers.

2. In the civilian community, the greatest volunteer participation was in educational and youth organizations. Data in Table 6 show more volunteering by women with three and four children than by women with no children or with only one or two. *More* children mean *more* PTAs, Sunday schools, and scouting activities.

3. Only 32 percent of wives with no dependents were volunteers, compared to 48 percent of those with dependents.

4. As expected, the percentage of mothers who were volunteers was the least for those who had preschool children (35%).

Who amongst the army wives in this study were able to put to good use their professional skills in volunteer activities? Twenty-one were nurses, 15 were teachers, six had clerical training, 3 were librarians, and 3 others were social workers; 2 were religious education majors. A bookkeeper, a recreation worker, a professional pianist, a beautician, a dietician, a speech therapist, and a professional model were others. In addition, there were many women in this study with academic backgrounds in liberal arts who felt that their contribution as volunteers was greater because of the general educational background which they brought to their work.

While less than 14 percent of the wives were making use of their formal academic preparation in their work as volunteers, the rest were not, for the most part, untrained workers. Almost 50 percent had received some pretraining or on-the-job training. About a third were trained in advance, either by the institution in which they would be working (such as a hospital) or the organization which they represented (such as the Red Cross). Many such groups have quite stringent requirements for their volunteers. Approximately 15 percent of the volunteers had some previous work, avocational, or volunteer experience which helped prepare them. Even though the data obtained show that about half of the work of the volunteer was on a routine and nonskilled level, 85 percent of the wives gave one or more ways in which they had acquired some special ability or skill for the work which they were doing as volunteers.

Data compiled on employment and volunteer service show that nearly half (48%) of those who were not employed participated as volunteers, while only 18.6 percent of those who were employed also served as volunteers. This is as might be expected. Surprising, however, is that 55.5 percent of those who were employed part time were also volunteers, a greater percentage than of those not

TABLE 5

RANK OF HUSBAND AND VOLUNTEER INVOLVEMENT OF WIFE

Rank	Total No.	No Volunteer Service		Volunteer Services					
				1 - 2		3+		TOTAL	
		Freq.	%	Freq.	%	Freq.	%	Freq.	%
Company Grade	292	205	70	84	29	3	1	87	30
Field Grade	403	191	47	167	41	45	12	212	53
General Officer	58	15	26	30	51	13	23	43	74
TOTAL	753	411	55	281	37	61	8	342	45

TABLE 6

DEPENDENTS AND VOLUNTEER SERVICE

School Age of Youngest Dependent	Total Families	Volunteer Services		Volunteer Services					
				1 - 2		3+		Total of Volunteers	
		Freq.	%	Freq.	%	Freq.	%	Freq.	%
None	109	74	68	26	24	9	8	35	32
Preschoolers in family	290	189	65	91	31	10	4	101	35
School Age	282	116	41	132	47	34	12	166	59
College age or over	72	32	44	32	44	8	12	40	56
TOTAL	753	411	55	281	37	61	8	342	45
No. of Children									
None	109	74	68	26	24	9	8	35	32
One-two	354	200	56	134	38	20	6	154	44
Three-four	217	100	46	91	42	26	12	117	54
Five or more	44	22	50	19	43	3	7	22	50
TOTAL	724	396	55	270	37	58	8	328	45

employed (see Table 7). It would appear that while those employed full time find themselves fully committed or occupied with their jobs, those employed only part time find enough satisfaction in activities outside the home to find the time also for volunteer service.

The feeling that army life stimulates a need for and interest in volunteer work was expressed frequently. Field Grade officers' wives, in particular, felt that there is more volunteer participation required in the Army than in civilian life, especially on or near an army post. Both Company and Field Grade officers' wives commented that volunteer requirements in the Army are too demanding and limited in depth because of frequent transfers. On the other hand, some wives felt that volunteer work allowed for greater flexibility, was more suitable and more available for army wives than was employment. The wives obviously had mixed feelings about volunteer work. Volunteer work was encouraged as part of the role of the officer's wife, but the personal benefits were not particularly rewarding. Volunteers often have more ability, skill, and knowledge than volunteer jobs seem to require—a decisive factor in the volunteer who turns to paid employment as more challenging and more rewarding.

Approximately one-third of the wives in this study had not worked since they

TABLE 7

EMPLOYMENT STATUS AND VOLUNTEER INVOLVEMENT

Employment Status*	Total No.	No Volunteer Services		Volunteer Services					
				1 - 2		3+		TOTAL	
		Freq.	%	Freq.	%	Freq.	%	Freq.	%
Not employed	602	313	52.0	232	38.0	57	10.0	289	48.0
Employed full time	70	57	81.4	13	18.6	0	0	13	18.6
Employed part time	63	28	45.0	31	49.0	4	6.0	35	55.0
Less than 10 hrs.	9	6	66.7	3	33.3	0	0	3	33.3
10-20 hours	16	5	32.0	10	62.0	1	6.0	11	68.0
Over 20 hours	16	5	32.0	11	68.0	0	0	11	68.0
Hours vary	22	12	54.5	7	32.0	3	13.5	10	45.0

*These figures do not include 18 wives who recently resigned because of change of station.

were married, another half had had "some" working experience—including the 20 percent who were currently employed. Half of those who were employed worked full time, and half were part-time workers.

Data show that employment for army officers' wives increased with educational level and degree attainment, a fact that is in line with recent Labor Department studies on all American women (U.S. Dept. of Labor, 1973 revised). Less than 11 percent of those persons who had not attended college were employed, while over 65 percent of those who had completed some graduate studies were employed. Or, in terms of academic degrees, only 14 percent of those with no degree were employed, while 50 percent of those wives who had earned *advanced* degrees were working. The majority of those working were employed by educational institutions (33%), medical services (21%), government (12%), or retail and wholesale trades (11%), or self-employed (10%). Half of those who were employed by the government worked for the Army.

The data indicate that the employed wives in this study were, by and large, working in positions commensurate with their educational background. Those wives who were college graduates and degree holders were working predominantly in the professional fields. Those persons with a Master's degree or higher were employed as teachers, librarians, real estate saleswomen, counselors, lawyers, an economist, and a museum curator. Not all wives were employed, however, in the same field in which they were academically prepared. While data in this study show that few women entered the labor market without some preparation or qualification for their specific job, only 60 percent of the women were employed in the same educational field in which they had studied while in school. Those who were working in other fields gave many reasons for this: convenience of job location or hours, inadequate education, change in interest, related jobs not available, or better pay. While many of these reasons are not unique to the military, some of the comments point to difficulties encountered by the wives because of their "temporary" or transient status in a community and their specialized occupations. While the fields of education and nursing were viewed by many of the wives as ideal for an army wife, others pointed out the difficulties of recertification for such positions with each change of state.

Data show that of the wives living off post, those living in urban settings were most likely to be employed. The availability of jobs in a metropolitan area, in addition to fewer military responsibilities, appear to be contributing factors. Those who live in small-town or rural areas, if employed, are more likely to be engaged in full-time rather than part-time jobs, as was shown in Table 4. Both data and comments appear to indicate that army wives in this study found the prospect of part-time employment attractive, but that many wives did not work because it was not available. Although some occupational fields lend themselves more favorably to part-time work than do others, wives in this study had been able to find part-time employment in many professional fields; however, the majority (75%) of the wives in clerical or office jobs were employed full time.

Wives did not question the salary they received for their employment, nor did they feel their salaries were out of line with those of others in the labor force. However, wives did feel that transient employment prohibits or retards advancement within the field, the end result of which is less salary. There was also a slight but noteworthy association between employment and time in residence. Of those wives who had moved within the past three months, 16 percent were employed; of those who had lived in their present residence for three months to one year, 22 percent were employed; and of those who had lived in the same place for *over* a year, 26 percent were employed.

The percentages of those wives employed in the four age categories follow: of those wives under 25, 15 percent were employed; of those wives between 25 and 34, 19 percent were employed; of those wives between 34 and 44, 19 percent were employed; and of those wives over 45, 18 percent were employed. However, employment when correlated with husband's rank revealed an inverse relationship; 25 percent of the Company Grade officers' wives were employed, 19 percent of the Field Grade officers' wives were employed, while only 5 percent of the wives of Generals were employed (see Table 8). The high

TABLE 8

**RANK OF HUSBAND AND AGE OF WIFE AS RELATED TO
EMPLOYMENT AND INTEREST IN EMPLOYMENT**

	Employment					Interest in Employment		
Husband's Rank	Not Empl.	Full Time	Part Time	Total Empl.	Percent Employ	No Int.	Yes Int.	Percent Interest
Company Grade	233	34	25	59	25	74	159	67
Field Grade	325	34	44	78	19	160	165	51
General	55	2	1	3	5	44	11	25
Age of Respondent								
Under 25					15	18	47	72.3
25-34					19	69	148	68.3
35-44					19	65	80	55.1
45 and over					18	126	60	32.3

correlation of age of wife and rank of husband would lead one to predict a similar employment ratio for both groups. This, however, was not the case. Nonemployment of the army officer's wife may be more a function of rank of the husband than age of the wife.

A summary of observations on the influence of rank and military assignment on the participation in both volunteer services and in the labor force is in order:

1. The *mobility* of the junior officer presents specific employment problems.

2. The wife of the officer *assigned on-post housing* finds she is expected to participate more in Army-related volunteer services than is the wife who lives off the post, detached from other military families.

3. The wife of a *commanding officer* finds extensive social obligations and responsibilities which tend to discourage employment.

4. The wife who is employed is less able to participate "voluntarily" in post activities, wives' club functions, and social events than is the nonworking wife.

The wives' responses as to why they work were grouped into several areas and are shown in Table 9. Some differences were noted in the responses given by the wives of junior officers as compared to the more senior officers' wives. Finance was the major reason why junior officers' wives worked. Inadequate salaries, frequent moves, need to purchase items such as furniture, contributed to the need for additional income. Field Grade officers' wives, as well as three Generals' wives, often stated their need to supplement the family income because of children in college as the reason for their employment.

"Personal satisfaction and mental stimulation" were most frequently given as reasons for working by the Field Grade officer's wife. The outside interest created by a job offers that stimulation. Company Grade wives frequently combined "the enjoyment and challenge of the job" with the wish or need to keep professionally current.

Although many wives in this study made reference to some of the problems associated with employment for the service wife or stated that they felt employment was not generally considered appropriate for the officer's wife, over half of the wives who were not working expressed some interest in entering the labor market in the present or future. Some interesting relationships in the data may be noted. A greater percentage of those wives with degrees were employed than those without; likewise, the unemployed wives with degrees showed greater interest in future employment than did those without degrees or college experience. The higher the rank of the sponsor, the smaller the percentage of wives employed and the less the interest in employment on the part of those not employed.

Although little difference was noted in the ages of the wives who were working, the interest in employment of those who were not declined steadily with the age of the respondent, as evident in Table 8.

TABLE 9

WHY WIVES OF ARMY OFFICERS WORK

Reason Given	Total Response	Rank Order of Responses		
		Company Grade	Field Grade	General
Personal satisfaction, challenge, interest	113	2	1	1
Financial	75	1	2	2
Professional experience, keep skills current	26	3	4	. . .
Husband on hardship tour	11	4	6	. . .
Security, interest when children grown	8	5	3	. . .
Have time to work now	7	6	5	3

Considering that so many wives seemed interested in working, it is worth noting some of the reasons why they were not presently doing so. The reasons most often cited were: (a) a variety of family and home responsibilities; (b) other commitments outside the home, such as volunteer services or social life; (c) personal attitude—happy as is, no need or interest; (d) lack of qualifications for meaningful employment; and (e) difficulties owing to transient nature of army life.

Many of the women who planned to work in the future had specific objectives in mind, such as: (a) to help pay for college (for self, husband, son, or daughter); (b) to have an outlet when children are no longer at home; (c) to have an outside interest; and (d) financial aid when husband is on an unaccompanied tour. The wives of young junior noncareer types anticipated a need and an opportunity to work when their husbands left the service and entered school or looked for a job. Younger wives also voiced their frustrations at trying to work while in the Army where the frequent transfers of junior officers made holding any meaningful position virtually impossible.

Wives whose husbands were, or had been, on hardship tours indicated a variety of reactions regarding the use of their time during their husbands' absence. Twenty-one of 60 wives in this study said they had gone back to school; 52 had entered the labor force. Others shared the feelings of a wife who stated, "I would like to work while my husband is in Vietnam but feel the need to stay with youngsters who need the security of one parent. Knowing I can work if I need to makes the unaccompanied tours easier."

Many wives commented on the relationship between their Army affiliation and employment, but attitudes varied greatly. Some women seemed to be employed in spite of the difficulties encountered; others found the problems incompatible with employment and remained out of the labor force. The wives felt that employers would not hire Army dependents because of the transient nature of the military. They also reported that they lost employment benefits in moves, that state employment qualifications and requirements were not uniform, career advancement was difficult, and jobs in career fields were often not available. A few wives felt that the scope and depth of experience, gained through the Army experience, increased their efficiency in a job; others, that mobility offered greater variety and job experience.

SUMMARY AND CONCLUSIONS

The army officers' wives in this study were well educated. Over 80 percent had some education beyond high school and approximately 40 percent had earned the Bachelor's degree. The occupational fields most frequently represented by them were education, nursing, and clerical work. While over 40 percent of the wives included in this study had had some education as married adults, half of all the wives expressed an interest in further study. Intellectual stimulation, personal growth, degree acquisition, and improvement of employment potential were cited as motivating factors.

For those wives with definite educational goals, frequent transfers caused difficulties in completing requirements, transferring credits, financing education, and finding suitable schools which met specific needs.

Nearly half of the wives in this study participated in volunteer services. Although about half of the work that they did as volunteers was of a routine nature requiring no special skills or training, many wives felt their educational background enhanced their role as a volunteer. Wives were more likely to perform volunteer services on the army post than in a civilian community; those who lived on the army post were more likely to be volunteers than were those living in civilian communities. Wives who volunteered in the community were most likely to be supporting youth programs; those wives on post were particularly active in women's cultural, social, and recreational programs. Organizations servicing the military community, such as the American Red Cross and Army Community Services, were well supported by officers' wives in this study.

While participation of the wife as a volunteer increased with the rank of the sponsor, participation in the labor force decreased with his rank. A relatively small percentage of army officers' wives were employed, although a fairly significant percentage were interested in employment at some future time. Lack of a challenging volunteer assignment was often seen as a decisive factor in the election of the volunteer to seek paid employment. Part-time employment seemed to be particularly attractive. Those wives who were college graduates were more likely to be members of the labor force than were those who had had little or no college experience.

The most frequently stated reason for working by wives of all ranks was financial. However, the disadvantages of employment appeared to be numerous. They centered around the loss of benefits—salary, fringe, seniority—caused by transfers; the difficulties in establishing any sort of a career; the lack of uniformity in state licensing and certification requirements which necessitated requalifying for employment; and discrimination by potential employers because of the transient existence of the military family. Many highly educated women were unable to find jobs available in their fields.

While there was reason to believe from this study that the military community expected the army officer's wife to participate as a volunteer, particularly if she resided on a military reservation, there did not appear to be a strong feeling regarding her participation as a member of the labor force.

Chapter 2

THE ADOLESCENT EXPERIENCE IN CAREER ARMY FAMILIES

PAUL DARNAUER

INTRODUCTION

The term "adolescence" triggers immediate responses from most Americans, responses which range from the longing to be an adolescent characteristic of younger children to the utter chagrin often felt by adults when having to deal with their children during this enigmatic period. To be sure, the major responsibility for adolescents is societally assigned to the family, but no one escapes concern about the issue. The mass media keep everyone apprised of adolescent-associated social problems: the hippie movement, drug use and abuse, violation of sexual mores, and apparently unrelenting attacks on customs and traditions.

The professional community, specifically, has concerned itself with understanding adolescent phenomena. As a result, the universals of "adolescenthood" are relatively well established. Concern with universals is important in a society that takes some pride in its international composition and involvements. These values, however, allow us to overlook what has long been emphasized in anthropology: understanding the effect of time, place, and socioeconomic variables on the universals. Redl (1969) reminded an international conference on adolescence that it is important to identify what of adolescence "is due primarily to geographical and social locus and the historical time at which . . . adolescence occurs" (p.83).

One such unique socioeconomic environment for adolescents in this country is the military and, specifically, the environment surrounding the career military family. Simple focus on the military family, however, overlooks yet another form of variability: that introduced by the mission and organization of the various military services (Army, Navy, Air Force, and Marines). Although there has been no systematic investigation of the adolescent experience as it occurs in a career military family, for many of the personnel charged with development

AUTHOR'S NOTE: This chapter is an adaptation of Darnauer, P. "The Adolescent Experience in Career Army Families," an unpublished doctoral dissertation prepared for the University of Southern California, 1970.

and operation of leisure-time and academic and counseling programs, such lack of data has not resulted in any particular concern; they have simply assumed that traditional theories of adolescence added to personal and corporate experiences were sufficient. At the same time, other individuals working with adolescent populations have been dissatisfied with such assumptions because they do not take into account many of the system influences. This study, which focused, on the Army, sought answers to the question, "What is it like to be an adolescent in a career army family?"

Although single, young men constitute the major portion of the Army, a conservative estimate is that a career-oriented group of at least 100,000 men are older and married.[1] As of 1968, 42.5 percent, or 623,000 military personnel, were married. Of that number, 349,100 were careerists whose dependent children exceeded 646,000.[2] Data on the number of children by age categories were not available; however, the investigator estimates at least 20 percent (129,000) were adolescents.

The major objective of this study was to identify the nature of the adolescent experience as viewed by adolescent members of army families and their parents. The major area of inquiry included the informal and formal friendship and leisure activities and the school experiences of these adolescents. It was expected that such inquiry would clarify certain aspects of family relationships, as well as certain aspects of the influence of the bureaucratic structure on army family life.

This exploratory study sought answers to the following questions about adolescents in career army families:

A. What do youth and their parents describe as the experience of these children in formal and informal friendship and group relations?

B. What do youth and their parents describe as the experience of these children in their school life?

C. How do these adolescents and their parents see the experience of these children as differing from that of adolescents from non-army families?

D. What are the differences between the perceptions of these adolescents and the perceptions of their parents with regard to the adolescent experience?

RELATED RESEARCH

The literature considered most pertinent to this study has the following themes: adolescence, child rearing and family functioning under specific environmental conditions, and social system theory as applied to the Army.

Adolescence

The developmental period of life, adolescence, has attracted and continues to hold wide attention. For purposes of more careful consideration, the literature can be divided into six subclassifications, the first of which is the theoretical formulation regarding adolescence. Representative of this grouping is the work of Erikson (1950, 1968, 1969), Gesell and his collaborators (1956), and the Committee on Adolescence of the Group for the Advancement of Psychiatry (1968). While these materials are usually research- and/or practice-grounded, their primary purpose is not to report research findings but to understand adolescence as a stage in the life cycle of the individual and to formulate explanatory theory.

Second, there are relatively broad studies of adolescents which tend to focus on youth from middle-class families. Included here are the reports of actual research in "River City," as conducted by Havighurst and his associates (1962); for the boy and girl scouts, which are interpreted by Douvan and Adelson (1966); and on the adolescent's view of himself, pursued by Strang (1957).

A third grouping of research consists of works on adolescent deviance. The purpose and focus of these studies are the understanding and/or correction of delinquency in its many and various forms. Representative works include those of Aichhorn (1938), Moles and associates (1959), and Peck and Bellsmith (1954).

Fourth, there are efforts concerned with professional practice with or in behalf of adolescents. This material is most frequently in article or monograph form, and its concern is with principles and techniques in treatment and problem-solving. In the literature of social work, Beck (1958) and Butler (1956a, b) represent this category.

Fifth, there are the discursive writings that highlight and criticize societal discontinuities or inconsistencies which have particular impact on the adolescent population. The springboard for these works is, again, research, but the intent is not particularly to report study findings, but to headline problems in an effort to promote change. The major work in this area has been done by Goodman (1960) and Friedenberg (1959, 1968).

Sixth, there is a large category of efforts that might be most simply labeled, "how-to-do-it as, or with, adolescents." These studies are generally in essay form and discuss such matters as physiology of puberty; how to live with teen-agers; dating; how, as a teen-ager, to get along with parents; and other subjects. Many of these works are impressionistic, anecdotal in content, and popular in style. A recently published, theme-applicable example from this grouping is *What Every Military Kid Should Know* (Gingras and Deibler, 1969).

Child Rearing and Family Functioning under
Specific Environmental Conditions

Few studies, outside of the field of anthropology, have looked at the influence of specific systems or phenomena on the adolescent experience. Those that have, had a focus that was primarily exploratory or descriptive. In a recent study of the kibbutz (Bettelheim, 1969), the influence of that closed system's child-rearing practices was considered in juxtaposition with Erikson's eight stages of life and the accompanying developmental crises. Bettelheim suggests that the kibbutz denies realization of ego-identity in interests of system preservation. That is, the tasks of adolescence are accomplished earlier in the life cycle (for example, separation from family and alliance with the peer group began in infancy and is a *fait accompli* by school age, and sexual identity naturally follows from the heterosexual living arrangement within the children's cottages), or else the tasks are not applicable (for example, occupational identity is assigned and ethics and values are prescribed for the individual while he remains in the kibbutz). Although the study has been criticized for its limited sample, its description of potential system influence on adolescent experience is clear.

Another study (Anderson, 1966) focused on the "open system" represented by a suburban, middle-class high school, and described three student subcultures. These subcultures represent solutions or compromises with adolescent tension, tension attributed to a "humanism-fatalism" imbalance. Anderson asserts that adolescents will be incompletely understood and only partially served unless there is greater sensitivity to the specific ways in which problems of adolescents are enmeshed in the larger social system.

The impact of the mobility phenomenon on children's school achievement has been the subject of two known research efforts (Partin, 1967; Snyder, 1967). Both report "movers" are generally the higher achievers, but in neither effort was the focus exclusively on adolescents. Also, both investigators described methodological refinements that are required before substantial confidence is placed in the findings (for example, better measures of potential and cultural deprivation). Nevertheless, a potential system influence on adolescents is underscored in their work.

The army and military family literature is, indeed, limited in nature. The situation and meaning of the military environment for career army personnel have been relatively well studied, but its implications for and effects upon the military dependent group are not clear. A few studies have focused on the children to determine whether mobility and/or father absence are related to problem behavior; for example, poor school performance, psychiatric disorder, etc. (Gabower, 1960; Lyon and Oldaker, 1967; and Pedersen, 1966). These studies, although lacking in age-specificity, indicate that a child's behavior is more closely related to the way in which the parents deal with him than to the conditions of the physical environment to which he is subjected (Gabower, 1960). The only reference from these studies specific to the adolescent of the military family indicated, without substantiating evidence, that boys in early adolescence have difficulty emotionally comprehending their fathers' absences and do not find that their mothers are sympathetic (Lyon and Oldaker, 1967). None of the authors is comfortable with the results, presumably because mobility and, particularly, father absence, would be expected to impose relatively severe stresses on a family.

Another study of military children (Kenny, 1967), aged 10 to 15, reported findings comparable to those of Gabower and also compared findings about intellectual functioning, emotional adjustment, and juvenile delinquency with findings from studies of nonmilitary groups. In each area, comparisons favored the military child. Kenny suggests that the findings are as expected because of an eliteness in the military population that is assured by military selection procedures; in other words, these findings are more population- than environment-specific.

In a study of problem-solving behaviors among career military families (Spellman, 1965), the majority of parent respondents believed that they had less trouble with their children (neither questions nor responses were age-specific) when compared with civilian families. The helpfulness of military discipline and the closed system or pervasiveness of military life were the most popular explanations for this difference. Although certain military families attributed troubles with children to the disruptions caused by mobility, the majority of respondents viewed mobility as a distinct asset for army children.

A study of coping patterns of families undergoing separation (Montalvo, 1968) also explored problems with children. One area of adolescent problems was described—adjustment of the adolescent to a new social environment. Specific stresses involved adolescent fear of risking rejection by friends and simultaneous personal difficulty in accepting peers who held prejudiced attitudes toward blacks and foreign nationals. This finding suggests that army adolescents may develop a more cosmopolitan outlook toward the superficial personal characteristics frequently used to identify whom one may have as friends.

The Army as a Social System

The central focus of this study is concerned with whether, how, and to what extent the adolescent experience is influenced by the Army social system—the umbrella under which some adolescents live because their fathers are career military personnel.

Parsons (1951) asserts that a social system consists of:

a plurality of individual actors interacting with each other in a situation which has at least a physical or environmental aspect, actors who are motivated in terms of a tendency to the "optimization of gratification" and whose relation to their situations including each other is defined and mediated in terms of a system of culturally structured and shared symbols (pp. 5-6).

Parsons explains that "actor" can be interpreted as individual or collective, depending upon the focus of interest. That the Army conforms to this definition requires little translation: the Army consists of a large number of people (officers, warrant officers, enlisted men, civilian employees, and dependents) who function as individuals as well as collective actors (units, offices, families). The base of operations—the environment—is usually a specific Army installation and is always defined, though in general terms, in army regulations. The activity of each actor varies but it is usually related to achieving organizational and, simultaneously, personal goals, such as assuring the country's defense, developing proficiency as a man-machine weapon, living as a family, assuring one's masculinity by participating in "manly" pursuits, or completing a selective service obligation—"optimization of gratification." An obvious aspect of the Army is its ordering through the use of symbols such as uniforms, insignia, hierarchical structure, and regulations which seem to cover all possible situations and contingencies.

Two characteristics of systems, implicit in Parsons's definition, require elaboration because of their significance for this study. The first characteristic has to do with the identification of a system and its interrelationships with its component parts. The Army in this study was viewed as the system in relation to which the army family functions as a subsystem. While the family has considerable autonomy, it neither becomes nor ceases to be an army family outside of the definitions established by the Army. The value of the Army to the family is apparent when considered in employer-employee terms. The interdependency is not so clear. It can, however, be identified by referring to Katz and Kahn (1966), who state:

We can describe the facts of organizational functioning with respect to five basic subsystems: (1) production subsystems concerned with the work that gets done; (2) supportive subsystems of procurement, disposal, and institutional relations; (3) maintenance subsystems for tying people into their functional roles; (4) adaptive subsystems, concerned with organizational change; and (5) managerial systems for the direction, adjudication, and control of the many subsystems and activities of the structure (p. 39).

Using this typology and its definitions, the army family can be considered a part of the Army "maintenance" subsystem. Its major purposes in that role are to meet the needs of the soldier-husband/father in the areas of affection, heterosexual expression, and parenthood, while he is simultaneously a member of the

Army. As a concept, the army family can also be viewed as a part of the "supportive" subsystem; for without the option of family life while serving within the system, fewer individuals would find the prospects of a military career appealing.

The point of view suggested above has a basic deficiency in that it is primarily unidimensional. A more useful approach, for purposes of this study, considers the interactions between various levels of systems from the standpoint of "problems" that must be solved at each level. Bell and Vogel (1960) suggest, in a work focused specifically on the family, that any social system must solve certain functional problems concerned with adaptation, goal gratification, integration, and pattern-maintenance of the system. For each problem, an exchange between a "subsystem of society" and the family is suggested. It is possible to identify some of the interconnections between the Army and the army family by referring to specific potential impacts that the system might have on the family. These can be considered as assets and liabilities, advantages and disadvantages, or "stresses" and "opportunities" (Montalvo, 1968). The stresses include periodic residential moves; accommodation to different and varying social, subcultural, economic, and physical living conditions; separation of husband and father from the family for extended periods; and occasional subjection to the uncertainties and potential hazards of combat training exercises and international hostilities with their threat of injury and permanent family dismemberment (Montalvo, 1968). To this list of stresses can be added accommodation to a value system that brings the career of the husband/father into jeopardy on any occasion of deviant behavior by other family members, a system that considers the husband/father on duty 24 hours per day and that espouses a duty-first, family-second ethic. These latter stresses, however, differ in degree only from those experienced by men in many positions in civilian life and are balanced by such potential benefits and opportunities as membership in a relatively closed social group with its own traditions and customs; use of exclusive recreational and social facilities; extensive travel and experiences in foreign countries; uninterrupted income; early occupational retirement; and military-subsidized vocational training and educational advancement (Montalvo, 1968).

The second characteristic to be discussed here is the tendency within systems to reward system-serving behavior and to punish or otherwise extinguish behavior that threatens the system. Generally these tendencies are seen in the problem-solving process and focus on system-wide survival rather than subsystem survival. The result is that where system-subsystem needs conflict, change occurs. The subsystem may continue to exist, but in modified form, the subsystem ceases to exist (is expelled by the system), or the subsystem produces system tension which must be resolved by some other means. These phenomena are described in the literature in such terms as family scapegoating (Bell and Vogel, 1960), costs of interaction with other system components (Parsons, 1951), and living with repressions bred into them by kibbutz education (Bettelheim, 1969). It is this tendency of the system to subjugate subsystem interests that was a basic stimulus for the present study, which is specifically concerned with the effect of the Army system on adolescents who are part of its family subsystem.

METHODOLOGY

Data Collection and Analyses

All data for the study were obtained during a structured interview with each adolescent and a separate, parallel interview with his or her parents. The single exception was school grades, which were taken from student record forms maintained by the Office of the Registrar at each school.

The interview guides were designed to obtain respondent opinion in four areas: general descriptive data, formal and informal friendship patterns, school experience, and general Army influence on adolescent life. Because of the exploratory nature of the study, all questions, other than those seeking specific descriptive information, included an initial stimulus inquiry with a "fixed-alternative" response followed by one or more "open-ended" questions which sought the explanation of the initial response. Replies of respondents were recorded at the time of the interview, using abbreviations and outline style to minimize loss of data. Where appropriate, and to the extent possible, responses were recorded verbatim. Upon completion of the interviewing, a coding system for reducing open-ended responses was developed.

All variables were analyzed by sex of the adolescent and rank of sponsor. Univariate analysis of much of the data was accomplished using nine other variables: adolescent age, family stability, parent-youth relationship (natural or stepparent), race, parent nationality, family mobility, parent interaction score,[3] location of residence (on or off post), and adolescent school performance. Bivariate consideration of the data was limited to areas of specific investigator interest. Where possible and appropriate, parent and adolescent replies were compared. Because the data were nominal and ordinal, the Chi-Square Test for significance of difference was the most appropriate test available. The Fisher Exact Probability test was used when appropriate.

The Community

Data for the study were collected at "Fort Recruit,"[4] a major West Coast Army post which is located geographically between a major cultural and recreational area and a thriving agricultural and growing industrial center in Newly Metropolitan County. In addition to its training mission, Fort Recruit provided facilities and logistical support for two major tenant organizations: a Department of Defense specialty school and an Army doctrine—and organization—evaluation unit. There were also several smaller activities.

The post population included almost 2,000 officers and 12,000 enlisted men who were in training status. The dependent population was over 10,000 in government quarters and almost 5,500 in off-post (nongovernmental) housing. Most personnel assigned to Fort Recruit could expect to obtain family housing within a reasonably short period (0 to 90 days), with actual time varying upon the housing requirements of the family. Families were not required to accept government quarters at the time of the study.

Adolescents eligible for the study attended senior high schools located in the civilian community that were civilian-staffed and administered by governmental or religious school districts. The relationship between the school authorities and Fort Recruit (the Army) was strictly liaison in nature. Most adolescents attended one of the two senior high schools operated by the school district in which Fort Recruit is located. These schools enrolled 2,994 students. Of those, 439 eleventh- and twelfth-graders came from Army homes; however, the school-specific data and other more specific data were not available. Some adolescents were in one of the three other public high schools or the two parochial schools in the area. Enrollment characteristics for these schools were not available.

SAMPLE PROFILE AND FINDINGS

The sample families consisted of a stratified random sample of 60 adolescents from 60 career army families and the parents of these adolescents. The sample included equal numbers of adolescents from officer families (30) and enlisted families (30) and equal numbers of boys and girls from each rank category. The specific ranks represented are shown in Table 1. That fathers had relatively high rank was an expected finding, since rank is closely related to length of service. Any father of adolescent children would be expected to have lengthy service unless he entered the Army at an advanced age.

The mean length of service among officers was 20.3 years (Standard Deviation [S.D.] = 4.3), and among enlisted men it was 20.7 years (S.D. = 5.0). Three-fourths of the families were white and in the other one-fourth, one or

TABLE 1

SPONSORS' RANK AND LENGTH OF SERVICE

Rank		Sex		Years of Service			
		Girl	Boy	14 or Less	15-19	20-24	25 and Over
Colonel	5	1	4	0	2	1	2
Lieutenant Colonel	10	5	5	0	4	2	4
Major	9	6	3	3	4	2	0
Captain	1	0	1	0	1	0	0
Chief Warrant Officer	1	1	0	0	0	0	1
Chief Warrant Officer	2	2	0	0	2	0	0
Chief Warrant Officer	2	0	2	0	0	1	1
Subtotal	30	15	15	3	13	6	8
First Sergeant	11	6	5	0	3	4	4
Sergeant First Class	13	5	8	0	4	5	4
Staff Sergeant	5	3	2	1	3	1	0
Sergeant	1	1	0	1	0	0	0
Subtotal	30	15	15	2	10	10	8
Total	60	30	30	5	23	16	16

both parents were nonwhite. In almost a fifth of the families, one or both parents were foreign-born. Comparisons of the racial and nationality character-istics of parents with general U.S. population characteristics is portrayed in Table 2. Some difference between military and general population racial charac-teristics was expected, particularly at the enlisted level, since the military has provided an integrated life style and more equal vocational opportunities than nonmilitary environments.

Over 75 percent of the individual marital partners in the study families had not previously been married. The total sample data are consistent with U.S.

population data reported by the U.S. Bureau of the Census on marriages and divorces.[5] For 70 percent of the families, the current marriage was the only marriage for both the husband and wife. Forty-eight adolescents (80%) lived with their natural parents. The remaining adolescents had a stepparent. No adopted children were in the sample.

Children

Half of the families had four or more children. The mean number of children per family was 3.75. Only one adolescent from any family was included in the sample. Nearly half of the adolescent subjects were the oldest of the children in their families. The age and grade characteristics of the study sample are shown in Table 3.

Location of Residence

Over 80 percent (49) of the families resided in government quarters: most quarters were located at Fort Recruit, but five officer-headed families lived at a subpost. The majority of those who lived off post occupied homes they were purchasing either in preparation for retirement or as a consequence of the sponsor's hardship tour.

Mobility

Over one-third of the families had lived in their present quarters for less than one year; however, ten had lived in the same residence over three years. The variation between the junior officer subsample and the total sample can probably be understood in terms of Vietnam War-induced mobility. Only eight families had moved less than four times since the adolescent began attending school, and no family had moved less than twice during the same period. Table 4 shows the number of moves the sample families had experienced since the subject-adolescent began school. The average of 5.8 moves per family was considerably higher than among the general U.S. population. Over two-thirds of the youths had moved at least once since beginning ninth grade, and nearly one-third made two or more moves. Seventeen families (28%) had previously been stationed at Fort Recruit: five were officer and twelve were enlisted families. For seven families (21%), all of whom were buying the homes they occupied in the civilian community, Fort Recruit had become "home."

TABLE 2

RACE AND NATIONALITY CHARACTERISTICS OF 120 INDIVIDUAL
PARENTS COMPARED WITH GENERAL U.S. POPULATION IN PERCENTAGES

Group	Race					Nationality		
	Total	White	Nonwhite[a]			Total	Native	Foreign
			Tot	Neg	Oth			
Sample Parents	100	78	21	11	10	100	91	9
U.S. Population	100	88	12	11	1	100	95	5
	$\chi^2 = 9.25$, df = 1, p <.01					$\chi^2 = 3.37$, df = 1, p <.01		

Source of U.S. Population data: U.S. Bureau of the Census, *Current Population Reports:* Series P-25, No. 416, "Estimates of the Population of the United States by Age, Race, and Sex" July 1, 1968 (Washington, 1968) p. 11; *U.S. Census of Population: 1960. Detailed Characteristics. United States Summary,* Final Report PC(1)-D (Washington, 1963), p. 349.

[a] Abbreviations are: TOT = Total, NEG = Negro, OTH = All other nonwhite groupings.

TABLE 3

ADOLESCENT AGE AND YEAR IN SCHOOL

Rank-Sex		Age				School Year			
		Total	16	17	18	10	11	12	NIS[a]
	Total	60	28	25	7	3	35	20	2
Officer:	Girl	15	7	7	1	1	8	5	1
	Boy	15	6	7	2	-	8	6	1
Enlisted:	Girl	15	7	6	2	-	11	4	--
	Boy	15	8	5	2	2	8	5	--

[a] NIS = Not in School.

Father Absence

All but three families had experienced at least one period of father absence. For nearly three-fourths of the families, a separation had been experienced since the subject-adolescent had attained adolescence, and over half the separations had occurred in that time. This fact reflects the influence of the Vietnam War. Data describing the time of father absence are summarized in Table 5.

School Achievement

School achievement of the subject-adolescents is shown in Table 6. Performance can be reported only in terms of grade point ratios, since no other comparable indices were available. This average is an extremely weak measure, since it equates grades made in academic course work (math, science, languages, and others) with those made in extracurricular pursuits (drama, chorus, journalism, and others) and applied courses (driver education, typing, and the like).

Comparison of sample and nonsample performance was made in an attempt to identify relative standings of twelfth-graders with the total senior class at one school. Of 17 twelfth-graders who attended Eisenhower, three ranked among the top 10 in the class of 360 students (standings of these were 1, 3, and 7). In terms of deciles: 5 were in the first; 4 in the second; 2 in the third; 1 each in the fourth, sixth, ninth, and tenth; and 2 in the eighth. Since the sample level of performance appeared high, all students in the top and bottom two deciles were identified as "army" or "non-army" and compared with the sample. From the analysis, it appears that the sample included an overrepresentation of "army" high performers. Less successful school performance was found among those adolescents who had a stepparent. Adolescents who moved infrequently or excessively performed less well than those who were moderately mobile. The poorer performance was particularly apparent among the infrequent movers. This finding is consistent with other reports of higher school performance among geographically mobile students (Kenny, 1967; Partin, 1967; Snyder, 1967).

Family Problems

An unanticipated finding of the study related to family problems. Of the 99 families contacted in conjunction with the study, 26 percent reported that they had, or were found through essentially incidental contact with the school or military authorities to have had, sufficiently severe intrafamily problems that the families had either sought, could have obtained, or should have requested extrafamily assistance in resolving the difficulty. In at least five instances,

TABLE 4

FAMILY MOBILITY SINCE ADOLESCENT BEGAN SCHOOL
(PERCENTAGES ARE CUMULATIVE VERTICALLY)

Rate of Mobility[a]	Total	Rank[b]						Sex	
		Officer			Enlisted			Girl	Boy
		Tot	Sr	Jr	Tot	Sr	Jr		
	60	30	15	15	30	11	19	30	30
High	11	7	1	6	4	1	3	9	2
Moderate	35	19	12	7	16	6	10	15	20
Low	14	4	2	2	10	4	6	6	8
Total Moves	349	189	86	103	160	58	102	189	160
Mean	5.8	6.3	5.7	6.9	5.3	5.3	5.4	6.3	5.3

[a]High mobility = 8 or more moves, moderate = 5 to 7, and low = 2 to 4 (2 was the fewest moves reported).

[b]SR = senior, JR = junior, and TOT = total.

TABLE 5

PERIOD OF LIFE WHEN ADOLESCENT EXPERIENCED FATHER ABSENCE

Item	Period of Life[a]		
	Early	Middle	Late
Number of Individuals Involved	14	34	43
Total Absences Experienced	14	37	51
Number of Initial Absences	14	25	17
Only Time Absence Experienced	1	9	15

[a]Definition of periods: Early = 0 to 6 years, Middle = 7 to 12 years, and Late = 13 or later years. When absence began in one period and extended into a subsequent period, it was counted in the latter.

TABLE 6

COMPARISONS OF ADOLESCENT ACADEMIC PERFORMANCE: ADOLESCENTS, COMPARED WITH ADOLESCENT GRADE POINT AVERAGE

Adolescent Performance Comparison

Grade Point Ratio [a]	Sample and Other Army				Sample and Non-Army				Army and Non-Army			
	Total	Better	Same	Poorer	Total	Better	Same	Poorer	Total	Better	Same	Poorer
Total	55[b]	18	30	7	56[b]	24	49	3	55	27	28	2
2.5 and Above Off	18	10	7	1	18	13	5	--	18	10	8	--
Enl	14	7	7	--	14	6	8	--	14	8	6	--
Subtotal		17	14	1		19	13	--		18	14	--
2.4 and Below Off	10	1	7	2	10	3	6	1	9	4	4	1
Enl	13	--	9	4	14	2	10	2	14	5	8	1
Subtotal		1	16	6		5	16	3		9	12	2

[a] Abbreviations are: OFF = Officer, ENL = Enlisted.
[b] "Could not compare" responses have been deleted.

TABLE 7

ADOLESCENT SCHOOL PERFORMANCE COMPARED TO MOBILITY

Grade Point Average		Total	Rate of Mobility		
			High	Moderate	Low
	Total	60	11	35	14
2.5 - 4.0		32	4	24	4
0.0 - 2.4		28	7	11	10

$$\chi^2 = 8.45, df = 2, p < .02$$

multiple problems existed. The adolescent actual-problem rate of 11 percent and probable-problem rate of 7 percent appear consistent with findings reported by Kenny (1967) in a study of personality assessment of "normal" military dependents in 5th to 10th grades. The finding also appears consistent with a Department of the Army report that at least 12 percent of army family households have a dependent child in need of special care and attention because he is emotionally troubled, physically handicapped, or mentally retarded (Montalvo, 1970).

ATTITUDINAL FINDINGS

The following is a description of the findings as they relate to the specific research questions investigated: adolescents' and parents' (1) descriptions of informal friendship relations, formal group involvements, and school experiences; and (2) comparisons of general experience with perceived experience of youths from civilian families.

Informal Friendship Relations

Almost half of the youths had friends who were adolescents in other army families. Place of residence, off or on post, was significant as a predictor of whether friends were from army families (on-post) or from civilian or both army and civilian families (off-post) ($\chi^2 = 13.00$, df = 2, p< .01). In either setting, most were satisfied with the composite of friends they reported.

Sixty percent of the youth indicated that they had a same-sex best friend and 80 percent said they had a group of friends. About half of the adolescents had both a same-sex best friend and a group of friends. A significant difference was found between boys and girls in terms of their preferences for same-sex best friend, a group, or both same-sex best friend and a group; most girls wanted a same-sex best friend (χ^2 = 6.68, df = 2, p< .05). Over two-thirds of the youths reported that they dated, but only half were satisfied with their dating frequency.

Few youths considered their fathers' position as influencing whom they selected as friends; however, there was considerably less consensus about the influence of association with the Army. Officer and enlisted youths differed significantly in their opinions about whether and to what extent their friendships were influenced by their "Army-ness"; officer boys most frequently described an influence (χ^2 = 5.70, df = 1, p < .05). All but four reasons given related to moving and occupying government quarters. In short, being the adolescent member of an army family influenced friendships because army families live where they live at the behest of army orders, and where one lived influenced friendship possibilities. Sixty percent of the youth said that officer, enlisted, and civilian categories were superfluous to their friend-selection process.

Three-fourths did not feel that race was important to their personal choice of friends. The same percentage reported that race, rank, and religion were not important in the friend-selection considerations of most army youth. This statistic, however, obscured the fact that over 40 percent of the girls reported these factors as significant considerations, and that a substantial majority of the respondents held that race, particularly, was more important to civilian adolescents than to army adolescents. Positive Army policies regarding racial integration were reported by the subjects to account for the difference between army and civilian attitudes.

Nearly two-thirds of the youths described no difficulty with their acquisition of friends; personal attributes of the potential friends were the usual explanation for variability in selection. Significantly less difficulty in making friends was reported by black and other nonwhite youths than those from white or interracial families (FEP = .0426, p < .05). Similarity of reports between adolescents and parents was close in the aggregate. When intrafamily responses were compared, the amount of agreement decreased and varied widely; the range was from 85 percent agreement about dating practices to 53 percent agreement on the inquiry about the grouping (officer, enlisted, or civilian) from which friends would be selected.

Formal Group Relations

Almost 60 percent of the youths said they were not actively involved in any organized peer group activity. Most of the "belongers" held membership in character-building or religious groups and had been involved with that activity, or at least one of their activities, in excess of one year. Ninety-eight percent reported religious affiliation, and half reported that they regularly engaged in religious pursuits. Parents reported the same amount of current and past involvements as did the youths, and intrafamily agreement approached 90 percent.

School Performance

A majority of adolescents from officer families rated their performance as superior to that of non-army students, and this represented a significant variation from one-fourth of the enlisted youths who said they did better. Responses were found to compare positively with actual school performance; however, enlisted teen-agers tended to depreciate their performance. Almost two-thirds of the parents who made a comparison considered army students academically superior to the non-army population. This finding was offset in part by 13 percent who rated army students as poorer. The "superior" group justified their rankings by pointing to advantages of travel, higher levels of parental interest in education, and higher adolescent aspirations. Six couples based their ranking on the impression that more army teen-agers were on the honor roll and received scholarships. Those who considered army youth poorer performers cited "mobility" as the cause. The academic rankings of adolescents by officer parents were significantly more favorable to army youth than were rankings by enlisted parents ($\chi^2 = 4.13$, df = 1, p < .05). Officer parents expected more in the way of performance from their children and assumed that performance which was in keeping with those expectations was general among army youth.

Advanced education appeared to be highly valued within the Army. The respondents revealed that their ambitions were to pursue higher education; furthermore, they felt that the Army encouraged educational achievement among its personnel who, in turn, encouraged it in members of their families. Over 67 percent of the boys and 57 percent of the girls in this study planned to attend college upon high school graduation. Comparable civilian data from the Douvan and Adelson study (1966) revealed that 46 percent of the boys, 32 percent of 17-18-year-old girls, and 34 percent of 14-16-year-old girls had college plans.

General Army Experience

Differences between Adolescent Life in Army and Non-Army Families: To aid the respondents' comparisons of teen-age life in an army family with teen-age experience as a member of a civilian family, all were asked about the existence of a civilian best friend or acquaintance. Three-fourths (45) of the adolescents indicated that they had a close friend or acquaintance who was not "Army." In addition, they were asked whether they considered an army family or a civilian family experience better for teen-agers. Seventy-six differences between adolescent life in army and non-army families were reported; 33 were considered favorable to army life and 39 were judged favorable to non-army life. Four did not cite differences. Almost half of the favored-army differences referred to a broader life experience and tolerance of differences in people. In the favored non-army grouping, over half referred to the requirement of frequent moves.

Most youths would not advise a peer about whether to choose an army or non-army family in which to spend his teen-age years, expressing that such decisions were personal and heavily dependent upon individual taste and personality. Of those favoring the Army, most described the advantages of travel, the economic advantages of post facilities, and the economic and emotional security of army family life.

Children who would advise others tended to be white, in the high and moderately mobile categories,[6] and among the low academic achievers.[7] When children who indicated they would not advise others were forced to a recommendation,[8] 23 selected an army and 8 a non-army family. One youth, who would not commit himself to a position, thought decision making relatively simple: "If you've got money, go civilian. If you haven't, go Army."

Advantages and Disadvantages for Teen-agers

Information about advantages and disadvantages was obtained by asking about "the things you can do" and "the things you cannot do" because "you are a teen-ager in an army family."

Advantages. Over three-fourths of the teen-agers saw advantages to army life. Of 71 specific advantages cited, 40 involved being permitted to use, or the economic advantage in using, post facilities (clubs, PX, theater, recreational); 17 specified travel opportunities, while 4 others focused on experience with varieties of peoples and cultures. Only one of 15 youths from the senior officer category did not report advantages. The same was true for one of 11 who lived off post.

Only seven parents did not report opportunities for teen-agers because of army status. They cited 92 advantages, 54 of which had a geographic mobility theme: 32 specifically mentioned travel, and 21 others reported breadth of knowledge and understanding as a result of contact with varieties of people and cultures (16 of these latter were posited by officer-parents). Twenty-nine parent comments had to do with the advantages of using post facilities.

Disadvantages. Three-fourths of the youth rejected the notion that there were any "things" they could not do as a teen-ager because they are "Army" that they could do if they weren't. More who reported disadvantages were from enlisted than officer families, but this difference was not statistically significant.

Among the recognized limitations, most frequently mentioned was the severity of real or implied social restrictions on the children because of potential family ramifications or because of military regulations.

Half of the parents identified disadvantages, however. The majority of the variation from adolescent response was provided by the officer-parents ($\chi^2 = 4.38$, df = 1, p < .05). This statistically important difference between officer and enlisted parents appeared to be related to broken families ($\chi^2 = 10.8$, df = 1, p < .01) and to parents of younger teen-agers ($\chi^2 = 6.95$, df = 1, p < .01).

Several explanations for the officer-related finding exist. Two possibilities are educational sophistication,[9] which would permit and encourage consideration of more alternatives; and nature of military duty,[10] which requires broader (officer), or narrower (enlisted), approaches in the thinking processes. Both are social class-related phenomena but seem to provide better insights than the umbrella concept.

Problems Encountered and Problems Escaped

Problems Encountered: A distinct majority (70%) of the girls and nearly 50 percent of the boys reported that they had encountered "teen-age problems" because they were "Army." The majority of the "problems" described had to do with moving; e.g., having to give up old friends and make new friends, and "getting adjusted after a move." Eight others described problems that were unique to Fort Recruit: lack of intrapost and area transportation, and limited work opportunities.

Parents, in proportions equivalent to those cited above, described army-related teen-age problems. More mothers than fathers reported problems, but the officer-enlisted difference was the one of greatest significance ($\chi^2 = 4.58$, df = 1, p < .05). Of the problems identified, 39 of 55 were related to mobility.

Problems Escaped. Almost two-thirds (38) of the youth did not think their "Army-ness" allowed them to escape from any teen-age problems. Twenty-two others, fourteen of whom were girls, disagreed. Nine who felt problems were escaped cited economic advantages: these adolescents said they didn't have to be concerned that their fathers would be laid off or on strike, or unable to provide medical care if required. For seven, there was no need for anxiety about living—"being stuck"—in the same community, with the same friends, or too close to relatives. These included over two-thirds of the officer-parents but less than one-third from the enlisted group. This officer-enlisted difference was statistically significant ($\chi^2 = 9.6$, df = 1, p < .01). Significantly higher propor-tions of parents from stable families, ($\chi^2 = 10.74$, df = 1, p < .01), natural parents (FEP < .001), white parents ($\chi^2 = 4.45$, df = 1, p < .05), parents who had Parent

Interaction Scores of 4 or 5, (χ^2 = 4.35, df = 1, p < .05), and parents of higher academic performers (χ^2 = 13.12, df = 1, p < .001) described unique "escapes" for their adolescent children. Parents cited economic insecurity, problems associated with continuity of residence (desire to travel, too close to relatives, tendency to stereotype), insecurity associated with less structure (army structure and restrictions have advantages), and difficulties within the civilian community as problems from which their children were shielded or allowed to "escape."

Army Career of Father or Father-Surrogate

Thirty-nine (55%) of the adolescents did not question their fathers' selection of an army career. Most reasoned in terms of their fathers' interests and involvements with the Army: "He has to do what he's interested in, I couldn't picture my father as anything but a soldier—that's his life." Other explanations included traveling and the opportunities geographic mobility provided (16), enjoyment of army life generally (15), feelings that life would have been rougher economically outside the Army (9), and belief that their fathers' career had not had any adverse effect on their lives (10). In contrast, 21 (35%) mentioned their wish that their fathers had civilian occupations. Of these, most had some objection to moving.

Three-fourths of the parents said their teen-agers had never wished seriously that their fathers had chosen a civilian career. Most indicated that the youths had never given them any reason to believe unhappiness with army life existed. Several reasoned that their teen-agers had always liked the Army and had been proud of their fathers' association with it. All sixteen who recognized youth unhappiness with army life attributed the unhappiness to mobility.

DISCUSSION

The findings suggested that, from the point of view of the adolescent, teen-age life as a member of an army family is not unique. Contact with a number of professionals and parents in the course of the investigation revealed that assumptions about the adolescent growing up in the army community may be erroneously built upon a commonly held stereotyped image of the army teen-ager. The data indicated that, in general, neither youths nor parents appeared to view adolescent life in the army family as dissimilar from adolescent life in civilian communities. The major difference or unique aspect of military life was the adolescents' vulnerability to relocations. Contrary to expectations, almost no mention was made of father absence, although most families had experienced at least one episode of absence, and for over three-fourths, an absence had been endured since the children had become teen-agers. Generally, the adolescent respondents did not define the unique aspects of military as favorably as did their parents. While officer-parents were more favorably disposed toward the Army, the enlisted-parents were more questioning and expressed sentiments more in line with those expressed by their adolescent children. It is highly probable that officer-parents were more committed to the Army way of life and Army values for several reasons: they had greater latitude of vocational choice when they elected an army career; they realized more of the rewards available from the army system; they tended to be in greater control over career alternatives; and they were more frequently in positions to influence or make policy decisions.

Discrepancies between the adolescents' reports and their parents' reports as to perceptions of army life were surprisingly great. Over 80 percent of the parent responses were found to be at variance with those of their adolescent children. Congruence was highest on adolescent social behavior (dating, groups of friends, organizational memberships), while discrepancies were greatest with regard to the nature of discussion with friends, army versus non-army extracurricular involvement, and academic performance. Parents appear to be in agreement with their adolescent children regarding issues over which they can exert influence, and they do more poorly in areas less subject to their parental control.

The major negative army influences on the life of the adolescent appeared to be geographic mobility and the requirement for compliance with army policy about rank differentials, racial equality, and personal behavior, particularly when using on-post facilities (government quarters as well as recreational and other services). Geographic mobility appeared to have both a negative and a positive influence on the adolescents' development of occupational goals and ethical values and their capacity for intimacy, as well as on their achievement of independence from family. The impact on occupational goals was seen in the reported disruptiveness of changing schools and absence of any real work experience opportunities. On a more positive note, there was opportunity to have broader life experiences which would have included exposure to varieties of occupational pursuits.

Capacity for intimacy, which involves sustained general interpersonal relationships as well as heterosexual relationships, was the factor which was most vulnerable to mobility. Both adolescents and parents, on behalf of their children, decried giving up old friendships and establishing new ones. Additionally, the adolescents reported increased frustration with these friendship losses at adolescence. In comparing the dating behavior of this sample with findings from the Douvan and Adelson study (1966), however, we find that although girls dated less (14-16-year-olds: sample = 64% versus 72%, and 17-18-year-olds: sample = 69% versus 91%), boys dated at the same or with greater frequency.

The adolescents' exposure to and adoption of values was measured in part by inquiries about race, rank, and religion. Many youths indicated that continuous relocations allowed them to have a broader perspective toward other peoples and races and thereby avoid the prejudicial stereotyping that was presumed or experienced among less mobile populations.

The adolescents' concern about compliance in the military community was not pronounced when contrasted with their concern about the impact of mobility. However, adolescents did express the dilemma they faced when attempting self-expression and experimentation at the risk of family reprisals owing to the impact on their fathers' careers. Several parents confirmed that their adolescent children could not "get into trouble" because such difficulty would have negative implications for the father's career in the military. These pressures tended to encourage rather rigid parent rule enforcement which at times increased or intensified family conflicts. A number of youths believed that restrictions of the military environment had been "good" for them.

Although this study cannot unequivocally delineate the specific aspects of the Army system and their influence on adolescent development, it seems reasonable to postulate that the demands of life in the military may delay such development. Bettelheim (1969) suggested that adolescent tasks were either accomplished before or superfluous to the kibbutz existence. Particularly among youths domiciled on army posts, the accomplishment of adolescent tasks may be postponed until after high school graduation. Movement toward occupational identity is forced upon the adolescent, since he must attend school at least until age 16; other developmental tasks, however, may be delayed. While sexual development, sex role typing, and consequent establishment of sex role identity must proceed, interpersonal friendships, both same-sex and heterosexual relationships, are permitted and encouraged, but their intensity and stability may be mitigated by the threat of a move. As a protective measure against the pain of leaving, adolescents may develop superficial relationships.

CONCLUSION

The Army has demonstrated an evolving awareness of, and sensitivity to, family problems which are the direct result of the military system's demands upon the family system. This awareness has produced some ameliorative programs: in 1965 the Army Community Service program was established; and in 1968 more centralized direction was introduced to guide Youth Activities army-wide. Although both of these programs have met some needs of army families, other needs persist. This study has highlighted problems for teen-agers that are related to changes of duty station.

While moving, per se, was considered a problem, particularly at adolescence, there appeared to be an underlying concern about transitioning children into, as well as stabilizing them within, the school system and the community. An area which appears to need some attention is the lack of a formalized arrangement by which youths become acquainted with what a new community has to offer. The data indicated that some youths perceive themselves to be second-class citizens of the Army. In one respect, this is an accurate assessment of the realities of life in the military: parents accept the risks of mobility and family separation when they elect career military status which put the family and the children in a subordinate position. Mission requirements of the Army will usually take priority over needs of families and children. However, in other areas of life, awareness of second-class citizenship can be reduced. Orientation programs do exist for parents at many duty stations, and parents are expected to pass information along. A similar welcoming and orientation for newly arrived youths would be beneficial. The Youth Activities program is a step in this direction of giving status to the children and involving them in the community.

The major value of this study for human service delivery is the observation that youths from army families perceive themselves predominantly typical, that is, similar to other adolescents. While they may move more frequently and be subject to the limitations and constraints of the military system, their problems are best understood on an individual basis. Masterson (1967) has indicated that the psychiatric diagnosis, "emotional turmoil of adolescence," is frequently an easy out from making a difficult diagnosis and undertaking more difficult treatment problems; however, this temporizing reveals little new about a patient and delays eventual treatment requirements. Similarly, ascribing the adolescent problems of army young people to the system under which they live is best considered a delaying tactic which serves neither the adolescent, his family, nor the Army. This study tends to emphasize that existing theories of adolescence are generally applicable to those youths who experience adolescence as members of army families.

The study also emphasizes the persistent theme of the importance of peer relationships and the pain that accompanies their dissolution owing to family relocations. At the same time, it suggests that the traumatic effects of geographic mobility at adolescence may be offset by a conscious effort to integrate the family and the children, in particular, into the receiving community, since the military community can offer some continuity.

On the basis of this study, it is fair to suggest that army youth do not perceive their experience as peculiar or unique. They do, however, observe obstacles to adolescent development and social adaptation that are amenable to system change.

NOTES

1. This figure was derived from those presented in Lang, 1964, pp. 42-74.

2. These figures have been developed from material in Department of the Army, 1968b, pp. 3-8.

3. All couples interviewed were assigned an interaction score by the interviewer. A score of "five" was awarded to those whose exchange was free, easy, and made room for difference of opinion. Those rated as "four" were less free to disagree but could reason together with the interviewer in an effort to achieve consensus on a specific inquiry. Couples who received a "three" replied to the interview questions but did not collaborate to arrive at replies. The "two" rating was assigned when the interview was dominated by one or the other of the parents with only occasional consideration for the partner. "One" was reserved for single-parent interviews or those where a husband or wife dominated the interview to the exclusion of the other and disparaged, verbally or nonverbally, contributions from the spouse sought by the interviewer.

4. Fictitious names were used to mask the identification of the actual military base and units involved in this study.

5. The rate of divorces to marriages has ranged from .23 in 1950 to .283 in 1968, and this rise has been consistent and gradual. For computation, the rates of 26 percent divorces and 74 percent marriages were used. Figures were obtained from: U.S. Bureau of the Census, *Statistical Abstract of the United States: 1969* (90th Edition) (Washington, 1969), p. 65.

6. Five of six high-mobility, 16 or 35 moderately mobile, and 1 of 13 low-mobility youths would advise. Four of the highs favored army life.

7. Seven of thirty-two high achievers and 15 of 28 low achievers would offer advice: $\chi^2 = 6.37$. df = 1. $p < .05$.

8. Only 33 of the 38 who would not spontaneously offer advice were requested to make a choice. The forced choice was added after five had been interviewed and all had declined advice giving.

9. Officers tend to have at least a baccalaureate degree, whereas enlisted personnel tend to have only high school educations.

10. Officers are charged with recruiting and career counseling, particularly with junior officer personnel. In addition, officers are frequently involved in decision making which is based on staff study processes (problem identification, selection of alternative courses with limitations and assets of each). Enlisted personnel are most frequently involved with day-to-day technical and personnel training functions which tend to call for a solution to a problem.

II

THE MILITARY FAMILY

UNDER STRESS

Chapter 3

ALIENATION: A FUNCTION OF GEOGRAPHICAL MOBILITY

AMONG FAMILIES

J E R R Y L. M c K A I N

INTRODUCTION

One of the more pronounced environmental-situational stresses encountered by modern families is geographical mobility. Daniel Bell (1967) for example, notes that the root fact necessary to understand so many other bewildering aspects which separate our times from the past is the "change of scale" of our lives. Toffler (1970) popularized conceptualizations similar to Bell's and specified it to geographical mobility. He notes:

> As technological change roars through the advanced economies, outmoding whole industries and creating new ones almost overnight, millions of unskilled and semi-skilled (and skilled) workers find themselves compelled to relocate . . . the disruption is often agonizing (pp. 87-88).

In substantiation of reactions occasioned by relocation, Toffler (1970) quotes Dr. Marc Fried, who observes:

> It is quite precise to speak of their reactions as expressions of grief . . . manifest in feelings of painful loss, the continued longing, the general depressive tone, frequent feelings of psychological or social or somatic distress . . . the sense of helplessness . . . anger . . . "similar to mourning for a lost person" (p. 88).

The military family, while no longer unique in this regard, is particularly susceptible to the potential stress of moving because of the frequency of the geographical change necessitated by the requirements of military service. For example, during the period 1 March 1967 through 29 February 1968, approxi-

AUTHOR'S NOTE: This chapter is an adaptation of McKain, J.L. "Feelings of Alienation, Geographical Mobility, and Army Family Problems: An Extension of Theory," an unpublished doctoral dissertation prepared for Catholic University of America, 1969.

mately 60 percent of Army personnel experienced one "permanent" change of station (OPOPM Report #2568E, 1968).

The possibility of adverse family reactions associated with a move is apparent to those engaged in service positions or professions within the military community. Not all families, however, react adversely to a move. The question then arises, what is characteristic of the family that manifests intra- and interpersonal problems associated with geographical mobility?

One of the social scientists who initially dealt with the subject of mobility in general, and touched on the aspect of geographical mobility in particular, was Sorokin (1959). He noted that geographical mobility has both positive and negative corollaries. On the one hand, it seems to be associated with broadening the mind and making life more intensive; on the other hand, it seems to cause emotional and interpersonal problems. In terms of pathology, and specific to the thesis of this study, Sorokin drew a definite relationship between pathology, alienation, and geographical mobility, stating that an increase or a decrease of mobility is a condition which considerably influences the chances of a "close intimacy with other men, the desirability of a real community of feeling, an urgent need of a unity of understanding, a close friendship." The implication in Sorokin's perceptive observation seems to be that there is a cause-and-effect relationship between mobility and alienation and pathology, and the stress of mobility is seen as the important variable. However, Sorokin also implies that the cause-and-effect relationship between the stress of moving and pathology is not direct; indeed, he notes that there are benefits to mobility, and he seems to imply that one's personal view of moving is an important variable.

Pedersen and Sullivan (1964), like Sorokin, tend to support the interpretation that it is the "definition" of the situation of mobility that is the important variable. They noted the influences of parental attitudes toward mobility in relation to the emotional adjustment of the mobile child. They compared histories of mobility in normal and emotionally disturbed children of military families. Although the two groups could not be distinguished with respect to incidence of mobility, Pedersen and Sullivan found that they differed significantly with respect to parental attitudes about mobility. Specifically, the mothers of the normal children were more likely to be accepting of mobility and satisfied with the military role as manifested by their identification with the military community than the mothers of the disturbed children. The latter difference between the two groups was also found for the fathers.

Another study by Gabower (1959) showed a relationship between mobility and behavior problems of children in Navy officers' families. Specific to alienation, she found that parents of children who were behavior cases were less active than parents of the control cases in such things as identifying with the community in which the family lived through participation in community activities.

Discussions with army social workers assigned to Army Community Services and with Post Billeting Officers brought out the additional situational dimension of the possible importance of the army family's living arrangements. For example, one Post Billeting Officer noted that whether a family lived off post or on post was an important element in its feelings of being a part of the army community. He expressed the opinion that if the military wanted to have a group of wives who felt a part of the Army and a part of their husbands' professions, quarters on the post should be provided early in the husbands' careers. The association between living arrangements, identification with the army community, alienation, and family problems was also pointedly noted by a civilian staff member of the Army Community Services office when he stated that "if one is interested in locating a lot of family problems, all one has to do would be to talk to the army wife who is living off post."

Hill (1958) also noted the importance of the family's attitude about the community and the family's interaction with the community. In a discussion of the social stresses on the family, Hill stated:

> It has always puzzled observers that some families ride out the vicissitudes of floods and disasters without apparent disorganization.... The key appears to be at the meaning dimension. Stressors become crisis in line with the definition that family makes of the event.... The families who adjusted least well ... were families whose relationship with relatives and neighbors had become tenuous.... These families lacked the nest of supporting families with which to share their troubles and were, therefore, forced to live alone in an enforced anonymity. Left to their own devices, crisis-stricken families in a new neighborhood withdrew into their narrow family circles and festered inwardly rather than risk being rebuffed (p. 141).

The studies and observations noted above suggest that the association between alienation and a stressful situation, especially geographical mobility, is of significance, and of primary importance is the individual's own definition of the situation.

Thus, it appears that four general questions may be potentially productive in the investigation of the association between the stresses brought about by geographical mobility and problems experienced by army families. First, is there an association between feelings of alienation and mobility in the military community? Second, are feelings of alienation influenced by residence, that is, by whether the family lives on a military post? Third, are feelings of alienation on the part of the army wife/mother an important variable in the incidence of family problems? And, fourth, are the feelings of alienation related to the army wife's identification with the military community?

The general questions noted above involve four major concepts: feelings of alienation, lack of community identification, geographical mobility, and family problems. These concepts and questions fall logically within the theoretical framework of anomie. While it is not the purpose of this paper to develop anomie theory specifically, it is necessary, because of the variety of theoretical interpretations, to have some understanding of anomie as it is used in this study, as well as to develop the major concepts within this organizing theory.

ANOMIE AND ALIENATION

The French sociologist Emile Durkheim is accredited with using the term anomie in his book *The Division of Labor in Society* (1947), first published in 1895. To Durkheim, anomie seemed to mean a condition of deregulation or relative normlessness in a social group. He viewed anomie as endemic in modern society owing to a lack of integration which has arisen because the division of labor fails to produce sufficiently effective contacts between people and adequate regulation of social relationships.

Merton (1957) discarded Durkheim's concept of man as an insatiable creature who can be controlled only by social restraints, and examined the actual social pressures upon persons to violate the accepted codes. While he retained Durkheim's idea that anomie was due to normlessness, he had other ideas of its causes. Merton viewed anomie as a breakdown in the cultural and social structure.

In addition to the more sociological emphasis of the theory, there is a large body of writing that appears to be psychologically oriented, emphasizing a state of mind rather than a state of society. The psychological aspects of anomie have been specifically examined by McClosky and Schaar (1957), who suggested that when socialization and the learning of norms are impeded by either a lack of ability to comprehend or an excess in the individual personality of anxiety, hostility, rigidity, i.e., "whatever interferes with learning the norms of a society," anomic feelings are increased. Impediments, then, may arise from an individual's social setting, from his personality characteristics, or from both.

Another important reformulation of anomie theory that seems to blend the individual's social setting and his individual personality characteristics is made by Talcott Parsons (1951). In a number of writings Parsons has extended the theoretical formulation of anomie and incorporated it into a broader theory of interactional analysis. Where Merton refers only to the stress occasioned by the discrepancy between institutionalized means and goals, Parsons develops several other forms—for example, when a person fails to reconcile his expectations of himself to the expectations others have of him.

Perhaps the most important work in the evolution of anomie theory, in terms of its psychological application, is that of Leo J. Srole (1956). Srole conceptualized anomie as:

a psychological state which refers to the individual's generalized pervasive sense of self-to-others belongingness at one extreme compared with self-to-others distance and self-to-others alienation at the other pole of the continuum (pp. 63-67).

He then postulated five attitudinal-ideational components of the anomic state of mind. Expressed as questions, does the anomic person feel that: (1) community leaders are indifferent to his needs; (2) little can be accomplished in a society whose social order is essentially unpredictable; (3) life goals are receding from him rather than being reached; (4) no one can be counted on for support; and/or (5) life is meaningless and futile?

Srole's scale has been employed in a large number of investigations and, along with Merton's typology of modes of adaptation (1957), is the most widely used instrument in the study of anomie. Investigators who have administered the Srole scale to various samples have uniformly reported that anomie is highest among certain sectors of the population (Bell, 1957; Meir and Bell, 1959; Roberts and Rokeach, 1956). Srole himself, in an early work, used a research model in which social malintegration stands as the independent variable and the mental state of anomie as the dependent variable. He theorized that to a large degree the state of anomie in an individual is dependent upon and determined by the condition of sociological integration at the points of the social system concurrently occupied by him (McClosky and Schaar, 1957).

In his later work, however, Srole broadened his formulation to include the possibility that anomie might be a function not only of social conditions but also of personality factors. Srole, then, is among those sociologists who have emphasized the subjective aspects of anomie which have been equated with the concept of alienation.

Although some exception (Nettler, 1957) has been taken to Srole's equation of anomie and feelings of alienation in the individual, the writer has selected Srole's definition of anomie for the purpose of the study of geographical mobility and family problems in the Army. The reason for this selection is that Srole's definition seems the most appropriate to the problem as formulated in the present study, and because of its operationalization and wide use in research.

GEOGRAPHICAL MOBILITY AND FAMILY PROBLEMS

A careful review of the literature on geographical mobility reveals no research, other than Pedersen and Sullivan's (1964) specific to the problems of the army family. In fact, the literature on spatial mobility and the family in general is very sparse. Studies that have been done on relocation, in general, have tended to confound mobility with other variables such as social class membership and horizontal mobility. Also, most of the literature refers to a study population identified as emotionally disturbed. However, the fact seems well documented that psychosocial casualty rates are associated with the disruption of social continuity accompanying relocation (Malzberg and Lee, 1956). Despite the lack of specificity to the army family in particular or to the family in general, and despite the confoundment of variables, the literature has much to offer the present study.

Geographical Mobility and Children

Teitze (1942) found that the rates of childhood disorders were higher for the group of children with the shortest time of residence in a house than for the study group with a longer period of residence in a house, but this relationship could not be demonstrated with length of residence in a city. Wilner (1962), who studied a group of children who had moved to a new development project and compared them with a group who remained in the slums, found that in a two-year period the group which had moved were more likely to be promoted in school, while the nonmovers were more often retained.

Additional support for the view that major change within the family group, in conjunction with mobility, has an adverse effect upon children was given by Bowlby (1952) and Weinberg (1961). Weinberg, for example, reviewed an array of literature concerning the mental health of refugees and displaced persons, and concluded that migration in family groups leads to a more favorable adjustment than solitary migration. He also noted that the reason for the move was important—involuntary migration itself has adverse effects.

Mobility under more ordinary circumstances is the focus of another group of studies which concern the child's social and academic adjustment to a new classroom setting. The dimensions emphasized are time of entry into the new classroom and the amount of residential and school mobility (Liddle, 1955; Smith and Demming, 1958; Smith, 1959; Young and Cooper, 1944).

Gilliland (1959) studied IQ as an intervening variable in the relationship between mobility and academic achievement and found that the transient children were significantly ahead of the nontransients in mean achievement and total achievement; in addition, with an increase in IQ and in the number of schools attended, an increase in the difference of the scores for transients and nontransients was noted. He also observed that transient children of professional parents gain much from mobility.

Adding to the variety of possible intervening variables have been the studies that dealt with the importance of parental attitude in association with moving. As has already been noted, perhaps the most significant study has been that of

Pedersen and Sullivan (1964), in which they found that the child's adjustment to a change of residence was in part dependent upon his mother's acceptance of the move. The writer also has previously observed that the element of parental attitude was perhaps involved in Weinberg's (1961) finding that if the move was involuntary, adverse effects resulted.

Kantor (1965), in commenting on the variety of frequently contradictory findings in the studies of academic and social adjustment of children, notes the possible confoundment of the findings by the influence of social mobility. In a study designed to distinguish between the effect of residential mobility as opposed to occupational, educational, and income mobility, she found that factors other than a change in residence appear to be related to change in the child's adjustment; the residential change itself is not sufficient to raise or reduce the child's disturbance level. However, she did find that families who change residence *within* a community have less well adjusted children, and frequently the child's maladjustment itself prompts the move.

Geographical Mobility and the Family

Although the literature on geographical mobility is limited in terms of the family, the literature that exists emphasizes the importance of the nuclear family's involvement with the extended family and the broader community in general. Litwak (1960), for example, dealt with the importance of the extended family. In his discussion of his findings, he mentioned how extended family ties offer emotional support throughout periods of transition and geographical mobility during which the nuclear family's social contacts are temporarily severed. In another study, Davis (1960) addressed the problems faced by the military wife traveling overseas and noted the increased importance of formal and informal military community resources.

Burchinal and Bauder (1965) referred to the importance of how well the mobile family fits into the social structure of its new home; they emphasized the importance of the interactional nature within the family unit and between the family and the larger community in adjusting to the move. Alienation and isolation are the important variables in family adjustment to the stress of geographical mobility. In regard to individual alienation within the family unit itself, role theory suggests that the basis of communication is the proper enactment of the reciprocal roles within the family (Spiegel, 1957). The family that cannot readjust its roles equitably in accordance with the demands of moving shuts off further effective communication that would allow for the needed changes; the result is an ever tightening circle of isolation of the individual members.

Relevant Studies on Family Problems

Among the labyrinth of literature that relates to family problems in general, but not specific to mobility, is a group of writings that has strong implications for a study of mobility and alienation. These are primarily clinical in their orientation and deal generally with concepts of stress within systems—family systems.

According to authors like Satir (1964) or Bell (1963), in the so-called functional family, goals tend to be defined as existing outside of the family and, generally, in socially approved terms; goals may be as specific as going to a movie or as general as providing a good education. Each member, by virtue of his presence and position in the family, has a unique contribution to make toward a family objective. Any change which steers family members off course tends to result in a redefinition by the other members of the same goal; however, the change may be seen as an indication that the goal should be altered if it suits the total family's objective. In either case, since the goal is the principal focus, the interrelationships among the family members tend to be readjusted in order to maintain integration. At the same time, goals are not sought at the total sacrifice of an individual's needs and development. The point that is being made is that by changing the interrelationships in functional families, the integration of the family is not threatened nor are the chances of their getting where they want to go lessened.

On the other hand, a dysfunctional family seems to be continually so threatened that it perceives changes which veer members off course as not only a threat to reaching a goal, but also as a threat to the very existence of the family. Consequently, much of their activity is devoted toward redefining their relationships so that their integration will be preserved. The difficulty may not be so much that these families lack interrelationships which can function as homeostatic controls and thus put them back on course, but rather that the interrelationships are totally preoccupied with maintaining the status quo. Changes occasioned by the transfer and absence of the sponsor introduces a situation whereby reorganization and realignment are needed to survive—a situation that is, of course, at cross-purposes to the original static balance which allowed for no change. The result is an anomic kind of situation where the goal and the means to obtain that goal are no longer complementary, and the family isolates itself in an attempt to maintain its tenuous balance.

Summary

Although a variety of impressions and findings that sometimes contradict one another have been noted in the review of relevant research, one theme seems to dominate the literature and is particularly pertinent to the theoretical framework of the present study. The theme, of course, is the reference, sometimes covert, to group belonging and association and to the discontinuity between goals and means. The literature also suggests that the confoundment of findings is due to intervening variables other than alienation. The writer suggests that in the following study the effect of at least two of these intervening variables, i.e., occupational mobility and reasons for moving, will be diminished because of the nature of the population. The families of this study, in general, moved because the Army directed them to move.

METHODOLOGY

Purpose

The purpose of this study was to shed light on the relationship of alienation to the incidence of marital and family problems, in general, and associated in time with moving. Furthermore, it was theorized that lack of identification with the military community might be a specific corollary of a generalized attitude of alienation. Thus, the correlation between the following variables was questioned: the wife/mother's feelings of alienation; her lack of military community identification; and family problems, both in general and associated in time with a move. Since the limitations of the study necessitated the respondents' retrospective (after move) and personal assessment of intra- and interpersonal family problems, the resulting bias had to be mitigated.

First, the question of whether the wife/mother's feelings of alienation and lack of community identification were related to family problems that had occurred at any time since the marriage had to be investigated. Second, the relationship between these same feelings of alienation and identification, and family problems that the respondents specified to a time frame approximating a move (but not specifically identified in the respondent's mind as caused by the move itself), had to be studied. Third, as a double check, the writer questioned if the correlation between alienation, lack of identification, and recent family problems (previous three months) would be significantly greater in those randomly sampled families who had just completed a move (within the past three months) than in those families relatively situated (twelve months or more) having completed a move at least twelve months prior to investigation. Finally, the writer questioned whether the wife/mother's feelings of alienation were related to her lack of community identification.

Principal Concepts

Feelings of Alienation. "Feelings of alienation" is a descriptive term referring to the subjective aspects of anomie theory, sometimes referred to as anomia. It is used, for the purpose of the present study, synonomously with Srole's definition of anomie, "the individual's pervasive sense of self-to-others belongingness at one extreme compared to self-to-others alienation at the other pole of the continuum."

Identification with the Military or Army Community. Identification with the Army is an attitude dimension which relates broadly to the individual's invest-ment in the military "way of life." It is an expression of preference for living in and having friends from the military community, and a feeling of satisfaction associated with the choice of a military career.

Geographical Mobility. A family was considered to be geographically mobile when the husband's military orders required a relocation of the family from one military post area to the post area selected for the data-gathering purposes of the present study.

Family Problems. Family problems refers to the army parents' perception of their own and their children's difficulties in enacting their various family and community roles. The term was operationalized through various instruments, to be specified later, that assessed both intra- and interpersonal problem areas, including the family's contact with medical and community family problem-solving resources. It was hypothesized that family problems accompanying geographical mobility are directly associated with those families where the wife/mother feels alienated from society and from the military community. Furthermore, it was hypothesized that these associations would be differentially distributed in the community according to place of residence.

Hypotheses

Specifically, the hypotheses addressed by the study were as follows:

I. There is a statistically significant direct correlation between the wife/mother's feelings of alienation and the incidence of family problems. That is, the greater the degree of the wife/mother's feeling of alienation, the greater the incidence of family problems.

II. (a) There is a statistically significant direct correlation between feelings of alienation and the incidence of family problems that the respondents have indicated retrospectively as having started or having been exacerbated about the time of a geographical relocation.

(b) The correlation between feelings of alienation and family problems that the respondents have indicated as having started or having been exacerbated within the past three months prior to the study, will be significantly greater in those randomly sampled families who have been situated for twelve months or more.

III. (a) There is a statistically significant direct correlation between the army wife's feelings of lack of identification with the military community and family problems associated in time with a move.

(b) There is a statistically significant direct correlation between the army wife's feelings of lack of identification with the military community and her feelings of alienation.

IV. There is a significant correlation between alienation and family problems associated with a move among those respondents living on the army post.

Data Collection and Instrumentation

A twofold scheme of gathering data was employed. The principal instrument was a questionnaire mailed to 200 enlisted army families who had been randomly selected in a stratified manner according to whether they had recently completed a move or whether they were geographically settled and whether they lived off post or on post. The second means for obtaining data was a personal interview with 29 of the 80 respondent wives.

Included in the mailed packet, in addition to questions regarding demographic data and confounding variables, were the Srole Anomie Scale (1956: 63-67); the Mooney Problem Checklist (see Buros, 1965: 146); Faber and Blackman's Index of Marital Role Tension (1960: 596-600); the Pedersen Attitude Scale (Pederson and Sullivan, 1964: 575-580), which assesses identification with the military community; the Clements Marital Problem Checklist and some items from the Clements Needs-Wants Inventory (1968); and a children's problems checklist selected from the Midtown Manhattan questionnaire (provided by Dr. Srole, 1962).

Regarding the three checklists—the Mooney Problem Checklist, the children's problems checklist, and the Clements Marital Problem Checklist—the respondents were given the opportunity to state whether or not the onset or exacerbation of the problem was associated in time with a move, i.e., they were asked to select one or more of four time frames ("0-3 months ago, 6 months ago, 12 months, 18 months or more . . ."). Comparisons were then made between problem onset and approximation to the time of a move. Additionally, as noted previously, comparisons were made between the two time-stratified subsamples.

All other questionnaire data were collected in terms of the subject's present time frame. Those instruments specific to marital interaction were necessarily composite scores of husband and wife. Additionally, all other assessments of "family problems" combined the independent perceptions of both husband and wife. The latter was done to reduce individual bias, and seemed more compatible with contemporary conceptualizations of the reciprocal and symbiotic nature of "problems" within family systems.

Interview data were collected in a generally open and unstructured atmosphere to provide depth and relevance in the study. Two trained interviewers collected the data which were tabulated immediately following the interviews. Interview items themselves were categorized according to the following: individual and family problems; alienation and identification, before and after the move; family goals and means, and personality traits selected from the Midtown guide (Srole, 1962).

Subjects

A random sample of 200 families was drawn and stratified according to length of time in the study area (less than three months or more than twelve months). The stratification was deemed desirable, as noted previously, to provide a comparison group to mitigate the bias introduced by the respondents' retrospective assessment of problems specific to a move. Eighty of these families responded to a mailed packet containing a lengthy questionnaire. From these 80 respondents, a random sample of 30, balanced for degree of anomia and duration in the study area, was selected for a follow-up personal interview. Twenty-nine agreed to be interviewed.

Analyses

Primary emphasis of the study was placed on the questionnaire data. The analysis of these data involved a detailed method of measuring the association between the major variables and traits within the various strata of the study. That is, correlations between feelings of alienation and the various categories of family problems were assessed in families living on and off the army post who had just arrived in the area, and those who had been located for 12 to 13 months. Point bi-serial correlational analyses were conducted on the questionnaire data, and the data obtained from the interviews were analyzed principally through content analysis.

FINDINGS

The following sections present in narrative and tabular form an analysis, described above, of the data pertinent to the hypotheses. While the main focus is on the hypotheses, sections will also be included which deal with the characteristics of the sample population and the correlations between the main study variables and other variables and attributes which are not specific to the hypotheses.

Population Characteristics

The wives/mothers were young, with a median age of 25.5; the average length of their marriages was five years, and they had a mean of 1.8 children. The majority of the respondent wives came originally from lower socioeconomic strata, although, as a whole, they were relatively well educated; 70 percent of the wives had a high school education or above and 30 percent had attended college. Their husbands had an average of 8.5 years in the Service with the largest number of men falling in the three- to five-year category. The largest group of noncommissioned officers was E-6, with E-5 being the mode for the specialists, proportional to rank and years of service strata in the Army as a whole. The majority of families had made six or more moves while in the Service.

Alienation and Family Problems in General

Data presented in Table 1 confirm the hypothesis that there is a direct and significant correlation between feelings of alienation and family problems not specifically associated in time with a move.

The correlation between alienation and family problems was particularly strong regarding the utilization of the Mooney Problem Checklist and the Clements Needs-Wants Inventory. Interestingly, for those families well situated in the area, there was an inverse correlation between alienation and use of community resources ($r = -.422$; $p < .01$). That is, those families who seem to need help the most use formally constituted resources least.

Alienation and Family Problems Associated with Moving

Data presented in Tables 2 and 3 tend to confirm the hypotheses (IIa and IIb) which proposed a strong and direct correlation between feelings of alienation and family problems associated with moving. Interestingly, those anomic families residing in the area for 12 months had a much higher correlation regarding children's problems. Also, of particular note was the lack of use of community resources, in general, but the strong use of medical resources by those anomic families who had just completed a move.

TABLE 1

CORRELATION BETWEEN FEELINGS OF ALIENATION AND FAMILY PROBLEMS

Traits	Length of Assignment to Post Area		
	3 Months N=37	12 Months N=43	All 3 & 12 Months N-80
Mooney Checklist Problems	.709**	.606**	.648**
Children's Problems	.372**	.399**	.388**
Marital Role Tension	.466**	.463**	.464**
Needs-Wants Discrepancy	.628**	.651**	.623**
Incidence of Marital Problems	.471**	.308**	.382**
Medical Resource Contacts	.134	-.163	.068 .
Community Resource Contacts	-.086	-.442**	-.273**

* = p < .05
** = p < .01

Lack of Community Identification and Family Problems Associated with Moving

The data indicated that the correlations between lack of identification with the Army way of life and family problems associated with moving are direct and strong (e.g., r = .564; p < .01) in those poorly identified (with the military community) families who had recently completed a move, but not significant (e.g., r = .138) in the families who had lived in the area for 12 months or more (see Table 4).

In comparing alienation and lack of identification with the military community (see Table 5), the analysis revealed that while there is a strong and direct

TABLE 2

CORRELATION BETWEEN FEELINGS OF ALIENATION AND

FAMILY PROBLEMS ASSOCIATED WITH MOVING TO A NEW POST

	Length of Assignment to Post Area		
	3 Months *N=37*	*12 Months* *N=43*	*All* *3 & 12 Months* *N=80*
Mooney Checklist Problems	.711**	.699**	.641**
Children's Problems	.251*	.611**	.392**
Incidence of Marital Problems	.443**	.627**	.436**
Medical Resource Contacts	.589*	-.163	.239*
Community Resource Contacts	.030	-.239*	-.125

* = $p < .05$
** = $p < .01$

correlation ($r = .357$ to $.517$; $p < .01$), these concepts are not identical entities. It was of interest, however, to find that alienation and lack of identification seem to function as similar entities in those families who had just completed a move.

Differential Location of Family Problems

Off-Post/On-Post Differences in the Coefficients of Correlation Between Alienation and Family Problems Associated with Moving. The data given in Table 6 tend to confirm the hypothesis that there is a difference between the correlation of alienation and family problems associated with a move among those respondents living off the army post and those living on the army post. The correlations are significantly different in all but the area of children's problems. It should be noted that while the correlations are significantly

TABLE 3

CORRELATION BETWEEN FEELINGS OF ALIENATION AND FAMILY
PROBLEMS WHICH OCCURRED DURING THE THREE MONTHS
(1 JUNE 68 - 1 SEPT. 68) PRIOR TO DATA COLLECTION
AND THE EVALUATION OF DIFFERENCE BETWEEN THE
COEFFICIENTS FOR EACH TIME PERIOD

| Traits | Length of Assignment | | | | Difference Between Z Coefficients | SEDZ | Z Ratio |
| | Pearson r Coefficients | | Z Coefficients | | | | |
	3 Mos. N=73	12 Mos. N=43	3 Mos. N=37	12 Mos N=43			
Mooney Checklist Problems	.711**	-.011	.89	-.01	.90	.073	12.33**
Children's Problems	.251*	.222*	.26	.22	.04	.073	.54
Incidence of Marital Problems	.443**	.092	.47	.09	.38	.073	5.20**

* = p < .05
** = p < .01

stronger in the off-post grouping in the area of Mooney Checklist Problems, the on-post families perceived a greater incidence to marital problems.

Off-post/On-Post Differences in the Coefficients of Correlation Between Lack of Identification with the Army Community and Family Problems Associated with Moving. The data given in Table 7 indicate the correlations of lack of identification with the Army and family problems associated with moving are *not* differentially located in the community according to place of residence. No significant difference was found between the Off-Post and the On-Post residents, except in the use of community resources.

TABLE 4

CORRELATION BETWEEN LACK OF IDENTIFICATION WITH
THE ARMY COMMUNITY AND FAMILY PROBLEMS ASSOCIATED WITH THE
THREE MONTHS PRIOR TO DATA COLLECTION AND EVALUATION
OF THE DIFFERENCE BETWEEN THE COEFFICIENTS FOR EACH TIME PERIOD

Traits	Length of Assignment				Difference Between Z Coefficients	SEDZ	Z Ratio
	Pearson r Coefficients		Z Coefficients				
	3 Mos. N=37	12 Mos. N=43	3 Mos. N=37	12 Mos. N=43			
Mooney Checklist Problems	.564**	.138	.63	.14	.49	.073	6.71**
Children's Problems	.249*	-.215	.25	-.22	.47	.073	6.43**
Incidence of Marital Problems	.346**	-.048	.37	-.05	.42	.073	5.75**

* = p <.05

** = p <.01

TABLE 5

CORRELATION BETWEEN LACK OF IDENTIFICATION
WITH THE ARMY COMMUNITY AND FEELINGS OF ALIENATION

Trait	Place of Residence		Length of Assignment		
	Off Post N=38	On Post N=42	3 Mos. N=37	12 Mos. N=43	All N=80
Alienation	.357**	.517**	.466**	.462**	.464**

* = p <.01

TABLE 6

CORRELATION BETWEEN FEELINGS OF ALIENATION AND
FAMILY PROBLEMS ASSOCIATED WITH MOVING TO
A NEW POST FOR WIFE OF ARMY PERSONNEL RESIDING
OFF AND ON THE POST AND EVALUATION OF THE
DIFFERENCE BETWEEN COEFFICIENTS FOR EACH
PLACE OF RESIDENCE

Traits	Length of Assignment				Difference Between Z Coefficients	SEDZ	Z Ratio
	Pearson Coefficients		Z Coefficients				
	Off Post N=38	On Post N=42	Off Post N=38	On Post N=42			
Mooney Checklist Problems	.710**	.605**	.89	.70	.19	.074	2.61**
Children's Problems	.480**	.395**	.52	.10	.10	.074	1.34
Marital Problems	.355**	.539**	.38	.60	.22	.074	2.98**
Medical Contacts	.067	.379**	.07	.40	.33	.074	4.46**
Community Resource Contacts	.232*	-.012	-.23	.01	.22	.074	2.98**

* = p < .05

** = p < .01

TABLE 7

CORRELATION BETWEEN LACK OF IDENTIFICATION
WITH THE ARMY COMMUNITY AND FAMILY PROBLEMS
ASSOCIATED WITH MOVING TO A NEW POST FOR THE
WIFE OF ARMY PERSONNEL LIVING OFF AND ON THE
POST AND EVALUATION OF THE DIFFERENCE BETWEEN
COEFFICIENTS FOR EACH PLACE OF RESIDENCE

Traits	Length of Assignment				Difference Between Z Coefficients	SEDZ	Z Ratio
	Pearson Coefficients		Z Coefficients				
	Off Post N=38	On Post N=42	Off Post N=38	On Post N=42			
Mooney Checklist Problems	.425	.388	.45	.41	.04	.074	.54
Children's Problems	.172	.187	.17	.18	.01	.074	.13
Marital Problems	.240	.338	.24	.35	.11	.074	1.49
Medical Contacts	-.067	-.035	-.07	-.04	.03	.074	-.40
Community Resource Contacts	-.411	-.027	-.44	-.03	.41	.074	-5.54**

** = p < .01

Interview Data

The interview data added a great deal of depth and clarification to the questionnaire findings (see Table 8). A content analysis of some 14 traits indicative of feelings of "belonging" revealed that only 28 percent of the anomic wives compared to 87 percent of the nonanomic wives indicated that they felt they lived "in a neighborhood." Similar patterns prevailed before and after moving.

An assessment of the wives' personality characteristics seemed to indicate that the anomic wife had significantly higher incidence of pathological personality traits (see Table 9). The anomic or alienated wives had a composite score of 35 immaturity traits, compared to a score of 11 for the nonanomic wives.

TABLE 8

FEELINGS OF BELONGING TO A PARTICULAR
LOCALE FOR ALIENATED AND NONALIENATED
ARMY ENLISTED WIVES

Traits	Wives Who Feel Alienated (N=14)	Wives Who Do Not Feel Alienated (N=15)
Since Moving		
Neighborhood feeling	4	13
Prefer closeness of small towns	12	12
Know one or more neighbors well enough to visit	8	15
Have as many friends as want	6	9
Have one or more close friends	5	12
Belong to one or more clubs or groups	2	13
Belong to Army social group	4	4
Belong to civilian social group	0	11
Took some specific action to help children get acquainted	1	1
Regard the civilian community as hostile toward military families	12	2
Before Moving		
Neighborhood feeling	10	13
Knew one or more neighbors well enough to visit	10	15
Had one or more close friends	9	14
Belonged to social group	4	11

TABLE 9

NUMBER OF PATHOLOGICAL PERSONALITY CHARACTERISTICS
OF ALIENATED AND NONALIENATED WIVES

Traits	Wives Who Feel Alienated (N-14)	Wives Who Do Not Feel Alienated (N=15)
Immaturity	35	11
Rigidity	40	13
Suspiciousness	41	8
Withdrawal	37	20
Frustration-depression	51	7
Neurasthenia	36	10
Anxiety-adult	181	51
Anxiety-childhood	62	31
Psychophysiological	72	25
Excess intake of stimulants	3	10

Similar differences were found with regard to other symptoms, such as 40 to 13 regarding rigidity and 41 to 8 regarding suspiciousness.

Alienation, then, seems to be a much more pervasive and enduring personality trait, less amenable than identification to alteration. However, the interview data suggested that identification with the Army seemed to function as an ego defense mechanism for some of the otherwise anomic wives.

There were also other findings that were not specific to the hypotheses but are of interest. First, alienation was found to be inversely correlated with the wife's social class origin (r = .426; p < .01) and education (r = -.250; p < .01). That is, the lower the social class origins and the education level obtained, the greater the degree of feelings of alienation. Second, alienation was found to be directly associated with a number of problems characteristic of the family of origin: deprivation of either parent by death, divorce, or separation before age 16 (r = .357; p < .01); behavioral problems (r = .464; p < .01); and emotional problems (r_{pbi} = .257; p <.05). Third, the number of moves experienced by the army family was not significantly correlated with any of the main study variables. Fourth, family problems associated with moving correlated significantly with the wife's social class of origin (r = .267; p < .01) and behavioral problems in family of origin (r = .388; p < .01).

DISCUSSION AND CONCLUSIONS

The finding that feelings of alienation and family problems are directly and strongly associated with one another supports anomie theory, which proposes that a variety of adverse social and personal problems can result from feelings of alienation. While it was beyond the scope of the present study statistically to assess the cause-effect relationship between alienation and family problems, the interview data suggested that alienation precedes contemporary family problems. This was particularly apparent in the anomic respondents' past histories, which indicated the presence of social deprivation and feelings of isolation and frustration that preceded their contemporary family problems.

The interviews also suggested that feelings of alienation, as assessed in the present study, are associated with pathological personality traits, such as anxiety, rigidity, and hostility, which tend to alienate the individual from satisfying interpersonal contacts. It is not clear from the statistical analysis of the data, however, whether the personality features cause the alienation or vice versa. This finding, while not specifically approached in the statistical analysis of the data, tends to support the psychological concept of anomie. The interviews, however, indicated that sociostructural features which tend toward alienation have the potential of exacerbating feelings of alienation and associated family problems in those individuals who are characteristically anomic.

Furthermore, the army family likely to experience the greatest incidence of family problems associated with geographical relocation is the family in which the wife/mother feels alienated from society and from the army community. It was not clear from the statistical findings alone whether the alienation preceded the move, although interview data would indicate that it did; the anomic wives were alienated and socially isolated prior to their most recent moves. From the findings of the questionnaire data and the interview data, it can then be concluded that mobility is a particularly stressful socioenvironmental feature for the anomic and psychologically isolated army wife. This finding and conclusion support the impression of the exacerbating influence of environmental factors. It also supports the impression drawn by the writer from the mobility literature that alienation and group identification are important factors in a family's adjustment to geographical relocation.

The findings also indicate that the wife's lack of identification with the Army and alienation are associated with marital and children's problems to a similar degree in those families who have recently completed a move, but not similarly associated in those families who are relatively well settled in the area. It may be concluded, therefore, that alienation and identification seem to function as similar concepts at the time of a move, but not after a family has had a chance to become adapted to a new area.

In general, the alienated family experiences the greatest incidence of family problems associated with moving when they reside off the military post. In contrast, some problems, such as marital tension, are greater in similarly characterized families living on post. While this finding generally indicates that place of residence is an important consideration in the study of alienation and family problems, it cannot be concluded that these same families would experience less family difficulties if they resided on post or less marital conflicts if they resided off post. The family's place of residence, on or off post, appears to have differential effects upon the family system. Whether the closed community setting in the military precipitates greater marital conflicts, and the open civilian community setting fosters more general family problems, cannot be determined by this study.

Considering the periodic similarity of function between alienation and identification and their respective associations with family problems, one finding specifically relevant to place of residence was that a family who had lived mainly on post in the past was more likely to be identified with the Army than was the family who had lived mainly in civilian communities. It is not clear, however, whether living on post increases one's identification with the army community, or identification tends one toward on-post residence.

Finally, the army enlisted families who appear to have the greatest difficulty in moving turn least frequently to community resources for help. Informal initiation of help and interaction by neighbors and peers seem, from interview data, to be more significant to them. It can be concluded that the formal agencies designed to offer help do not reach those families who perhaps need it the most. Whether or not these families would respond to formal contact is not clear. The interview data, however, suggested that the anomic wife and family are more likely to respond to the informal contacts of peers.

Chapter 4

MOBILITY IN THE MILITARY: ITS EFFECT UPON

THE FAMILY SYSTEM

RAYMOND M. MARSH

INTRODUCTION

This study, which is exploratory and descriptive in nature, was designed to delineate problems and hardships endured by the nuclear family of military personnel undergoing enforced geographic mobility. It was postulated that a predisposition to experience family hardships during the moving process would be dependent upon differences in family characteristics, type of transfer, and the distance moved, and that families who have less contact with family community resources would experience more hardships than families that use formally established community resources or obtain assistance through informal social networks.

The significance of studying family hardships resulting from geographical mobility is apparent when one considers the extent of mobility throughout the nation. It is estimated that approximately one in seven individuals in this country moves each year (Rossi, 1955). This so-called milling around the country is due to a variety of reasons; the most frequently cited reasons being the search for employment or increased opportunities in the job market and dissatisfaction with the housing situation or disenchantment with the neighborhood. In addition, family relocations required by private industry and the defense establishment contribute significantly to geographic mobility in the United States. Public programs also account for a considerable number of family relocations. It is estimated, for example, that approximately 100,000 families are forced to move each year because of urban renewal and highway construction. A more recent development is the effort to encourage and facilitate the relocation of families residing in rural areas where there is an absence of industrialization. A substantial portion of voluntary moves are simply a result of

AUTHOR'S NOTE: This chapter is an adaptation of Marsh, R.M. "Family Disruption During the Moving Process," an unpublished doctoral dissertation prepared for Brandeis University, 1970.

the normal process of change in the family cycle (expansion or contraction of family size). The so-called push-pull factors (racial discrimination, unemployment, poor housing, inadequate public assistance benefits, etc.) related to internal migration by the nation's poor are now receiving increased attention from urban economists and social planners, as well as the providers of welfare services (Lansing and Mueller, 1967).

In spite of the increasing interest in geographical mobility and problems encountered by migratory families, the disruptive influences operating on families during the moving process and while settling into a new community, although frequently deplored, are rarely documented. Empirical studies are scarce and their findings inconclusive.

The Complexity of Moving

Even under the most favorable circumstances, families on the move have a variety of complex tasks to perform. While new and, perhaps, different relationships must be established between the family and the new as well as the old community, administration of customary family affairs must continue without interruption. For example, on the one hand, household goods and personal possessions must be packed and relocated; the old residence must be disposed of; and involvement in relationships, activities, and institutions in the old community must be terminated. On the other hand, entry into the new community means finding a suitable residence, beginning employment in a new place, acquiring friends and reestablishing contact with a church, a hospital, schools, utility services, and shopping facilities. Amidst all this transitional activity, the family must also continue functioning as a unit.

In addition to the performance of these rather basic tasks, there may be unique problems or intrafamily difficulties which increase the difficulties of the moving process. For example, the moving process might be further complicated by chronic illness in the family, by a handicapped child who needs special or remedial education, or by the need to sever close family ties. The complexity of geographical mobility may also be affected by mediating variables such as a forced relocation, by a sudden move with limited time to plan the move, or by a relocation to a community viewed by the family members as an undesirable place to live or work.

The Rationale for Studying Military Families

The movement of military personnel and their dependents is a constant major activity within the military system. In 1968 the Army alone, with a strength of 1,468,032, moved 59.5 percent of its personnel at least one time. Of the

873,659 male personnel who were moved, 42.8 percent had one or more dependents (U.S. Army, 1968). Like their civilian counterparts, military personnel and their dependents facing a relocation are required to confront a series of both expected and unexpected obstacles which may affect the complexity of tasks to be performed during the process of moving. For example, military regulations control, to some extent, the procedures that military personnel must follow when they are being transferred from one station to another. Furthermore, despite the availability of social and support services to the military person and his family while the move is being planned and executed, family differences as well as local variations in post policies and available resources reduce the uniformity and predictability of the experience, and therefore add to the complexity of family adjustment and adaptation.

There is a need to examine the nature and the extent of family hardships occasioned by geographical mobility in the military. Families who are forced to relocate as a result of reassignments, such as overseas assignments, as well as routine changes, should be of particular interest because the military system has formalized its responsibility for assisting these families. The degree to which the military community is responsive to the individual family varies and the quality of service and assistance that families can expect to receive from most of these programs is not uniform. This research recognizes that a need exists to examine systematically the effects of moving on the individual family and to determine the types of services and other resources that should be improved upon or be made available in order to minimize family hardships. It is assumed that findings from this research can be generalized to public programs such as urban renewal, highway construction, and other projects that require forced relocation and involve program planning for families who migrate or are forced to relocate themselves.

PAST RESEARCH

Considering the large numbers of families who move within this country each year and the disruptive nature of the moving process itself, there appears to be a paucity of research on problems actually encountered by families who are in the process of moving and settling into new communities. There are, however, a number of studies and theoretical discussions that are relevant to this inquiry.

Social mobility, both vertical and horizontal, has long been of interest to social scientists. Their interests, largely theoretical, provide some information which leads to a better understanding of the problem area that is the focus of this research. Generally, these scientists make a distinction between migration and mobility: migration usually refers to physical removal from one location to another, so that it may be a short move within the city or county or a long-distance move involving relocation in another region or country; social mobility is used to indicate a shift of a person's status in the social structure and is frequently referred to as vertical mobility, i.e., the movement may be upward or downward. Migration is always "horizontal in nature," meaning that one physically relocates his geographical position without any necessary change in his social status. The term "relocation" is most frequently employed by social planners and is usually used in conjunction with programs of clearing families from areas slated for urban renewal or highway construction projects.

The social science literature generally focuses upon three general components of the study of residential mobility: (1) reason for moving—involuntary, voluntary, dissatisfaction with dwelling, changes in composition of the family, employment opportunities, etc.; (2) intervening factors—community status, role opportunities, degree of disruption of social system involvement, education, occupation, income, credit, social psychological expectations of individuals, knowledge, skills, attitudes, values, creativity, interaction of families with a social structure, interaction of the nuclear family with the extended family, marital relationships, family cohesiveness, role flexibility, life styles, commitment to family goals, etc.; and (3) postmigration adjustments—consumption, leisure patterns, conformity to norms, extended and nuclear family role patterns, occupation, income, housing, social participation, political role, aspirations, satisfactions, complaints, fears, anxiety, etc. (Burchinal and Bauder, 1965). Few researchers have emphasized the family's adjustment process immediately after transition into a new community in an attempt to learn what disruptive influences were occurring and how the family was responding to them.

Three major studies which pertain to geographical mobility of military families were approached from the social-psychological perspective. Gabower (1959) was primarily concerned with behavior problems of children of Navy officers as they relate to social conditions of navy family life, including mobility. Pedersen and Sullivan (1964) studied the effects of geographical mobility and parental personality factors on emotional disorders in children. They used a sample of army families and hypothesized that the children whose parents experience the greatest number of geographical moves would experience the greatest number of emotional problems. In comparing a group of disturbed children with a group of children with no history of emotional difficulties, they found that the groups could not be distinguished with respect to incidence of mobility. They did find, however, that they differed significantly with respect to the mother's attitude toward mobility; mothers of disturbed children had a more negative attitude toward mobility in the military. Pedersen and Sullivan (1964), however, specifically cautioned the reader from making generalizations of their findings to other groups because they feared that the element of self-selection for the control group may have affected their findings. McKain (1969) studied feelings of alienation and family problems associated with geographical mobility in a group of recently relocated army families. His analysis revealed that there was a significant correlation between feelings of alienation and family problems associated with moving, and that families who seemed to have the greatest number of problems also tended to be minimally involved in the use of community resources to assist them with these problems.

The literature indicates that there are obvious gaps in the research on mobility, serious bias in the samples selected in previous studies, and contradictory findings in many of the studies that have been done to date. Generally, researchers agree that further inquiry is needed because of the lack of an integrated theory and the lack of hard data on the families who move and their reestablishment in the receiving communities. It seems clear that if social institutions are to provide assistance to families in making transitions during the process of migration, they must know more about the nature of the problems that are experienced. Services must be fashioned and policies established that will be socially sensitive to the stresses and disruptions experienced by highly mobile families in our society.

OPERATIONAL FRAMEWORK

This study was primarily designed to obtain data that have practical implications for more effective planning of services for military families. An effort was made to assess the relationship between hardships experienced by the family, attitudes toward moving, the degree of neighboring, and the extent to which the family felt settled in the new community after a period of two months. Three indices were developed in order to quantify these measures: the dependent variable, family hardships; and two major independent variables, extent of neighboring and attitude toward relocation.

The research concentrated on an examination of the allocation of resources, a lack of which would contribute to family hardships. The attribute of hardship was measured by the following empirical referents: the family is forced to live apart during the moving process; the cost of moving exceeds allowances payable by the Army; the family must borrow funds in order to complete the move; the family must wait more than 29 days for assignment of post housing or before finding suitable housing in the civilian market; medical treatment for a family member must be interrupted by the move; the family is forced to sell household goods to conform with weight allowances; the family is forced to purchase additional items (in excess of dislocation allowance) to furnish new residence; the family's shipment of household goods is delayed; a family member's schooling is interrupted during a semester; a family member's essential part-time employment is terminated; interpretation by the family that the new post will not be a desirable place to live; and interruption of the family's pay and allowances owing to transfer of records.

The assumption is that, since the military requires its personnel to be mobile, it must provide supportive services to assist the family in relocation. It was postulated that if the social structure failed to provide the required social and economic resources for the family, then hardships would be generated and the family may experience crisis. Thus, one of the implicit questions being raised by this study is whether existing supports are sufficient. Existing services, which include provision of transportation for families and household goods (including payment of claims for damages), government quarters, dislocation allowances, and a variety of social services in a sense reflect some of the Army's policies and programs in the planning for its personnel and movement of their families. Other indications of policies dealing with the movement of personnel are such things as: the amount of travel time allowed, granting of compassionate reassignments and delays of permanent changes of station that would cause undue family hardship, and advancing military pay under specified conditions. Taken collectively, these policies and programs reflect the sensitivity of the Army to the problems of family relocation and represent the allocation of required resources to help meet families' needs during the moving process. The further assumption is made that it is desirable that these resources be allocated in such a manner as to prevent family hardship. The occurrence of family discord as a result of geographic mobility may require additional resources (both internal and external to the family unit) to assist them in reorganizing and reestablishing family equilibrium.

It is not contended that all geographical relocation represents a "life crisis" or hardship that the nuclear family cannot appropriately handle with its own internal resources. As a matter of fact, it has been suggested in the literature review that relocation can represent increased opportunities for the family (Little, 1970). Military families, reunited after a hardship tour or relocated at their own request in order to be near a dependent relative, represent moves that unite and support the nuclear family. It is reasonable to assume, nevertheless, that in a period of transition there is some degree of disruption of previously maintained social and interpersonal relationships, and a series of interactions between the family and its environment must take place as the family seeks to establish equilibrium in a new environment. This study examined the hardships, if any, the family endured during the process of transition.

It was postulated that there is a predisposition to experiencing family hardships in the moving process depending on differences in the characteristics of the family's attitude toward moving and the distance of the move. Furthermore, families who experience hardships as a result of the move but who make greater use of supportive services and neighboring, and have a positive attitude toward relocating at the new post, will have fewer family hardships than those families who have less contact with their neighbors, have a negative attitude toward relocating at the new post, and make less use of services available to assist them in moving and settling into the community.

METHODOLOGY

Two pretested and self-administered questionnaires were prepared for data collection. The first questionnaire was presented to the service member while he was being "in-processed" at the unit personnel office immediately after arrival at his new duty station. The purpose of the instrument was to determine if any major family problem had occurred during the actual move itself. Additionally, it provided descriptive data on the subject and his family. Two months after the arrival of the military member, a second questionnaire was presented to him for completion. With the focus of obtaining additional social characteristics, this instrument was designed to elicit information on possible hardships that the family experienced during the moving process and settling into the community. It also obtained information regarding the use of social services, the degree of neighboring, and the extent to which family members felt they had become settled into the community since their arrival.

The study was conducted at a relatively isolated army post located in a semirural area about 50 miles from a major northeastern city. As at other army posts of comparable size, there was a broad range of social welfare activities, medical facilities, post exchanges, family housing, schools, a commissary, a bank, and other essential services to support a military facility of approximately 10,000 personnel and their families.

The study population consisted of every enlisted military family arriving at the post during the three-month study period. Of the 332 personnel who initially met the eligibility criteria for the study, 145 were later declared ineligible and 3 refused to participate.[1] A total of 205 families were finally selected for the study sample.

Major Indices of Family Adjustment

Three indices were developed for this study: a family hardship scale, an attitude toward relocating scale, and a neighboring scale.

Family Hardship Scale. The items included in this scale measure family hardships, that is, the degree to which the family system was stressed (children's schooling; borrowing money was necessitated). A factor analysis of these fifteen variables was undertaken to provide additional evidence that the items chosen to compose the scale represent a unitary measure of family hardship. The interpretation of the factor loadings (Marsh, 1970) suggests that the items selected to develop the index of family hardships have an acceptable degree of content validity. That is, they seem to demonstrate that a consistent theme of hardships underlies the items in the scale. In order to determine the reliability of the scale based on internal consistency, an alpha coefficient was computed. An alpha coefficient of .634 was obtained.

Attitude Toward Relocation Scale. In order to measure the family's attitude toward relocation, an index of twelve items was designed to measure the family's attitude toward the new community in which they were living, opinions of the type of duty assignment, and reactions to the working conditions in the new community. Factor analysis of the 12 items revealed the scale measures the family's satisfaction with the new post, commitment to the military, satisfaction with living quarters, and familiarity with the new post. The alpha coefficient in this instance was .726, an acceptable level of reliability.

Neighboring Scale. A neighboring index was constructed for the purpose of measuring the extent to which the family interacted informally with friends and neighbors. The seven-item index, when factor-analyzed, indicated an emphasis (of measures) upon interaction with new neighbors, establishing new friends, and helping newcomers. The alpha coefficient, .610, represented an acceptable level of reliability.

FINDINGS

The frequency distribution of the items on the Family Hardship Scale (Table 1) revealed that the most heavily scored items were: cost of move was greater than the payable allowances provided by the Army; the necessity for the family to borrow money in order to pay the cost of the moving; delay in regular monthly pay because the finance record was lost or in process of being transferred; and separation of family during the process of moving. Of the 914 points scored on the scale, 412 were made on these items, thus indicating that most of the hardship lay within this portion of the index. Only 13 families failed to score on the scale and only one family scored as high as twelve points.

Table 2 presents the frequency distribution of scores on the twelve items contained in the Attitude Toward Relocation Scale. Item 3 was more frequently

TABLE 1

FREQENCY DISTRIBUTION OF SCORES ON FAMILY HARDSHIP SCALE

Items	Number	Percent
1. Cost exceeded allowances	130	63.4
2. Borrowed money to cover cost of moving	81	39.5
3. Unable to find house for a period exceeding 29 days	73	35.6
4. Family separated during move	68	33.1
5. Pay delayed owing to moving	60	29.2
6. Family separated because of no house	57	27.8
7. Household goods lost or damaged	55	26.8
8. Bought extra household goods	52	25.3
9. Hardship caused by pay delay	51	24.8
10. Medical care interrupted	41	20.0
11. Family separated over 29 days	39	19.0
12. Sold items to meet weight allowances	29	14.1
13. Preferred assignment elsewhere	23	11.2
14. Unable to find part-time job	22	10.7
15. Children's schooling interrupted	20	9.7

TABLE 2

FREQUENCY DISTRIBUTION OF SCORES ON ATTITUDE

TOWARD RELOCATION SCALE[a]

	Positive	%	Negative	%
1. Respondent's anticipation that he will like working conditions at new post	55	26	155	76
2. First impressions of new post immediately upon his arrival	85	41	120	59
3. Respondent's anticipation that he will like his military duties at new post	88	43	117	67
4. Feelings toward having a job that requires moving periodically	24	12	181	88
5. Respondent's immediate reaction when notified he was being transferred to new post	62	30	143	70
6. Family's first reaction when notified they were moving to new post	62	30	143	70
7. Family's current feeling about living at new post	66	32	141	68
8. Respondent's familiarity with new post before arrival	31	15	174	85
9. Rating of present home	85	41	120	59
10. Commitment to the military as a career	36	17	169	83
11. Satisfaction with military duties	62	30	143	70
12. Respondent's feelings now about living at new post	63	31	142	69

[a]The study population scored 1,476 on this index for a mean of 7.20. The standard deviation, 2.792, with a variance of 7.798; the skewness was -0.491, with a kurtosis of -0.680.

cited than the other items; 88 percent of the sample indicated their anticipation of liking the military duties at the new post. Eighty-five percent of the population had a positive impression of the new post immediately upon their arrival and a like number rated their current house as being better than their previous one. Only 24 percent of the sample indicated that they did not mind having a job that required them to move periodically.

Table 3 presents the frequency distribution of the scores on the seven items designed to measure the extent to which the family interacted informally with friends and neighbors. "Stop and talk with neighbors" received the highest number of positive responses, with 47 percent of the sample responding positively to this item. The next highest positively scored item was "Number of new friends increased here."

In order to explain the variance in family hardship, the data was analyzed further. A correlational analysis revealed a positive correlation between family

TABLE 3

FREQUENCY DISTRIBUTION OF SCORES ON NEIGHBORING SCALE[a]

Variable Description	Scored	Percent
1. Stopped to talk with neighbors	97	47
2. Entertained neighbors	76	37
3. Made close friend since arrival at new post	57	28
4. Exchanged or borrowed tools or household items from neighbors	77	37
5. Helped other newcomers in settling	45	22
6. Number of friends increased since arrival	79	38
7. Changed close friends since arrival at new post	76	37

[a]The study population scored a total of 1037 points on the neighboring index. The mean was 5.058 with a standard deviation of 1.597. The variance was 2.550 with a skewness of -0.743 and a kurtosis of -0.051.

hardship and rank ($r = .282$, $p < .01$), length of service ($r = .271$, $p < .01$), age of the father ($r = .271$, $p < .01$), years parents were married ($r = .220$, $p < .01$), number of children ($r = .249$, $p < .01$), and the age of the first child ($r = .365$, $p < .01$). There was a negative relationship between attitude toward relocation and family hardships—the better the attitude toward relocation, the less hardship ($r = -.225$, $p < .01$). Of additional interest is the finding that sixteen independent variables (Table 4) were significantly correlated with the family's attitude toward moving to the present post. Of particular importance were the high correlations between a positive attitude and the respondent's feeling that the assignment would enhance his military career; the new post is the assignment of choice; and the family's reaction toward leaving the old community.

A "best" regression equation for explaining the degree of family hardship was computed with a number of independent variables entered one at a time in a step-wise fashion. In the order of their importance, the variables were: amount of time respondent waited for permanent housing; age of first child; distance family moved; unforeseen costs while traveling; attitude toward relocating to this post; familiarity with the post prior to arrival; amount of money spent in buying household goods after arrival; damages to household goods while in transit; amount of money borrowed to cover cost of moving; and the number of children. The multiple correlation for the regression equation was .74, which indicates that about 55 percent of the criterion variance is explained by these ten variables.

When the study group was divided into three groups according to rank,[2] significant differences were found with regard to attitudes and family hardship, specifically between grades E7-E9 and E1-E3. The senior noncommissioned officers (E7-E9) were the least happy with their military assignment and expressed a preference for being stationed at another post; their children's schooling was interrupted more; and their household goods were lost or damaged more. As a consequence, the higher-ranking noncommissioned officers (NCOs) also had to buy more household goods than did the lower grades. Although a significantly larger number of senior NCOs were separated from their families for periods longer than 29 days, there were also a significant number of lower-grade enlisted personnel who were separated from their families because they could not find houses in the new community. The latter group's separation, however, was for a shorter period of time than that of the more senior NCOs. A comparison of the middle-grade NCOs (E5-E6) and the upper-grade NCOs reveals the following significant differences: the senior NCOs are unhappy with their assignment and prefer to be at a post elsewhere in the United States. They are more frequently separated from their families than the E5-E6 and their separation was for longer periods of time.

For a more precise assessment of family hardship as a function of rank, the

TABLE 4

VARIABLES RELATED TO RESPONDENTS' POSITIVE ATTITUDES

TOWARD MOVING TO A NEW POST

Variable Description	*r*	*p*
1. Family hardships	-.225	.01
2. Neighboring	.190	.01
3. Specifically asked for new post	.443	.01
4. Assignment enhances military career	.510	.01
5. Respondent is familiar with new post	.305	.01
6. Received advanced information on health facilities	.257	.01
7. Received advanced information on housing	.273	.01
8. Prior to arrival had close friends at new post	.298	.01
9. Friends provided advanced information	.262	.01
10. New commander was rated as helpful	.305	.01
11. New first sergeant rated as helpful	.303	.01
12. New Unit officer and NCOs rated as helpful	.248	.01
13. Amount of damages to household goods	-.403	.01
14. Amount move costs over payable allowances	.300	.01
15. Family's positive reaction to leaving old community	.758	.01
16. Family feels that it is settled	.316	.01

study sample was divided into five groups (E1-E4; E5; E6; E7; E8-E9). There was a significant difference in the groups on their overall scores on the Family Hardship Scales. Overall, the E6s had the highest scores, implying that they experienced more hardships according to the index than did the other grades. No significant differences were noted in the groups when their mean scores were compared on the other two indices—attitude toward relocation and neighboring. Specific differences were noted in the use of post services ($F = 4.326$, $p < .002$), wait for permanent housing ($F = 2.539$, $p < .041$), and a number of new friends acquired ($F = 1.739$, $p < .001$). The E6s again received the highest scores. Significant differences among grades are noted in Table 5.

It was previously suggested that the use of community resources, either the formally established agencies or the informal social network composed of neighbors and friends, may mitigate some of the problems of moving and family hardships, and the data strongly suggest this. A significant correlation between the use of services and family disruption was found ($r = .14$, $p < .05$). Furthermore, the E6s, who expressed the greatest hardships, also made significantly greater use of services ($F = 4.88$, $p < .001$).

At the beginning of this study, it was postulated that a predisposition to experience family hardship during the moving process would depend on differences in family characteristics, attitude toward moving, and the distance moved. The findings support this proposition. Family hardship was positively correlated with father's rank ($r = .20$, $p < .01$), length of service ($r = .29$, $p < .01$), father's age ($r = .27$, $p < .01$), length of marriage ($r = .22$, $p < .01$), number of children ($r = .25$, $p < .01$), and age of the first child ($r = .37$, $p < .01$).

Findings in this research clearly support the hypothesis that families facing more complex family developmental tasks (Hill and Rodgers, 1964) experience greater family hardships. The older respondents in this study were those with larger families and school-age children. It is interesting to note that the most senior NCOs had less hardship than the E6s. The E6s had fewer resources available than the E7s. That is, their basic pay was less, more constraints were placed upon them in finding a suitable home on post because housing was assigned according to rank—and the E7s, E8s, and E9s had priority. The E6 families in this study had the most children (the 108 children in this grade constituted 45.7 percent of all respondents' children). The E7s, E8s, and E9s, on the other hand, had only 22 percent of the 236 children in the sample.

Other Problem Areas

One of the stated purposes of this research was to delineate the problems experienced by families while moving and settling into a new community

TABLE 5

SIGNIFICANT DIFFERENCES (F-TEST) ON SELECTED VARIABLES

OF FAMILY HARDSHIP, BY RANK

	Rank	
Variable	*Lowest Score*	*Highest Score*
1. Cost of move exceeded payable allowances	E-5	E-6
2. Needed to borrow money to cover cost of move	E-8	E-6
3. Awaited house for over 29 days	E-1 – E-3	E-6
4. Household goods lost or damaged	E-1 – E-3	E-6
5. Necessary to purchase additional household goods	E-1 – E-3	E-6
6. Hardship created because of delay in pay	E-7 – E-9	E-6
7. Children's schooling interrupted	E-1 – E-4	E-6
8. Unforeseen expenses incurred while in transit	E-7 – E-9	E-6
9. Amount of money spent in excess of moving entitlements	E-1 – E-3	E-6
10. Amount of money borrowed to defray cost of moving	E-7 – E-9	E-6
11. Damages to household goods while in transit	E-1 – E-3	E-6
12. Amount of money spent in buying household goods to furnish new house	E-1 – E-3	E-6
13. Family separated for more than 29 days	E-5	E-7 – E-9
14. Preferred assignment elsewhere	E-1 – E-3	E-7 – E-9
15. Family separated because of not having a house	E-5	E-1 – E-3
16. Mechanical difficulty with car in transit	E-5	E-1 – E-3

because of their implications for changes in or improvement upon Army policy and planning for the provision of family services.

Unforeseen expenses while in transit were most prevalent for those personnel at the rank of E6. Twenty-eight percent of the total study population, however, reported having unforeseen expenses, and they attribute these expenses to: change of orders after travel had already begun, unexpected high cost of motels, road tolls, and taxi fares. Eighteen persons reported having mechanical trouble with their automobiles, and the cost of repairing the mechanical difficulty ranged from $10 to $500, with a mean of $83.64. Six families were involved in automobile accidents, and the damages ranged from $50 to $1,000, with a mean of $395. Fifty-five families reported that their household goods were lost or damaged in transit. This expense ranged from $10 to $1,500. Fifty-four wives reported having medical problems that necessitated specialized treatment during the period of moving and settling into the community: sixteen wives were pregnant, 10 had acute medical conditions, and 28 had chronic medical conditions. Eighteen children were reported to have problems of such severity as to warrant specialized educational or medical care.

The expenditure of personal funds to defray cost of moving was the highest scored item in the Hardship Scale. Concomitantly, having to borrow money was highly correlated with family hardship. The amount of money the family had to borrow was significantly related to the amount of personal funds the family used to defray the cost of moving. The extent of damages to household goods was highly correlated with the amount of money the family borrowed. The amount of money borrowed was also highly correlated with the cost of repairing an automobile because of mechanical difficulty and with the cost of repairing the automobile because of an accident. Obviously, families who borrow money during the process of moving do so in order to pay for unforeseen and emergency costs associated with their move.

The disturbing financial status of the families can further be described by the following findings. Forty-seven (23%) of the family heads had a part-time job at their last duty assignment in the United States. Of these, 21 (45%) worked because their military pay was inadequate; 17 (36%) worked in order to liquidate indebtedness; and 9 placed their earnings from the extra work into savings. To add to the hardships, 22 respondents reported they had had difficulty establishing credit since their arrival at the new post. One of these had unfavorable credit references, 3 were unable to obtain credit references, and the remaining 18 were not granted credit because of their low grade (E1-E4).

SUMMARY AND CONCLUSIONS

On the basis of the findings reported here, some basic conclusions may be drawn:

First, payable allowances and benefits do not cover the full cost of moving. This appears to be a consistent finding independent of rank, attitude toward relocation, the number of social services used, family size, and other characteristics that may make the moving process a more complex one.

Second, most enlisted military personnel must borrow money in order to cover the excessive cost of moving. The amount of money borrowed is highly correlated with contingencies such as unforeseen expenses during the process of moving and settling into the new community, which occur with regularity. This indicates that military personnel (except for the grades E7-E9) live on marginal incomes; and when additional expenses are introduced by moving, financial resources are strained beyond their limits. Considering the frequency with which military people move and the findings of this study, geographic mobility may be one of the major factors which undermine the economic security of the military family.

Third, families who seem to experience the most hardships as a result of moving also make the most use of available community resources in order to mitigate the hardships. Social agencies serving the military community, like those in the civilian society, appear to serve the function of assisting the individual and his family with problem situations.

Fourth, on the other hand, findings indicate that social welfare services, such as the Army Community Services, Red Cross, Army Emergency Relief, etc., may not be sufficient to provide more remedial services to families disrupted during the process of moving. While social services to families appear to be a valuable asset to the military family, an increase in financial benefits to offset the full cost of relocation for all military personnel appears to be needed to minimize family hardships.

Fifth, in examining family hardships, we must be cognizant of the fact that most of the hardships identified in this study are beyond the immediate control of the serviceman and his family and thus are not easily offset by social supports in the community or by a more positive attitude toward the relocation.

The inescapable impression, derived from viewing the frequency and the types of hardship families experience during moving, is that the military requires them to move but fails to subsidize fully the move and, therefore, forces the family into a financial crisis that necessitates their borrowing money. This situation is aggravated further by failure to pay the military member on time and sufficiently during the moving process. Failure to provide immediate housing forces the family to live in high-cost housing and thus contributes to the problem.

Additionally, respondents frequently complained that the Army failed to provide advance general information on the living conditions, availability of housing, the exact location of the post, additional transportation, and opportunities for second jobs or jobs for wives, in order that the family might realistically plan their move. Vincent (1967), in writing on the role of social policy and the mental health of the family, emphasized that families, under special circumstances, are forced to adjust to certain policies because they have no alternative. This seems to be the plight of the military family in relation to moving. Families appear to adapt to the inadequate allocation of resources and the hardships of moves.

The pattern of adjustment varies from family to family. Lower-grade enlisted personnel adjust by accepting and enduring a prolonged separation from their families until housing and financial stability are achieved. The upper grades adjust by their willingness to be separated from their families for a temporary period of time until housing becomes available. Findings reflect that families adjust also by: selling items of household goods in order to be within their weight allowance; buying additional household goods in order to furnish their houses at the new location; obtaining part-time jobs in order to supplement their incomes; borrowing money in order to defray the cost of moving and to cover automobile problems and damages to household goods while in transit; and bringing their families to live in available guesthouses or expensive motels. They not only exhaust their financial resources but also become indebted in the process.

Results indicate that families who experience hardships are more likely to wait more than 29 days for a permanent house, have school-age children, experience unforeseen expenses while in transit, and have to travel a long distance. These data are of relevance to military personnel and career experts, community planners, and providers of services, since they can aid in identifying potentially vulnerable families. With a minimum of knowledge about the family and the receiving community, it is possible to determine the probability of a family's experiencing hardships, and policies and services can be formulated or modified to minimize this situation.

The present study also documents the importance of the availability of housing for all personnel. The lack of housing is one of the most important factors in contributing to family hardship. This finding has far-reaching implications, because it clearly identifies the need for housing for all married military personnel and at a cost they can afford. It is not simply a matter of morale, although this too is important, but it is a necessary requirement to reduce the hardship experienced by the family. Warning against or preventing the serviceman from bringing his family into a new community when housing is not available does not prevent hardship; it only ignores the critical importance of the family and the realities of family life. Delaying the family's arrival into the new community is not a satisfactory solution to the prevention of hardship, because uncertainty and extra living costs are inherent in separation. At some point, the family and household goods must be transported to the new community; and during this period of transition the family is still subject to such hardships as: unforeseen costs, mechanical failure of the automobile, accidents, damaged household goods, and interruption of medical care and school.

Guesthouses for temporary lodging are not entirely satisfactory for extended periods. Families in this study frequently referred to the additional costs of eating at the post exchange and other restaurants while staying at the post guesthouse. At the policy level, a major disadvantage of providing temporary housing to incoming families is that this diverts resources that could best be used for the provision of additional permanent housing. Findings of this study support giving priority to the provision of permanent housing. Furthermore, the importance of the serviceman's familiarity with the post prior to his arrival implies the need for assurance that advance information can be made readily available.

The findings revealed that the occurrence of unforeseen expenses was significantly correlated with experiencing hardships. The report of unexpected high costs of motels and road tolls implies a need for improved and expanded technical assistance to families in planning their moves. The extent of damages to household goods was significantly correlated with the need to borrow money; therefore, the rapidity with which the financial claim for reparation is processed and settled may determine the incidence of the family's need to borrow money. The importance of accurate and timely payments to military personnel, particularly during periods of movement, is obvious. The fact that a sizable number of individuals reported a delay in pay implies a continuing need to improve the rendering of this vital service.

It can be concluded that many of the families in the study sample experienced a crisis situation as a result of the stressful nature of these problems. It was not within the scope of this research to examine the degree or the severity of family crises, but the study did provide evidence that hardships resulting from the move occurred in the vast majority of the families who participated in the study.

NOTES

1. Fifty-seven individuals who completed the first questionnaire, anticipating that their wives would come later, did not complete the second questionnaire because it was subsequently decided that their wives would not join them. Eight subjects were transferred within a sixty-day period and, therefore, were not available to complete the second questionnaire. Sixteen individuals were discharged from the Army and thus were not included in the study. Twelve individuals were eliminated because they reported that they had separated from their spouses and/or instituted divorce proceedings. Six subjects were absent without leave

and thus not available. Two subjects were hospitalized with serious illnesses and were unable to complete the second questionnaire. Another 23 individuals were eliminated because their wives already lived in the area and the families had not changed residence. Three refused to participate.

2. Enlisted ranking system ranges from E1 through E9, with the highest being E9. In parts of this study the ranks were grouped: E1-E4 = lowest grade; E5-E6 = middle grade; and E7-E9 = senior grade.

Chapter 5

PROLONGED FAMILY SEPARATION IN THE MILITARY:

A LONGITUDINAL STUDY

HAMILTON I. McCUBBIN
BARBARA B. DAHL

The Department of Defense and the family in the military system, two profoundly important social institutions, compete for the same resource—the serviceman. In time of war, the former takes control while the family waits for the termination of conflict or for the man to fulfill his commitment to his country, an obligation which, in its extreme, may even result in his death. The Vietnam conflict, because of its length and its unpopularity with a vast sector of the American citizenry, placed even greater stresses upon the families whose sons, husbands, and fathers were serving their country. When one considers the sensitivity of the public to the manner in which this war was conducted and the contagiously strong feelings against American involvement in Vietnam, it is not surprising to find that a number of researchers have focused their attention upon this war and its complexities.

As the war continued, the number of family casualties—Americans bereaved by the death of an immediate family member—mounted. Lieberman (1971a, b) reported estimates of family casualties as of 1971: 30,000 widows and orphans, 80,000 parents, 60,000 grandparents, and approximately 80,000 brothers and sisters; at least 250,000 Americans experienced the loss of an immediate family member! Much smaller in number, but of definite significance, were the 608 [1] held in limbo by the classification of their sons or husbands as prisoners of war

AUTHORS' NOTE: This chapter is an expanded and integrated version of two previous reports: (1) "The Returned Prisoner of War: Factors in Family Reintegration," which appeared previously in the *Journal of Marriage and the Family,* 1975 (August), pp. 471-478; and (2) "Children of Returned Prisoners of War: The Effects of Long Term Father Absence," paper presented at the American Psychological Association Annual Meeting, Chicago, Illinois, August, 1975.

(PW). Although little has been written about this situation by scholars of the American family, this is not necessarily unexpected given the absence of data on the military family. Furthermore, the public seems to accept tacitly casualties and the disruption of families as a fact of war.

On the other hand, the importance of determining the effects of war upon the family has been acknowledged by social scientists (Bey and Lange, 1974; Boulding, 1950; Hill, 1949; Lieberman, 1971a, b; Waller, 1944). Considering the intensity of discussions already devoted to the subject of the military family (Bennett et al., 1974), the evolution of social institutions devoted to keeping alive the public consciousness of the plight of these families (Powers, 1974), and the volumes of printed rhetoric proclaiming the importance of the military family, one cannot help but be concerned about the paucity of data for this population. Its priority relative to the political and medical aspects of the war was certainly lower than specialists in family research would have considered desirable.

In light of the importance of and need for studies on the general subject of the Southeast Asian conflict and the adjustment of the military family to the war, longitudinal research had been proposed for the study of families of prisoners of war as an ongoing research effort initiated by specialists of the Family Studies Branch of the Center for Prisoner of War Studies (Plag, 1974). The present chapter deals with data derived from this longitudinal study and focuses upon family adjustment to separation and reunion.

RESEARCH LITERATURE

Family Adjustment to Separation and Reunion

Over the years behavioral scientists have continued to extrapolate and document lessons learned from prisoner of war experiences. The classic studies of the trauma of concentration camps (Bettelheim, 1953; Eitinger, 1964; Frankl, 1968), prisoner of war experiences (Biderman, 1967), stresses of captivity (Schein, 1957; Schein, Schneir, and Barker, 1961), and coping behavior in captivity (Ballard, 1973) indicated the significance of these unique experiences and their possible influence upon the longitudinal adjustment of repatriated prisoners (Schein, Cooley, and Singer, 1960; Segal, 1973). In contrast, there is a paucity of research attempting to answer questions surrounding the adjustment of families of prisoners of war (PW), family adjustment during the internment period, and the role families play in the long-term rehabilitation of repatriated prisoners.

Although existing research on the general problems of family adjustment to father separation in the military indicates the importance of this line of inquiry (McCubbin, Hunter, and Dahl, 1975), the adaptation of the PW family to an indeterminate and unprecedented length of father absence has only been alluded to in past research. Even though PW families were present at Schilling Manor, Allen (1972) did not isolate these families for special study. Recent papers by Spolyar (1973), Hall and Simmons (1973), and Brown (1972) attempted to describe the grieving process, adjustment problems, and coping behaviors both of families of prisoners of war and of servicemen missing in action; however, none of these studies was based on any systematic assessment of such families, and specific consideration was not given to families of those held as prisoners of war.

More recently, studies concerning families of returned prisoners of war (RPW) from the Vietnam conflict have emphasized the stresses associated with the prolonged separation and the importance of these stresses in determining how families adjust after reunion. Family problems and stresses which emerged during the separation period, while the husband was held captive in Southeast Asia, have been linked to the initial readjustment problems of the returning prisoner of war (McCubbin, Hunter, and Dahl, 1975). These researchers have emphasized that problems unique to the families in the PW situation, particularly the prolonged and indeterminate absence of the father/husband, have encouraged families to develop behaviors which might actually lessen the probability of a successful postreunion adjustment. The waiting wife, functioning as head of the household, often matures, develops greater independence and self-confidence, and provides a life style for her family in the absence of a husband or father.

In another study (McCubbin and Dahl, 1974b, c), returnees' self-reports of ability to endure the hardships of captivity were positively correlated with family adjustment at time of reunion. However, it is still unclear from the family research conducted by the Center for Prisoner of War Studies (McCubbin, Dahl, Metres, Hunter, and Plag, 1974) what combination of factors best explains the nature of family reintegration following a prolonged separation. It remains to be determined why some families overcome the stresses of separation and reintegration with time, while others experience severe disruptions and have great difficulty achieving stability. On the basis of his WW II study, Hill (1949) concluded that the processes of adjustment involved in family reunions after prolonged separations could not be properly understood without taking into consideration the family's history, characteristics of family members, their adjustment to the separation period, as well as the family dynamics at the time reunion occurred.

Children's Adjustment to Separation and Reunion

While studies on father absence have stressed the importance of (a) the age of the child during father absence, (b) the sex of the child, and (c) the length of father absence, their results are contradictory, findings being confounded by type of father absence—i.e., death, divorce, desertion, or military service—the availability of father substitutes, and by other environmental factors (Baker, Cove, Fagen, Fischer, and Janda, 1968; Hetherington, 1972; Lynn, 1974; Santrock, 1972; Trunnell, 1968a, b).

Some researchers, in discussing father separation, focus on the absence of the instrumental leader in the family (Parsons and Bales, 1955; Zelditch, 1955). They point to father as the parent who stresses delay of immediate gratification in the interest of greater future rewards. Father is seen as the parent who represents for the children the rules and principles of society. Still other scientists (Bandura and Walters, 1959; Biller, 1968; Mowrer, 1950; Sears, Rau, and Alpert, 1965) emphasize the importance of a masculine model in the home, not only for the boy's sex-role development but for the girl's as well. Social workers, in a study by Stephens (1961), described fatherless boys as anxious about sex and as effeminate. According to one study (Douvan and Adelson, 1966), adolescent boys living with their mothers, as a defense against anxiety about their insecure masculinity, swaggered and put up a front of exaggerated self-confidence; they rejected men and rebelled against adult authority.

The unfavorable consequences of father absence may manifest themselves at an earlier age in boys than in girls. The absence of the father may cause problems as the young boy shifts from mother to masculine identification. In a study of father-absent eight- and nine-year-old Norwegian sailor and whaler children (Lynn and Sawrey, 1959), the father-separated boys, insecure in their masculinity, struggled to resemble the father but reacted with compensatory masculine bravado. In addition, the father-absent boys showed poorer peer adjustment than either the father-present boys or the father-absent girls. There were no findings to suggest the negative influence of father absence on the girls' femininity. Tiller (1961), in another study of father absence among Norwegian children, found that although both the boys and the girls were negatively affected by lack of father's presence, the boys manifested more detrimental effects than the girls.

Although the girl, in response to the absence of an adult male with whom to relate, may not manifest problems early, difficulties in relating to males might be expected to surface during adolescence when interest in the opposite sex heightens. Hetherington (1972), in her investigation of the effects of paternal absence on personality development in adolescent daughters, compared three groups of adolescent girls: (a) those from intact families; (b) those from divorced families; and (c) those from families in which the father was absent because of death. Results indicated that daughters without fathers felt less personal control over the course of their lives and reported themselves as more anxious than girls from intact homes. The main finding, however, was that the effects of father absence were manifested by an inability of these adolescent girls to relate appropriately to men and male peers.

Paternal absence occurring in the early years, i.e., the "formative years," is frequently associated with more detrimental consequences than when it occurs later (Anderson, 1968; Seplin, 1952). As with Hetherington's (1966) earlier findings in a study with father-absent boys and in her 1972 study, described above, the loss of the father when the girls were young (before age five) was more damaging than later father separation (after age five). Pedersen and Sullivan (1964), in one of the few studies of the effects of father absence on military children, found that 59 percent of the children referred to a child guidance clinic for emotional disturbance had had some period of extended paternal absence during their first five years of development.

Many investigators have also shown a relationship between the length of absence and children's emotional adjustment. In another study of children whose fathers were absent owing to military service, Gabower (1959) found that fathers of disturbed children were gone more frequently and for longer periods of time. Trunnell's study (1968) of children under 18 years of age seen for psychiatric diagnosis in an outpatient clinic revealed that the longer the father was absent and the younger the child at the time of his absence, the greater the degree of psychopathology.

Investigations conducted by the Center for Prisoner of War Studies, before and after the return of American prisoners from Southeast Asia, pointed out the importance of utilizing a longitudinal approach when studying the long-term effects of separation on children of these men (McCubbin, Hunter, and Dahl, 1975; McCubbin, Hunter, and Metres, 1974); however, the existing studies are basically descriptive in nature (Benson, McCubbin, Dahl, and Hunter, 1974; McCubbin, Hunter, and Metres, 1974). At present, there are no studies comparing this population (PW) of children with a normative group.

It is paradoxical that, while professionals are expected to continue the extension of comprehensive medical, legal, psychological, psychiatric, and social work services to repatriated prisoners and their families, we as yet lack clarity regarding the nature and extent of the problems the families faced in the past, the family dynamics associated with their adjustment to the prolonged separation, the family's adjustment to father's (PW) return, and the impact of separation and reunion upon the children's emotional and social development. Knowledge of the history of family adjustment is essential to the establishment of counseling and treatment relationships and to the development of family services.

The present research was directed toward studies of family adjustment and reintegration occasioned by husband/father absence and subsequent reunion. In the face of prolonged and indeterminate absence of a husband/father, how do families adapt as a unit? What are the residuals of this experience in terms of the family's ability to reintegrate and to renegotiate role relationships following the return of the servicemen? What are the long-term effects of both separation and reunion upon family stability and upon the emotional health of its individual members, particularly the children? Deriving answers to questions such as these constitutes goals of the present investigation.

METHODOLOGY AND RESULTS

Because of the complexity of the methods and sampling involved, this longitudinal investigation, the study of the family's adjustment to separation, the factors involved in family reintegration following husband's (PW) return, and the children's adjustment to separation and reunion, it was essential that the methods and results be presented independently.

PHASE I

Family Adjustment to Separation

Phase I of the study reported here, in part, represented an effort to determine the nature and extent of adjustment problems experienced by families of prisoners of war in Southeast Asia. These families were studied solely because they were in a unique situation of adapting to the prolonged and indeterminate absence of a husband (PW), not because they had been referred for help with emotional, financial, or medical problems. The underlying assumption was that when a family is called upon to adapt to the absence of a husband/father listed as a prisoner in a war zone, the occurrence of adjustment problems (in the broadest sense) must be expected. The study was conducted during the period from April 1972 to December 1972, by the staff of the Center for Prisoner of War Studies (CPWS) before the repatriation of American PWs from Southeast Asia. Families included in the study were drawn from the total population of men listed as prisoners of war (PW) by the Service Departments of the Army, Navy, and Marine Corps. The sample was limited to families of *pro*creation (those in which the PW serviceman had a status of spouse) because of their "dependent" status and the responsibility of each of the armed services to provide them comprehensive care during the serviceman's absence.

The sample consisted of 100 families, approximately 50 percent of the total number of wives of servicemen listed as PWs by each service—Army, Navy, and Marine Corps. The vast majority (76 percent) of the sample was represented by Navy families, followed by the Army (16 percent), and, in turn, the Marine Corps (8 percent). The sample included 204 children. Ninety-two percent of the sample were families of commissioned officer personnel; an additional 1 percent were those of warrant officers; and 7 percent were families of enlisted personnel.

A structured interview format was used for conducting each family interview. Single in-depth interviews, ranging in length from two to eight hours, were conducted with PW wives located throughout the Continental United States, Hawaii, Puerto Rico, and Europe. The 100 interviews were conducted by the professional staff of the CPWS Family Studies Branch, consisting of a Navy psychiatrist, civilian clinical psychologists, military and civilian social workers, with assistance by clinical social workers of the U.S. Army. The Army social workers were selected on the basis of their extensive experience with military families and were given additional orientation with respect to the PW situation and training in the application of the structured interview schedule.

The interview schedule was used to ensure the systematic collection of data. The questions elicited specific demographic information and data related to family history as well as psychological, social, and medical factors conceivably related to family and individual adjustment. During the nine months of data gathering, the interview schedule was revised on two occasions, resulting in varying numbers of respondents on particular items. Those families indicating active social, psychological, medical, legal, or financial adjustment problems were referred to appropriate civilian or military resources for continuing assistance.

Family Adjustment to Separation—Results

The Situation. The situation common to these families was that each had been confronted with a military report of casualty followed by a listing of their husbands/fathers as prisoners of war. The length of absence of these men extended from one year to over eight years. Fifty-four (54 percent) of these absences had extended over a period of from five to eight and one-half years.

PW Family Characteristics. The ages of wives in this sample of families ranged from 20 to 49, with an average of 31.1 years at the time of the interview. The educational level of the majority of wives was in excess of fourteen years; over one-third had earned college degrees. The average length of marriage before separation was five years. Prior marriages were infrequent for both husbands and wives (6%). At the time of the interview, extended families (both or either parent) existed for most of the PW husbands (90%) and wives (95%). Religious affiliations varied, however, with both husbands (66.4%) and wives (61.5%) being predominantly Protestant. While the families averaged two children, 20 (20%) had no children. The 204 children ranged in age from less than 1 year to 25 years, with the majority between the ages of 8 and 15.

Coping with the Unknown: Role Adjustments. Families adapted to new responsibilities with modifications in family roles accompanied by related anxieties, frustrations, and feelings of insecurity engendered by the husband/father absence. Not surprisingly, the majority of the wives (76.7%) reported the lack of husband's companionship as the most difficult problem with which they had to cope. Concomitantly, difficulties with feelings of loneliness, making decisions alone, lack of suitable social outlets, concern for personal health, and guilt feelings about their change in role were emphasized by the wives as additional problem areas. Traditional responsibilities were intensified for the wife who, as a result of the situation, was tasked with the dual mother-father role. Twenty-nine were employed on either a full- or part-time basis; however, over two-thirds of the group (67%) were unemployed. Disciplining of the children, handling of family finances, and the health of the children were cited as additional disturbing family problems. Role adjustment problems are presented in Table 1.

During this period of prolonged husband absence, the wives involved themselves in a wide range of activities which, for the most part, appeared to enhance self-esteem and occupy them mentally and emotionally. Participation in national and local efforts to clarify their husbands' casualty status provided a social and emotional outlet for the majority of the wives. Their responses indicated that hobbies, television, and social group functions were additional activities which ranked high, with military service club activities receiving less emphasis than the other four areas mentioned.

Adaptation of the family to its inherent social responsibilities required that family members, the wife in this particular situation, have the authority to negotiate all legal transactions. This area of responsibility proved to be one of unexpected difficulty. Although less than one-third of the families emphasized legal problems as a major area of difficulty encountered during the period of husband/father absence, when these problems did occur, they affected the family's financial stability and credibility and mitigated the family's ability to plan for the future. Working against the traditional identity of the dependent wife, the PW wives were called upon to assert themselves, gain control of the family, and establish themselves as the rightful and legal representatives of their absent husbands and the family.

TABLE 1

ROLE ADJUSTMENTS

Adustment Problems	Number of Respondents	Number of Positive Responses	Percent
Lack of husband's companionship	60	46	72.3
Feelings of extreme loneliness	60	28	48.2
Making decisions alone	60	25	39.8
Lack of social outlets	60	19	27.7
Disciplining children	60	14	18.7
Time for dual mother-father role	60	10	18.1
Handling family finances	59	5	13.9
Health of wife	60	5	10.8
Health of children	60	3	4.2

Wife's Perception of the Marriage. In contrast with the wives' retrospective assessment of their marriages prior to casualty, in which over three-fourths (79.6%) of the group indicated satisfaction with the marriage, only 44.8% felt satisfaction with the marriage at the time of the interview. This change in feelings about the marriage was evident in other areas, such as the increase (12.1%) in the number of wives planning divorces, as shown in Table 2.

Physical and Emotional Health of the PW Wife. In general, the wives maintained surveillance over their health, and on the average, had received a thorough physical examination within the fifteen-month period preceding the interview. At the time of the interview the wives were asked to evaluate, retrospectively, their health status during their husbands' absence. Data from the interviews showed that a smaller percentage of the wives (3%) rated their general health as a handicap during the period of husband absence than they would have rated it prior to the husbands' casualty (6%).

Emotional and psychological adjustment appeared to be an area of greater difficulty. Out of 12 emotional symptoms covered by the interviewer, nearly two-thirds (64%) of the sample reported having experienced five or more symptoms during the period of husband absence (see Table 3).

TABLE 2

PW WIFE'S PERCEPTION OF HER MARRIAGE

Wife's Assessment	Precasualty		At Time of Interview	
	Number	Percent	Number	Percent
Divorce/separation requested	0	0.0	0	0.0
Divorce/separation planned	1	1.7	8	13.8
Uncertain about future of marriage	4	6.8	1	1.7
Major problems, poor relationship	2	3.4	15	25.9
Minor problems, fair relationship	5	8.5	8	13.8
Good relationship	13	22.0	6	10.3
Excellent relationship	34	57.6	20	34.5
Total	59	100.0	58	100.0

Additional indices of emotional adjustment noted were that over half the group (50.6%) were taking or had taken tranquilizers during their husbands' absence, and 40.5 percent had experienced body weight fluctuations of 15 pounds or more during that period. Almost half the group (49.2%) indicated they were nonsmokers. Of those who smoked, 22 percent reported they now smoked more heavily than they had prior to the husband's casualty. Slightly over 8 percent were nondrinkers. Among the drinkers, 27.7 percent found they consumed alcoholic beverages more frequently since casualty than they had prior to casualty. For 5 percent of all the wives interviewed, alcoholism was reported to be a potential, if not an already existent, problem. Over one-third (36.1%) of the group reported frequent feelings that life was meaningless, and 33.9% reported entertaining suicidal thoughts at some time during their husband's absence, although only 20.3% felt they had ever really seriously considered suicide.

TABLE 3

PW WIFE'S EMOTIONAL SYMPTOMS

Symptoms	Number of Respondents	N	Percent
Depressed, "down in dumps"	83	100	83.0
Jumpiness, "uptight"	71	100	71.0
Fitful Sleep	55	90	61.1
Difficulty falling asleep	60	100	60.0
Waking, not rested	51	90	56.7
Bored	44	88	50.0
Rapid mood fluctuations	47	100	47.0
Headaches	40	100	40.0
Feeling life is meaningless	35	97	36.0
Poor digestion	35	100	35.0
Shortness of breath	22	100	22.0
Accident-prone	16	88	18.2

Adaptation to Emotional Stress. The sample of 100 wives reported a wide range of symptoms related to emotional and social adjustment that they found to be moderately or severely difficult to manage. In many instances the families sought professional help to cope with the situation.

Interview data revealed that 37 percent of the wives were either receiving treatment (5%) for emotional problems or had been in treatment (32%) at some time during the husband's absence. Based upon evaluations made by the interviewers, which reflected either direct or indirect evidence of disabling anxiety, depression, psychosomatic complaints, guilt feelings, or dysfunctional family interactions, an additional 44 percent of the wives appeared to be in need of psychological assistance (see Table 4). Further, based upon the interviewers' evaluations of present problems and the wives' reports of anticipated future problems, it appeared probable that approximately 75 percent of the families would benefit from marriage or family counseling at the time of release of the PWs and during the period immediately thereafter.

Adjustment of Children of PW Families. The physical and emotional adjustments of children of prisoners of war are important indices of both individual and family adjustment. Children's problems represent another source of stress for both the mother and the family unit. Only three of the mothers (6.7%) reported that the physical health of children presented major problems during the husband's absence. The most frequently reported physical health problems among this group of 204 children were the common childhood diseases, accidental injuries, and surgery.

In contrast with the children's physical status, their emotional adjustment appeared more problematic. One-half of the PW children were judged by their mothers to have had significant emotional problems during the period of father absence. For the families with children, the most frequently reported symptoms reflecting adjustment difficulties were unwarranted and frequent crying (10.8%), fear of the dark (10.8%), nightmares (9.3%), nail-biting (8.8%), shyness (7.8%), and rebelliousness (7.4%). Social and interpersonal adjustments of the children were also areas of concern to the mothers. Fourteen children (6.9%) were reported to have displayed behavior problems in the school setting and an equal

TABLE 4

PSYCHOLOGICAL/PSYCHIATRIC COUNSELING RECEIVED
BY OR RECOMMENDED FOR PW WIVES

Status at Time of Interview	Number	Percent*
Wives receiving treatment	5	5.0
Wives who received treatment in past, but not now in treatment	32	32.0
Wives who never received treatment	62	62.0
Wives for whom treatment was recommended who were not in treatment	44	44.0
Families who might need counseling at time of repatriation	75	75.0

*N = 100

percentage had difficulty with peer relationships (6.9%). Behavior problems at home (5.4%) and poor relationships with mother (6.4%) or other adults (3.4%) were areas of additional concern for the mothers.

Use of Children's Services. In general, the mothers attempted to seek the assistance of mental health professionals when they felt their children had emotional problems. Of the 69 children judged by their mothers to have displayed emotional or adjustment problems, 37 children (53.6%) had received or were receiving professional counseling. The interviewers made a clinical judgment of the children's need for psychological or psychiatric assistance on the basis of mothers' comments and their reports of the children's behaviors and symptomatology during father absence. On the basis of the clinical judgments made at the time of the interview, it would appear that 40 (19.6%) of the 204 children would have benefited from professional counseling (see Table 5).

Concerns about Family Reunion

The wives' concerns about reuniting with their husbands provided an index of future adjustment difficulties. For the wives, it represented a critical time of accounting for their stewardships during the husbands' absence. For other wives,

TABLE 5

PSYCHOLOGICAL/PSYCHIATRIC TREATMENT RECEIVED
BY OR RECOMMENDED FOR PW CHILDREN

Status at Time of Interview	Number	Percent*
Children receiving treatment	9	4.4
Children who received treatment in past but not now in treatment	16	7.8
Children who were never in treatment	179	87.7
Totals	204	100.0
Children for whom counseling was recommended who were not already in treatment	40	19.6

*Based upon the total number of children in the sample N = 204

repatriation meant facing the increased possibility that their husbands were not coming back. The wives' primary concern about the postrepatriation period was what their husbands' reaction would be to their increased independence (46.0%). Handling of finances and dating were further concerns voiced by the wives. A few of the wives expressed concern over the husbands' evaluation of the manner in which the children had been reared (see Table 6).

Repatriation also meant the wives had to come to terms with their fantasies about the husband's physical and emotional status. The majority (68.7%) of the wife group emphasized their concern over the husbands' ability to adjust to the rapid social change which had occurred during their absence. Slightly over half the wives indicated concern about their husbands' health, and over one-third noted their own anxieties about their husbands' ability to assume the husband and father roles and to continue a career in the military. Of those families with children (N = 80), one-third of the wives expressed concern about their husbands' ability to cope with their children's problems.

The wives emphasized the need for family and individual services at the time of their husbands' repatriation. Heading the list of desired services were occupational counseling (63.6%), educational counseling (62.6%), and psychological counseling (57.6%) for the returning men. Over half of the wives emphasized the need for job retraining for the husband, while slightly under half acknowledged the need for marriage and family counseling and legal counseling at the time of repatriation. Other anticipated needs were financial and spiritual counseling.

TABLE 6

WIVES' CONCERNS ABOUT REPATRIATION

Concern	Positive Responses	Percent*
Becoming too independent	28	46.0
Not saving more money	13	21.3
Dating	12	20.0
Manner in which children raised	10	16.0
Drinking too much	3	5.0

*N = 61 due to revised questionnaire

PHASE II

Phase II of the investigation was designed to determine what combination of factors best explain the dynamics of family reintegration following a prolonged separation. Families of prisoners of war who were interviewed in 1972, to assess the dynamics of their adjustment to prolonged separation, were involved again in the longitudinal study in 1973, twelve months following their husbands' (PW) return.[2] Specifically, in this phase, four groups of data were used as predictors of family adjustment 12 to 16 months following the return of American PWs from Southeast Asia (SEA): demographic data, indices of family adjustment to separation, psychiatric evaluations of the fathers/husbands (returnees) at the time of their return, and the returnees' perceptions of the hardships of captivity.

Family Reintegration Following Prolonged Separation—Method

Subjects for this phase of the investigation consisted of 48 Navy families of returned American prisoners of the Vietnam War. The families were selected on the basis of the following criteria: (1) the wives of the returned prisoners (returnees) of war, prior to the repatriation of their husbands and before having received word of their husbands' eventual return, had discussed their feelings and hardships experienced during the separation with the staff from the Center as part of the 1972 survey; (2) the returnees had received a complete psychiatric examination immediately following their repatriation from Vietnam; and (3) the returnees had participated in a one-year follow-up study of family adjustment by completing a questionnaire mailed to them approximately 12 months following their return.

In comparing the original sample of families and this follow-up sample with regard to nine characteristics,[3] only length of time spent in captivity showed a statistically significant difference, returnees participating in the follow-up inquiry having spent more months in captivity. Other variables highly correlated with months in captivity, such as pay grade and age, were not found to be significantly different. On the whole, differences between respondents were not pronounced and were not considered to be ones which would result in data biases.

For the purpose of deriving a composite of variables to explain the degree of family reintegration following years of separation, social change, and possible changes in the individual family members, it was essential to emphasize the use of longitudinal data which take both time and change into consideration. Data were obtained from five independent sources: (1) master files of personnel records which provided the needed background information on the returnees; (2) in-depth interviews[4] conducted in 1972 with wives of PWs; (3) medical records[5] which indicated the psychiatric status or functioning of the returnees based on examinations made at the time of their repatriation; (4) a Captivity Questionnaire[6] completed by the returnees regarding their perceptions of the stresses associated with the captivity experience; and (5) a follow-up mailed questionnaire[7] completed by the returnees 12 to 16 months following their repatriation and family reunion in early 1973.

The predictor variables were the following; I. *BACKGROUND/PRE-CASUALTY VARIABLES*. Husband's characteristics: (1) age at time of casualty; (2) rank/rate at time of casualty; (3) years of formal education; (4) degrees/diplomas earned; (5) previous marriages; and (6) preparation for separation—number of tasks completed by the husband to prepare his family for separation (power of attorney, legal will, etc.). Wife's characteristics: (7) age at time of casualty; (8) years of formal education; (9) degrees/diplomas earned; and (10) previous marriages. Family characteristics: (11) length of courtship; (12) length of marriage; (13) quality of marriage—wife's retrospective rating of the quality of marriage before casualty; (14) number of children; and (15) reasons for the last tour to SEA—personal request versus military requirement. II. *CAPTIVITY/SEPARATION*. Husband's adjustment to captivity: (16) time spent in captivity; (17) time spent in solitary confinement; (18) perceived physical abuse in captivity; (19) perceived psychological coercion in captivity; (20) perceived threats and promises in captivity;[8] (21) adaptability—personal qualities (self-understanding, tolerance, patience, etc.) which the men valued and felt might have aided them in enduring the hardships of captivity; and (22) value of family in coping—the degree to which the husbands felt that letters and thoughts of family, home, and future aided them in enduring the hardships of captivity. Wife's adjustment to separation: (23) length of separation; (24) number of letters received from her husband; (25) number of role adjustment problems; (26) number of legal problems; (27) number of financial problems; (28) symptoms of strain and tension—number of emotional tensions experienced by the wife; (29) social activities—the number of social activities in which the wife took part during the separation period; (30) independence—the number of "independent" activities in which the wife engaged (working, etc.); (31) self-reliance—the degree to which the wife relied on herself, rather than outside help, to cope with the hardships of separation; (32) participation in PW/MIA activities—the degree to which the wife participated in local and national PW/MIA activities designed to facilitate the husband's return; (33) perceived quality of the marriage—the wife's assessment of her marriage at time of the interview (during husband's absence); (34) relationships with own parents—wife's assessment of the quality of her relationship with her parents; (35) relationship with in-laws—wife's assessment of the quality of her relationship with her husband's parents; (36) emotional adjustment—whether or not the wife experienced emotional difficulty for which she was recommended for professional counseling; and (37) anticipated hardships of reunion—the number of apprehensions and concerns expressed by the wives regarding family reunion (marital conflict, child adjustment, husband's health, etc). Family characteristics: (38) maintaining father's role—the amount of effort exerted by the family to maintain father's image and role in the family (photos, discussions, planning for the future); (39) children's emotional adjustment—whether any of the children had been in, were presently in, or were recommended for professional counseling. III. *REPATRIATION/REUNION*. Husband's emotional stability: at time of repatriation as evidenced by the psychiatrists' assessment of the returnee's (40) interpersonal functioning, and (41) affect. The predictor variables, the source of each variable, and the classification of these variables relative to time are presented in Table 7.

The degree of family reintegration was the criterion used in this study. Hill (1949), in his study of family adjustment to the crises of war separation and reunion, developed a questionnaire to measure the relative success of the returning servicemen in their adjustment to family reunion. Specifically, Hill's questionnaire was designed to provide an index of the serviceman's success in developing or reestablishing bonds of coherence and family unity of which the husband-wife relationship, the division of labor within the home, the reallocation of roles, and the father-child relationship are paramount. Hill (1949) defined adjustment to reunion as the process of opening the family ranks to include father, realigning power and authority, reworking the division of labor and responsibility, sharing the home and family activities with father, renewing the husband-wife intimacies and confidences, assuming father-child ties, and bringing balance between husband-wife, mother-child, and father-child relationships. Hill's Family Reunion Questionnaire was modified for the present study; additional items were introduced, particularly with regard to father-child relationships, and a few items in the questionnaire were altered to focus upon the returning PW and his family.

The resulting 50 items of the Family Reunion Questionnaire were tested individually (N = 66)[9] with respect to their discriminant function, i.e., the degree to which they discriminated between families who experienced family discord, separations, or divorces, and those families which remained intact. The resulting 17 statistically significant items were factor-analyzed to find a set of independent dimensions with which all the relationships existing among the pool of items could be described in the simplest manner. A 17 x 17 correlation matrix with unity in the main diagonal was subjected to a principal components factor

TABLE 7
PREDICTOR VARIABLES AND CRITERION

	Background Information Precasualty	Captivity/Separation	Repatriation/Reunion	Follow-Up
I.	HUSBAND/PW/RETURNEE education△ rank△ previous marriages* age△ preparation for separation⁰ degrees/diplomas earned△	time in captivity++ physical abuse++ psychological coercion++ threats and promises++ adaptability⁰ value of family in coping⁰ time in solitary confinement△	interpersonal functioning+ affect+	
II.	WIFE age* previous marriages* education* degrees/diplomas earned△	length of separation△ letters from PW△ role adjustment problems* legal problems* financial problems* social activity* independence* self-reliance* participation in PW/MIA activities* emotional adjustment* anticipated hardships of reunion* tension and strain* perceived quality of marriage* relationship with own parents* relationship with husband's parents*		
III.	FAMILY/MARRIAGE length of marriage* quality of marriage* reasons for last tour* length of courtship* number of dependent children*		maintaining father's role* children's adjustment*	FAMILY REINTEGRATION⁰

+Psychiatry Exam [Feb-May, 1973]   ++Returnee Captivity Questionnaire [Feb-May, 1973]   *Family Interview [Apr 1972-Jan 1973]   ⁰Mailed Follow-Up Questionnaire 1974 [May-July 1974]   △CPWS Master Files analysis by which two factors were extracted. A normalized Varimax procedure (Kaiser, 1958) was used to rotate these two factors to simple structure. To determine the stability and reliability of these factors, the 17 items were factor-analyzed on the basis of data obtained on an independent sample (N = 50) of returnees from another branch of the armed services. The principal components analysis and Varimax rotation revealed the same two independent factors.

Factor I, the most pervasive factor in terms of the number of items (12) making up the scale, was provisionally called the Husband-Wife (H-W) Reintegration Scale. The H-W Reintegration Scale was composed of items describing the returnee's perception of the quality of the husband-wife relationship, the quality of family communication, and the meaningfulness of his role in the family. Factor II was labeled the Father-Child (F-C) Reintegration Scale. This scale of 5 items was an index of the returnee's assessment of the children's development, his feelings about the children, and the degree to which they were able to relate to each other. This study is limited to total Family Reintegration, a criterion which was created by combining the two scales to represent an index of the returnee's perceived integration into his family system.

In order to establish the degree of relationship between the predictor variables and the criterion of family reintegration, Pearson product-moment correlations were calculated. This procedure permitted the identification and elimination of those variables having little or no relation to the dependent variable. Linear multiple regression procedures[10] were utilized for the purpose of analyzing the unique contribution of each of the predictors in accounting for variance in the index of family reintegration.

Family Reintegration Following Prolonged Separation—Results

Thirty-four of the original forty-one background, captivity, and separation variables showed negligible relationships with the criterion and were eliminated from the regression analysis. The remaining seven significant variables shown in Table 8 were obtained from each of the major categories of predictors: (1) quality and length of marriage before casualty and number of dependent children were related to background characteristics; (2) quality of marriage during separation, maintenance of father/husband role during the separation period, and wife's emotional adjustment were related to the family's adjustment to separation; and (3) the returnee's "thoughts of family, career, and the future—their value in coping during captivity" were related to the returnee's captivity experience.

A regression equation was derived in which the beta weights of the predictors were statistically significant at or beyond the .05 level. The resulting three variables shown in Table 9 yielded a multiple correlation of .70 ($p < .001$). Hence the combination of three variables—wife's assessment of the quality of marriage before casualty, wife's emotional dysfunction during the separation period, and length of marriage prior to casualty—was significantly greater than any of the variables taken independently.

A reexamination of the remaining thirty-eight variables and their associations with the three significant predictors revealed unique relationships which clarified their importance and meaningfulness. The variables significantly related to length of marriage before casualty were the husbands' age ($r = .51$, $p < .05$) and rank ($r = .47$, $p < .05$). The wives' education, demonstrated by the number of degrees/diplomas earned ($r = .30$, $p < .05$), and length of courtship before marriage ($r = .35$, $p < .05$) were significantly correlated with the wives' assessments of their marriages before casualty. The major variables affecting the wives' emotional dysfunctions during the separation period are presented in Table 10.

The fact that wives' emotional dysfunctions during the separation period emerged as the final significant, but negatively related, predictor of family

TABLE 8

CORRELATIONS OF THE SIGNIFICANT VARIABLES
WITH THE CRITERION OF RETURNEE-FAMILY REINTEGRATION

Predictors	r	p <
Wife's assessment of the quality of the marriage during the separation	.53	.01
Length of marriage	.52	.01
Wife's assessment of the quality of the marriage before casualty	.50	.01
Maintenance of father/husband's role during the separation	.45	.01
Value of thoughts of family, career, and future in coping with captivity	.36	.05
Wife's emotional dysfunction during the separation period	-.31	.05
Number of dependent children	.30	.05

TABLE 9

MULTIPLE REGRESSION STATISTICS FOR VARIABLES
COMPRISING REGRESSION EQUATION FOR PREDICTING
RETURNEE-FAMILY REINTEGRATION

Variables	Validity	Beta Weight	t Value
Length of marriage before casualty	.519	.448	4.076***
Wife's assessment of quality of marriage before casualty	.505	.371	3.304**
Wife's emotional dysfunction during the separation period	-.306	-.231	-2.096*

Multiple Correlation R = .70

*p < .05
**p < .01
***p < .001

TABLE 10

CORRELATIONS OF BACKGROUND AND FAMILY
VARIABLES WITH WIFE'S EMOTIONAL
DYSFUNCTION DURING THE SEPARATION PERIOD

Variables	r	p <
Wife's symptoms of tension	.53	.01
Quality of marriage during separation	-.50	.01
Wife's relationship with own parents	-.33	.05
Adjustment problems during the separation period: role adjustment problems, legal problems, and financial problems	.30	.05

reintegration suggests the importance and disturbing complexity of the separation period. The wives were confronted with major dilemmas which were not easily reconciled without emotional struggle.

PHASE III

Phase III of the present investigation was concerned with the question of how the children of returned prisoners of war, who had experienced unprecedented periods of father absence owing to wartime separation, have fared. More specifically, the investigators examined the personal and social adjustment of these children as compared to a normative group.

Children's Adjustment to Prolonged Separation and Reunion—Method

Children were drawn from the initial representative sample of 100 families of prisoners of war originally interviewed by the Center for Prisoner of War Studies in 1972. The criteria for selection were: (1) the families had experienced father absence as a result of the father's having been taken prisoner during the Vietnam War; (2) the families had at least one child who experienced father absence; and (3) the families had experienced the return of the father from his prison experience. Of the families whose children were eligible for this part of the investigation, i.e., families with children between the ages of 5 and 18, 91.5 percent (43) participated. Families were predominantly Navy (74%), followed by the Army (21%) and the Marine Corps (5%). Thirty-eight were families of commissioned officers, two were families of warrant officers, and three were families of enlisted men. The subjects were 99 children, 55 boys and 44 girls, ranging in age from 5 to 17 years at the time of testing. The mean number of years of father absence for this group was 5.3 years.

Subjects were administered the appropriate level of the California Test of Personality (CTP), Form AA, according to their ages and grade levels. Twenty-four children were given the primary level (grades kindergarten through 3); 31 children were given the elementary level (grades 4 through 7); 18 children were given the intermediate level (grades 8 and 9); and 26 children were given the secondary level (grades 10 through 12). The children's testing was a part of the family follow-up interviews and, thus, all testing took place in the family's home. All interviews were conducted between March 1974 and January 1975, approximately 12 to 22 months after the father's return. Each subject was instructed to complete the test on his own by either circling the appropriate response, YES or NO, or by indicating his choice to the examiner. Although no time limit was set, the majority of children took approximately 30 minutes to complete the test.

The California Test of Personality was chosen (1) because of its reported validity and reliability in numerous studies (Buros, 1970) and the availability of established norms for various age groups and grade levels; (2) because of its appropriateness for a wide range of ages; and (3) because of its organization around the concept of life adjustment as a balance between personal and social adjustment. The CTP is divided into two components: The Personal Adjustment Scale and the Social Adjustment Scale. The first component of the CTP is designed to measure six dimensions of personal adjustment: self-reliance, sense of personal worth, sense of personal freedom, feeling of belonging, freedom from withdrawal tendencies, and freedom from nervous symptoms. The scales in the second component of the CTP are designed to measure six aspects of social adjustment: social standards, social skills, freedom from antisocial tendencies, family relations, school relations, and community relations. The number of correct responses is the raw score for each of the twelve component scales. A Total Personal Adjustment Score is obtained by adding the raw scores for the six personal adjustment component scales; a Total Social Adjustment Score is obtained by adding the raw scores for the six social adjustment component scales; and a Total Adjustment Score is computed by combining the Personal and Social Adjustment Scale totals.

In order to determine whether all total group means, as well as means for each level of the CTP, fell significantly below or above the normative mean, the Student t ratio was used. Pearson product-moment correlations were computed to determine the relationship between length of father's absence and the children's social and personal adjustment.

Children's Adjustment to Prolonged Separation and Reunion—Results

Table 11 indicates that, as a group, the RPW children's scores on the CTP, when compared with the median scores of the normative group established for the CTP, were found to be uniformly below the norm in the realms of Total Personal Adjustment [t (98) = -3.28, p < .005], Total Social Adjustment [t (98) = -5.46, p < .005], Total Social Adjustment [t (98) = -5.46, p < .005] and overall Total Adjustment [t (98) = -4.39, p < .005].

An analysis of the component scales reveals that, as a group, they obtained significantly lower scores on two of the four component scales dealing with personal adjustment: sense of personal freedom [t (98) = -3.16, p <.005] and

TABLE 11

COMPARISON OF THE COMBINED RPW GROUPS
WITH THE NORMATIVE MEDIANS

CTP Scales	t	P
Personal		
Self-reliance	-.48	N.S.
Sense of personal worth	-.64	N.S.
Sense of personal freedom	-3.16	<.005
Sense of belonging	-1.40	N.S.
Freedom from withdrawal tendencies	-3.50	<.005
Freedom from nervous symptoms	-.92	N.S.
Total Personal Adjustment	-3.28	<.005
Social		
Social standards	-.58	N.S.
Social skills	-1.43	N.S.
Freedom from antisocial tendencies	-5.43	<.005
Family relations	-4.50	<.005
School relations	-4.98	<.005
Community relations	-2.81	<.005
Total Social Adjustment	-5.46	<.005
Total Adjustment	-4.39	<.005

freedom from withdrawal tendencies $[t(98) = -3.50, p < .005]$. Additionally, the group scored significantly lower on four of the six component scales dealing with social adjustment: freedom from antisocial tendencies $[t(98) = -5.43, p < .005]$, family relations $[t(98) = -4.50, p < .005]$, school relations $[t(98) = -4.98, p < .005]$, and community relations $[t(98) = -2.81, p < .005]$. To determine whether these findings could be accounted for by specific families, the number of children of the same family who fell at the norm or 20 percentile points above or 20 percentile points below the norm was determined. The distribution did not reveal any pattern which would suggest that the findings could be accounted for by select families.

Table 12 presents a comparison of children's scores within each level (primary, elementary, intermediate, secondary) of the California Test of Per-

TABLE 12

COMPARISON OF EACH RPW GROUP
WITH ITS NORMATIVE MEDIAN

CTP Level	CTP Scale	$\bar{X}$	Norm Median	t
Primary (N=23)	Self-reliance	5.17	5.50	-1.11
	Personal worth	5.87	6.00	- .48
	Personal freedom	5.78	6.00	- .63
	Belonging	6.00	6.00	.00
	Withdrawal tend.	4.35	5.50	-2.81***
	Nervous symptoms	5.17	5.50	- .92
	Social standards	6.87	6.50	1.46
	Social skills	6.00	6.00	.00
	Antisocial tend.	5.65	6.00	-1.16
	Family relations	6.61	6.00	2.44**
	School relations	6.17	6.50	-1.36
	Community relations	6.09	6.50	-1.18
Elementary (N=32)	Self-reliance	7.00	7.50	-1.21
	Personal worth	8.47	8.00	.98
	Personal freedom	8.88	10.00	-2.90***
	Belonging	9.44	10.30	-2.57**
	Withdrawal tend.	7.31	7.00	.50
	Nervous symptoms	8.44	9.00	-1.04
	Social standards	10.34	10.50	- .65
	Social skills	8.38	9.00	-1.44
	Antisocial tend.	8.06	10.00	-4.34***
	Family relations	8.47	10.50	-3.59***
	School relations	7.66	9.00	-3.02***
	Community relations	9.25	10.50	-3.13***
Intermediate (N=18)	Self-reliance	9.89	10.50	- .13
	Personal worth	11.22	12.00	-1.15
	Personal freedom	11.17	12.00	-1.41
	Belonging	13.06	13.00	.09
	Withdrawal tend.	10.28	12.00	-2.05*
	Nervous symptoms	12.06	12.00	.08
	Social standards	12.72	13.00	- .57
	Social skills	10.50	11.00	- .64
	Antisocial tend.	10.33	12.00	-2.13*
	Family relations	10.33	13.00	-2.76***
	School relations	10.94	12.00	-1.59
	Community relations	11.94	12.00	- .09

Table cont'd

CTP Level	CTP Scale	$\bar{X}$	Norm Median	t
Secondary (N=26)	Self-reliance	10.42	10.00	.91
	Personal worth	13.04	12.00	-2.94***
	Personal freedom	11.19	13.00	-2.72***
	Belonging	12.58	13.00	-1.07
	Withdrawal tend.	10.15	12.00	-3.21***
	Nervous symptoms	10.77	11.00	- .35
	Social standards	13.15	13.50	- .91
	Social skills	11.62	12.00	- .76
	Antisocial tend.	10.04	12.50	-3.51***
	Family relations	11.04	12.50	-2.54**
	School relations	9.88	12.00	-4.25***
	Community relations	10.77	12.00	-1.82*

*   p <.05
** p <.01
*** p <.005

sonality with normative data for each level. As evident, significant differences were obtained in all of the grade levels, with greater differences noted in the realm of social adjustment. Children in three of the four levels, elementary, intermediate, and secondary, scored below the norm on the "family relations" scale and also obtained scores below the norm on the "freedom from antisocial tendencies" scale. Two of the four levels, elementary and secondary, scored below the norm on the "school and community relations" scales.

With respect to personal adjustment, children in three of the four levels, primary, intermediate, and secondary, obtained scores below the norm on the "Freedom from withdrawal tendencies" scale, and children in the elementary level scored below the norm on the "sense of personal freedom" and the "sense of belonging" scales. However, it is interesting to note that children in the secondary level scored above the norm on the "sense of personal worth" scale.

Correlational findings indicated the longer the period of father absence, the better was a child's Total Personal Adjustment ($r = .300$, df = 98, $p < .01$), Total Social Adjustment ($r = .319$, df = 98, $p < .01$), and Total Adjustment scores ($r = .318$, df = 98, $p < .01$). In addition, findings using component scale scores indicated that the longer the absence of the father, the better were children's family relations ($r = -.254$, df = 98, $p < .01$) and the more self-reliant he became ($r = .289$, df = 98, $p < .01$).

DISCUSSION

In summarizing previously mentioned studies and in examining recent studies by the Center for Prisoner of War Studies, we drew the following conclusions: (1) the normal patterns of coping with father/husband absence were disturbed by the unprecedented and indeterminate length of his absence; (2) major adjustments in family roles and interaction were prominent and had, over time, become strongly entrenched patterns that usually led to a new way of life; (3) the PW wives modified their assessment of their marriages and developed new sets of expectations for the future of their present marriage or the initiation of a new marital contract; (4) the wives experienced emotional difficulties during the waiting period, and these strongly reflected the complexity and difficulty of their coping with the situation; and (5) much of the social acceptance, stability, and continuity taken for granted in the intact family were lacking or severely taxed in the family of a prisoner of war. The military family without a father lived in double isolation—as a social deviant in the military system and as an enigma to a civilian community struggling to reconcile the appropriateness of the military conflict which left this family fatherless. It appeared quite obvious that the family's functioning was influenced profoundly by the stresses brought about by the months and, in most cases, years of waiting—so obvious, perhaps, that it had either been taken for granted or forgotten and had never received careful scrutiny.

Husband/father absence within the PW situation appears to be unique; the unprecedented length of absence and its unknown and unpredictable outcome added to the complexity of the more usual separation during a routine unaccompanied tour of duty. The families were confronted with basic questions which needed to be answered to their personal satisfaction. Should they plan for the husband's eventual return or a confirmation of his death? In most cases families had to prepare for both. The shifting of family roles and responsibilities suggest the evolution of a family unit without the father. The closing of ranks within the family was suggested by Hall and Simmons (1973) as part of their clinical portrait of PW/MIA families. Hill (1949) also noted that this pattern of "closing ranks" was a common phenomenon among families experiencing father separations during World War II. While these may be indices of normal adjustment, Hill also noted that the type of reorganization which made for successful separation adjustment appeared to hinder adjustment at time of reunion.

The emotional and adjustment problems experienced by the children of PW families were not noticeably high. However, it would be premature to conclude that the separation had negligible or no effects upon the children. The French (Marcoin, personal communication, 1972 and 1975), in their assessment of PW families of the Indochina War, found both behavior and academic difficulties among their children long after the repatriation of their fathers. Special education programs were developed specifically to assist these French children. The possible deleterious effects of father separation upon child adjustment were also underscored by Gabower (1960) in her controlled study of behavior problems of children in Navy families.

Variations in the social and psychological hardships experienced by the families indicated that the PW situation did not produce a crisis in every case. Frequent prior military tours by the husband, resulting in his absence, may have provided some wives with the experience needed to cope with the situation. Thus, adjustment may be eased by a sort of rehearsal or graduated immunization. Family life would continue, for the family who experienced frequent separations, with only a minimal break in the usual routines. In contrast, totally dependent wives, unaccustomed to the responsibilities brought about by the casualty, would be confronted with a crisis and would perhaps respond to the situation by withdrawing, thereby neglecting a host of other family responsibilities. The meaning of the PW situation varied from family to family. If, prior to casualty, husband, wife, and children had been in constant conflict, the father's absence might even be a relief, in spite of guilt feelings about his loss. However, where the family had previously worked and functioned as a unit, sharing responsibilities as well as recreation, the casualty would come as a traumatic shock, and adaptation would be extremely difficult. Where the father's role had been an integral part of the functioning of the family unit, his casualty would be a major loss.

Realistic appraisal of the wives' concerns and apprehensions about repatriation also suggested that the anticipation of reunion posed a threat to one or more of the rewards that the separations had provided, e.g., the opportunity to assume greater freedom, an independent income with the latitude to determine its use, and the avoidance of any confrontation with their husbands about the manner in which the wives conducted themselves during the husbands' absence. These apprehensions were also mentioned by Isay (1968) in his study of the submariners' wives. The French social workers (Marcoin, 1972 and 1975) cited similar problems as major areas of difficulty and as factors contributing to family discord following the repatriation of the French PWs from Indochina. Therefore, the significant relationship between these survey findings and the stresses in the husband-wife relationship following the husband's (PW) return, which was examined in Part II, is certainly not surprising.

It is of considerable interest to note, however, that in Part II of this investigation, among the variables, length of marriage has the highest correlation with the criterion of family reintegration—a finding which is inconsistent with the results of other investigations. Terman (1938), on the basis of his classic studies regarding personality and background correlates of marital happiness, questioned the importance of length of marriage as a predictor. Hill (1949) tested the predictive validity of length of marriage, an index of familism, but was not able to confirm its importance in family adjustment to separation and reunion. In the context of the present study, a possible explanation for the discrepancy in findings might be that the process of family reintegration for returned prisoners of war is unique. The prolonged and indeterminate separations, averaging five years, produced changes in family systems, modifications in wives' personalities and expectations for the marriage, and generally altered family life styles. Thus, family reintegration following this extreme type of separation would appear to involve a basic—overt and covert—reexamination as well as renegotiation of the marriage. Such a process necessitates taking into consideration the foundation of the marriage, its evolution, strengths, weaknesses, tensions, and fears—factors which are integral components of the length of marriage.

Studies of families during the Depression (Angell, 1936) and World War II (Hill, 1949) pointed to the importance of adequate marital adjustment and family organization to meet the crises of daily life as well as separation and reunion. The isolation of marital satisfaction before casualty as the second independent predictor of family reintegration is, in part, a confirmation of these earlier studies. A satisfactory marital situation before casualty provides a foundation for withstanding, enduring, and overcoming the stresses of separation and subsequent family reintegration. In considering the positive relationship between length of courtship and the wives' assessments of quality of marriage before casualty with the unique contribution of length of marriage, it would appear that the establishment of a relationship strong enough to endure the stresses of separation and the trials of reintegration was accomplished early in the marriage.

These findings add to the credibility of efforts to establish family counseling programs during the separation period (Powers, 1974) and give further credence to our past and present efforts to provide continuous services to families of men who have returned as well as to those families who were not so fortunate (Hunter and Plag, 1973; McCubbin and Dahl, 1974a). It is interesting to note that the emergence of the wife's emotional dysfunction as a major predictor also lends support to the extensive efforts on the part of the French military to extend social work and family counseling services to families of the French PWs held in Vietnam during the Indochina War.

It was reasonable to predict that the stresses associated with separation and reunion would have an effect upon the children. The results of Phase III, indicating that children who had experienced extended periods of father absence exhibited significantly greater difficulty with their adjustment than the norm, are in agreement with studies investigating the detrimental effects of long-term father absence (Gabower, 1960; Pedersen and Sullivan, 1964; Trunnell, 1968). The finding that, when the group as a whole was examined, more of the scores which fell below the norm were in the realm of social adjustment, would support those investigators who view the father as the instrumental leader in the family, as the parent who represents for the children the rules and principles of society (Parsons and Bales, 1955; Zelditch, 1955). It would be expected that the children taking the intermediate and secondary levels of the test (i.e., children between the ages of 13 and 18) would, indeed, score low on such scales as family relations, freedom from antisocial tendencies, and freedom from withdrawal tendencies, since such patterns are typical of the alienation so characteristic of adolescence. However, it should be emphasized that, because these groups have been compared to age-appropriate norms, we may conclude that this sample has indicated even greater alienation. The findings that children in the secondary level scored above the norm on their sense of personal worth might be explained by the fact that, since this group represents the oldest children within these families, perhaps they were also those who became the more responsible members of the family and thus more mature. This, then, might give them a feeling of being well regarded by others and a feeling that they were respected by their families, teachers, etc., as suggested by Hillenbrand (1970).

The finding that the RPW group as a whole scored below the norm in the realm of school adjustment is interesting from the standpoint of observations shared by French social workers (Marcoin, 1972, 1975) who, in their assessment of prisoner of war families of the Indochina War, found both behavior and academic difficulties among the children long after the repatriation of their fathers and, consequently, felt the need to establish special education programs specifically designed to assist these children.

The correlational findings dealing with length of father absence are also of interest. The fact that longer periods of father absence were not more detrimental to the adjustment of the child contradict findings of earlier studies, such as those by Gabower (1959) and Trunnell (1968). It may be that within the RPW group, longer periods of father absence placed greater demands on the children of these families—greater responsibility within the family unit, more opportunities to contribute to the family well-being, as well as to the ability to do things independently of others—leading to a sense of security and self-respect in connection with the various family members. This would be particularly true of the older children within the family. Hence, the findings that the longer the period of absence, the better the family relations of the child and the more self-reliant the child became are not totally unexpected.

CONCLUSIONS

There are two basic reasons for predicting that the returned prisoner of war (RPW) and his family would experience the difficulties of readjustment: the special status held by the RPWs, and the fact that after a prolonged absence, in some instances as long as eight years, the returnee had to face not only an extremely changed society but also a family whose patterns of adaptation to the stresses and increased responsibilities of father absence had virtually become a new way of life.

The few recent personal reports of family experiences of American returned prisoners of the Vietnam War (Plumb, 1973; Rutledge and Rutledge 1973; Chesley, 1973; Gaither, 1973) and a recent study by the Center for Prisoner of War Studies (Metres, McCubbin, and Hunter, 1974) confirmed the hypothesis that family reunions would be stressful. The public's demands upon the returnees, changes in personalities and values, and discrepancies in expectations of both husband and wife were realistic obstacles to a successful family reunion and may be among the major contributing factors to the surprisingly high estimates of divorces[11] among the recently returned prisoners of war.

As a general rule, as time passes, marriage partners, through confrontation, communication, negotiation, and compromise, grow closer together. The void caused by the captivity experience not only prevented this normal process of marital adjustment but, in many instances, also created an even wider gap which would have to be narrowed in the postrelease period if the marriage were to survive. Although both partners had one major goal during the separation period—day-to-day survival—it is highly probable that this goal resulted in a polarization of life styles owing to the significant differences between the situational demands for survival for the prisoner of war and those placed upon his family in terms of their emotional and physical abilities to cope with daily routine. Indeed, the stresses of captivity and the stresses unique to the families in limbo encouraged each, the man and his family, to develop independently behaviors which may not be totally congruent for postrelease adjustment. During captivity the man lost his independence and became totally dependent upon his captors for even the most basic needs. Relative to life in the United States, the prisoner of war had been placed in a time capsule. His wife, on the other hand, functioned in the role of head of the household and, as a result, matured, grew independent, gained self-confidence, and developed a style of life for a family without a husband or father. Interestingly enough, the social changes which evolved during this time, in particular the movement toward women's liberation, appeared to legitimize and support the wives and their development in this direction. In fact, social change may have been a major factor in aiding the wives' overall adjustment. When the prisoner of war came home to his wife, it seemed almost inevitable that even feelings about basic family decisions, goals, and values would be at variance.

Wives were in control of the reintegration process; some, after weighing their personal feelings about the quality of their marriage before separation, and considering their personal aspirations as well as the hardships they endured during the separation, had determined in advance of their husbands' return that they had no recourse but to terminate the marriage and begin a life for themselves. Although final decisions were often delayed until the husband and wife had had the opportunity to share their feelings openly, the outcome usually remained the same. For these families, the returning husbands were basically excluded from the decision-making process and, in most cases, tacitly accepted a decision which had previously been determined.

For the majority of the families, however, the process of reestablishing their marriages and family structure involved extensive renegotiations between marital partners. Although outweighed by other strong predictors, it did appear that the maintenance of father's role in the family unit during the separation period was important in the reintegration process. In families who left fathers' role open for renegotiation, the husbands appeared to experience greater opportunity to reestablish themselves in the family, to regain some control over the marital relationship and the family unit, and, ultimately, to have some influence upon deciding the future of the marital contract. For most families, however, the reintegration process is not complete, and for some the process will continue well into the future.

It is the opinion of the investigators that a comparison group is needed to determine whether the data on family adjustment and child adjustment would differ in any way from the adjustments made as a result of father absence brought about by a "normal" unaccompanied tour. Longitudinal data are needed regarding family and child adjustment to father absence in the military, independent of father absence brought about by military conflict. Data of this nature would be extremely valuable to the military in planning unaccompanied tours overseas and in the provision of services to families.

The findings concerning the wives' emotional health during separation and the children's personal and social adjustment following reunion point out the stresses inherent in separation and reunion and the importance of past and present efforts to extend services to families of returned prisoners of war, as well as to families of servicemen missing in action. In addition, the role of family research in the systematic, long-range planning of services to families throughout the military system was substantiated.

NOTES

1. From figures established immediately prior to the signing of the peace treaty (January 28, 1973).

2. Of the 100 PW families interviewed in 1972, 84 (84%) had their husbands return in 1973. Data for this phase of the study were available only for families of Navy RPWs.

3. Characteristics were: (1) pay grade at time of capture; (2) age at capture; (3) time (months) in captivity; (4) years of education; (5) Academy graduate (vs. non-Academy); (6) Protestant (vs. other); (7) marital status at time of capture; (8) military status at capture (Regular vs. Reserves); and (9) assignment at capture (Pilot vs. non-Pilot).

4. Family Assessment Form (FAF), a 177-item structured interview schedule used during the period April 1972-January 1973.

5. Initial Medical Evaluation Form (IMEF), Form 7, a 13-category inventory completed by the evaluating psychiatrist following the initial psychiatric examination at time of the serviceman's (PW's) return from SEA.

6. Returnee Captivity Questionnaire (IMEF, Form 6), a 35-item inventory administered at the Medical Centers processing returned PWs.

7. Survey of Returned Prisoners of War Section G, a 62-item inventory developed by the USAF in collaboration with the Center for PW Studies.

8. Predictor variables 18, 19, and 20 were obtained through a factor analysis of the Returnee Captivity Questionnaire which isolated three factors: perception of psychological coercion, perception of physical abuse, and basic threats and promises in captivity.

9. Data were available on 66 respondees who were married at time of casualty and completed the Family section (G) of the follow-up questionnaire; however, only 48 met all of the selection criteria for inclusion in this study.

10. Regression Analysis Program prepared by C.H. Nute and D.D. Beck, Navy Medical Neuropsychiatric Research Unit, San Diego, California.

11. As of October 1974, the divorce/separation rate for RPWs of the Army, Navy, and Marine Corps was 26.9 percent.

III

THE FAMILY IN THE
MILITARY COMMUNITY

Chapter 6

FAMILY SEPARATION IN THE ARMY: A STUDY OF THE PROBLEMS ENCOUNTERED AND THE CARETAKING RESOURCES USED BY CAREER ARMY FAMILIES UNDERGOING MILITARY SEPARATION

FRANK FLORES MONTALVO

INTRODUCTION

In America, during any one year, there are thousands of Army families that have been temporarily separated because of the absence of the soldier. These families potentially face serious problems of readjustment to living in the civilian community, as well as to the absence of the father and husband. This study focused on the problem-solving experiences of fifty-five career Army families in which the husbands and fathers were absent owing to their military assignments overseas. It was addressed primarily to learning the nature of the resources that were used by these families when they encountered problems in maintaining vital ongoing family functions. The fundamental question that guided this inquiry was: how were these families surviving and managing the impact of family dismemberment and family relocation? The potentially more stressful periods of family living in the Army occur under conditions of family separation. Therefore, knowledge of the range of family problems encountered, the types of problem-solving resources needed, and the nature of the families' adjustment during this time can contribute toward initiating and coordinating preventive and corrective services.

One of the objectives of military social service programs is to coordinate military services with those of social agencies within the civilian community. It is also the military's responsibility to inform and acquaint the civilian community

AUTHOR'S NOTE: This chapter is an adaptation of Montalvo, F.F. "Family Separation in the Army: A Study of the Problems Encountered and the Caretaking Resources Used by Career Army Families Undergoing Military Separation," an unpublished doctoral dissertation prepared for the University of Southern California, 1968.

[147]

with the problems of army families and to assist in developing resources in the community on their behalf. Consequently, one of the objectives of this study was to identify the full range of resources, civilian or military, that army families need to cope with separation.

In most societies, carrying out the normal functions in the family is predicated on the existence of a well-functioning family unit with a normal complement of parents (Herbst, 1960). The deleterious effects of temporary family dismemberment in the military may be experienced by the wife, the children, and by the family as a whole (Hill, 1949). On the other side of the coin, the family's problems may be communicated to the absent father, and therefore affect his well-being, morale, and work performance. The uncertainties of the husband's occupation, the repeated readjustments required in moving family and household to new localities, and the recurrent absence of the father are among the potential sources of strain in the family.

Most army families confronted with military separation are forced to leave military communities, if they were living in them, and exchange close friendship ties and known sources of help for the uncertainties of a different community. The family's decision as to where to live while waiting for the family to be reunited is a difficult one to make. A poor decision and unfavorable choice of neighborhood in civilian communities may take their toll in poor family functioning. Yet, we know little or nothing about the family during separation, and how it may or may not be supported by community resources, and the ultimate impact of the decisions families make with regard to relocation during the husbands' absence. There are currently few objective studies available about today's army family and its problems and none has addressed itself to the resources that are used by career army families who encounter problems while undergoing significant periods of family separation.

THE ARMY FAMILY

According to available information, 93 percent of officers with ranks of captain and above are married. Of enlisted men in senior ranks, 80 percent are married. Furthermore, 88 percent of these officers and 80 percent of these enlisted men are supporting one or more children. In the usual sense of the term, the soldier is a "family man." In terms of numbers, this involves over 350,000 soldiers and over 860,000 wives and children. Almost all these families experience residential mobility; thus, approximately one-half million new army family members—soldiers, wives, and children—may be affected annually by extended military separation. Although it is true that the absence of the husband/father for extended periods of time may be experienced by the families of other occupational groups, unlike the military, few civilian families simultaneously disengage themselves from their supportive social network of primary relationships when separation takes place.

The Army Family's Subculture and Caretaking Resources

The nuclear family is regarded as neither self-sufficient nor independent in its relationship with its environment—that is to say, it is an open system (Bell and Vogel, 1960). The family seems to be, in addition, particularly handicapped in dealing with emergencies (Hill, 1958). Thus, when emergencies arise and its internal resources are exhausted, where and to whom in the environment does the nuclear family turn for help?

It has been suggested that the family is selectively open to transact with other agencies, including kin and professional caretakers, and that "agencies can be ranked on their accessibilities to the interior of the family: immediate kin highest, family friends and neighbors next, the family physician, the family pastor, the family lawyer, and so on" (Hill, 1958). Formal agencies, such as school, health clinic, social agencies, and the like, are least accessible. However, the question arises as to why certain resources should be preferred over others.

Scholars tend to emphasize that the nuclear family in modern society is in relative isolation from supporting social networks while it attempts to cope with environmental demands (Burgess and Locke, 1953; Parsons and Bales, 1955). To some, society is perceived as an environment in which the family goes about coping and adjusting alone and separated from other families. The internal dynamics and external relationships of the family are explained more by the personality of its members and their internal role configuration than by influences of the enveloping social-environmental systems of which the family is a part. The simplistic notion that the "outside world" has little influence upon family behavior is certainly questionable. Studies directed toward discovering the supporting role of the extended kin have raised questions about viewing a nuclear family as the model type (Fellin, 1964; Litwak, 1960; Sussman, 1959; Sussman and Burchinal, 1962). Bell and Vogel's theoretical perspectives and an accumulating inventory of empirical studies regarding the family's interdependence with the social environment (Blum, 1966; Bott, 1957; Gans, 1962; McKinley, 1964; Rainwater, 1966; Zimmerman and Cervantes, 1960) contend that the nature of the social environment directly influences and shapes the family's identity, values, attitudes, behavior, style of living, and preferred sources of support in maintaining itself as a functioning unit. One must consider the army family's attempts to cope with stress within the context of its social environment and relationships.

The Dimensions of the Caretaking Resources

A caretaker in the community may be defined as anyone who provides services to people experiencing tensions owing to the problems they encounter, with the expressed aim of reducing them. In more abstract terms they are referred to as social and help resources. In this study, both custodial and therapeutic activities are subsumed under the caretaking function. Help aimed at improving the family problem complex is referred to as care*giving*; while help directed at providing protection, security, and nurturance is referred to as care*taking*. Gans (1962) offered two methods of categorizing caretaking resources: first, in terms of their organizational structure's being formally or informally developed; and second, in regard to their origin's or auspices' being internal or external to the user's subculture.

Formal Caretaking—Caretaking resources include agents who are trained for this purpose and who operate within formally structured agencies and institutions in the community. Such assistance may take such forms as medical and psychiatric treatment, casework, group work; occupational, social, legal, and economic counseling; educational and vocational guidance; and financial aid, and are considered formally organized in that they are developed specifically for health and welfare purposes. The agents are financially remunerated from some source (public or private); they require a degree of specialized skill acquired through training; and the caretaker and the recipient in need of service take on the formal roles of helper and client.

Informal Caretaking—Caretakers may also be classified as informal resources. They include family relatives, peers, neighbors, and personal associates who provide assistance during times of need. Informal resources are made up of purposeful primary relationships. Primary relationships are "relatively intimate, face-to-face encounters of varying degrees of permanency and structure. . . . The primary relationship may be conceptualized as an episode of interaction, usually between two (but sometimes more) participants, that is personal, reciprocal, and intimate and tends to recur with some periodicity" (Blum, 1966:77-86). They are not, however, specifically organized for this purpose, have not undergone specialized training in this regard, do not expect or receive monetary compensation for their aid, and do not assume an institutional role as helpers.

Formal vs. Informal Caretaking—The lack of routinized activities in the caretaker function and the lack of formal relationship between the caretaker and the recipient allow for the assistance to be given spontaneously, immediately, at no financial expense, and without the user's assuming the potential stigma associated in our culture with the formal, public role of being in need of help and being unable to manage on one's own.

Tyhurst has stated that "turning to the psychiatrist may represent an impoverishment of resources in the relevant social environment as much as an indication of the type of severity of disorder" (1957: 164). It should also be recognized, however, that turning to a formal resource when no other is available may have been preceded by a period of inactivity when the condition did, in fact, worsen and require services beyond the scope and management of informal resources.

These points are important in this study, since they emphasize the preventive role in mental health that effective informal resources play. By providing direct emotional support and by supplying services and facilities which reduce the family's concern with physical and economic survival, they may prevent the development of primary difficulties. The family's concern about being labeled "sick" or "inadequate" may also be lessened. It would seem that the more the family can expect help from among its peer families and its relatives, the more primary and derivative problems it can avoid.

The Subculture of the Career Army Family

In order for the informal social networks to be more readily utilized by the members as a source of help, the individuals must have feelings of interdependency and caretaking relationships which are reciprocal with each other. Such sentiments and behavior are found among people with similar ideology, expectations, and norms. The nuclear family is such a group.

Subcultures are responses families make to the opportunities and deprivations that they encounter. They consist of an organized set of responses developed out of their efforts "to cope with the opportunities, incentives, and rewards, as well as the deprivations, prohibitions, and pressures" which the natural and social environment offers them (Gans, 1962: 249). Each subculture tends to develop its own resources to support families in their attempts to cope with the stresses involved in utilizing the available opportunities. These caretaking resources are interpreted as being internal to and consistent with the family's style of life.

When families in the subculture are in need of services, they prefer to seek them first from the internal caretaking system. The access and use of internal resources legitimize the families' memberships in the subculture and lead to the families' identifying with subcultural values and goals and supporting the caretaking system. Greatest reliance is placed on informal resources made up of primary relationships. These statements contradict the notion that families seek help from whatever resource is available to them. Rather, they tend to have preferences as to where and from whom they seek help and what resources they develop and support. Breakdown in the families' supporting networks and their source of member legitimization would tend to lead, by this construct, to feelings of estrangement, isolation, and alienation from the subculture.

Military families may be said to possess a common subculture insofar as they share similar life experiences with other families in the military establishment. All are subject to similar social pressures and sanctions leading to their conformity to the values and norms espoused by the profession. Propinquity to each other in restricted residential communities where work and home acquaintances overlap and interact with each other tends to produce a close-knit network of social relationships. The group's traditions, customs, and wearing of a uniform as a visible distinction between member and nonmember, tend to minimize differentiation among the members and emphasize group identity, group solidarity, and to distinguish the military family from all others in society. Although the pattern of using caretaking resources was derived from studies of social class behavior, the military is not to be equated with any particular class. The central assumption of this study is that the military community possesses a separate and distinct subculture.

Stresses and Opportunities—Among the demands of the military occupation which are peculiar to the profession and which are expected to be encountered by its members are the following: periodic residential moves which reduce the opportunities for establishing lasting ties with civilian friends and family relatives; accommodation to different and varying social, subcultural, economic, and physical living conditions requiring flexible standards in one's living arrangements; separation of husband and father from the family for extended periods with the attendant adjustment in family roles and member satisfaction; and occasional subjection to the uncertainties and hazards of combat training exercises and international hostilities with their threat of injury and permanent family dismemberment.

Equally distinctive are the families' benefits and opportunities, such as, membership in a relatively closed social group with its own traditions and customs; use of exclusive recreational and social facilities, restricted organizational resources such as community housing at nominal rent with furniture, appliances, groundkeeping, maintenance, and security services; medical facilities and use of the commissary and post exchange; extensive travel and experiences in foreign countries; uninterrupted income; early occupational retirement; military subsidized vocational training and educational advancement; and the opportunity to render a public service. Together, the stresses and rewards help distinguish the career army' family's style of life from that of its civilian counterpart.

Even within the military there may be further distinction between differing subcultural commitments, with the expectations for deprivations and rewards differing on that basis. While the distinction between career and noncareer members is not clearly visible, those who have initiated commitments to service life by volunteering, rather than being drafted, and by "going Regular Army" and assuming a different status from reservists, tend to accept greater subjection to potential stress, as well as expect greater attention within the military reward system. To the careerist, soldiering is a profession and residential moves are accompanied by changes and advancement in work duties and responsibilities; family separations are frequently a part of earning coveted assignments to military specialty schools; and exposure to danger is concomitant with the exercise of professional expertise. Consequently, the career Regular Army families tend to express the greatest commitment and involvement in the military subculture. They tend to be more accepting of the stresses involved as being "part of the job" and look to the subculture for the rewards and benefits of being a member.

Ties Between Work and Home—Relatively few social studies have discussed extensively the life style of the army family in relation to its enveloping social system (Janowitz, 1960). The sharp segregation between work and home found commonly in urban centers is minimized in the Army. Frequent is the statement "a soldier is on duty twenty-four hours a day." It is also implicit that the behavior of family members should not interfere with the soldier's military duties nor threaten group cohesion by discrediting the military as a profession. Therefore, the conduct of family members may subject the soldier to disciplinary action and sanction by his superior. The soldier is held accountable for his family's behavior.

Some of the rewards mentioned above also provide opportunities for reinforcing the tie between work and home. Military families frequently reside together within the confines of a military post, which is under the jurisdiction of the post commander. The housing communities are physically separated from the homes of civilian families. The presence of work associates as neighbors and friends, of a neighborhood environment with like and visible symbols of one's standard of living, and of communal recreational facilities tend to provide multiple opportunities for supporting the values, attitudes, and behavior patterns which are preferred, and for correcting individual deviancy in this regard.

The military clubs provide an arena where social roles are learned and performed, where family friendships are developed and extended into wider networks, and where group identity and cohesion are most apparent. The bridging of relationships is very apparent in the military custom of the official, often monthly, social reception at the club for the incoming and departing officers and their wives in an organization. Its purpose is to facilitiate the families' social entrance into their new military community and to provide a social vehicle for the community's expression of loss and interest in the departing families' future. It functions to soften the social impact of geographic mobility among transient military families by offering them tangible evidence of the continuity of their life style and of their membership in the subculture regardless of their location. While propinquity may be a main socializing factor in the housing community and in recreational facilities, participation in club affairs is an open invitation for and an expected method of socialization into the military subculture.

The union between work and home becomes mutually reinforcing, for as the values between the systems are shared, communication between them also tends to increase (Arensberg and Kimball, 1965). At work and home the, family members are thus subject to a strong set of sanctions and normative controls.

The Military Subculture and the Civilian Community

The consequence of developing a distinctive life style is to create a life apart from the rest of society and from the members' previous subcultures. As military life becomes an increasingly dominant influence in family affairs, the army family relies more and more on the military community as a reference group and as a source of support, and becomes more estranged from civilian influences. As Janowitz observed, "the community's cohesion thwarts social integration with civilian society" (1960: 204). Viewed as a relatively closed social system, the military shares this process of separateness and identity with other subcultures in our society.

Blum's (1966) recent paper, which draws conclusions regarding primary group participation based on various studies into social class subcultures, including Bott's (1957), is particularly appropriate to our study of military families. Reference has previously been made to informal resources' being among the first used by families encountering problems. The nature of participation by families in primary relationships within and outside of their subculture will tend to define the network of informal caretakers that the families have available. Blum's conclusions are significant in this respect, indicating that people who come in recurrent and varied contact with others similar to themselves tend to be more isolated than individuals who come in contact with a variety of people who are different from themselves. Relationships within the military community are more likely to be more personal and intimate than are contacts in the civilian community. One form of cross pressure between two social systems is seen by Blum (1966) as the person's exposure to two differing value systems. Resolution of the conflict is accomplished by "minimizing the inconsistencies and by disassociating himself from the group that prescribes norms that conflict with those prescribed by the more highly valued group" (Blum, 1966). It is the threat of undermining the normative consistencies derived from his close-knit social network which leads the individual to withdraw from participation in the wider society. This phenomenon tends to reinforce the military families' tendency to identify more closely with other military families.

Applying Blum's summary to army families, the following propositions can be made about their primary relationship pattern and its consequences:

(1) The primary relationships among army families are more personal and intimate than their relationships with civilian families;

(2) The army families are vulnerable to cross-pressuring situations which can be avoided only through their withdrawal from participation in groups whose norms and values are inconsistent with their highly valued system;

(3) The army families are likely to be isolated from activities, issues, and associations in the civilian communities because their close-knit networks minimize their contact with others differing from themselves, and prevent the cultivation of loyalties to other social systems; and

(4) The army families are likely to experience feelings of alienation and isolation when they reside in the civilian communities and are separated from their close-knit social networks.

Limitations of Viewing the Military as a Subculture

There is strong evidence indicating, at the same time, that modern army life has significantly changed in recent years from the smaller, isolated, company-town atmosphere of previous times. The large and permanent size of the Army, the relatively high turnover rate of military personnel with varying degrees of service commitments, the changing occupational requirement for managerial and technological competence rather than for exclusively warrior and heroic performance, the recruitment of members from a wider social spectrum, the requirements and inducements for further civilian education among its officers, and the reliance on housing within the civilian community to augment limited on-post facilities are some of the factors which have worked against greater socialization into a common and separate subculture (Janowitz, 1960). An important limitation implied here is the fact that, by and large, socialization into the military subculture occurs after childhood when the individual has chosen an occupational career. Its distinctive features are not generally inculcated early in life. In this sense it is more in keeping with the changes that families experience when they move into different subcultural strata in our society. Thus, while family life may appear worlds apart from the others, the members retain familiar roots in the civilian community.

Formal Resources in the Military

As with other subcultures, the military has attempted to provide support for its members' families as they encounter problems while pursuing their chosen occupation. This activity has been considered important enough that a special staff section in the Army, Army Community Services, has been given the responsibility for developing programs which strengthen family life (U.S. Army Regulation 608-1, 1965). The development of such specialized services within the organizational structure of the Army appears to be due to several factors.

The increase and permanent size of the military has not only increased the number of families who encounter problems but has also rendered traditional, informal, semiorganizational resources limited in their scope. The military community has changed. It has become too large, too mobile, and too impersonal to rely on voluntary self-help (Janowitz, 1960). Formal resources and caretakers in the Army are seen as internal to the military value system and are seen as existing to support the Army style of life. These formal caretakers are professionally trained in their service activities and are also members of the military occupation. This is not in contradistinction to the civilian middle-class community, except that in a society where occupational and family roles are so closely bound, the distinction between formal and informal caretaking may be less fixed.

Formal caretaking resources in the military have similar characteristics to bureaucracies in civilian life. There is a tendency for services to be impersonalized and for clients to be treated as "cases" rather than as individuals. The close relationship between formal and informal resources does not imply the complete amalgamation of one into the other; only that there is a greater opportunity for each to influence the other. In the military, this is reflected in a close interdependency between caretaker and client, and the latter views all formal resources as being in his figurative possession to tap and his right to use. This includes the resources provided by other armed services for which he is eligible.

Mutual Help as a Tradition—The informal social networks in the Army also perform important caretaking functions. The tradition of military families' helping each other on an informal basis during periods of stress remains strong in spite of an increase of secondary group relations. The recognition of this tradition and of its survival value has led to its institutionalization, to a certain extent. When a member is transferred to a different community, he is assigned "a sponsor" (a military officer or enlisted man usually in the same unit), who attempts to facilitate the newcomer's transition into his new environment by helping him with individual and family needs. The formalization of a tradition may have been due to the dispersion of primary relations within the expanding Army, but it is facilitated by the close ties between work and home. It should be noted that this procedure tends to be perfunctory, since more often than not the offer of help by the member's future workmates is spontaneous.

The wife's extrafamily role as helper continues—as a neighbor, friend, and member in voluntary organizations such as the women's club, and in religious affiliations. The distinction between formal and informal resources is further blurred when officially recognized organizational resources, such as the Army Community Services, employ volunteers from the subculture, i.e., wives of servicemen, to carry out some of its functions. This caretaking activity directly reflects the close union between work and home life and the close-knit social network found in the military community. The tradition of mutual help approaches the degree of obligation and responsibility among many of its members. It may not be overstating the case to propose that the extent to which mutual help is expected among the members of a collectivity is the extent to which they can describe themselves as belonging to a community. It seems a natural outcome of a sense, in the military, of common destiny and group identity coupled with separation from previous-life associates and from the coexisting subcultures in civilian communities.

Because the community provides the primary source of continuity to family life while occupational requirements introduce potential disturbances in family routine, the Army has tended to establish resources for the important areas of family functioning. Many of these were cited before in terms of such benefits as housing, consumer, medical, and welfare resources. In addition, the community organizes infant nurseries, school facilities for children, and a variety of recreational and religious activities for the soldier and his family.

There is recognition of the growing importance of family life in the Army and its relationship to the profession. At the same time, recently enacted health benefit programs attempt to augment the military facilities with civilian services. The Military Medical Benefits Amendments of 1966 provide for civilian medical care for active-duty personnel and others through partial payment for outpatient and inpatient treatment (U.S. Public Law 89-614). The recently developed Health Resources Information Branch, Office for Dependent Medical Care, Denver, Colorado, operates an exchange to supply information concerning location, cost, and services available from nonprofit civilian facilities in regard to problems of handicapped children belonging to service families. The listings are national and international, recognizing the mobility of military families, and are developed to support the objectives of the Army Community Services program.

In spite of the extensions of formal services to military families, it remains to be seen to what extent they are utilized or are functionally available to the military families. Even when residency requirements established by institutions are adjusted to the mobile army family, and when the army family is helped to assuage its hesitancy to use civilian resources, there may remain a reluctance of various civilian agencies to serve military families. Social workers in the armed services are well aware that some of the civilian resources take too much to heart the military adage, "We take care of our own." While it does do this to a great extent, the Army's primary mission prevents it from filling all the gaps and meeting all of the needs of the military family.

Finally, the role of family relatives, especially parents, is less certain. If it is similar to that played during periods of need in other subcultures, relatives would tend to fill the gaps in military and civilian assistance and to augment resources which are limited or uncertain that are provided by the subcultures.

The Army Family and Its Subcultural Resources

As a subcultural system, the army community develops, maintains, and staffs its own resources to support the member family in its attempt to cope with the stresses the family encounters while it attempts to meet the demands of its various social situations and satisfy the requirements of the profession. The resources consist of closely knit social networks of relationships and of institutions that are provided as resources for help by the military organization. These caretaking resources are interpreted by the army family as being internal to and consistent with its style of life. As such, they are supported and preferred to nonmilitary resources when a family needs help and when both services are equally available. Union between home and work tends to lead to personalization of formal resources and to formalization of informal resources. The latter occurs in the development of a tradition of mutual help which is officially supported and provided for by the military establishment.

The intimate primary relationships developed during careers in the military lead to increasingly greater group loyalty and solidarity among army families, to preferring military facilities as a source of formal help, to estrangement from the civilian community, and to experiencing feelings of isolation when separated from the military social network and the valued informal resources.

As with other subcultures, the army family relies on its kinship network to fill in for unavailable resources and to augment limited, depleted, or uncertain resources in the military community. The accessibility and use of military resources, and the members' participation in their development and maintenance, help legitimize the family's membership in the military social system. Separation from them or denial of their use would raise questions as to the extent of the family's membership in the subculture.

Purpose of the Study

This study focused on problem-solving experiences of career army families in which the husbands and fathers were absent owing to their unaccompanied twelve-month military assignments overseas. The purpose was to determine the following: the extent to which the problems were attributed to the absence of the soldier or to the family's relocation into a new community; the nature of caretaking resources that were used to resolve problems; if there was a difference in the customary pattern of using resources by army families; and the relationship between the use of resources and the nature of the problems faced, the extent of involvement in the subculture, and the wife's emotional responses to the separation experience. These factors were thought to be relevant to the family's adaptation to dismemberment under specific conditions: they had moved residence as the result of separation; they were living in urban, civilian communities; and they could not join their husband for at least one year because of his assignment. The information collected about four specific areas of family functioning—child care and development, home management, community relations, and adult need satisfaction—was based on the wives' subjective perceptions of the families' ongoing life experiences.

METHODOLOGY

The sample consisted of 55 out of the available 154 separated families. Data were obtained through semistructured research interviews designed to compare information on four vital areas of family functioning, resources used, and social characteristics of the families. Two scales were devised. Narrative summaries of each family's experience supplemented the analysis of statistically significant differences within the sample.

The Interview Guide

A series of questions, developed through pilot interviews, were designed to cover the problems encountered in four vital areas of family functioning and to determine the nature of the resources used by the wives to meet them. Areas in family functioning were kept as mutually exclusive as possible, although, in reality, it was recognized that they were interdependent and overlapped with each other. Thus, all matters relating to the children's development were recorded in that area, and the family's relationship to the community was restricted to the mother's perception based on her experiences as an adult. The latter area, in turn, was a more objective appraisal of community relations than her feelings about satisfying her social and personal needs. Similarly, her evaluation of home management was approached from the point of view of her ability to attend to the physical side of the family's needs by keeping the home running. A final set of questions requested the wives' suggestions for developing needed resources and means by which army wives could be of help to each other. The questions provided a sense of closure to the interviews and an opportunity for the wives to express their desire to help others, which was the main incentive provided for questions eliciting their participation.

The subcultural involvement of the families required the development of a scale to estimate indirectly the extent of the families' socialization into the subculture, and the extent of their separation from civilian ties and influences. The indices used are based on the description of the army family and its subculture used in this study. The social characteristics tabulated and compiled in the course of the study, in addition to those used in the subculture scale, were (a) the wife's age, (b) number of months separated, (c) number of children living in the home, (d) family's life cycle, (e) first and second reason for moving to study site, (f) status of work of the mother, (g) living and housing arrangement, (h) educational level, (i) wife's national origin of birth, and (j) the family's racial or ethnic group.

Criteria Used for Selecting Subjects

The criteria used for a family's inclusion in the study were that the family's military member was committed to an army career and was currently assigned to an unaccompanied (by family members) overseas tour of duty; in addition, the family had volunteered to be interviewed. If the officer had attained at least the rank of captain, he was considered to have career intentions. Families whose sponsors had attained the rank of warrant were also included. All warrants were expected to have been former enlisted men. The officers' families, therefore, whose husbands and fathers had achieved the following ordered ranks were included in the sample and considered career families: warrant, captain, major, lieutenant colonel, colonel, general officers. If the enlisted man had attained the rank of sergeant (E5) or above, he was considered to have career intentions. The families whose sponsors had achieved any one of the following ordered ranks were included in the study: sergeant (E5), staff sergeant (E6), sergeant first class (E7), master sergeant and first sergeant (E8), and chief master sergeant and sergeant major (E9).

Separation Experience—All members of the families not only had their sponsor overseas, but they also had moved in connection with the separation, and their residence was in a civilian community. Most of the families moved from military to civilian communities, but some moved from one civilian community to another. The important criterion was that residential mobility took place.

Each household was sent a letter which requested voluntary participation in the study and was worded to appeal to the desire of the wives to contribute to the development of help resources in the Army designed specifically to benefit separated families. A preliminary questionnaire accompanied the letter and constituted the reply form used for volunteering. The preliminary information gathered in this manner included the sponsor's current rank, the number of children in the home, the months the family had been separated, and the family's new address and phone number if it had moved.

The primary purpose of the research design was to collect valid information which would reflect accurately the families' experiences and enable the researcher to answer the basic question posed for investigation: how were army families surviving and managing the impact of family dismemberment and family relocation?

FINDINGS

Characteristics of the Families

The typical family in this study was Caucasian—76% of the families were white, and 24% were black, Filipino, or mixed—and included two children living in the home, the eldest of whom was of school age and preadolescent. The family had decided to move in order to be near its extended family to whom it felt close; two-thirds of the families gave as their reason for moving "nearness to relatives." It maintained, however, a separate residence in a rented house. The mother in the family was native-born (67% were native-born), was not working (75% were not employed during their periods of separation), and tended to have been a career army wife for less than ten years (the mean number of years that the wives spent as army wives was 9.5). She was under thirty years of age (almost half of the wives were between the ages of 21 and 30) and had attended college (70% of wives had graduated from high school and over half had at least some college education). The father had a junior status with the enlisted rank of sergeant; over one-half of the families' sponsors were enlisted men, with the rank of E6 being the most prevalent; among the officers, the rank of captain represented the mode. The family's friendship ties over the years were with other military families and it preferred to live in a military residential community; 70% preferred living in a military community. As mentioned earlier, it fully expected extended absences to take place on the part of the sponsor owing to his commitment to a military career. Out of a possible twelve-month period of separation, 60% of the families were separated for six or less and 40% for seven or more. The six-month period, as the halfway mark, tended to be viewed by the wives as the critical period, and for this reason the adjustment of those above and below this bench mark were examined in this study. The mean number of months of separation was 5.6.

To what extent do families attribute their problems to the absence of the husbands and to what extent do they attribute them to their separation from the military subculture? The research data indicated that, while separation from the husband/father was felt deeply, separation from the informal caretakers provided by the subculture also had a significant impact on the families' perceptions of problems encountered and on their ability to meet them. Seven out of ten problems, whether they were due to the husbands' absence or to relocation, were seen by the career families as preventable had they been living in a military community and had they been able to draw upon its interpersonal resources.

Only seven families reported being free of major problems. One-half of all families encountered severe enough stress to create adjustment difficulties in maintaining family functions. Contrary to expectations, the absence of the sponsor was not generally regarded as stressful a situation as relocating into a new social environment. Both situations, however, were interrelated and created special problems for the families' adaptations. Current military housing policy restricting separated families from residing on post appears to be at variance with the spontaneous, informal caretaking system developed within the subculture. Native- and foreign-born wives tended to attribute their problems to different factors—the former to the sponsor's absence and the latter to relocation. Both, however, thought that they would not have had their problems if they had lived in the military community, and both tended to see the primary relationships in the military community as their prime source of help. Thus, it appeared that regardless of the nature and causes attributed to problems and the different social circumstances found among the career wives in the study, the military subculture, with its interpersonal relationships and its tradition of mutual help, plays a potentially significant and primary role in helping families cope with the stress of military separation.

Resource Preference

Community resources were used by about 61 percent of all of the families. The families did not, however, show any pronounced preference in their use of civilian or military resources (see Table 1).

Degree of Stress and Nature of Resources Used

There was a marked tendency for severely stressed families, when they sought help, to use military resources significantly more often than families under

TABLE 1

RESOURCES USED FOR RESOLVING ALL PROBLEMS

Resources	Number Of Problems	Percentage
Military	22	18
Family	25	20
Civilian	28	23
None	48	39
Totals	123	100

moderate stress. The latter preferred to use nonmilitary resources almost exclusively—both civilian resources and family relatives were used to an almost equal extent. This latter finding emphasized the importance of the families' successful transition into the civilian community and the importance of the resources within it in support of the families. While important, it was not surprising to find that severely stressed families were reluctant to make use of any resource; resources were not used for almost one-half of those problems encountered by severely stressed families.

It seemed that the failure to use resources was strongly related to the worsening of the problems encountered. In many cases it appeared that an earlier use of resources would have helped to circumscribe the problem to within more manageable limits; in some, the problem was severe from the beginning and no resources were sought at any time. The reasons given for not using resources varied. Some wives were not aware of them in the community; many were reluctant to use those which were available because of feelings of estrangement; and a third group preferred to "live with the problem" until the family was reunited. Regardless of the reasons given for not using resources, the trend indicated support for the contention that families experiencing crises tended to be more socially isolated from resources and tended to fester from within during periods of stress.

Birth Origin and the Use of Resources

For all problems encountered, there was little difference in regard to birth origin (foreign- vs. native-born wives) as far as failure to use resources was concerned. Foreign-born wives failed to use resources for 37 percent of their problems, while native-born wives failed to do so for 42 percent of their problems. There was, however, a statistically significant difference in the nature of the resources used by the two groups. For problems for which resources were used, the foreign-born wives used military resources and relatives for about four out of five problems, while the native-born wives used military resources and relatives for somewhat over one-half of their problems. On the other hand, the former used civilian resources for only one out of five of their problems, while their American-born counterparts turned to the civilian sector for two out of five of their problems.

While the main categories of caretaking resources were used to an equal extent by the families in the study, important differences were noted in the use of resources by American- and foreign-born wives. The former tapped civilian over military resources by about two to one. Greater flexibility in their use of resources while separated from the military subculture was indicated by their greater ease in using interpersonal caretakers in the civilian community. The foreign-born wives maintained their preference for military over civilian resources in spite of changes in their subcultural environment. Family relatives were also preferred. There was distinct difficulty in using personal resources in the civilian community, reflecting their continual estrangement in that setting. Neither group showed a preference for using formal resources.

These patterns tended to illustrate family adaptation to the separation experience. Almost all families expressed a desire to have military resources available for all problems, especially those provided by the social networks in the military community. In response to not being able to rely on resources within the military community setting, the American- and foreign-born wives behaved differently. The former attempted to make the transition between the separate subcultures and encountered some difficulties. The latter made few attempts in this direction, preferring to seek out and maintain contact with military friends in civilian communities or with relatives. They reported few, if any, friends living in military housing. For all families, extended kinship ties appeared to mediate the transition and provide islands of security during the adaptive processes.

Family Relatives as Resources

In all areas of family functioning, the wives reported being most aware of relatives as resources for support and problem solving. Although two-thirds of the families decided to move to specific areas of the U.S. to be near their families, only one problem in five encountered by the entire group was taken to relatives for their assistance. Twice as many problems were taken outside of the extended family as within. Many families, however, emphasized the importance of the companionship and the "emotional presence" of the extended family during the course of their separation experience. Relatives, especially parents, were viewed as providing security, protection, and emotional nurturance and were sought less for therapeutic or caregiving purposes. During the separation period, the extended family played roles which were uncomfortably close to past parent-child relationships. Therefore continual concern was expressed by the wives over clarifying the boundaries between their own families and those of the extended kin. In addition, generational differences and dissimilarities in life experiences led many of the wives to feel uncomfortable with the role of family relatives as caretaking resources. While they were frequently seen as necessary, they were also regarded as limited in the extent to which they could meet the wives' adult needs.

In general, the educational level of the wives was not associated with the nature of the resources used by the wives in the study. However, there was an association between wives' education and the use of kinship tie as a source of support. The less well-educated wives used family relatives most often and in preference to friends, by a ratio of two to one, while the more educated group used friends somewhat more often than they did kin ties as a source of help for their problems. Both groups of wives used formal resources to an almost equal extent. The data on the use of informal resources are presented in Table 2.

TABLE 2

LEVEL OF EDUCATION OF WIVES BY NATURE
OF INFORMAL RESOURCES USED

Level of Education	Number of Problems For Informal Resources Used		
	Family	Friends	Total
High school or less	14	7	21
More than high school	11	14	25
Totals	25	21	46

$\chi^2 = 1.53$; df = 1; p < .30, Not statistically significant

The Use of Informal and Formal Resources

In general, personalized untrained caretakers in the form of family relatives and friends were preferred by all families for three out of five of the problems they reported. The data appear to support the hypothesis that families turn to informal resources more than formal ones when confronted with problems. Previous studies of social class behavior in regard to using caretakers suggested that formal, institutional resources were seen as external to the working-class value system and were used sparingly. In this study, both educational groups used formal resources (civilian and military) for solutions to their problems to an equal extent. The absence of significant differences suggests that both formal resources (civilian and military programs) were regarded as internal to the army families' value system regardless of the social class into which objective indices may place them. As such, the military may represent a distinct subcultural caretaking system where formal institutional resources are equally available to and used by all army families.

Awareness and Use of Resources

The degree to which the wives were aware of community resources to assist them, if needed, was significantly related to wives' actual use of these services (Table 3) in the sample's overall awareness of military versus civilian resources.

TABLE 3

AWARENESS OF MILITARY AND CIVILIAN RESOURCES BY
USE AND NONUSE OF RESOURCES FOR ALL PROBLEMS

Awareness of Military and Civilian Resources	Number of Problems for Resources		
	Used	Not Used	Total
Either or both	55	19	74
Neither	20	29	49
Totals	75	48	123

$\chi^2 = 12.54$; df = 1; p < .001.

TABLE 4

ORIGIN OF BIRTH BY THE USE OF INFORMAL MILITARY
AND CIVILIAN RESOURCES

| Origin of Birth | Number of Problems for Informal Resources Used | | Total |
	Military	Civilian	
Foreign	5	1	6
United States	3	12	15
Total	8	13	21

Significance level using Fisher test was .05. See Sidney Siegel, *Nonparametric Statistics for the Behavioral Sciences* (New York: McGraw-Hill Book Company, Inc., 1956, p. 99).

Birthplace

The wives' use of resources appeared to be a function of whether the wives were foreign-born. Although both groups indicated an equal level of awareness of resources, the foreign-born wives tended to emphasize military resources more often; native-born wives mentioned civilian resources more often.

While most families expressed a desire to have military resources available for all problems, the foreign-born wives used this resource most often and felt somewhat inept in turning to the informal caretakers in the civilian community for help. The American-born wives, on the other hand, were especially flexible in adapting to the civilian community by using informal resources within it more often than their foreign cohorts. They tended to express greater comfort in having resources available to them in the social environment, even though their overall use of resources was proportionately no greater than the foreign-born wives'. Both groups looked for family relatives to be a source of custodial care to the same extent.

Changes in the Pattern of Using Resources

Spellman (1965) observed that intact, career Army families living on post preferred using military-based resources over civilian resources by a margin of three to one if they had problems. One objective of the present study was to determine if a selected group of separated families followed a similar pattern for all problems while living in a civilian community. It was assumed that their on-post preference was similar to those in the previous study. Comparison was made between the observed number using civilian and military resources in the study population and the expected frequency based on the three to one ratio. The figures in Table 5 satisfy the requirements of the research objective, and the results indicated that a change was noted in the study families' pattern in using resources—from a marked preference for military resources to a slight choice for civilian ones. That is, less than one-half rather than three-quarters of the problems were referred to military resources.

Thus, for the families in this study, their assumed on-post pattern of using resources while separated from their sponsors was not transferred off post. This finding should be tempered by the fact that military resources were geographically distant from the families and the military community was virtually nonexistent for them. The expected patterns, however, did develop under more

TABLE 5

OBSERVED AND EXPECTED FREQUENCIES BY USE OF
MILITARY AND CIVILIAN RESOURCES FOR PROBLEMS

Frequency	Number of Problems for Resources Used		Total
	Military	Civilian	
Observed in study	22.0	28.0	50
Expected	37.5	12.5	50

$\chi^2 = 20.02$; df = 1; p $< .001$.

circumscribed conditions, which were more closely analogous to those in the previous Spellman (1965) study. His results reflected the comparative, expected use of resources by families who were suppositionally confronted with child guidance and marital problems requiring the help of more formalized therapeutic resources. The child care and adult need satisfaction areas in this study were similar types of problems, the maladjustment classification was an equal level of severity, and the use of formal resources was analogous. For the twelve such problems, eight were referred to military resources and four to civilian ones. While the difference was not statistically significant, it suggested that for severe, internal family problems, formal military resources were still preferred by army families even when living off post and undergoing family separation.

Contrary to general assumptions, as much as one-half of the problems encountered by father-separated families were attributed to the families' relocation into new communities rather than to the separation. Military and civilian resources and family relatives were used to an equal extent, although families that did not face maladjustments in family functioning used nonmilitary resources almost exclusively. The equal use of civilian and military resources indicated a change in the army families' preferred use of military resources when they are united and living in military communities. The nature of the problems faced was not associated with the resources used, although the more severe adjustment difficulties were referred mostly to military resources. There was a strong indication that the families which were heavily involved with the military subculture tended to minimize their dependence on relatives as a source of assistance. The wives who responded with emotional difficulty to separation made less use of resources than those who responded better.

The families that were able to make fuller use of civilian resources, because they were able to develop social relations within the community, encountered fewer problems and adapted best to the separation experience. For most, however, there was a rapid withdrawal from the civilian community and its potential resources after an initial attempt at integration. Their marginal status within the community became most clearly defined when the families became aware that geographic and social separation from the military community made their subculture's (military's) resources inaccessible. The close-knit network of relationships within the Army was seen by the wives as providing significant protection against the stresses of family dismemberment. Separation from the military community appeared more stressful than the soldiers' absence from the home. As a result, they believed that most of their problems could have been prevented if they had been better integrated into military community life. The foreign-born wives were as successful in coping with stress as the native-born wives, although they exhibited a different pattern of using resources.

Military Separation as a Neglected Social Problem

Determining the impact of the separation experience on families is related to the value one places on family stability, family development, and our judgment as to how severe a general problem should be before one becomes concerned. Certainly, the families in the sample behaved well socially, causing a minimum of difficulty in communities, and they were not a source of concern among health and welfare institutions. The usual index rates of disruption, such as delinquency and mental illness, were negligible. On these bases, the research families were ignored. They caused little damage and visible disruption to military and civilian social systems. Within the military system these families would be ignored. If they had created difficulties this study might have been undertaken possibly long before now and the services needed would already have been provided.

The military social structure and subsystems within which the family operates provide the sources for both its destruction and its growth. The sociocultural environment presents the army family with conflicting values and expectations which cannot be easily resolved, at least without high social costs. On the one hand, society places great emphasis on preserving the integrity of the family and its effective functioning in order to ensure its contribution to society. At the same time, social recognition is given to the soldier's role in implementing national goals, and society sanctions extended separations from wife and family during the performance of his military duties. Both these values cannot be fully attained by the family without substantial adaptations and emotional as well as financial costs to the family system. Most of the costs remain hidden.

The military subculture has attempted to minimize the cost to the family by providing specialized resources and services during times of need. However, problems, maladjustments, and emotional distress have occurred when these resources were unavailable for effective use during separation. In this regard, four out of five families encountered problems beyond the families' capacity to cope—one-half of them were under severe stress, and one-third of the wives responded with emotional difficulties to the separation experience. Most important, the wives thought that seven out of ten problems could have been prevented if adequate subcultural resources had been available and used.

The Subculture's Informal Caretaking System

A principal finding derived from the study was that the families believed strongly that a distinct informal subcultural caretaking system existed within the military community. This system was composed of a close-knit network of help-reciprocating families that shared the values and attitudes required to maintain and support a tradition of mutual help among its members. This tradition was expected to be activated whenever any member experienced difficulties in overcoming the stresses that his style of life involved. The distinctive feature of this tradition was that service was provided on the basis of need without the explicit agreement of direct payment to the provider. Since there was an implicit expectation that all participants would be ready and willing to return like service to others at some time in the future, membership in the subculture was a necessary condition for eligibility. All members were potential recipients and providers of service. The debt accrued as beneficiary was owed to the caretaking system; it could never be paid in full; and there was sufficient faith in its continuance that some payment was expected to be made at some time. The recurrence of potential stresses maintained a constant need-level among the members; the close-knit network of relationships provided a continuing source of willing caretakers; and the strong sense of group solidarity tended to obligate the members to uphold and contribute to the maintenance of the mutual help tradition. The "bond of services" which was provided became the common purpose which helped to unite the members even further (Hiller, 1947: 115). It was at this point, and at this level, that the adage, "We take care of our own," began to have real meaning for the families in the study.

As long as the reciprocity principle was maintained, the caretaking activity was not interpreted as charity, since the recipients did not class themselves as dependent, and they believed that they were willing to return services at some time. It was thus a right that was earned, or capable of being earned, through participation in the system. There was strong emphasis on the part of the separated families on their capacity to contribute to the system, and they regarded this as their obligation and duty as career army wives. Their desire to maintain interdependent, rather than dependent, relationships also led to their emphasis that helping and being helped should be done within the context of socializing and comradeship. The wives mentioned that it would be easier to give and receive help if the families were engaged in social and recreational activities together. The "social club" nature of mutual help groups seemed to carry latent functions in addition to meeting social and personal needs. The function was not directed to cloak the caretaking activities, but to facilitate them.

In view of the importance of reciprocity in maintaining the caretaking system's continuity, two additional reasons are seen as being important. First, it provided the members with the opportunity to test out the others' willingness to help. Second, interdependence required an equal capacity to reciprocate services, and engaging in social activities together implied equal status among the members. Help could be asked for and accepted more easily if the members were less concerned with having dependent status relative to other members.

SUMMARY AND CONCLUSIONS

This description was based on the perceptions of the separated families and not on their observed participation in the caretaking system. While they were in a position to comment on what resources they needed and which were missing, the existence of a tradition of mutual help was not demonstrated directly and remains open for in-depth study. The following propositions are offered with regard to the nature of the caretaking system within the military community:

(1) When career army families living in military communities encounter family problems beyond the scope of their own resources, they seek other member-families in
the community as sources of help significantly more often than would civilian
families facing a similar situation;

(2) Participation in the informal caretaking system by the family is positively associated with the husband's commitments to a military career;

(3) Member-families accept help significantly more often when they can demonstrate a
capacity to reciprocate services than when they cannot.

Because of the army family's temporary residence, its separated status, and its military affiliation, it tended to be ascribed a peripheral status within the civilian community. Its role was uncertain and poorly defined; obligations and expectations unclear. Those who were best able to bridge the gap into civilian life, because of personal attributes or, more important, because of community receptivity, appeared best able to adjust to the separation experience. For most, however, there was a rapid withdrawal from the civilian community and its potential resources after an initial attempt at integration. Since much of this response was based on the research families' perceptions of their negative encounters with various civilian families, research regarding the attitudes of the latter toward army families would allow a more accurate estimation of the realities of the army families' viewpoints.

The conclusion is twofold: First, that the experiences of the army families within the civilian community were, to a great extent, a reflection of the anonymity and social distance which is characteristic of urban environments. Their perception of rejection was acute because it contrasted sharply with their accustomed close-knit relationships in the Army. Second, families played a part in closing out the civilian community. They could also close ranks within the family because they could foresee their eventual reintegration within their military subculture at some future time. This tended to hasten isolation. The peripheral status that they described was thus partly elective and assumed, even though it denied them access to potential resources for problems that were encountered during the separation experience.

The peripheral status became most clearly defined when the families became aware that geographic and social separation from the military community tended to make the subcultural resources inaccessible. The opportunities for continued association with the military community and mutual help among army families were not possible for some. The families felt less a part of the Army and many strove in words and deeds to reaffirm their membership in the subculture in order to reduce their feelings of uncertainty, uselessness, and pervasive concern that they were being forgotten by their valued military community. For some, this meant a bitter resignation to their marginal status and its grim acceptance as a "normal part of army life." There was a distinct lack of any perception of their having a meaningful role in any community and the feeling of living in limbo until the family was reunited and reaccepted into the military social system. Family relatives were temporarily helpful in ameliorating the problems and tensions associated with the separation experience. When they were unavailable or their helping capacities exceeded, and the family retained its distance from the civilian community, military resources were sought. To some, the latter was psychologically the "only family we have left."

Thus, the separated families' inability to participate in the informal caretaking system not only limited the potential resources available to them but also contributed toward their demoralization by increasing their dependency on nonreciprocating resources; reduced their sense of worth by denying them the opportunity to function usefully and meaningfully within their primary group; and created uncertainty about their status in the subculture and the value that the latter placed upon them. The findings in this study further support an important generalization in the mental health field: "the disruption of the smaller social context may be more invidious than major cataclysms" (Cumming, 1968: 12). The close-knit network of relationships within the Army provides significant protection against the stresses of separation. The career army family's separation from the military community was seen here as at least as disruptive as the absence of the sponsor from the home.

The informal caretaking system is an important adaptive subcultural response to the exigencies of military life. Its availability suggests the need for allowing the soldier's family to remain in the military community when he is assigned overseas and for recognizing the family as a continuing member of the subculture. This support system's operation is a significant element in any family's social reality and ability to master problems.

Chapter 7

UTILIZATION OF PROBLEM-SOLVING RESOURCES

AMONG MILITARY FAMILIES

SETH SPELLMAN

INTRODUCTION

Prior to World War II the Armed Services, in spite of the widespread unemployment of the thirties, had never grown larger than 200,000 men, except during periods of active warfare (Vidich and Stein, 1960). It thus does not appear to have had a significant impact on the larger American scene. Since the end of World War II, however, the military establishment has become increasingly important as an instrument of American policy and as a consumer of goods and services (Janowitz, 1959; Walter, 1958). This increasing importance has, of course, necessitated larger numbers of men being under arms. One of the consequences of having large numbers of men under arms is that many of them will be married and will likely be accompanied in their military assignments by wives and children. Many individuals have chosen, for a variety of reasons, to make a career of military service with the Army. Their families may be characterized as military families. It is this segment of the military population with which this study is concerned.

PROBLEM

The essential questions regarding these families to which this study seeks answers are as follows: To what extent are career army families, living on a military reservation, aware of help resources located in the military community,

AUTHOR'S NOTE: This chapter is an adaptation of Spellman, S. "Orientations Toward Problem-Solving Among Career Military Families: A Study of the Knowledge of Available Resources in a Military Community and Perception of the Social Cost of Using Them For the Resolution of Family Conflict," an unpublished doctoral dissertation prepared for Columbia University, 1965.

and what is their perception of the social cost of using such facilities? The study intends to describe the distribution of knowledge of help resources, the perception of social cost at various organizational levels, and to isolate, where possible, those social characteristics of career military families most immediately related to these distributions.

THEORETICAL CONSIDERATIONS

In the ordinary arrangements of our society, there is a distinct separation between the authority of the workplace and the home. There are, to be sure, reciprocal influences of the workers' activities both on the job and in the home. This has been pointed out by many authors (Bettelheim and Sylvester, 1950; Dyer, 1962; Friends and Haggard, 1948). The authority of the workplace is expected to stop with the workers' receipt of a money payment, and as has been indicated by Goffman: "the spending of this (money payment) in a domestic and recreational setting is at the discretion of the worker and is the mechanism through which the authority of the workplace is kept within strict bound" (Goffman, 1958).

When a member of the Army moves his family into government-owned housing on a military reservation, he brings it under the authority of the military to an extent which is greater than that experienced by his civilian counterpart in regard to employer authority. The family is subject to certain rules and regulations formulated by the Army. The authority of the workplace then, to an important extent, does not stop with the receipt of a money payment by the husband/father but extends directly into the area of family living.

The military rank of the husband/father is directly related to the kind of living arrangements to which his family will be expected to adjust. To an important extent, the rank of the husband/father will determine how the family is expected to behave and what it is expected to value. It will also, of course, determine the level and type of job assignment at which the husband/father works.

The U.S. Army is a hierarchical organization. As in most large, formal organizations, the level at which one performs determines the scope of information which he receives and consequently, in an important way, bears upon his perspectives of the organization. One of the central assumptions of social organization theory is that a person's informational perspectives are crucially limited by his position in the particular large-scale organizations in which he participates (Janowitz and Delaney, 1957). Where there is a distinct separation of the authority of the workplace and the home, one should not necessarily expect to find uniformities in the perspectives of individuals similarly located in one organization, except as their perspectives refer to the job situation. Such individuals would be expected to have wide-ranging and varied perspectives and attitudes relative to help resources and their use which were not necessarily conditioned in the first instance by the single organization in which they work.

When one works, lives with his family, makes important domestic purchases, and to a large extent enjoys recreational pursuits all under one authority, one is encompassed by that authority to an uncommon extent. In such a case, it seems important to ask if uniformities, attributable to organizational location, exist in the attitudes and information perspectives of such individuals. It also seems important to ask whether the wives of men who are similarly located exhibit uniformities of attitude and informational perspectives (Whyte, 1956). There is empirical evidence that individuals similarly located do exhibit relative homogeneity with respect to certain attitudes (Festinger, Schacter, and Back, 1953). There is also considerable evidence that decisive pressures are exerted by the social structure of which one is a part, to bring about conformity with the normative orientations in those structures (Cartwright and Zander, 1953; Merton, 1957).

RELATED RESEARCH

No systematic investigations could be located which dealt, as a central concern, with the orientations of the career military family living on a military reservation relative to the handling of interpersonal conflict. Two studies were located which focused on specific aspects of military family life but in neither instance did the families in the study live on a military reservation. Gabower investigated the social situations which are characteristic of Navy life in an attempt to determine "why among navy children living under similar conditions, some developed behavior problems and others did not" (Gabower, 1960). This study, as the title indicates, was concerned only with the officer family and with children in a patient or client status. It was not concerned with what the families knew about available resources in the military community, nor was it concerned with attitudes toward the use of military community help resources.

The second study which has been concerned with the military family was an exploratory investigation of the marriage and family life of officers and airmen in a Strategic Air Command Wing (Lindquist, 1952). Its central focus was the effect on wives and children of the husband/father's temporary and sudden absences from the home. The study was limited to wives of men who were, at the time, on temporary duty outside the United States. All of the wives lived in a civilian community located near an Air Force base. In considering the use of community and Air Base services, Lindquist states: "Counselors in agencies and organizations were not known to these women. There was fairly general agreement that they could not expect much help from the base ... if advisory services for families were available in the city, they were not known to the wives" (p. 24). Lindquist, however, was dealing with a relatively small sample and made no attempt to determine the differential distribution of those perspectives.

Three studies conducted among civilian populations are directly relevant to the present investigation. In fact, as originally conceived, the present research was to have been a replication of one of these studies. In conjunction with the Midtown Community Mental Health Project, Margaret Bailey investigated community orientations toward casework (Bailey, 1958). Her study was concerned with the public relations of social casework, as a helping profession which partakes "of a larger cultural complex around the whole question of help with personal and interpersonal problems." This was a two-part investigation consisting of a survey, which made use of a precoded instrument, and an exploratory interview, which was open-ended and designed to obtain greater depth of content concerning the nature and quality of community understanding of social casework.

Baily found that only 39.5 percent of the survey respondents (N = 1,660) suggested use of one or more sources of professional help for child guidance problems, and 32.8 percent for marital difficulties. In each instance, the problem presented to the respondent was described as "serious." In spite of this qualification, about one-half of the respondents suggested solutions within the family. For problems in child guidance, Bailey found that the doctor and the psychiatrist were most frequently suggested as sources of professional help, and the social caseworker was the least frequently suggested. The clergyman was the preferred source of help for marital difficulty and, again, the social caseworker was mentioned least often. Bailey found, however, that acquaintance with casework agencies as resources offering services to those with interpersonal problems was much higher than expressed inclination to use casework help. To the extent that the problem under investigation here is the same as that treated by Bailey, this study may be viewed as a replication of hers. The methodology and theoretical orientations of the studies differ, however.

The second study of direct relevance to this research is the Wolins study of welfare problems and services in Berkeley, California (Wolins, 1954). Since the primary aim of the Wolins study was the description and evaluation of welfare needs and available community services, there is a significant difference between the orientation and methodology of his study and this one. One of his concerns, however, was an attempt to gather information about the community's knowledge of welfare services and willingness to use these services. As with the Bailey study, caution must be exercised in trying to compare the Wolins findings with findings of this investigation.

The third study, which is of importance to the current research, is in regard to how Americans view their mental health (Gurin, Veroff, and Feld, 1960). That study addressed itself to the question, "how mentally healthy do adult Americans think they are?" The answers to this and many related queries were sought by interviewing a probability sample of Americans. Much of the material in two sections of this study, "Readiness for Self-Referral" and "People Who Have Gone For Help," deals directly with the questions being raised in this investigation. An opportunity is thus afforded to measure the opinions of career military persons living on a military reservation against opinions expressed by Americans, in general, as to attitudes toward the use of professional help and knowledge of available help resources.

PURPOSE

The purpose of this study was to determine the extent to which military families are aware of agencies of professional groups in the military community that have as one of their functions the task of assisting families with problems in child guidance and marital difficulty. A further purpose was to determine their evaluation of the social cost involved in using professional help in general, and their evaluation of the social cost involved in using specific professions in particular, regarding help for problems in child guidance and marital difficulty. This study will not be concerned with the universe of problems which occur in the study population. Rather, the author's concern is to determine (1) the distribution of cost evaluations toward professional help for two types of interpersonal problems, and (2) the distribution of knowledge relative to available resources for problem solution in a military community.

HYPOTHESES

Within the context of the purposes of this study and the theoretical position outlined above, the following hypotheses were advanced:

I.   Knowledge of help resources and attitudes toward the use of professional help are
     not randomly distributed throughout the military population but are differentially
     concentrated at various levels in the organization hierarchy.

II. Among individuals of the same rank status, knowledge of resources and attitudes
     toward the use of professional help will be differentially distributed according to
     age, sex, education level, and length of stay in the community.

III. Military wives and soldier-husbands/fathers will differ as to preference for use of
     military or civilian resources for problems in marital relationship and child guid-
     ance.

SAMPLE

Only career military families living on a military reservation are included in
this study. The study is further limited to career members of the U.S. Army and
their families. For inclusion, the enlisted man was required to have completed at
least seven years' service and the officer was required to have completed three.
This study was further limited to career army families living at Fort Dix, New
Jersey, but was not limited to clients or patients, as the latter were not of central
concern in the study. It was anticipated that some of the respondents would
either have made use of military community help resources in the past or may
have been making use of them during the study.

Making use of the stratification inherent in military ranking, a systematic
stratified sample was selected, by dwelling unit, from Fort Dix billeting records.
This procedure was conducted in conformity with the rules of probability
sampling. Separate subsamples were selected for each of the four relevant rank
status groups (Field Grade, Company Grade, Senior Noncommissioned Officers,
and Junior Noncommissioned Officers).

The total sample selected was as follows:

110 Field Grade
124 Company Grade
217 Noncommissioned, E7 through E9
204 Noncommissioned, E4 through E6
———
655 Total

Following the selection of dwelling units, the sample was randomly divided
so that approximately half the sample of participants would be wives and half
would be husbands. This was accomplished by designating the wife in each
alternate dwelling unit as the respondent. Letters were then delivered to each

dwelling unit selected. These letters indicated the general nature of the study, its sponsorship, informed the occupants of their selection, and designated which of the marital partners the investigation would include. The respondents were also told that they would be informed subsequently as to where and when their participation was desired.

Since the entire population of Field Grade and Company Grade respondents meeting the population criterion had been selected, it was not possible to make sample substitutions in these groups. Among the junior and senior enlisted respondents, however, substitutions in the sample were possible and a total of sixteen substitutions were made. A systematic method for making substitutions in the sample was provided in view of the transiency of military populations. For each dwelling unit selected for participation, two alternative units were selected. In each instance, the first dwelling unit meeting the population criterion and *immediately preceding* the dwelling unit selected in the sample was designated as first alternative if substitution became necessary. The first dwelling unit meeting the population criterion and *immediately following* the unit selected in the sample was designated as second alternative. Of the sixteen substitutions made, all were first alternatives. Seven of the substitutions were occasioned by the initially selected respondent's having been a foreign-born person recently arrived in this country. The other nine substitutions were necessary owing to the fact that the dwelling unit selected was actually found to be vacant. Of the 655 dwelling units selected, 512, or 78 percent, actually participated.

THE INSTRUMENT

The data collection instrument used in the investigation was a 27-page, 187-item questionnaire. The instrument was administered in a centralized setting to groups ranging in size from 5 to 50 over a 17-day period. The investigator was present as each group completed the questionnaire.

Both fixed-alternative and open-ended questions were used. Items included in the questionnaire were developed as a result of structured interviews, conducted with subjects considered representative of those with whom the questionnaire was to be used. These interviews had been conducted at Fort Jay and Fort Hamilton, New York, during the preceding January and February. The instrument as used in the study was pretested at Fort Dix, New Jersey, and required an average of about one hour to complete. Of the questionnaires completed by respondents, 507 were found to be usable.

The statistical technique most used was the Chi-Square Test for differences between the observed frequency distributions and the expected ones, and the Chi-Square Test of independence. In all tests for significance, the .05 level of confidence was used as the criterion for rejecting null hypotheses.

RESULTS

Hypothesis I

The question with which the study was concerned in the first hypothesis was whether or not groups of individuals who were variously located in the organization were equally aware of health and welfare services, and whether the services were equally acceptable to people located at various levels in the hierarchy. Since the hypothesis deals with both knowledge and attitudes, it was separated for testing in the following way:

IA Knowledge of help resources is not randomly distributed in the military population but is differentially concentrated at various levels in the organizational hierarchy.
IB Attitudes toward the use of professional help are not randomly distributed but are differentially concentrated at various levels in the organizational hierarchy.

Hypothesis IA: Respondents were asked a series of questions, both general and specific in content, regarding the services available in the community which could be used in the resolution of serious marital problems and serious parent-child problems. When the respondents were requested to list as many resources on post as they could which were available for use in resolving marital conflict, fewer than half in each group could mention any particular resource other than chaplain. The mean number of responses per respondent is higher among the officer groups than among the enlisted groups and indicates that the officer groups either named more resources than enlisted groups or named particular resources more often. The percentage distributions appear to indicate that the officer groups more often named the clinically oriented help resources, i.e., "doctor" ($\chi^2 = 30.9$, df = 1, p <.001), mental hygiene clinic ($\chi^2 = 55.0$, df = 1, p < .001), psychiatrist ($\chi^2 = 20.0$, df = 1, p < .001), and social worker ($\chi^2 = 10.2$, df = 1, p < .01); while the enlisted respondents appear to have more frequently stressed the nonclinically oriented "official" resources, i.e., Commanding Officer and Army Emergency Relief.

To control statistically for the general tendency to make more mentions of all resources by the officer respondents, the number of responses by officers was weighted in each category by the ratio of the number of responses of enlisted respondents to the number of officer respondents.[1] These data indicate that the officer groups not only mentioned more resources in the military community but also that, even when this tendency was statistically controlled, they were relatively more likely to mention clinically oriented resources than were enlisted respondents. Weighting the officer responses also reveals that when the tendency of officer respondents to make more mentions is statistically controlled, a significant difference is revealed in the mention of chaplains as a resource.

When these data are compared with those reported by Bailey (1958), it must be concluded that these respondents were more knowledgeable regarding resources available in the community for their use in resolving marital conflict. Whereas Bailey reported that only 32.8 percent of her respondents could suggest one or more sources of professional help for marital difficulties, over 90 percent of the respondents in this study mentioned one or more sources of help for marital conflict. It must be pointed out, however, that none of the groups seemed very strongly aware of certain resources available in the military community, and as previously noted, with the exception of chaplains, none of the resources was named by as many as 50 percent of the respondents.

Table 1 shows the pattern of response to an open-ended question which required the respondent to list as many resources on post as he could which were available for use in resolving parent-child conflict. Again, it is immediately apparent that the mean response rate per respondent increases with rank. As rank increased, either more resources of all types were mentioned, more particular types of resources were mentioned, or particular types of resources were more frequently mentioned.

There are three factors in Table 1 worthy of note. First, the Field Grade group did seem generally attuned to all type of resources located in the community, and particularly to psychiatry. Second, while Field Grade officers represent a high-income group compared to others in the military community, income is not a factor in the use of military community resources. The fact that the Field Grade group, like Gurin's (Gurin, Veroff, and Feld 1960) high-income groups, seemed particularly attuned to psychiatry appears to substantiate, to some extent, Gurin's suggestion that it is not income per se that leads to the increased salience of psychiatry; rather, it may be a reflection of the social climate in which the high-status groups live. Third, an apparently linear relationship exists between rank status and the mention of psychiatry. This, too, is in agreement with the findings of Gurin and his associates and offers further confirmation of the central theme of the Hollingshead and Redlich report (1958).

When the distributions in Table 1 are compared with the initial findings regarding services to assist with marital conflicts, it may be seen that there was

TABLE 1

PERCENTAGE DISTRIBUTION BY RANK STATUS AND THE MENTION OF COMMUNITY RESOURCES AVAILABLE FOR USE IN RESOLVING PARENT-CHILD CONFLICT

Resource Named	Junior NCO	Senior NCO	Company Grade	Field Grade
Chaplain	63	77	77	79
"Doctor"	23	32	51	42
Psychiatrist	3	7	12	27
Psychologist	1	2	8	9
Nurse	0	2	0	4
Pediatrician	1	0	9	8
Social Worker	3	2	19	8
Judge Advocate	13	13	10	11
Military Police	1	0	5	11
Red Cross	10	9	8	6
School or Teacher	36	41	50	53
Mental Hygiene Clinic	4	6	30	23
Commander	14	13	18	15
Informal Resources	15	18	18	21
Mentioned no resources	21	12	6	3
Mentioned one or more resources	79	83	94	97
	100	100	100	100

Table cont'd

Of those mentioning one or more:				
Mentioned clinical resources only	1	1	2	1
Mentioned nonclinical resources only	62	51	14	20
Mentioned both clinical and nonclinical resources	37	48	84	79
	100	100	100	100

an increased tendency for all respondents to mention more clinically oriented resources and fewer authority-oriented resources. This finding suggests that they were more inclined to define parent-child conflict in clinical terms than they were to define marital conflict in such terms. In considering help resources for parent-child conflict, no definite trend is evident in the mention of clinically oriented resources only, but in mentioning nonclinically oriented resources only, it may be observed that there was an increasing tendency to confine one's response to nonclinically oriented resources as rank decreased. It may also be seen in Table 1 that the Company Grade respondent was more likely to mention both nonclinical and clinical resources than other rank groups, and there is also some indication that this group of respondents, more often than the rest, confined their responses to clinically oriented resources only.

One further fact about these data should be noted. Though knowledge of resources is not randomly distributed in the population, none of the groups can be considered as strongly aware of help resources in the community. Few respondents could go beyond naming the chaplain, school, or teacher or "doctor." This is a finding also reported in the Gurin study, where it was indicated that institutions explicitly created to offer psychological guidance and help with interpersonal conflict are less often known or consulted than those for which psychological guidance and interpersonal help is not a major function (Gurin, Veroff, and Feld, 1960). When we compared these findings with the Bailey findings we must conclude, however, that most of the respondents in this study were more knowledgeable regarding their community resources than were the respondents in the Bailey study. Bailey reported that "only about two-fifths (39.5 percent) of the respondents suggested use of one or more sources of professional help for child guidance problems" (Bailey, 1958).

Since the open-ended questions that asked respondents to name available resources which they considered appropriate for use in marital conflict and parent-child conflict were quite unstructured, they may not have been sufficient to stimulate full responses. To obviate this possibility and to confront the respondents with a real problem situation, at a later point in the questionnaire a series of vignettes were presented and the respondent was requested to name as many resources available in the community as he could which might be appropriately used in attempting to resolve the difficulties. One of the vignettes was concerned with interpersonal conflict precipitated by impending retirement.

A man is to retire within a year. He and his wife are in serious disagreement about what they will do after retirement. All of their children are grown up and have families of their own. The couple have begun to have violent quarrels and although they have always been very close to each other, now they seem to be drifting apart. Both of them want to solve the problem but don't seem able to do so themselves. To whom on the post might they turn for help in solving this problem? (Name as many as you can.)

The responses given to the structured question were in agreement with the responses obtained to the open-ended question regarding resources for marital conflict. The officer groups more often named the clinically oriented helping person, while the lower-ranking respondents more often tended to restrict their responses to the military commander, lawyers, and informal resources.

Another of the vignettes described a child problem and was designed to give the respondents a more specific frame of reference in which to answer.

A 10-year-old child has trouble getting along with children and as a result has almost no friends. He seems to try to play with other children but always ends up in a fight. His mother worries about him, and feels that he is a "sad" child. To whom on post might the parents turn for help?

Responses revealed that within the context of a more specific situation, the pattern of response in regard to a child problem changed. Particularly, it shows that both groups of enlisted respondents now mentioned professional helping persons more often and correspondingly mentioned lawyers, commanders, and informal help much less than had previously been the case. The officers continued the pattern of mentioning professionally trained helping persons relatively more often than enlisted respondents. It was found that highly significant differences existed between the enlisted and officer respondents in the mention of psychiatrists ($\chi^2 = 22.2$, df = 1, p $<$ .001), psychologists ($\chi^2 = 22.2$, df = 1, p $<$ .001), social workers ($\chi^2 = 8.4$, df = 1, p $<$ .01), and the mental hygiene clinic ($\chi^2 = 4.2$, df = 1, p $<$ .05). The officer respondents were much more likely to mention those resources than were the enlisted respondents. The differences between the groups in naming chaplain, "doctor," school or teacher, and informal resources were not significant.

Hypothesis IA was supported. Knowledge of help resources was not randomly distributed but was differentially concentrated at various levels in the organizational hierarchy.

Hypothesis IB: Hypothesis IB was concerned with the distribution of attitudes toward professional help. While personality variables are important in the attitudes an individual may hold and/or express, his attitudes are also importantly influenced by the groups of which he is a part. In terms of the attitudes held toward use of community resources for the resolution of interpersonal conflict, the individual is very likely to take the social cost of using such facilities into account. What will his friends and neighbors think of him? How will making use of community resources affect his official standing in the organization? What do other members of his group expect of him when he is faced with family conflicts? Does he feel that going for help is the proper thing to do, or does he feel that the individual should handle his problems without help from someone outside the family? Does he feel it preferable to receive interpersonal help from outside the system (civilian community), or does he prefer receiving help from within the system (military community)?

The hypothesis assumed that respondents who were located differently in the organization were exposed to different influences and would express differing attitudes toward the use of military community resources. That is, their perception of the social cost involved in making use of these resources would vary.

Use of Resources Officially Damaging. Clearly one of the attitudinal dimensions toward use of military community resources was the extent to which respondents believed that the need to use such resources would be detrimental to them. In attempting to determine whether respondents believed that the need for help would be detrimental to them, we asked them to agree or disagree with the following statement:

> A person may be a very good soldier, but if he has a serious problem in his marriage and his commander finds out about it, it will be held against him and may hurt his career.

The percentage distribution of responses to this statement by rank status and the Chi-Square Test for significance indicates that the four groups did differ significantly in their response to this statement ($\chi^2 = 51.9$, df = 3, p $<$ .001). Data reveal that there was progessively less agreement as rank status increased. This difference tends to provide some evidence that officers were less inclined than enlisted groups to believe that having serious marital problems would be detrimental to their military careers.

Acceptance or Rejection by Friends or Neighbors. To ascertain what the respondent believed the reaction of friends and neighbors would be if he experienced a serious family problem, we presented the following statement for agreement or disagreement:

> Other Army families are very understanding when a serious problem occurs in a family living near them.

The percentage distribution of responses to this statement by rank status and the Chi-Square Test of significance reveals that the four groups did differ in how they believed neighbors would respond if a serious problem occurred in a family living near them ($\chi^2 = 12.5$, df = 3, p < .01). Although most of the respondents agreed that their neighbors would be understanding of them, it is of interest to learn where, proportionately, most of the agreement lies. As rank status increased, so did the tendency to agree with the statement. This finding provides some evidence that officer respondents were more likely than enlisted groups to believe that the military family communities in which they lived would not be condemnatory of them if a serious family problem occurred.

Expectations of Others. An attempt was made to ascertain whether the respondents believed that going for help was expected of them when a situation arose which they could not solve through self-help alone. They were asked to agree or disagree with the following statement:

> Other Army families expect that if a family can't solve its problems themselves they will seek help from someone trained to help with that kind of a problem.

Differences between the four rank status groups were significant ($\chi^2 = 11.9$, df = 3, p < .01). Apparently all groups believed that they were expected to seek professional help if self-help failed, although they held this belief to significantly different degrees. There was a slight tendency for the higher-rank groups to endorse this view more often.

Acceptability of Military Community Resources. To test the distribution of attitudes toward use of military community resources, the respondents were asked to indicate agreement or disagreement with the following two statements:

> If I had a problem in my marriage and wanted someone professionally trained to help me with it, I would prefer going to a civilian professional person rather than to a professionally trained person in the Army.

> If I had a problem with my child and wanted someone professionally trained to help me with it, I would prefer going to a civilian professional person rather than to a professionally trained person in the Army.

There was a strong tendency of all groups to disagree with these statements. Further, although the differences are not statistically significant, the trend of the data indicates that there was some increasing tendency to disagree as one went up in rank.

Rejection of civilian resources did not necessarily mean that military resources were acceptable for use by the respondent. It is possible that some military resources would be acceptable to them and others would not. To investigate this aspect of their attitudes, the questionnaire included the following series of statements with which the respondents were asked to agree or disagree:

> If I had a serious problem in my marriage and wanted a clergyman to help me solve it, I would prefer going to a military chaplain rather than to a civilian clergyman.

> If I had a serious problem in my marriage and wanted a psychiatrist to help me solve it, I would prefer going to an army psychiatrist rather than a civilian psychiatrist.

> If I had a serious problem in my marriage, and wanted a psychologist to help me solve it, I would prefer going to an army psychologist rather than to a civilian psychologist.

> If I had a serious problem in my marriage and wanted a social worker to help me solve it, I would prefer going to an army social worker rather than to a civilian social worker.

Data indicate a great deal of similarity in the way the different groups responded to these statements. They consistently expressed a preference for the professional person who is located within the military system. The Chi-Square Test for significant differences reveals, however, that when considering help by a psychiatrist, the groups did differ significantly ($\chi^2 = 8.4$, df = 3, p < .05). Internal inspection of that part of the data suggests that the Company Grade group differed markedly from the others in their rate of endorsement of psychiatric help by the Army. Approximately one-third of this group rejected help by army psychiatrists, whereas the rejection rate did not exceed 20 percent in any other group. With the exception of help by social workers, the Company Grade group was lowest in percentages of agreement with using army chaplains, army psychiatrists, and army psychologists. With the exception of the Company Grade group, however, there was a tendency to express higher levels of agreement as rank increased.

It has been demonstrated that these groups differed significantly on three of the five attitudinal dimensions used in the study and that on the remaining two dimensions, the trend of the data was as predicted. It is concluded that hypothesis IB was partially supported. Perception of the social cost of using professional help was not randomly distributed but was differentially concentrated at various levels in the organizational hierarchy.

Hypothesis II

Attention has previously been called to the fact that the data so far presented, although indicating significant differences between the various rank groups, also indicate that the groups were considerably alike in their knowledge of and attitudes toward the use of military community help resources. The investigator questioned whether this homogeneity would continue if the data for each group were separately examined in terms of the respondent's age, sex, education, and length of stay in the community.[2] The first three of these variables are quite commonly recognized criteria by which people are socially differentiated. Although military rank is the transcendent criterion by which people in military communities are differentiated, age, sex, and education are to some extent related to military rank; within the various rank groups, we assumed that they were related to knowledge of help resources and attitudes toward their use. This assumption constituted the second hypothesis of the study and was stated as follows:

Hypothesis II.   Among individuals of the same rank status, knowledge of resources and attitudes toward the use of professional help will be differentially distributed according to age, sex, educational level, and length of stay in the community.

As with the first, this hypothesis also dealt with two dependent variables, which it was believed desirable to examine separately. For purposes of testing the hypothesis, it was therefore restated as follows:

IIA. Among individuals of the same rank status, knowledge of resources will be differentially distributed according to age, sex, educational level, and length of stay in the community.

IIB. Among individuals of the same rank status, attitudes toward the use of professional help will be differentially distributed according to age, sex, educational level, and length of stay in the community.

Hypothesis IIA: It has been demonstrated by Gurin and his associates (1960) that the definition applied to a problem is related to the sex, age, and educational level of the individual experiencing the problem. Younger people, women, and the higher educated are all more likely to define a problem in mental health terms and are more likely to seek out professional help when confronted with a problem. Assuming that the population from which this sample was drawn would be similar in important ways to the representative sample of Americans included in the Gurin et al. study, among individuals of the same rank status, the younger respondents, women, and the higher educated will more often name professional resources than other respondents. Particularly, they will more often name clinically oriented resources.

Sex and Education. Among officer status respondents, men mentioned a greater total number of resources for the resolution of marriage conflict than did women. When the respondents considered resources which were available for use in resolving difficulties with their children, it was found that women named proportionately more professional resources than did men, and that men much more often named nonprofessional resources than did women.

The modal response in naming resources available for use in resolving parent-child conflict was the mention of nonclinical professional resources. Officer status respondents, particularly officers' wives in the youngest age range, were somewhat more likely to name clinically oriented resources than respondents who were older. Woman mentioned proportionately more professional resources, both clinically oriented and nonclinically oriented, at each educational level in which they appeared, than did men. In examining the resources named by respondents as being available for use in resolving parent-child conflict, we again found that women at each educational level named proportionately more clinically oriented resources than men. However, the frequency with which clinically oriented resources were named by men showed no essential change from one educational level to another, whereas women tended to increasingly name such resources as educational level increased. As educational level increased, both officers and officers' wives tended to mention proportionately more clinically oriented resources. At the lower educational levels, officers' wives mention proportionately more nonclinical professional resources than did men. Men, on the other hand, mentioned proportionately more nonclinical professional resources at each educational level than did the women. In terms of the officer status group, these findings are not at variance with previously cited research. The finding that women were more inclined than men to name professional resources and that the mention of clinically oriented resources increased with education is in direct agreement with the Gurin et al. study (1960). A significant difference was demonstrated to have existed between officers and officers' wives in the mention of clinically oriented resources ($\chi^2 = 7.3$, df = 2, p < .05), but not between enlisted men and enlisted wives. However, men mentioned proportionately more resources at each educational level than did enlisted wives. These men also mentioned more resources as educational level increased. Enlisted status respondents, of both sexes, could name few clinically oriented resources at any educational level. These respondents were concentrated at the lower education levels and the failure to differentiate them on the education variable, for marriage conflict, may have been a reflection of this fact.[3]

In Table 2, it is evident that men of both rank groups, at each age level, named more resources of all types than did women. However, among officer status respondents, young women named clinically oriented resources proportionately more often than other respondents of that rank status (see Table 3). Women at the youngest age level of both rank groups named proportionately more professional resources of both types than did men, at that age level. Officers tended to name proportionately more nonclinical professional resources

TABLE 2

AVERAGE NUMBER OF RESOURCES NAMED AS AVAILABLE FOR
USE IN RESOLVING MARRIAGE CONFLICT: BY RANK, AGE, AND SEX

Rank and Resources Named	Age and Sex 21-34		35-44		45 and over	
	Men	Women	Men	Women	Men	Women
Officer Status						
Clinically Oriented	1.30	.97	1.49	.72	1.35	.77
Nonclinical Professional	2.00	1.26	1.82	1.37	2.13	1.38
Nonprofessional	.88	.23	.91	.26	1.17	.31
Number of Cases:	(34)	(39)	(45)	(43)	(23)	(13)
Enlisted Status						
Clinically Oriented	.38	.25	.39	.27	.45	.38
Nonclinical Professional	2.25	1.37	1.67	1.47	1.80	1.38
Nonprofessional	1.57	.50	.89	.78	.70	1.00
Number of Cases:	(72)	(60)	(97)	(49)	(20)	(8)

at the younger age level and to name proportionately more nonprofessional resources as age increased. Enlisted wives named proportionately fewer non-clinical professional resources and more nonprofessional resources as age increased. Enlisted men, on the other hand, named more nonclinical professional resources and fewer nonprofessional resources as age increased.

Length of Stay in Community. The response of wives was examined for the relationship between the amount of time during marriage that they had lived on a military reservation and their naming of resources available for use in resolving marriage conflict. Findings indicated that among neither officers' wives nor enlisted wives were those who had lived mostly in the military community most likely to name clinically oriented resources. Among both groups, the wives who

TABLE 3

PERCENTAGE OF RESPONSES BY RANK, AGE, SEX, AND
TYPE OF RESOURCES NAMED AS AVAILABLE FOR USE
IN RESOLVING MARRIAGE CONFLICT

| Rank and Resources Named | Age and Sex | | | | | |
| | 21-34 | | 35-44 | | 45 and over | |
	Men	Women	Men	Women	Men	Women
Officer Status						
Clinically Oriented	32	41	36	30	30	31
Nonclinical Professional	47	51	42	58	44	54
Nonprofessional	21	8	22	12	26	15
	100	100	100	100	100	100
Number of Cases:	(34)	(39)	(45)	(43)	(23)	(13)
Enlisted Status						
Clinically Oriented	8	12	13	10	15	13
Nonclinical Professional	54	65	57	59	60	50
Nonprofessional	38	23	30	31	25	37
	100	100	100	100	100	100
Number of Cases:	(72)	(60)	(97)	(49)	(20)	(3)

had lived in both military and civilian communities during their marriages were more likely to name clinically oriented resources than were other wives.

Among enlisted wives, those women who had lived an approximately equal time in civilian and military communities during their marriages named fewer resources than the other two groups; while those who had lived mostly in civilian communities tended to name more resources than the others. When the relationship between the length of time that wives had lived in military communities and their proportionate response in naming resources available for resolution of child conflict is examined, officers' wives who had lived an approximately equal time in military and civilian communities named proportionately more clinically oriented resources than others and were less likely to name nonclinical professional resources than others. Officers' wives who had lived mostly in civilian communities and those who had lived mostly in military communities did not differ appreciably in the proportionate mention of either type of resource. Among enlisted wives, the greater proportion of clinically oriented resources were named by wives who had lived mostly in military communities.

When the question of knowledge of available resources was considered, the observed differences among respondents of the same rank status were not statistically significant. However, these differences were in the expected direction in terms of resources known by respondents at varying sex, educational, and age levels. These results have also, for the most part, conformed to the findings of other research. No consistent differences in the mention of resources were found which could, with confidence, be attributed to length of stay in the community as a marriage partner. From these findings it may, therefore, be concluded that Hypothesis IIA was partially supported.

Hypothesis IIB: Hypothesis IIB was concerned with the differentiation of respondents of the same rank status in their perception of the social cost of using military community resources. The differential response frequency of officers and officers' wives to a statement that having serious marital difficulty would have detrimental consequences for a military career, if known to the military commander, was examined. Although the majority of both groups disagreed with the statement, and thus indicated that they did not believe that having serious marital difficulty would be harmful to their careers, the Chi-Square Test indicates that significant differences existed between officers and officers' wives in their perception of the social cost of serious marital difficulty that becomes known to the military commander. Officers were twice as likely as officers' wives to agree with the statement ($\chi^2 = 4.8$, df = 1, p < .05). Enlisted status respondents did not differ significantly on the basis of sex.

Age, education, and length of stay in the military community as marriage partners did not prove to be significantly related to the response of officers and officers' wives. However, among enlisted status respondents, age was significantly related to the belief that serious marital difficulty would be harmful to the respondent's military career. The older enlisted respondent believed it to be costly significantly less often than did younger enlisted respondents ($\chi^2 = 6.1$, df = 2, p < .05). Enlisted men and enlisted wives between 21-34 years of age differed significantly in their response ($\chi^2 = 4.6$, df = 2, p < .05). These younger wives much less often believed that marital difficulty would be harmful to their husbands' careers than did enlisted men of that age range. Education and length of stay in the military community as marriage partners did not prove to be significantly related to the response of enlisted status respondents.

The belief of respondents of both rank status groups that they would be understood by their friends and neighbors in the event that they experienced serious family problems was not related to the respondent's sex, age, education, or length of stay in the military community as a marriage partner.

The majority of respondents, of both rank groups, believed that they were expected to seek professional help when unable to resolve family conflict through use of their own resources. This belief was not demonstrated to be related to the respondent's sex, age, educational level, or length of stay in the military community as a marriage partner for either rank group.

The majority of respondents of both rank groups rejected the use of civilian resources for marital conflict. However, enlisted men and enlisted wives differed significantly in the extent to which they rejected the use of such resources in favor of military resources ($\chi^2 = 6.0$, df $= 1$, p $< .05$). Enlisted men preferred the use of civilian resources much more often than did enlisted wives. Officers and officers' wives did not differ significantly in their expressed rejection of civilian resources in favor of military resources for marital conflict. For neither rank group was the respondent's age, education, or length of stay in the community as a marriage partner shown to be significantly related to the expression of preference between civilian and military community resources for problems in marriage.

For neither rank group was the respondent's sex, education, or length of stay in the community as a marriage partner shown to be significantly related to the expression of preference between civilian and military community resources for parent-child conflict. However, among enlisted status respondents, age was significantly related to the expression of preference ($\chi^2 = 9.4$, df $= 2$, p $< .01$). Enlisted status respondents between 35 and 44 years of age preferred the use of civilian resources for parent-child conflict much more often than did enlisted respondents at other age levels. Enlisted respondents 45 years of age and older were much less likely to express preference for the use of civilian resources than were younger enlisted respondents. Among officer status respondents, age was not significantly related to the expression of preference between civilian and military community resources.

Among individuals of the same rank status, the perception of the social cost involved in the use of military community resources was not shown to be differentially distributed according to educational level or length of stay in the community. This perception was shown to be significantly related to the respondent's sex and age for some of the measures. Hypothesis IIB was supported to a minimal extent.

HYPOTHESIS III

Hypothesis III dealt with differences in preference for military or civilian help resources which may be attributable to differences in the sex of the respondents. Men who are career members of the Army are integrated to a greater extent in the military structure than are military wives. Wives, on the other hand, are frequently engaged in voluntary activities in the community which may bring them into contact with help resources.[4] To ascertain whether differences existed in the preferences of the two groups for help from military or civilian resources, the following hypothesis was tested:

III. Military wives and soldier-husbands/fathers will differ as to preference for use of military or civilian resources for problems in marital relationship and child guidance.

Since this hypothesis deals essentially with two response categories, it was restated as follows for testing:

IIIA Military wives and soldier-husbands/fathers will differ as to preference for use of military or civilian resources for problems in marital relationship.

IIIB Military wives and soldier-husbands/fathers will differ as to preference for use of military or cilivian resources for problems in child guidance.

Hypothesis IIIA: The two sex groups did differ significantly ($\chi^2 = 3.8$, df = 1, $p < .05$) in their choice of civilian or military help resources. Men preferred civilian resources more frequently than did women for problems in marriage. This greater tendency on the part of the male respondents to prefer help from outside the system may have been related to a belief that their formal responsibilities within the system took precedence over responsibilities centering in the family, and that to seek help from military resources would have led to their being defined as deviant. To investigate these possibilities, the respondents were asked to agree or disagree with the following two statements:

If there is a conflict between the requirements of the Army and the requirements of the family, the requirements of the Army should come first.

A person may be a very good soldier but if he has a serious problem in his marriage and his commander finds out about it it will be held against him and may hurt his career.

Data indicated that many more males than females believed that their formal military responsibilities took precedence over family responsibilities when the two demands were in conflict ($\chi^2 = 9.3$, df = 1, p < .01). However, it is of interest that while 70 percent of the male respondents agreed with the statement, 56 percent of the female respondents also agreed. There is, then, some indication that among career military families, it is fairly generally expected that the military responsibilities of the husband/father will take precedence over family responsibilities when demands from the two areas (job and family) conflict. Highly significant differences did exist between male and female respondents in their judgment that marital disharmony would be harmful to their military careers if known to the command officer ($\chi^2 = 14.4$, df = 1, p < .001). Although most respondents of both sexes disagreed with the statement, 43 percent of the males agreed with it, while only 26 percent of the females agreed.

It may be concluded that military wives and soldier-husbands/fathers did differ as to preference for use of military or civilian resources for problems in the marriage relationship. Hypothesis IIIA was supported.

Support of Hypothesis IIIA established that the respondents generally preferred the use of military rather than civilian resources when serious marital difficulties occurred. However, the question arises as to whether specific resources in the military community might stimulate a differential response pattern. In other words, are all help resources in the military community equally preferred over their counterparts in the civilian community? To investigate this question, the respondents were asked to agree or disagree with the following series of statements:

If I had a serious problem in my marriage and wanted a clergyman to help me solve it, I would prefer going to a military chaplain rather than to a civilian clergyman.

If I had a serious problem in my marriage and wanted a psychiatrist to help me solve it, I would prefer going to an army psychiatrist rather than to a civilian psychiatrist.

If I had a serious problem in my marriage and wanted a psychologist to help me solve it, I would prefer going to an army psychologist rather than to a civilian psychologist.

If I had a serious problem in my marriage and wanted a social worker to help me solve it, I would prefer going to an army social worker rather than to a civilian social worker.

There were no signficant differences between the sexes in the preferences of army chaplains and army psychiatrists. They did differ significantly in the extent to which they preferred army psychologists ($\chi^2 = 5.7$, df = 1, p < .05) and army social workers (χ^2 11.2, df = 1, p < .001) rather than civilian professionals. Among the male respondents, 26 percent disagreed with going to an army psychologist rather than to a civilian psychologist. The female respondents disagreed in 17 percent of their responses to the statement regarding psychologists. It thus appears that males were more inclined than females to prefer civilian psychologists. This inclination is even more marked in response to the statement of preference for army or civilian social work help. Here we find that 30 percent of the males preferred help from civilian social workers rather than army social workers. The females indicated in 17 percent of their responses a preference for civilian social work help. A possible explanation for the male respondents' more often preferring to seek professional help in the civilian community lies in their formal relationship to the system. This relationship leaves the male respondent vulnerable to social and occupational penalties.

Hypothesis IIIB: Hypothesis IIIB stated that military wives and soldier-husbands/fathers would differ as to preference for use of military or civilian resources for problems in child guidance. To test this hypothesis, the respondents were asked to agree or disagree with the following statement:

> If I had a problem with my child and wanted someone professionally trained to help me with it, I would prefer going to a civilian professional person rather than to a professionally trained person in the Army.

Twenty-nine percent of the males agreed with the statement while only 22 percent of the females agreed. Although this trend is consistent with the previous finding that males were more likely to prefer help from resources located outside the military system, differences between males and females were not statistically significant.

Therefore, it may be concluded that military wives and soldier-husbands/fathers did not differ as to preference for use of military or civilian resources for problems in child guidance. Hypothesis IIIB was not supported.

DISCUSSION

Mannheim (1940), in attempting to assess the state of contemporary social knowledge, postulated that the type of knowledge available to a social actor is conditioned by his position in the particular large-scale organizations in which he participates. In an empirical test of this assumption, Janowitz and Delany (1957) demonstrated that individuals located at lower levels of hierarchical organizations possessed "functional" knowledge which made possible day-to-day operations, and individuals located at upper levels possessed "substantive" knowledge which enabled the administrator to maintain the organization and to adapt its policies to changing social circumstances. This study was a further empirical test of Mannheim's postulate. To the extent that Mannheim's postulate was limited to an organizational variable, i.e., organizational location, this study was an extension of his postulate, since in addition to the organizational variable, variables referable to the personal characteristics of the individual, i.e., sex, age, education, and length of stay in the community, were claimed to be importantly related to the knowledge of resources and to the perception of the normative orientations referable to their use.

In general, considerable anxiety, particularly among the lower-ranking enlisted status group, appears to accompany the use of help resources within the military community. This anxiety is apparently related to a rather widespread belief that family conflict, either marital or parent-child, which comes to official attention will be dealt with in a punitive way by commanders and with lack of interest on the part of the professional consultant.

Although a definite relationship existed between rank status and the dependent variables, most of the professional resources of the community, and particularly those resources specifically concerned with offering help with interpersonal conflict, had little salience for most respondents. The finding that respondents in the upper levels of the organization knew more of the resources located in the community than did those at the lower levels reinforces the finding of Janowitz and Delany (1957) and offers further suggestive evidence for the validity of Mannheim's thesis. In addition, this finding is in agreement with previous research which has demonstrated that individuals in higher socioeconomic positions tend to be more aware of those agencies offering help with problems in the interpersonal and intrapersonal relations (Bailey, 1958; Gurin, Veroff, and Feld, 1960; Hollingshead and Redlich, 1958).

The clergyman (chaplain) was the only resource mentioned by a substantial number of respondents for help with marriage conflict. Other than teachers, the clergyman and nonpsychiatric physician were the only resources mentioned by substantial numbers for help with problems in the parent-child relationship. These findings, while arrived at by different methodological means, are in direct agreement with the findings of Bailey (1958) and Gurin et al. (1960) and once again point up the consistency with which people of radically different social circumstances name these resources as available for use in time of personal trouble.

A definite relationship appears to exist between rank and the type of resources that can be named as available. Lower-ranking enlisted status respondents were much more likely to name those resources traditionally associated with military operations and the military community than were respondents at higher ranks. The respondents of lower rank were more likely to limit their response to naming the chaplain, Red Cross, the lawyer, and the military commander than were higher-rank respondents. Officer status respondents not only knew more specialized professional resources but also generally knew more resources of all types than enlisted respondents. Respondents with the highest military rank were particularly aware of psychiatric help. In this regard, they were quite similar to the high-status respondents in the Gurin et al. study (1960) and in the study by Hollingshead and Redlich (1958). Studies conducted with civilian populations have shown that high-status respondents are consistently more attuned to psychiatric resources than are lower-status respondents. Gurin has suggested that it is not the ability to pay, per se, that leads to the increased salience of psychiatry, but rather that this may be a reflection of the social climate in which the high-status groups live. Ability to pay for services is not a factor in the use of military community resources, and the fact that psychiatry was named with increasing frequency as rank increased, offers empirical evidence in substantiation of Gurin's suggestion that ability to pay is not the determining criterion.

Respondents in this study placed differential emphasis on resources according to the type of interpersonal problem presented to them. Clinically oriented resources were named much more often for use in parent-child conflict than they were for marital conflict. This suggests that the respondents were much more inclined to define parent-child conflict in such terms. Just why this should be so is unclear. It has, however, been pointed out in previous research that difficulty in the parent-child relationship is more likely to be interpreted by the parents as reflecting inadequacy in themselves, and is also more likely to be referred for psychiatric treatment than is marital difficulty (Gurin, Veroff, and Feld, 1960).

While most respondents in this study did not believe that serious marital difficulties would have detrimental consequences for their military careers, considerable numbers did hold this belief, and there was a direct relationship between rank and the prevalence of the belief. Junior noncommissioned officers were most likely to believe that such conflict would be officially harmful to them. As rank increased, fewer respondents believed that serious marital conflict would have detrimental consequences for them within the system. While lower-ranking enlisted respondents were more likely to believe that marital conflict would be detrimental to them, they also were more likely than others to believe that their neighbors would not be supportive of them and were least likely to believe that they were expected by friends and neighbors to seek professional help if unable to resolve their family difficulties alone. The majority of the lower-ranking enlisted members did not believe that marital difficulty would be officially harmful to them, did believe that their neighbors would be supportive and understanding, and did believe that they were expected to seek professional help if self-help failed. The fact that they differed significantly from other rank groups in the extent to which these beliefs were held may indicate that they were not integrated into the system to the same extent as higher-rank groups. These respondents make up the lowest supervisory level. They thus, in general, are subject to a greater degree of control, earn less money, and probably have an increased opportunity to have observed or experienced detrimental consequences arising from family difficulties. Clearly, this is only one of several possible lines of interpretation. To test such an interpretation, one would need, for example, some measure of differential integration in and commitment to the military system, the extent to which different rank groups are subject to control in family living areas, the differential incidence of officially reported family difficulties, and the frequency with which negative sanctions are applied, by rank, for officially known family conflict. This is an area deserving of further study.

A number of important differences between men and women of the same rank status have been reported in the findings of this study. The most consistent sex difference in the data has been that women were more likely than men of their rank status to be aware of clinically oriented resources and were less likely than men of their rank status to evaluate the social cost of using military community resources as being high.

It is not surprising that important differences between the sexes in awareness of professional resources and perception of social cost have been found among these respondents. Studies conducted in civilian communities have repeatedly demonstrated differences between the sexes in perception and awareness of social arrangements (Lindzey, 1954; Gurin, Veroff, and Feld, 1960; Whyte, 1956). However, the differences between the sexes in this study were also related to their rank status and thus to their organizational location. Officers' wives were more aware of clinically oriented resources than any other respondents. Officers were more aware of clinically oriented resources than enlisted wives; and enlisted wives were more aware of clinically oriented resources than enlisted men. Thus, while the wives of both rank status groups were more aware of these resources than were men of their rank status, officer status respondents of both sexes were more aware of them than were enlisted status respondents.

The participation of wives in the activities of the military community is limited to those functions not directly involved in purely military operations. Such functions as are available for wives are usually concerned with the maintenance of family solidarity, the maintenance of military community institutions specifically concerned with "welfare" and morale, and the supply of social and emotional support. Gurin et al. (1960) have suggested that women can be expected to be more attuned than men to the psychological facets of experience: a greater awareness of stress in interpersonal relations, more intense feeling of uncertainty, and greater introspectiveness. Given a greater sensitivity among women about personal relationships and a focusing of community participation into expressive rather than instrumental areas, it follows that women would be more aware than men of those institutional arrangements specifically concerned with the resolution of interpersonal conflict (Parsons, 1952). The evidence provided by this study indicates that women were more likely than men of their rank status to be aware of such resources.

Studies conducted in civilian communities have generally shown a greater readiness on the part of women to make use of clinically oriented resources for the resolution of interpersonal conflict than is evidenced by men (Parsons, 1952). Does a total institutional setting, in which fairly stringent sanctions may be imposed for violation of normative expectations, alter this pattern of response? The evidence of this study is that it does not. Women of both rank groups were less likely than men of their rank status to believe that use of help resources in the community would eventuate in the application of negative sanctions. Officers' wives were least likely of all respondents to believe that marital conflict would have detrimental social consequences for them within the military community. Officers were less likely to believe that marital conflict would have detrimental consequences than were enlisted wives; and enlisted wives were less likely to believe it socially detrimental than enlisted men. Thus, the evaluation of the social cost of using military community resources was highest among enlisted men and lowest among officers' wives.

Studies of resident populations of total institutions have generally been limited to a consideration of organizational variables and involuntary populations. The population considered here was made up of voluntary members of the institution. It seemed important, therefore, to investigate the influence of personal characteristics on knowledge of the organization and perception of the social cost to the voluntary members who make use of organizational facilities. Studies conducted in civilian communities have repeatedly demonstrated the importance of personal characteristics in the response of participants. Yet, the influences of age and education have largely been ignored in considerations of the total institution populations, while the resident's length of stay in the community and the involuntary nature of his stay have been emphasized (Wheeler, 1961).

Among the general civilian population, those studies which have been made repeatedly have demonstrated that younger people and women are more likely to know of personal help resources than other members of the community (Gurin, Veroff, and Feld, 1960). In this study, women between the ages of 21 and 34, of both rank groups, were more aware of professional resources than men. The awareness of clinically oriented resources was markedly greater among these women than among men of the same age. As age increased, however, men of both rank groups were as often or more often aware of professional resources than were older women. The finding that women were more inclined than men to name professional resources and that the mention of clinically oriented resources was related to age is in agreement with the findings of Gurin and his associates (1960).

Age was not related to whether officer status respondents believed that marital conflict would be detrimental to their military careers. Age was significantly related to this belief, however, among enlisted status respondents.

Enlisted status respondents who were 45 years old or older were much less likely than younger enlisted respondents to believe that marital conflict would be officially harmful to them. Enlisted men between 21 and 34 years of age were more likely than any other respondents to believe that marital conflict would hurt their official standing with the Army. Perhaps the younger upward-oriented enlisted respondent, with less time in the system, is much more aware of the possible deterrents to his upward movement than the older respondent who has been in the system longer and whose career pattern is established.

Age was not related to whether respondents of either rank group believed that their friends and neighbors would be understanding of them in the event they experienced serious family conflict. However, the data suggest that respondents 45 years of age and older, of both rank groups, were somewhat more likely to believe they would be understood than younger respondents. Age was also not related to the belief that friends and neighbors expect that professional help will be sought when self-help fails. Again, however, the data indicate that respondents 45 years of age and older, of both rank groups, were somewhat more likely than younger respondents to believe that they were expected to seek professional help.

Among officer status respondents, age was not related to the preference for help from military or civilian resources for marital problems or for parent-child conflict. Among enlisted status respondents, age was not related to the preference for help from military or civilian resources for problems in the marital relationship. However, for problems in the parent-child relationship, enlisted status respondents between 34 and 44 years of age were much more likely than other age groups to prefer help from civilian resources.

Within each rank group, educational level differentiated the respondents. Among officer status respondents, as educational levels increased, more professional resources were known to be available for use in resolving both marital and parent-child conflicts. Officers' wives exceeded officers at each educational level in the proportion who know professional resources to be available for use in each type of family conflict. Among enlisted status respondents, men at each educational level exceeded women in awareness of professional resources available for use in marital conflict. On the other hand, enlisted wives at each educational level exceeded enlisted men in awareness of professional resources available for use in parent-child conflict. Among men of both rank groups who named clinically oriented resources, there was an important increase in the frequency with which such resources were named as educational level increased. The higher the educational level, the more clinically oriented resources were named by men of both rank groups for use in resolving both types of family problems. In neither group was educational level related to the perception of the social cost of using military community resources for the resolution of family conflict. It will be recalled that age was also largely unrelated to this perception.

The differences observed between military wives who had lived for varying periods of their marriages in military communities were quite small. However, some definite trends in the data were observable. Officers' wives who had lived for extended periods in both military and civilian communities were more aware of all types of professional resources than were officers' wives who had lived mostly in military communities or mostly in civilian communities. Among enlisted wives, altogether more resources were known to be available for use in marital conflict by those wives who had lived mostly in civilian communities. Resources available for use in parent-child conflict were more frequently known by enlisted wives who had lived most of their marriage in military communities. For both types of family problems considered, those enlisted wives who had lived mostly in military communities knew proportionately more clinically oriented resources than other enlisted wives. The length of stay in the military community as a marriage partner was not related to the perception of the social cost involved in making use of military community facilities.

Rank status and the respondent's sex were the variables which most clearly differentiated the respondents in both their knowledge of available resources and the perception of the social cost resulting from their use. While education and age were related to knowledge of available resources, these variables were not related to the perception of social cost. The length of time during marriage that the respondent had lived in the community as a marriage partner was not related to perception of social cost; and only a very weak relationship was demonstrated between length of stay in the community and knowledge of resources. These findings suggest that the organizational variable, rank status, exceeds the respondent's personal characteristics as a predictive measure of what resources are known and evaluation of the social cost of their use.

For problems in the marriage relationship, men preferred help from civilian resources significantly more often than women. There was no statistically significant difference between men and women in their preferences for help with parent-child conflict; however, the trend of the data indicated that men, somewhat more often than women, preferred to receive such help from civilian resources. The majority of both men and women believed that if there is a conflict between the requirements of the Army and the requirements of the family, the requirements of the Army take priority. However, men and women differ considerably in the extent to which this belief is held. While 70 percent of the men believed that Army requirements take priority over the family, only 56 percent of the women held such a belief. It appears, then, that among career army families, it is generally expected that the military responsibilities of the husband/father will take precedence over family responsibilities when demands from the two areas conflict.

Men and women differed to a considerable extent in the belief that serious family difficulty would be officially damaging to the military career. While only 26 percent of women held this belief, 43 percent of the men believed that serious family conflict would be detrimental to their official standing.

Men and women did not differ significantly in their preference for help from military or civilian clergymen or psychiatrists. However, they did differ significantly in preference for help from military or civilian psychologists and social workers. Women, significantly more often than men, preferred help from military psychologists and social workers. It appears, then, that women living in the military community, while not officially members of the Army, are more aware of and more assured in the use of resources specifically concerned with offering help with interpersonal conflict than men who hold official status in the organization.

CONCLUSIONS

An investigation of the literature shows that few explicit attempts have been made to examine systematically and to explain the career military community (Janowitz, 1959). Its nature has largely been taken as "given," something to be accepted without systematic explanation, and its influence on the individual's current behavior and opinions as unproblematic. As suggested earlier, however, the military community is important as an object of study in its own right; and, specifically, its influence on the opinions and behavior of individual community members is an important social welfare concern. The findings relative to Hypothesis III suggest that large numbers of the men in this study looked upon the use of military community resources as inimical to their positions in the organization. Their relatively greater preference for the use of civilian community resources may be understood as an attempt to avoid the violation of what they believed to be normative behavior within the organization. If this explanation is correct, then on the theoretical side, serious questions may be raised about the processes of socialization into the role of a career soldier. Given the fact that the Army is almost continuously attuned to recruiting the career soldier to reenlist, how does it happen that he believes, in such large numbers, that the use of resources specifically provided to offer help with interpersonal conflict will have detrimental consequences for his career?

On the practical side, the fact that soldiers, considerably more often than their wives, prefer the use of civilian resources for use in the resolution of family conflict indicates a serious block to the extent to which professional resources can be most effectively used. Looking at the differential distribution of information relative to the availability of help resources and the differential perception of the social cost of using resources, it is clear that the lower-ranking, least-educated persons among the population have less information about the availability of resources and a perception of the greatest social cost of using resources. This subgroup has fewer personal resources for resolving interpersonal difficulties and, therefore, a presumably greater need to make use of existing community resources. However, they are most likely to be cut off from the use of community resources by a lack of information and by an unfavorable evaluation of the social cost to them of making use of community resources. A considerable lack of information relative to the resources available, and a substantial amount of fearfulness and anxiety among all groups, appear to accompany the use of military community resources. The extent to which this fearfulness is present, however, increases as rank decreases. Programs designed to increase the level of information about help resources and to make their use more acceptable must, therefore, be primarily aimed at lower-ranking groups, although they must be sufficiently broad to include all strata of the community. It would seem that the use of community resources must also be disassociated from the official status of the user, and this disassociation effectively communicated to the population served. This would seem to be information valuable to those attempting to formulate broad social decisions for meeting the interpersonal needs of military families. It would also seem to be information valuable to therapists and other professional persons attempting to be of help to clients referred to them by authority figures. Help giving must be structured in such a way that the client or potential client does not perceive the receipt of help as damaging to his or her official status in the organization. The perception of damage to one's status may present an initial resistance by the client with which a therapist must deal before assistance with the real conflicts can be accepted.

NOTES

1. The weighting ratio was calculated by dividing the mean number of responses by officer into the mean of responses by enlisted respondents. $2.65/3.36 = .78$, the weighting factor.

2. Length of stay in the community was examined only for the female respondents. This variable is defined as the extent to which the respondent has lived in her family group in the military community, i.e., whether she has lived mostly on post during her marriage, mostly

off post during her marriage, or an approximately even amount of time on post and off post. The male respondents were not examined for this variable for, in order to be included in the study, they must have served several years within the system.

3. Among male enlisted respondents, 63 percent had less than a high school education. Among enlisted wives, 43 percent had less than a high school education.

4. Wives and mothers in the military community, as in civilian communities, serve as Red Cross volunteers, hospital volunteer helpers, welfare volunteers in military units and wives' clubs, etc.

IV

THE MILITARY FAMILY IN TRANSITION

Chapter 8

DIVORCE AND DISSOLUTION IN THE MILITARY FAMILY

JOHN WESLEY WILLIAMS, Jr.

Divorce and family dissolution are phenomena which have been of great interest to social scientists. Sociologists have examined these phenomena in terms of stigma, cohesiveness, disjunctive affiliation, and the effects on the structure of society as well as correlational analysis with such concepts as mobility, religion, security, education, occupation, race, and income. Psychologists have long been concerned with the trauma of divorce as well as intermediate and long-lasting effects on the personality. Anthropologists have investigated ways in which different societies handle divorce as well as similarities in cultural patterns. There is a prodigious amount of literature on divorce and family dissolution. Most of it is macroanalysis and focuses on such areas as statistics, causative factors, and associational variables.

There is a paucity of marital dissolution research on distinctive, specific groups in American society. Goode's (1956) study of 425 divorced urban mothers in Detroit was perhaps an attempt in this direction, but Goode never suggested that divorcées in Detroit could be looked upon as members of a well-defined group. Monahan (1955) also approached this problem in his study of childless couples, but again, to define "childless couples" as a distinguishable group is somewhat misleading. Another study tangential to this problem was the one by Kephart and Monahan (1954) in which they investigated divorce among religious and mixed-religious groups.

These and other studies have pointed toward analysis of specific groups as far as divorce is concerned but have fallen short owing to the diverse and heterogenous nature of the populations chosen. As Goode (1970) says, "Unfortunately, there exist no reliable data for divorce in specific occupations for the country as a whole." By this is meant such groups as professional athletes, college professors, lawyers, military officers, and the like. There would be much to be learned from such investigation. This chapter focuses on divorce and family dissolution among one particular group in American society—United States Air Force officers. Data pertaining to the society, in general, and to Air

AUTHOR'S NOTE: This chapter is an adaptation of Williams, Jr., J. W. "Divorce in the Population of the United States and in a Homogeneous Subset of that Population (United States Air Force Officers) 1958-1970," an unpublished doctoral dissertation prepared for State College, Mississippi, 1971.

[209]

Force officers, in particular, will be presented. Divorce rates for the two categories will be compared.

Over 4,000 Americans break up their marriages every day of the year (Vital Statistics Report, HEW, 1974). Comparison of the divorce rate for the United States with the rest of the civilized world shows that the United States has a distinctly high rate. (In some instances, the terms "ratio" or "number in divorced status" are used, owing to the ambiguity of the word "rate".) For the years 1930-1970, divorce rates for the United States were highest of all countries who report their annual divorce totals to the statistical offices of the United Nations (*Demographic Yearbook,* 1970). Examination of Table 1, showing the number of divorces from 1958 through 1970, reveals that the number of divorces increased every year but two during this period. Decreases during these two years, 1959-1960 and 1961-1962, were slight—.5 of 1 percent and .2 of 1 percent, respectively. The increase from 368,000 divorces in 1958 to approximately 708,000 in 1970 was almost a 100 percent increase. Increases in total numbers give us only a limited amount of information, however. The rate per 1,000 population proves a better way to observe the change, owing to the fact that it takes into account the change in population. From Table 2 it can be seen that the rate changed from 2.1 per 1,000 population in 1958 to 3.5 in 1970. This is more than a 70 percent increase (note that only from 1961 to 1962 did

TABLE 1

DIVORCES IN THE U.S., 1958-1970*

Year	Number of Divorces
1958	368,000
1959	395,000
1960	393,000
1961	414,000
1962	413,000
1963	428,000
1964	450,000
1965	479,000
1966	499,000
1967	523,000
1968	584,000
1969	639,000
1970	708,000

*Vital Statistics Reports, HEW, 1958-1970

TABLE 2

DIVORCE RATE PER 1,000 TOTAL POPULATION 1958-1970*

Year	Number of Divorces	Rate per 1,000 Total Population	% Change in Rate
1958	368,000	2.1	
1959	395,000	2.2	+4.8
1960	393,000	2.3	+4.5
1961	414,000	2.3	0.0
1962	413,000	2.2	-4.3
1963	428,000	2.3	+4.5
1964	450,000	2.4	+4.3
1965	479,000	2.5	+4.2
1966	499,000	2.5	0.0
1967	523,000	2.7	+8.0
1968	584,000	2.9	+7.4
1969	639,000	3.2	+11.0
1970	708,000	3.5	+9.0

*Vital Statistics Reports, HEW, 1958-1970

the rate go down). It should also be noted from Table 2 that the rate began to increase at a faster pace about 1966; e.g., note the 11 percent increase in the one-year period from 1968 to 1969.

Although the divorce rate per 1,000 population is a useful way to present data, a more exact way is to show the divorce rate per 1,000 married females 15 years of age and older. As is shown in Table 3, there was a substantial increase from 1958 to 1970. Again, it can be observed that the rate increased almost every year. The overall increase in the divorce rate for this time period was approximately 65 percent.

A comparison of the marriage rate per 1,000 population with the divorce rate

TABLE 3

DIVORCE RATE PER 1,000 MARRIED FEMALES 15 YEARS OF AGE AND OLDER*

Year	Number of Divorces	Rate per 1,000 Married Females	% Change in Rate
1958	368,000	8.9	- - - -
1959	395,000	9.3	+4.5
1960	393,000	9.2	-1.1
1961	414,000	9.6	+4.3
1962	413,000	9.4	-2.1
1963	428,000	9.6	+2.1
1964	450,000	10.0	+4.2
1965	479,000	10.6	+6.0
1966	499,000	10.9	+2.8
1967	523,000	11.2	+2.8
1968	582,000	12.4	+10.7
1969	639,000	13.4	+7.0
1970	708,000	14.9	+11.0

*Vital and Health Statistics, 1958-1974

per 1,000 population should help answer the question of whether the increase in divorce is being accounted for simply because of the increase in marriage. Table 4 presents the number of marriages and the change in marriage rates from 1958 to 1970. Note that the number of marriages increased every year from 1958 through 1970. The smallest percentage increase in number (1.9 percent) occurred in 1962, and the largest (6.8 percent) in 1968. The average percentage increase during this time period was 3.8 percent. A better way to examine the change is by examining the rate per 1,000 population. This rate increased from 8.4 in 1958 to 10.6 in 1969. Thus it appears that the rate is increasing. A better idea of the change can be had by observing the degree to which the rate itself changed. In the column on the far right it can be seen that after a 1.2 percent increase in the rate from 1958 to 1959 a three-year period followed in which no increase in the rate occurred. The greatest increase occurred from 1967 to 1968, when the rate jumped from 2.2 to 6.2; however, it fell back to 3.0 in 1969. The average change was 2.2 percent per year. These figures do not become very meaningful until comparison is made with the percent change increase in the divorce rate over the same period of time.

Another way to determine the divorce trend is to observe the divorce rate per 1,000 marriages. Table 5 shows that there were 1,451,000 marriages in 1958 and 368,000 divorces. This produces a divorce rate per 1,000 marriages of 253. This is probably the basis for the popular belief that the divorce rate is about one in four. In 1970 there were 2,158,000 marriages and 708,000 divorces, producing a rate of 325. The rate changed from one in four in 1958 to one in three in 1970 (Glick, 1975). While we recognize that the divorces which occurred in 1970 did not involve the people who married in 1970, this 12-year trend presents strong evidence that about one in every three marriages is ending in divorce. It can also be seen from Table 5 that the great increase in the divorce rate is not simply a function of an increasing number of marriages.

One additional table (Marital Status of the White and Nonwhite Population 14 Years and Older) is presented in order to further establish that divorce is increasing at a rapid rate in American Society (see Table 6). The percentage of divorced males and females in the population has been steadily increasing since 1958. This is true for both the white and nonwhite populations. Thus, divorce, both as an event and as a status, increased dramatically between 1958 and 1970. In numbers alone the increase was more than 90 percent. The rate per 1,000 population rose over 70 percent while there was an increase of 66 percent for married females 15 years of age and older. A rise was also seen in the divorce rate per 1,000 marriages—a change from about one in four to approximately one in three. The divorce rate increase far outpaced that of the marriage rate. Although the upward trend in the divorce rate began in 1957, the year 1967 marked the beginning of the greatest increase since the World War II era. Rates

TABLE 4

MARRIAGES – NUMBER, RATE, AND PERCENT CHANGE 1958-1970

Year	Number of Marriages	% Change in Number	Rate Per 1,000 Population	% Change in Rate
1958	1,451,000		8.4	
1959	1.494,000	+3.0	8.5	+1.2
1960	1,523,000	+1.9	8.5	0
1961	1,548,000	+1.6	8.5	0
1962	1,577,000	+1.9	8.5	0
1963	1,654,000	+4.9	8.8	+3.5
1964	1,725,000	+4.9	9.0	+2.3
1965	1,800,000	+4.3	9.3	+3.3
1966	1,857,000	+3.2	9.5	+2.2
1967	1,927,000	+3.8	9.7	+2.2
1968	2,059,000	+6.8	10.3	+6.2
1969	2,146,000	+4.2	10.6	. +3.0
1970	2,179,000	+1.5*	10.7	+1.0

*Provisional

for both whites and nonwhites were up during this period. There is no evidence that divorce rates are leveling off; in fact, a regression analysis of data from 1958 through 1980 predicts a divorce rate per 1,000 marriages well into the 400s by the late 1970s. We are already seeing such rates in some parts of California. In the next section we will examine variables associated with divorce in an attempt to define factors related to divorce.

TABLE 5

DIVORCE RATE PER 1,000 MARRIAGES*

Year	Marriages	Divorces	Divorce Rate per 1,000 Marriages	Percentage Change in Rate
1958	1,451,000	368,000	253	- - - -
1959	1,494,000	395,000	264	+4.0
1960	1,523,000	393,000	258	-3.0
1961	1,548,000	414,000	267	+3.0
1962	1,577,000	413,000	262	-2.0
1963	1,654,000	428,000	259	-1.0
1964	1,725,000	450,000	261	+0.7
1965	1,800,000	479,000	266	+2.0
1966	1,857,000	499,000	268	+0.8
1967	1,927,000	523,000	271	+1.0
1968	2,059,000	582,000	283	+3.0
1969	2,146,000	639,000	299	+6.0
1970	2,158,000	708,000	325	+9.0

*Vital and Health Statistics, 1958-1974

FACTORS RELATED TO DIVORCE

There is an abundance of material available on the subject of divorce; however, not only are there few recent studies, but also few of the studies completed can be classified as empirical research. A quick review of variables previously found related to divorce is presented here in order to give the reader a

TABLE 6

MARITAL STATUS OF THE WHITE AND NONWHITE POPULATION
PER 1,000 POPULATION (14 YEARS AND OVER)

Year	White				Nonwhite			
	Percent Married		Percent Divorced		Percent Married		Percent Divorced	
	Male	Female	Male	Female	Male	Female	Male	Female
1958	70.6	66.6	1.6	2.3	62.4	60.9	2.5	2.8
1959	70.5	66.8	1.7	2.4	60.9	61.2	2.7	3.2
1960	69.9	66.5	2.1	2.7	62.1	60.1	2.4	3.6
1961	69.9	65.8	1.9	2.7	62.0	60.9	2.0	3.8
1962	70.2	66.0	2.0	3.1	60.5	59.3	2.5	3.8
1963	69.7	65.6	2.0	2.7	61.0	58.9	2.7	4.3
1964	68.8	64.8	2.1	2.8	61.5	61.0	2.3	4.0
1965	68.8	64.4	2.1	2.8	60.8	59.8	2.9	4.0
1966	68.9	64.8	2.1	3.0	58.9	58.8	3.6	3.8
1967	68.9	64.3	2.1	3.1	59.8	58.7	2.7	4.0
1968	68.3	63.5	2.3	3.1	54.5	54.5	2.7	4.3
1969	68.4	63.3	2.2	3.2	56.3	54.6	2.6	4.0
1970	68.6	63.6	2.3	3.3	56.5	54.9	2.7	4.2

*Vital and Health Statistics, HEW, 1958-1974

better understanding of why divorce occurs. Although we will probably never be able to say what "causes" divorce, we can specify conditions associated with divorce and point out significant correlations among several variables.

Levinger (1970) offers the proposition that cohesiveness is inversely related to divorce, i.e., the lower the cohesiveness, the higher the rate of dissolution. He states that marital cohesiveness is analogous to group cohesiveness and that the strength of the marital relationship is a function of the attractions within and the barriers around the marriage. For many years, lawyers in the United States have maintained that the number-one cause of divorce is financial problems. Schroeder (1939) found a significant correlation between divorce rates and average income; that is, divorce rates were higher for those in the higher income group. In an analysis of the 1960 census data, Udry (1966) found an inverse relationship between income and marital instability. Goode (1956) constructed a "proneness to divorce" table by income which showed that those who were most divorce-prone were those in the lower income brackets.

There is also evidence in the literature that divorce is associated with occupation. Kelly (1969) points out that "jobs that provide a high level of intellectual or creative satisfaction, good income and regular hours create conditions most favorable to marital happiness." Likewise, in an analysis of the 1960 census data, Udry (1966) found that, generally speaking, there is lowest marital instability in the lowest status occupations for men, and highest stability in the high status occupations. Goode (1956) also shows that professional groups which have the highest socioeconomic rank have the lowest divorce rates.

Education is another variable that is mentioned by several investigators as being correlated with divorce. The more educated a person is, the more likely he is to have a well-adjusted marriage, and the less likely he is to become divorced (Clinard, 1957). Burgess and Cottrell (1939) reported a consistent relationship between increased chances of success in marriage and a rising level of educational achievement for both husbands and wives. A survey by Monahan (1961) showed that divorce was lowest among the college educated.

Still another factor, community stigma, appears to play an important part in the divorce decision. Several references to this concept are found in the literature. Levinger (1970) states that one of the barriers against divorce is community disapproval and that such disapproval seems more characteristic of rural than urban communities. Kirkpatrick (1963) found that those who are free from social controls are more likely to divorce. The fact that the group we associate and live with has a great influence on our decisions is brought out by Whyte (1956) in his description of life in the modern suburb. He notes that the visibility of the marriage has a beneficial effect on relations between husband and wife. Ogburn and Nimkoff (1964) suggest that in places where the inhabitants are personally acquainted and see each other face to face often, marriages are more stable, mainly because in such primary groups the opportunity for the opinion of others to play a part in regulating a person's conduct is much greater.

Tied in with the relationship between higher socioeconomic status and divorce is *security*. In most cases, those couples who have a high income, high education, and a professional occupation feel more secure than those whose income is low and whose potential for advancement is lower. A life relatively free from financial worries would certainly cause fewer conflict situations than one where inadequate income is a constant irritation. Hollingshead (1950) mentions that economic security is one of the principal goals of the American middle-class family and that this is probably tied in with the fact that divorce is rare for this group. In a study of 200 couples in the Los Angeles area, Williamson (1966) showed that couples with a higher average monthly income were better able to cope with life's problems, and that those who had savings, little or no indebtedness, and a fair amount of life insurance were more likely to have fewer marital problems. Locke (1951) also showed a positive relationship between security and marital success, noting that homeownership, life insurance, stocks, savings, the presence of appliances and status symbols, and the regularity of the husband's job were important factors.

The *legal* cause of the divorce is seldom the *actual* cause; most divorces are awarded on the basis of mental cruelty, desertion, drunkenness, insanity, adultery, neglect to provide, and conviction of a felony. When Goode (1956) asked his respondents, "What was the cause of your divorce?", almost all responses fell into the following categories: personality, authority or cruelty, desertion, triangle, home life, consumption, values, nonsupport, alcoholic drinking, and relatives. Terman (1938) listed 35 common grievances, including such factors as in-laws, unfaithfulness, lack of affection, selfishness, lack of consideration, management of income, insufficient income, religious beliefs, and alcoholic drinking. According to Levinger (1970), there are sources of alternate attraction that serve as causes of marital dissolution. He includes in this category: preference for other sex partner, opposing religious affiliations, wife's opportunity for independent income, and disjunctive kin affiliations. From the studies mentioned above, it appears reasonable to suggest that the marital bond is strengthened if the couple increases its physical and psychological distance from both sets of parents. Cohen and Hodges (1963) point this out when they say, "When kin are close, we would expect to find greater distances between spouses."

DIVORCE IN THE AIR FORCE OFFICER POPULATION

Now that we have examined data which show conclusively a rising divorce rate and have considered possible causative factors associated with this increase, we will turn to an examination of divorce in one particular group in American society—United States Air Force officers. This particular subset was chosen for several reasons. First, there is widespread belief among American citizens that professional military officers are somehow "different" from civilians. Second, many authors point out the significant positive relationship between mobility and family disorganization (divorce). It is thus logical to believe that the inordinate amount of mobility among military families would lead to family crises. Third, members of the military, themselves, seem to believe that military families have high divorce rates. Although several studies have indirectly suggested a high amount of family dissolution in particular commands which experience frequent family separations, there are few empirical data available.

Theoretically, the lack of residential stability among these families *should* lead to high divorce rates, and yet short, periodic separation may in fact act to *strengthen* the marital bond instead of to weaken it. Fourth, military officers are a subset of the overall population. They have characteristics that set them apart—e.g., uniforms, hair styles, high mobility, more family separation, more patriotism, more tradition, etc.—and Janowitz (1960) in his book, *The Professional Soldier,* suggested that military officers have a different value system than civilians. Thus, they form a cohesive unit and are set apart by interactions and relationships based on common interests, values, and norms. Fifth, since the military system permeates many areas of our everyday lives, a conscientious effort should be made to learn more about it and to account for differences between civilians and military men as far as one of society's major problems, divorce, is concerned. Last, the problem of divorce in the military takes on greater significance as the nation moves toward an all-volunteer force. If it is discovered that divorce and family dissolution are rare in a military environment, this fact is a positive aspect of military service; if it is discovered that the divorce rate among military men is much higher than for their civilian counterparts, then efforts can be made to discover causative factors. However, it should be pointed out that there are factors that affect the completeness, and, thus, the interpretation of the data. For the Air Force, divorce is still a sensitive area, and, additionally, like many other large bureaucratic organizations, it has only begun to collect and computerize data with sociological significance. Prior to approximately ten years ago, data were available only from the published results of sample surveys.

Significance of the Problem

The significance of this problem for sociology is obvious. A comparative analysis of the military subset and the overall population may provide sociology with an in-depth analysis of marital status and influential variables in a homogeneous group in our society. Second, it may also provide insight into the question of whether or not all groups in society have about the same divorce rates. Third, it may help determine the effects income, education, occupation, and several other variables have on divorce rates.

RESULTS

Available data cover an eleven-year period from 1960 to 1970. Data for 1960 through 1965 are from sample surveys; data for 1966 through 1970 are from 99 percent complete populations. Not included in these data are those officers who were widows or widowers, annulled marriages, or whose marital status was unknown (less than 1 percent for any given year). Table 7 shows marital status for Air Force officers for 1960-1970. Note that only about 1 percent of Air Force officers are divorced at any given point. The dramatic increase that has occurred in the United States population does not appear to have occurred in this subset. However, it is possible that the percentage of divorced may be masked by those who quickly remarry.

Divorce and Education

Since the literature on education level and marital status points out a strong relationship between divorce and education, that relationship for this particular group was examined. Table 8 shows marital status for Air Force officers by education level and indicates an almost monotonic increase in divorce as education levels go down. The mean divorce ratio for those with doctorate degrees is 0.7, while for those with less than a college degree it is 1.6. This inverse relationship is consonant with what is generally true in American society; i.e., as education rates go down, divorce rates go up. Education levels for Air Force officers compare quite favorably with the overall American population. Over 80 percent of Air Force officers have a college degree (see Table 9). Almost 20 percent hold graduate degrees.

Divorce and Grade (Rank)

Another relationship of interest is the one between divorce and rank. Owing to the visibility of the marriage, social control, and socioeconomic factors, it was hypothesized that higher-ranking officers should have lower divorce rates. From Table 10, showing status by rank, we can see that divorce ratios among higher-ranking officers are lower than among lower-ranking ones, which supports previous findings that lower divorce rates are associated with groups with higher socioeconomic status. The somewhat higher rate for Majors is probably due to the fact that, as a group, they are in a period of married life when divorce generally occurs. Lieutenants have not yet entered the vulnerable years.

Marital Status and Rated/Nonrated

Within the Air Force there are men who fly (rated) and those who do not (nonrated). Nonrated officers generally have a more stable work style (definite

TABLE 7

OFFICER FORCE MARITAL STATUS 1960-1965

Marital Status	1960		1961		1962		1963		1964	
	N	%	N	%	N	%	N	%	N	%
Married	*	86.3	*	87.7	*	86.6	113,627	85.3	112,789	83.8
Single	*	13.6	*	12.4	*	13.5	17,051	12.8	19,381	14.4
Divorced	*	*	*	*	*	*	1,465	1.1	1,615	1.2
Legally Separated	*	*	*	*	*	*	400	0.3	135	0.1
Widowed	*	*	*	*	*	*	400	0.3	270	0.2
Annulled	*	*	*	*	*	*	*	*	*	*
Unknown	*	*	*	*	*	*	266	0.2	403	0.3
Total	*	99.9	*	100.1	*	100.1	133,209	100.0	134,593	100.0

*Unknown

Table cont'd

Year												
	1965		1966		1967		1968		1969		1970	
	N	%	N	%	N	%	N	%	N	%	N	%
	108,673	83.4	107,208	81.2	108,545	79.4	109,001	79.4	106,023	79.1	100,879	78.9
	19,913	15.3	23,277	17.6	26,503	19.4	26,386	19.2	26,100	19.5	25,243	19.7
	1,436	1.1	1,067	0.8	1,352	1.0	1,504	1.1	1,519	1.1	1,505	1.2
	130	0.1	106	0.09	77	0.1	77	0.1	78	0.1	62	0.1
	130	0.1	188	0.14	179	0.1	210	0.2	199	0.1	157	0.1
	*	*	*	*	*	*	*	*	3	0.0	8	0.0
	261	0.2	145	0.1	10	0.0	28	0.0	63	0.0	31	0.0
	130,543	100.0	131,991	99.9	136,666	100.0	137,206	100.0	133,985	99.9	127,885	100.0

TABLE 8

EDUCATION LEVEL AND DIVORCE MEANS: 1966-1970

Level	Ratio
Doctorate	0.7
Master's Plus	0.8
Master's	0.9
Graduate Work	1.3
College Graduate	1.0
Less than College Graduate	1.6

TABLE 9

EDUCATION LEVEL OF U.S. CIVILIANS AND
AIR FORCE OFFICERS, 1969

Population (N)	Median Yrs. of School Completed	College Degree or More	5 Years or More of College	Graduate Degree	Less than 4 Yrs. of High School
Air Force Officers (153)	16.5	83%	21%	18%	0.2%
U.S. Civilians (154)	12.4	21%	10%	UNK	27.0%

TABLE 10

GRADE (RANK) AND DIVORCE: MEAN DIVORCE RATES: 1963-1970

Rank	Ratio
General	0.2
Colonel	0.8
Lt. Colonel	1.1
Major	1.5
Captain	1.3
Lt.	0.8
Warrant Officer	1.3

hours and at home on the weekends) than those officers who fly. Sociological theory suggests that higher divorce rates are associated with disruption; therefore, we would expect more rated officers to be divorced. As indicated in Table 11, a strong relationship appears to exist between flying status and marital status. These data support the proposition advanced by Monahan (1955) that divorce-proneness among occupational groups relates to the stability of the husband's home life.

Marital Status and Command

The Air Force is broken down into several smaller units, referred to as *commands*. Each command has certain obligations and responsibilities, e.g., the primary mission of the Aerospace Defense Command (ADC) is to defend the nation in the event of an air attack. Divorced status means for officers in these various commands from 1966 to 1970 are presented in Table 12. Examination of these data reveals minimal differences in divorce ratios across commands; however, there are a few which should be pointed out. Sociological literature points out that where there is greater family instability and disruption there is likely to be greater chance for divorce. This appears to be supported by the data on the Tactical Air Command (TAC) and the Military Airlift Command (MAC). In both cases the rates have shown a steady increase. For TAC the ratio moved from 1.0 (N = 102) in 1966 to 1.7 (N = 222) in 1970. For MAC the ratio moved

TABLE 11

RATED/NONRATED AND MARITAL STATUS, 1966-1970*

Flight Status	Marital Status									
	Single		Married		Divorced		Legally Separated		Total	
	N	%	N	%	N	%	N	%	N	%
1966										
Rated	5,723	8.1	64,478	90.7	695	1.0	64	0.1	70,940	99.9
Nonrated	17,506	28.8	42,677	70.3	391	0.6	36	0.1	60,610	99.8
1967										
Rated	5,730	8.3	62,005	90.3	773	1.1	49	0.1	68,557	99.8
Nonrated	20,714	30.5	46,071	68.5	577	0.9	27	0.0	67,789	99.9
1968										
Rated	5,976	8.9	60,141	89.6	850	1.3	39	0.1	67,006	99.9
Nonrated	20,400	29.1	48,825	69.8	654	1.0	38	0.1	69,917	99.9
1969										
Rated	5,400	10.1	56,072	88.3	849	1.4	45	0.1	63,366	99.8
Nonrated	19,695	28.0	49,933	70.9	674	1.0	33	0.0	70,337	99.9
1970										
Rated	6,441	10.7	52,568	87.7	830		31	0.1	59,870	99.9
Nonrated	18,802	27.7	48,311	71.1	675		31	0.1	67,819	99.9

*Does not include annulled, widowed, or unknown.

from 1.0 (N = 119) in 1966 to 1.4 (N = 165) in 1970. During this period ratios for all other commands changed very little. For both TAC and MAC aircrews, disruption was a way of life during this time period, owing to their heavy involvement in the conflict in Southeast Asia. Most TAC crew members served at least one full year at one of the remote bases in Southeast Asia (many served two full tours). When not actually serving in this theatre of operations, they were at training bases away from home requalifying in the latest weapons systems. This life style contributed significantly to family disruption and undoubtedly accounts for a significant proportion of the increase in the divorce ratio for this command. A similar situation exists in MAC. Although few MAC units were stationed in Southeast Asia, most of them spent considerable time flying in and out of the area. Many crew members were home only a few days out of each month and could make few family plans that were not subject to change or cancellation. This finding lends support to the sociological proposition that the chance for divorce is higher where there are disruption and instability of family life.

Divorce and Regular vs. Reserve Status. There is a tendency for reserve officers to have slightly higher divorce rates than regular officers (see Table 13). This finding supports the proposition that divorce rates are higher where there is less security. Reserve officers are in a somewhat tenuous position. They may be released from service at the convenience of the government and have no guarantee that they will be allowed to remain on active duty long enough to retire. Chances for promotion are not as good as for regular officers and their status is not as high.

Divorce and Source of Commission. Table 14 shows that those officers who were commissioned through programs not requiring a college degree had a greater tendency to be in the status "divorced" than those who were required to have a degree. This finding supports the hypothesis that higher divorce rates are found in lower educated groups.

Divorce and Religion. Air Force officers who belong to the Catholic or Jewish faiths have lower divorce ratios than those in any other religious category. Those officers with no preference for religion or who claimed no religion had the highest ratios. This finding supports the proposition that being attached to a religious body of some kind is correlated with lower divorce rates.

Divorce and Race and Sex. No significant differences showed up between blacks and whites. This suggests that in situations where these two groups have equal income, education, living conditions, etc., many of the statistical differences between them vanish. Female officers had higher ratios than males, but it cannot be determined from available data whether they entered service in a divorced status or divorced while in service. It may be that they do not remarry in the same numbers as males.

Divorce and Southeast Asia (Vietnam) Tour. More officers who served a tour in Southeast Asia are in divorced status than those who had not; however, this may be a spurious relationship, in that flying personnel probably made up the bulk of the officers assigned there at any one time, and it has already been established that flying officers have higher rates than those who do not fly, even though the differences are not great.

Comparison of Divorced Status Between Air Force Officers and the U.S. Population, Ages 20-50, 1960-1970. Owing to the fact that there is a lack of detail in census and Public Health Service data on divorce, direct comparison of these two groups is difficult; however, there is a limited amount of data that does permit comparative analysis. Tables 15 through 17 show this comparison.

TABLE 12

COMMANDS AND DIVORCED STATUS MEANS (1966-1970)

Command	No. Divorced	% Divorced
Aerospace Defense Command	81	1.0
Air Training Command	138	0.8
Alaskan Air Command	122	1.3
Air Force Academy	90	0.9
Strategic Air Command	244	1.0
Tactical Air Command	177	1.4
Security Service	13	0.9
Headquarters, USAF	26	0.9
Military Airlift Command	144	1.3
Pacific Air Command	146	1.1
USAF in Europe	35	1.2
Systems Command	110	1.1
Air University	41	0.7
Air Force Logistics Command	35	1.0
USAF Special CONUS Units	46	1.0

TABLE 13

DIVORCE RATE FOR REGULAR AND RESERVE OFFICERS
PER 1,000 MARRIAGES

Year	Regular Officers	Reserve Officers
1966	9	10
1967	10	14
1968	12	16
1969	12	16
1970	14	16

TABLE 14

FIVE-YEAR DIVORCE MEANS FOR SOURCES OF COMMISSION: 1966-1970

Source of Commission	% Divorced Rate
Officers Candidate School	1.5
Aviation Cadets	1.4
Direct Appointment, Civilian	1.3
United States Naval Academy	1.3
Warrant Officer	1.2
Direct Appointment, Military	1.0
United States Military Academy	0.8
Officers Training School	0.8
Reserve Officer Training Corps	0.8
United States Air Force Academy	0.4

TABLE 15

COMPARISON OF
DIVORCED STATUS BETWEEN MALE AIR FORCE OFFICERS
AND MALES IN THE U.S. POPULATION, AGES 20-54, 1960-1970

Population		1960	1961	1962	1963	1964	1965	1966	1967	1968	1969	1970
							Divorced					
U.S.	N	730,000	837,000	894,000	915,000	944,000	941,000	955,000	975,000	1,064,000	1,126,000	-----
	%	1.9	2.2	2.3	2.3	2.4	2.4	2.4	2.3	2.6	2.8	3.0*
A.F.	N	---	---	---	1,465	1,615	1,436	1,067	1,352	1,504	1,519	1,505
	%	---	---	---	1.1	1.2	1.1	0.8	1.0	1.1	1.1	1.2

*Provisional

TABLE 16

NUMBER OF DIVORCED MEN PER 1,000 MARRIED MEN
(ALL MALES AND AIR FORCE OFFICERS, Ages 20-54, 1960-1970)

	Divorce Rate	
Year	All Males	Air Force Officers
1960	2.6	NA*
1961	2.7	NA
1962	2.9	NA
1963	3.0	1.3
1964	3.1	1.4
1965	3.2	1.3
1966	3.3	1.0
1967	3.1	1.2
1968	3.5	1.4
1969	3.4	1.4
1970	3.2	1.5

*Not Available

TABLE 17

DIVORCES PER 1,000 U. S. MARRIED MALES, AGES 20-54,
AND PER 1,000 MARRIED AIR FORCE OFFICERS,
AGES 20-54, 1963-1969

Year	Number Married	Number Divorced	No. Div. Per 1,000 Married
		U. S. Males	
1963	30,982,445	915,000	29
1964	31,180,000	954,000	31
1965	31,123,000	941,000	31
1966	31,676,000	959,000	30
1967	31,976,000	975,000	31
1968	31,030,000	1,061,000	34
1969	32,494,000	1,126,000	35
		Air Force Officers (Male)	
1963	106,830	1,377	13
1964	107,150	1,534	14
1965	103,430	1,364	13
1966	106,696	1,009	10
1967	108,107	1,239	11
1968	108,297	1,368	12
1969	105,384	1,371	13

Although these figures are not age-specific, they do provide some basis for comparison. They suggest that Air Force officers have lower divorce rates than the overall population.

DISCUSSION

It is not within the scope of this chapter to attempt to explain the upward trend in the divorce rate in the United States population; however, any such explanation would have to include such considerations as changing divorce laws, lessening social stigma for divorced persons, and the fact that divorce is in the process of becoming institutionalized.

The small percentage of Air Force officers in divorced status can be partly explained by reference to several sociological concepts. Primary among these is that of integration, i.e., the societal integration that takes place through shared norms, values, and beliefs. Williams (1960) makes this clear when he says, "a basic postulate is that the integration of a society can be defined in terms of the sharing of common prescriptions for conduct, belief, valuation." He states further that a society is a human aggregate possessing a common ultimate-value system; that a society is possible because people share "a common world of experience"; and the continuing operation of any social aggregate does depend upon a minimal sharing of normative orientations. Integration, then, is operationalized as "the extent to which interests, values, norms, beliefs, symbols, and other social and cultural variables are shared." According to Williams (1960), divorce, extremely high mobility, and other forms of small-group dissolution are evidence of instability of normative patterns in the basic units of person-to-person contacts.

Levinger (1970) discusses this concept in terms of group cohesiveness. He says that marital cohesiveness is analogous to group cohesiveness and can be defined accordingly. He emphasizes the point that group cohesiveness is "the total field of forces which act on members to remain in the group including the attractiveness of the group itself and the strength of the restraints against leaving it." Thus, according to Levinger, the strength of the marital relationship would be a direct function of the attractions within and the barriers around the marriage. He also suggests that the less socially visible the couple is, the more likely it is to break up. Scanzoni (1965) supports this concept and implies that when both partners tend to belong to the same reference group and to interact with the same "significant others," the possibility of conjugal conflict is lessened. He also says that to the extent marriage partners are mutually involved in external networks or clusters of interests, they will be influenced by the cultural elements of these networks, i.e., be integrated with them and thus share a common universe of values and norms.

In the military environment, the sharing of a common culture and adherence to common norms, values, and beliefs is profound. The Air Force officer corps is a homogeneous, stable group in which a common set of standards and goals is shared by practically all members. These norms, values, standards, and goals are generally shared by wives. Although the officer force to some degree cuts across all social classes, there is a strong feeling of commonality of kind. In fact, young officers are socialized by both their peers and their superiors to direct their loyalty toward the group and toward the mission. This loyalty to the country, to the Air Force, and to the unit may carry over into loyalty to the wife. The Air Force husband and wife are made to feel as a "team," and that the accomplishment of the mission is dependent on *them*, not just on the husband. The wife is made to feel that her role is valued. Most wives are proud that their husbands are Air Force officers, and feel they are contributing in their own way to their husbands' success as well as to the mission of the Air Force.

The relatively high income and the fringe benefits received by the Air Force officer and his family, as well as the outstanding retirement system, promote strong feelings of security—a concept that is highly correlated with low divorce rates. Even though the military has moved away from the "garrison" concept (where all men and their families lived on post with very little contact with civilians), most of the social interaction is still with fellow officers and their wives. This is probably more true for those who live on base than for those who live in the civilian community. Although practically all families have civilian friends, the Officers Club and especially the Officers Wives Club is usually a very important part of the couple's lives. Many formal and informal activities occur here, and most of these activities reinforce the couple's feeling as a team. The fact that both partners participate mutually in many external activities, sharing the same reference group and significant others, contributes to marital cohesiveness. The close scrutiny which results from housing patterns on bases, the fairly high degree of social interaction with other couples in the same unit, and the more intimate knowledge of what is happening in other people's lives (especially on small bases) make marriages more visible in the military environment. High-ranking officers, astronauts, war heroes, etc., are especially in the public eye and would be expected to have lower divorce rates.

Previous research has suggested that when the couple is separated from both kin groups, the marriage has a better chance of success (Cohen and Hodges, 1963; Scanzoni, 1965; Thomas, 1956). Air Force couples fit this criterion very well. The very nature of military service is such that the partners usually live great distances from the kin groups. The fact that the couple must work out their own problems free from interference and advice from kin groups is functional for the marriage.

Marriage partners in the military are mutually involved in many external networks and clusters of interest. There are many institutionalized social activities which require the presence of the officer and his wife. Social theory suggests that when the couple participates together in activities, strength is added to the marital bond.

According to sociological theory, the great amount of mobility associated with military family life should lead to high rates of disorganization, including divorce. There are reasons why this is not necessarily true for Air Force officers and their families. When civilian families move to a new location, they generally move into a completely new life style. This includes a new job; a different type of housing; new neighbors with different values, beliefs, and ways of doing things; a new shopping situation; a different culture; etc. For the military family this is not generally true. Most Air Force bases are similar and the life style changes little from one to another. The officer often moves into the same job he had at the previous base, he moves into about the same type of housing he had before, the shopping center on base is usually identical to that on the base he just left, the new people the family interacts with hold about the same values and norms as those they just left, the life style is similar to that previously led, and the same kinds of goods and services are available. There are the normal inconveniences of moving, but there is much less overall disruption of the family than in civilian life. If the family does not live on base, this concept would not be quite as applicable, but the overall working and living situation would still have many similarities to the former environment.

The disruption of the family is alleviated also by the formal organizations the Air Force has set up to aid the family when a move occurs. A Family Service Organization is set up on all bases to help the family with problems that arise as a result of its move. This organization will lend the family kitchen equipment, provide baby-sitting service, assist with finding housing, provide information on the base the departing family is going to, provide brochures on local shopping and sightseeing, provide information on base facilities, and in general, assist the new family in its adjustment to the new environment. Family Services also provides a "newcomer's orientation" in which questions concerning the new base are answered and the family is made to feel welcome. The Officers Wives Club on most bases also has a welcome committee which assists in getting the new family settled. These and other services lower the amount of disruption caused by moving to a new location. These internal supports may act as inducements for the couple to remain in the group and as factors to ease the friction and disruption caused by the high mobility rate. In this way the Air Force becomes something like an extended family, offering comfort and assistance even when the husband is deployed. It is possible that this sense of group cohesiveness carries over into marital cohesiveness.

The relatively high education, high income, and strong sense of security are important factors for consideration when attempting to explain the lack of high divorce rates among Air Force officers. A lack of serious financial problems, according to previous research, contributes highly to marital happiness and stability. Since this research study points out that Air Force officers score high on these variables, this finding adds verification to the hypothesis that there is an inverse relationship between socioeconomic ratings and divorce.

SUMMARY

In this chapter propositions suggested by previous researchers, developed into hypotheses, tested through statistical analysis, are found to support many previous findings dealing with divorce in our society. As a result, more credibility has been given to the following general statements:

(1) As education levels go up, divorce rates go down (for males only).
(2) As income increases, the proneness toward divorce decreases (for males only).
(3) The more visible the marriage, the less the chance for divorce.
(4) Divorce-proneness among occupational groups relates to the stability of the husband's home life.
(5) Lower divorce rates are found where there is a great amount of security.
(6) Divorce rates are lower among Catholics and Jews.
(7) Where socioeconomic conditions are similar, blacks and whites have about the same divorce rates.
(8) There is some reason to believe that lengthy separation of the husband and wife is correlated with higher divorce rates.
(9) In cases where the couple shares normative orientations and belong to the same reference group, the chance for divorce is lessened.
(10) When the couple is separated from both kin groups, the marriage has a better chance for success.
(11) Frictions caused by high mobility rates may be alleviated by internal supports supplied by the groups to which the couple belongs.

Although this study suggests the divorce rate among Air Force officers is low, direct comparison with civilians of equivalent socioeconomic standing was difficult owing to a lack of detailed data on the civilian population. Also, because divorce remains a sensitive issue within the military system and factors, thus, exist which affect the completeness and interpretation of the data, the need for further research in the area of family dissolution becomes apparent. The propositions supported in this research effort, however, do provide "building blocks" for a theory that may eventually predict and explain divorce in American society.

Chapter 9

INDIVIDUAL AND FAMILY PROBLEMS RELATED TO

RETIREMENT FROM THE MILITARY SERVICE

J O H N S. M c N E I L

Most of the population equates retirement with aging, reduced income owing to unemployment, dependency, and the constructive use of leisure time. Very little has been written about the individual who, because of his occupational choice, may retire from his primary career at a much earlier age. One such occupational group is composed of career Armed Services personnel. Military retirement is based upon a length of service principle, in contrast to age plus length of service in other occupations. Current law allows career military personnel to retire after twenty years of active duty. Retirement, therefore, has a special meaning for the career military man and his family that differs markedly from other occupations.

During the rapid military mobilization of World War II, millions of men and women entered the Armed Forces who would not have done so if there had been no national crisis. Many of these individuals decided to remain in the military service after the end of the war and a substantial number eventually decided to make their career in the Armed Forces. During the 1960s, thousands of these persons became eligible for retirement by virtue of having completed twenty years of active duty.

The increase in numbers of retired military personnel has grown at such a pace that the usual attrition by death has not been able to control the size of the retired rolls. In 1900 there were only about 3,000 persons on the military retired rolls; by 1925, this figure had increased to more than 19,000; and by 1950, it had soared to more than 132,000. Thus, in a period of fifty years the number of people on the retired rolls had multiplied more than forty times. In 1960 there were 255,000 retired military personnel and in 1970 there were 750,000.

Military retirement can be studied from several foci: its impact upon society,

AUTHOR'S NOTE: This chapter is an adaptation of McNeil, J.S. "Adjustment of Retired Air Force Officers," an unpublished doctoral dissertation prepared for the University of Southern California, 1964.

its impact upon the military establishment, and its impact upon the military retiree and his family. The focus in this chapter will be upon the impact of military retirement on the retiree and his family; however, some attention will be given to its effect upon society.

If a lifetime is perceived as the period extending from infancy and childhood, through adolescence and young adulthood, to middle adulthood and old age, then middle adulthood, the time when the career serviceman retires, is generally considered to be the time of highest status and greatest productivity. It is expected that the nondisabled adult male will be gainfully employed until he reaches the "normal retirement age," which is considered to be sixty-five years of age. The career military man, who retires from the Armed Forces during middle adulthood, is expected to retire to another occupation, not to a life of leisure.

Age, thus, is the hub around which most decision making revolves. At the time of retirement the typical officer is between 40 and 49 years of age and has a maximum of one dependent school-age child living at home. The typical enlisted man who retires has a wife and two or three dependent school-age children living at home and is a few years younger than the recently retired officer. This factor of age, however, is a relative entity. The military retiree is considered young when compared with individuals who retire at the usual age of sixty-five, but when he begins to seek employment, he may be considered too old. It is well known that many industries are hesitant to employ individuals over forty-five years of age, and some even put the cut-off at age thirty-five.

Age is also intricately interwoven with the life cycle stages of the family. Of the various formulations developed suggesting the phases of family life cycles, Hill and Rodgers (1964) propose eight stages ranging from the establishment of the marriage, expectancy of the first child, childbearing, preschool family, school-age children, adult trainees, young adult launching, and middle years to aging years. At the time the career serviceman retires from the Armed Forces, the family may be traversing several of these stages. Ages of dependent children may range from infancy to young adults. Although retirement is conceived of in this formulation as occurring during the aging years, obviously it occurs at an earlier stage with the military retiree, and other factors may add to the family's adjustment problems. For example, at the time the family is facing retirement from the military, the wives are often menopausal or premenopausal. Both parents, at this point in life, are usually preparing to adjust to the recognition that children have less need for parental protection or guidance. For the wife, who primarily has always been a homemaker, adjustment may be more difficult. The husband, who is in the throes of his own adjustment problems, may be less able and/or willing to meet the needs of his wife. Thus, the preretirement preparatory period and the time immediately subsequent to retirement have the potential for being emotionally hazardous for all family members. Each member of the retired military family experiences some degree of stress as these multiple stages of the family cycle impact simultaneously. Age, familial responsibility, and social pressure force the retired serviceman to seek employment.

REASONS FOR RETIREMENT

Managerial personnel policy may require retirement for varied reasons, such as age, disability, or reductions in personnel strength levels, or to create promotional opportunity for younger employees. Second, retirement may occur because the employee arrives at a voluntary decision to retire once he has attained retirement eligibility. In the first instance, the individual has no choice in the retirement decision, and these actions often are perceived in a negative light by the individual. In the Armed Forces, although the retiree is young by standards utilized for retirement purposes in civilian industry, military policy implies that he is old or "over the hill." When retirement is involuntarily initiated because of personnel reduction or personnel flow requirements, the element of quality control arises. Supposedly those employees who are retained are a greater asset to the organization than those involuntarily retired. The retiree and his family must deal with the implied stigma attached.

Career military persons who retire voluntarily do so for many reasons. It has been emphasized that most seek employment in civilian industry following retirement from the Armed Forces. Employment choices are curtailed considerably the older the retiree is at the time he seeks employment. Many persons plan their retirement by the time they are 45 years of age because of the tendency for industrial concerns to place a cut-off at this age level for bringing new personnel into the organization. Age, again, becomes critical relative to family pressure. High school age children are very resistant to changing schools and not being able to graduate with their class. Wives are often ready to secure a home and become established in a community. Familial pressure at this time in life may precipitate the decision to retire, should reassignment to another military installation be required. Some retirement decisions are made because of disagreement with policy. Individuals who have attained retirement eligibility may handle their disagreement with the changes, which inevitably occur in any social system, by exercising the option to initiate action for voluntary retirement. Still another reason for individuals retiring is that they may see limited or no opportunity for advancement. Included in this group would be persons who feel they have not attained the rank they expected and those persons who have been promoted to the top of their hierarchy but are sufficiently ambitious and cannot tolerate being plateaued. Examples of these would be noncommissioned officers who have been promoted to pay grade E9, or officers who are colonels and envision minimal opportunity for elevation to the General Officer corps. Financial gain can also be an influencing factor in opting for retirement if the man has a transferable skill that brings a good price on the labor market. A combination of retired pay and salary from the civilian job may place some retirees at a higher income level.

Thus, reasons for retirement vary, but the act of retirement is processed because the serviceman either has a mandatory retirement date, or makes a voluntary decision to retire.

GROWTH OF THE SIZE OF THE RETIRED ROLLS

The military retirement program was established initially during the Civil War. Prior to this legislation, pensions were authorized for individuals who were disabled in combat to the extent that they were unable or partially unable to earn a living. Approximately forty years after the Revolutionary War, Congress passed legislation that provided pensions for elderly financially needy veterans. A "pauper clause" placed responsibility upon the veteran to prove his financial need. This precedent has continued following each war. On July 14, 1861 President Lincoln signed into law the General Law Pension System Bill which created the military retirement program as we know it today. Initially, only officers were included, but in 1885 enlisted personnel became eligible for retirement benefits. Except for liberalizations of retirement eligibility provisions, the law enacted over a hundred years ago has retained its basic structure.

Although large numbers of persons undoubtedly sought military careers during the period of the Depression of the 1930s (see Table 1), relatively few persons were on the military retired rolls until after World War II. Policy regarding national defense is again reflected in the size of the retirement rolls since 1960 (see Table 2); the recent increase in the size of the military retired rolls has averaged approximately 60,000 per year, and this rate of increase is expected to remain relatively constant for the next fifty years.

Another perspective of the retired rolls is seen in Table 3. Totals are given for each rank as well as direct costs of the retirement program as of June 1973. The most common rank at which officers retire is Lieutenant Colonel, and the most common rank at which enlisted personnel retire is Master Sergeant. Approximately twice as many enlisted personnel are on the retired rolls as are officers, but this is expected, since there are more enlisted personnel than officers. Additionally, enlisted personnel, on the average, retire at an earlier age than officers.

TABLE 1

SIZE OF RETIRED ROLLS BY FIVE-YEAR INTERVALS
FROM 1900 TO 1960

Year	Number
1900	3,029
1905	4,102
1910	5,405
1915	6,739
1920	10,035
1925	19,369
1930	32,838
1935	37,437
1940	48,374
1945	64,456
1950	132,828
1955	180,817
1960	255,089

Source: Actuarial Accountant of Office of Assistant Secretary of Defense for Manpower and Reserve Affairs.

TABLE 2

SIZE OF RETIRED ROLLS 1961-1973
WITH PROJECTIONS TO 1978

Fiscal Year	Actual Budget	Average Number
1961	,,	275,914
1962	,,	313,436
1963	,,	358,830
1964	,,	410,853
1965	,,	462,463
1966	,,	508,566
1967	,,	564,280
1968	,,	624,496
1969	,,	691,688
1970	,,	750,144
1971	,,	806,139
1972	,,	867,190
1973	,,	946,080
1974	,,	1,017,271
1975	Projected	1,076,000
1976	,,	1,135,000
1977	,,	1,190,000
1978	,,	1,241,000

Source: Actuarial Accountant for OASD for Manpower and Reserve Affairs

TABLE 3

MONTHLY RETIRED PAY BY RANK
AS OF 30 JUNE 1973

Retired Pay Grade	Number of Persons	Monthly Amount	Average Monthly Retired Pay
Officer (O)			
0 - 10	131	$ 255,777	$ 1,952
0 - 9	360	613,503	1,704
0 - 8	1,867	2,582,703	1,383
0 - 7	1,794	2,019,202	1,126
0 - 6	49,691	45,519,506	916
0 - 5	94,460	63,676,741	674
0 - 4	66,732	36,324,963	544
0 - 3	30,023	12,772,947	425
0 - 2	16,590	5,351,429	323
0 - 1	5,442	1,407,103	267
Warrant Officer (W)			
W - 4	10,463	6,431,071	615
W - 3	9,861	4,217,886	428
W - 2	14,360	5,303,832	369
W - 1	4,676	1,383,845	296
TOTAL OFFICERS	306,450	$187,904,508	$ 613
Enlisted (E)			
E - 9	28,655	$ 14,842,943	$ 518
E - 8	65,281	26,478,074	406
E - 7	240,225	75,949,619	316
E - 6	171,691	45,662,300	266
E - 5	83,397	17,807,301	214
E - 4	24,440	3,807,752	156
E - 3	10,240	1,476,107	144
E - 2	3,951	347,489	88
E - 1	942	100,543	107
TOTAL ENLISTED	628,882	$186,472,128	$ 297
GRAND TOTAL	935,272	374,376,636	400

Source: Actuarial Accountant of OASD for Manpower and Reserve Affairs

RETIREMENT RESIDENCES

Military retirees and their families show a decided preference in terms of the geographic location they select as a retirement residence. Selection of a retirement residence is influenced by several factors, including proximity to military installations, desirability of the climate, and availability of employment opportunities. Approximately 17 percent of retirees settle in California, and slightly less than 8 percent in Florida and Texas, respectively. Similarly, approximately 8 percent retire in the Virginia-Maryland-District of Columbia areas. Four areas thus provide the retirement residences for about 40 percent of all retirees. These figures, however, reveal a shift in preference when compared to similar data regarding retirement residences compiled in 1960. At that time, approximately 25 percent of military retirees were settled in California, 10 percent in Florida, 8 percent in Texas, and 5 percent in the District of Columbia area. Undoubtedly, this shift has been influenced by the high cost of living in some of these areas and the decreased opportunity for employment. The Southern states seem to attract a large number of military retirees. Approximately 20 percent retire in the southeastern geographic area. The states attracting retirees with climates that are considered to be more rigorous are those that have significant quantities of military resources within their borders. Retirees do not settle randomly throughout the state, but tend to cluster in or around areas adjacent to military installations.

RETIREMENT AND EMPLOYER RESPONSIBILITY

Neither private industry nor the military service has ever really resolved satisfactorily the question regarding the extent of employer responsibility toward prospective retirees, retired persons, or their families. Opinions vary from those who believe the employer has no responsibility, to those who argue the employer should assure, to every extent possible, maximum adjustment in retirement. Since the passage of the Social Security Act, most employers have come to accept the right of employees to pension benefits, In spite of this trend, thousands of industrial employees have learned at the point of retirement that their expected pension is not available. Recent federal legislation is intended to minimize the possibility of this tragedy.

The military service has never been fully committed to an individualized preparatory assistance approach during the preretirement phase. Individuals approaching retirement are briefed and provided reading materials, and limited job referral resources are provided utilizing the existing state employment agencies. Assistance is sometimes available for things such as resumé preparation. Although Program Transition, a program where young, active-duty personnel completing their military obligation were released from normal military duty functions so that they might learn a skill which could be sold in the civilian labor market, was extended to include prospective military retirees, more recently, budgetary retrenchment has forced the discontinuance or severe restriction of most individualized programs in the retirement preparatory phase.

During the postretirement period, the military's responsibilities have fluctuated. A case in point is the provision of medical care for the retiree and his dependents. Medical services have always been provided to dependents and retired personnel on a space-available basis. This procedure worked quite well when the number of persons on the retired rolls was relatively small. However, at present at many military installations, medical care for retirees and their families is practically nonexistent. Although retirees and their dependents are included under the coverage of the military medicare program (CHAMPUS), the retiree's coinsurance share is larger and his benefits fewer than those for dependents of active-duty personnel, especially those benefits relating to handicapped children. Another crucial postretirement benefit is the eligibility of surviving dependents to receive cash payments derived from the deceased retiree's pension rights. Such a program is in effect in the military services through the Family Protection Plan and was developed as an actuarially sound survivorship annuity. If the retiree participates in the plan, each month an actuarially determined percentage of his retired pay is deducted to pay for the annuity he has selected. Annuities are available in the amounts of one-eighth, one-fourth, or one-half of the retiree's retirement pay. The plan has been criticized as being too expensive and too restrictive. A very small percentage of eligible retirees elect to utilize this form of insurance protection for their families. For the maximum annuity of one-half of his retired pay, depending upon the ages of the retiree and his wife, the cost of the family protection can be as much as one-quarter of the monthly retired pay check. Recently, however, some of the more objectionable features have been liberalized.

Within the past twenty years, the overall direction of the military service on the employer responsibility continuum has been toward less responsibility. This is evident in the nibbling away of fringe benefits and the changes already made and being contemplated in the method of computing the amount of retired pay received. Until 1958 pay was tied to active-duty pay. Each time there was a pay raise for active-duty personnel, retired pay was recomputed on the current active-duty pay scales. Now retired pay is raised on the basis of the Consumer Price Index. As a result, individual retirees receive considerably less in retired pay than they would have under the old system.

Experience has shown that many retirees desire and need more assistance than has been made available to them. There is greater need for help in the areas of resumé preparation, job placement, vocational guidance and counseling, financial planning, and counseling to assist in dealing with the psychological shock of retirement. Adequate assistance programs should begin many months, or even a few years, prior to actual retirement and continue afterward when needed. Theoretically, the best retirement planning begins the day the career military person enters on active duty. One program no longer in operation that was beneficial to many retirees was the policy of allowing individuals approaching retirement to select the geographic area of choice for their final duty assignment. This gave the family a head start on retirement. Obviously many things could be done to assist the retiree, but such programs are low-priority items.

SOCIETAL PARADOXES

The retiree and his family are placed in a double bind through use of societal paradoxes. For example, there is a decided cultural, familial, and individual push for the military retiree to seek full-time employment. Simultaneously, there is a counterpressure which makes it more difficult for the retiree to secure suitable employment and/or adjust adequately to his retired status. Society insists that the retiree be gainfully employed because he is too young to retire to leisure. Yet, often, he is seen as being too old even to be hired as a new employee and, if so, his age minimizes his potentiality for many promotional opportunities. This inequity toward the worker persists in spite of federal legislation to the contrary and research that documents the values of hiring people over forty. Sheppard (1970) concluded that the worker over forty has greater experience and better judgment in decision making, and more objectivity about personal goals and abilities; "as older men, they have already satisfied many of their needs for salary and status and are able to concentrate more on job responsibilities." Employers also may attempt to buy the work skills of the retiree at wages below the standard level for the civilian population. The rationale seems to be that, since the retired person already has some income, this amount should be subtracted from salary that would be paid to a worker who was not receiving a retired paycheck. As a result, the retiree is not evaluated relative to his contribution to his employer but rather on the basis of how much money he should need to live at a level similar to his coworkers. When the retiree succeeds in finding employment, his retired pay is envied by his coworkers while there may be the implication that it is undeserved.

The retiree is expected to relinquish vestiges of his former military identity; in particular, the use of his Armed Services rank which he earned through the years. In contrast, a retired physician, minister, or college professor maintains the use of these titles. Similarly, the honorary title of "Kentucky Colonel" is held in high esteem and used with no hesitancy. When conversing with individuals who have not been career military personnel, references to prior experiences in the military may not be relevant. For example, one retiree's wife related having been criticized following a PTA meeting where she reported procedures that had been done in a PTA group while she was in an overseas country. The local people had seen the wife in the light of bragging about her foreign travels. The wife, on the other hand, was trying to participate actively in hopes of being accepted into her new community.

Many societal paradoxes are variable and influenced by time, place, circumstance, and individuals involved. Some aspects affect all retirees and are actually codified into federal legislation, i.e., Dual Compensation Laws and Conflict of Interest provisions. Dual Compensation laws, specifically aimed at retired Regular officers, do not affect enlisted personnel or retired reserve officers. Similarly, Regular officers who were retired for injury incurred during wartime combat are exempted. This legislation was designed to discourage retired Regular officers from another source of income from the federal government. Since 1894, when the first Dual Compensation laws were passed, a retired Regular officer has been required to forfeit a large portion of his retirement pay if he holds a federal government job. As a result, relatively few retired Regular officers are employed by the federal government.

Conflict of Interest legislation also dates to the decade preceding the twentieth century; the first such law was passed in 1896. Conflict of Interest legislation is intended to prevent the employment of retired military personnel by companies that do business with the federal government and, more specifically, with the Department of Defense. Many retired personnel object strenuously to these laws because of the implication that the individual would be in a position to influence military friends to buy services or products from the retiree's company of employ. Retired military personnel argue that the legislation impugns their integrity and interferes with their quest for employment.

THE NEED TO WORK

For the military retiree there is an emotional as well as a material need to work. In our culture, society demands that able-bodied adult males be gainfully employed in some type of productive work. Thus, anxiety and frustration are augmented for the retiree who is unemployed. Families of retirees are not prepared for the unemployed retiree. Wives complain about having the retiree underfoot all day, thereby disrupting the usual household routine. Younger children, especially, often have difficulty understanding their father's presence in the home during normal working hours. Retirees themselves, if in the home all day, may become critical of their wives' activities.

Problems also may arise when the wife must work to meet financial obligations. Many wives accept this as a matter of course and see working as a time-limited experience. Other wives may prefer to work outside the home. In some families there is a complete reversal of roles, and the wife becomes the primary wage earner while and the retiree assumes the household functions. The husband may feel castrated by his new role, and the wife may feel considerable hostility toward her husband. If the children are fairly young, they may find it difficult to decipher the altered roles of mother and father. The emotional impact does not affect just one member of the family but is likely to impinge upon each individual within the home.

The material need to work is epitomized by the desire to maintain an accustomed standard of living. Frequently, earnings from the civilian job, when combined with retired pay, may not equal previously received gross active-duty military pay. Table 4 indicates how much the typical retiree must earn on his civilian job to maintain his accustomed standard of living. Retired individuals at each grade level must seek civilian employment if an appreciable reduction in income is to be avoided. The higher the rank, the more that must be earned on the retirement job.

Confirming employment prior to the effective date of retirement is desired by many career military personnel. Success in this regard meets economic as well as psychological needs. Securing employment prior to retirement, however, seems to be the exception rather than the rule. In fact, the retiree should expect his job search to continue for several months following retirement. This period, in which the retiree spends seeking suitable employment, can be an agonizing time, with the retiree experiencing varying mood swings and levels of activity. Clinical observations by the author indicate that the retiree goes through four distinct phases in his search for appropriate employment. Initially there appears to be a period of optimism accompanied by considerable job-hunting activity. During this phase, the retiree tends to view other similarly unemployed retirees as persons who are not really serious about working and, therefore, have not vigorously sought work, believing that anyone who wants a job can find a job. This belief encourages him to try harder. In the second stage, practically all leads, potential leads, or even hints of leads may be pursued. Activity of this nature is reflected by increased anxiety which frequently represents wasted effort and energy. As this second phase continues, the effect of repeated

TABLE 4

EARNINGS REQUIRED TO EQUAL
ACTIVE-DUTY PAY
JANUARY 1974 RATES

Retired Pay Grade	Monthly Active-Duty Pay at 20 Years of Service	Monthly Retired Pay at 20 Years of Service	Required Monthly Earnings to Equal Active-Duty Pay
Officer			
0 - 8	$3,204	$1,433	$1,771
0 - 7	2,830	1,246	1,584
0 - 6	2,245	954	1,291
0 - 5	2,013	863	1,150
0 - 4	1,758	737	1,021
Enlisted			
E - 9	1,277	523	754
E - 8	1,139	459	680
E - 7	1,022	405	617
E - 6	915	356	559
E - 5	799	302	497

rejections begins to take its toll. In the third phase, the retiree begins to doubt his worth and employability and spends fewer hours in job-seeking activity. This phase may be constructive, however, in that greater selectivity and more orga-nized behavior allow increased attention to those prospects with greater possi-bility of success. More important, he avoids multiple rejections. Simultaneously, though, he may feel somewhat guilty about not spending more time in actual job seeking. Planning may not seem to be quite the same as actually visiting a potential employment site and being interviewed by the personnel people. Wives may interpret the retirees' behavior during this phase as not caring about getting a job or as complacency on the part of their husbands. Where the wife is engaged in pursuits outside of the home, the husband may assume an increasing share of the household tasks and antagonism between the two may increase. Some wives feel compelled to seek employment themselves; as a result, the retiree's ego may be further deflated. During the fourth phase, there is often a reduction in job expectations, and the retiree makes a more realistic appraisal of such factors as the potential labor market in his locale. He is more willing to lower his salary minimum and is more favorably inclined to accept employment in geographic areas that were his second or third choices in terms of desirability. The family, too, if they resisted a move previously, may be less resistant during this phase. Retirees are more vulnerable to employer exploitation at this time. In some ways the retiree's morale is at a new low, the financial situation may be critical or approaching desperation, and familial pressure is at a new high. Any friendship gesture that may even suggest charity or sympathy is likely to be hostilely rejected.

MILITARY RETIREMENT AS A CONTINUUM

Military retirement may be seen as a continuum that begins with the preretirement period and extends through a period of role confusion to a period of adjustment or maladjustment. Individuals approaching retirement may respond to this eventuality in individualized fashions, which essentially tend toward active or passive preparation. The extent of planning may be evaluated relative to how effectively the prospective retiree has prepared in four areas: (1) retirement activity, (2) retirement residence, (3) finances, and (4) appraisal of health. For most retired military personnel, the primary retirement activity will be seeking employment. This entails a careful evaluation of individual skills and interests and how these may be utilized in nonmilitary occupational pursuits. Active planning necessitates some realistic decision regarding retirement activity and residence. When there is urgent need for additional funds, it becomes quite difficult to make decisions selectively and wisely. The condition of health need not be a major factor except for those individuals who are retired because of medical disability, or for those cases where family members have medical problems that require special considerations.

Retirement from the military service, for most career personnel, presents an uncertain future. Approaching an unfamiliar situation can be an anxiety-producing experience. Constructive channeling of this anxiety will, in all probability, propel the prospective retiree toward actively preparing for retirement. A lack of channeling will impede effective preretirement preparatory activity. Individuals may or may not be aware of the effect that approaching retirement has on their emotions. Preretirement anxiety may be evidenced as much as five or six years before actual retirement. As retirement becomes imminent, the intensity and frequency with which it is reported are increased. Preretirement symptoms appear often enough to be grouped as a "syndrome" (McNeil and Giffen, 1965a). While the symptoms are not of themselves unique the precipitating cause—early retirement—is. The more common symptoms are complaints of anxiety, irritability, apprehension, job ineffectiveness, loss of interest, increased alcohol intake, depression, somatic complaints for which no physical basis can be found, and even overt psychotic illness. The somatic complaints frequently center around the gastrointestinal tract or cardiovascular system. Involuntarily retired personnel may present severer symptoms. They, in effect, perceive they are being rejected by the military service and being told they can no longer produce in a satisfactory manner. The intensity and type of symptoms seem to be rooted in the basic personality; the more mature the personality, the fewer the symptoms that will surface. The poorer the integration, the greater will be the inability to function or plan properly (McNeil and Giffen, 1965a).

The period immediately following retirement from the Armed Forces is a most difficult time for the retiree. He is in the throes of adjusting from a military career to a civilian setting. This period can be labeled a time of role confusion. Role in this context refers to an individual's behavior in various situations. When roles are clearly defined, we have a clear picture of expected behavior. If there is uncertainty of role performance on the part of both the individual (retiree) and society, this uncertainty produces role confusion. In role confusion, we are assuming that the individual concerned is willing and able to perform the role but lacks sufficient knowledge to do so. Role confusion is contrasted with role conflict; here the role performance is known but for some reason the individual does not perform the expected role. The retired military person usually wants to make an adjustment to civilian life but is hampered because his role has not been clearly defined (McNeil and Giffen, 1967).

Society has failed to define or structure a realistic role for the retired military person. He is usually visualized as either occupying a lucrative position in a large corporation that does volume business with the Department of Defense or as living a life of leisure on a comfortable pension. To society the retired military person's role is placed at extreme ends of a continuum where the majority do not fall, and society overlooks the space between these poles where, in actuality, the greatest percentages are to be found.

There is a marked contrast in roles between a military and a nonmilitary setting, between active duty and retired status. This contrast in roles is dramatized when one reflects briefly upon the military structure itself. There is a built-in status structure within the military establishment. Each individual's role is predetermined through tradition and written regulation. The uniform and its accompanying insignia determine the role of the individual in relation to all other persons within military society. Deviation from expected role performance is dealt with swiftly and at times harshly. Upon retirement, this symbolization and structuring of roles is lost. It is also extremely unlikely that the retired individual will make a lateral transfer in his new career, to a status equal to that which he previously held. Generally, the retiree must start at the bottom of the ladder, which represents a considerable loss of psychic income.

There are several reasons why the retiree usually starts at the bottom. Among these reasons is the fact that most industries tend to promote from within their own ranks. A new employee, generally, must prove his value to the company by moving successively through increasingly responsible positions. Another factor is the extent of transferability of skills. Skills used in the military service are not always immediately transferable to civilian occupations. It is estimated that approximately 25 percent of all military specialties are combat duties (Janowitz, 1960) and, therefore, nontransferable to civilian industry. A third factor is the extent of civilian prejudice against military retirees. It is often believed the military retiree relies upon authority and force rather than arbitration and negotiation to resolve conflict. This prejudice is also displayed through the tendency of civilian employers to underpay the labor of the retiree. He may find himself assuming a lower status position with consequently less authority and responsibility. He may find that considerable emphasis is placed upon individual achievement, whereas in the military service there tends to be greater reliance upon teamwork and group effort.

The military retiree is at a further disadvantage because he has not been accustomed to bargaining for wages. In the Armed Forces, salary scales are legislated by Congress and everyone of similar rank and seniority receives equal pay. Many retirees enter the civilian labor market with expectations of commanding a salary commensurate with that which they received while on active duty. It is a disturbing experience for retirees to learn that their worth to the potential employer is valued so lowly. Where the individual expected to have a greatly increased income upon retirement, he finds that his retired pay and earnings from civilian employment combined may be less than his active-duty pay. This is especially true for the serviceman who had received incentive or hazardous-duty pay in addition to base pay and allowances. In our culture, type of employment and earnings are indices of social position. The loss of psychic income becomes concretized through actual loss in earning power.

The retired military person may be the focus of opposition originating from his fellow employees. The retiree may be seen as an outsider who has not "grown up" with the company; yet, he either occupies a promotional position or he is in active competition for it. If the retiree has a supervisory position, he must be very careful not to pull rank in order to avoid being caricatured as a maladjusted "old soldier." Resentment may also be present if it is thought that the retiree, by holding a position, is preventing a civilian who has no additional source of income from being employed.

Members of the retiree's family also experience role confusion. A wife assumes the status level of her husband and shares his position in the social system. The military wife, who has become accustomed to expect special treatment because of her husband's rank, experiences some moments of alarm and dismay when this is no longer afforded to her. Children also experience a phase of readjustment and need, in many instances, to search for a new identity (McNeil and Giffen, 1967). An actual case example will serve to illustrate the retirement syndrome.

CASE EXAMPLE—The 40-year-old wife of an officer was seen in the hospital Family Clinic crying and visibly depressed; she expressed to the examining physician some suicidal ideation. She was referred to the Department of Mental Health for further follow-up, diagnosis, and treatment. Her husband had received a mandatory date for retirement from the service, and likewise he was becoming tense and upset. The wife complained that they no longer seemed to be able to communicate with each other and that her husband was drinking more. He had remarked to her that he believed that her personality was changing. During her husband's military tour, she had been an active member of the Officers' Wives Club and engaged with her husband and their friends in many of the activities available. Upon her husband's retirement, her symptoms became worse. She seemed to be more tearful and upset. She related that her husband either was unable or did not want to seek employment, and merely remained around the house. Although the patient was not a compulsive housekeeper, she enjoyed running her house on a schedule. Her husband's being at home markedly interfered with her functioning.

The husband was also seen at the Mental Health Clinic, and some of the problems that are fairly common in individuals going from active status to retirement were discussed with him. He was encouraged to seek employment actively, but for a while the situation did not change. The retiree occasionally would look for jobs, but he considered these beneath his ability and capability. The wife was encouraged to try to pursue her previous outlets and activities with her friends and to include her husband in these activities. Finally the husband received word that he had been accepted for a job that was to his liking. The marital relationship seemed to improve and the symptomatology that his wife presented some eight months previously began to resolve. The last information received indicated that both were progressing satisfactorily; he was still gainfully employed and she was entering into activities in the community again.

Most retirees undoubtedly make a good adjustment to civilian life. The quality of this adjustment, however, is difficult to evaluate. It is doubtful that one can completely give up an experience that has patterned the greater portion of an adult life without some observable signs or symptoms. Some insight into the extent of the adjustment can be gained if consideration is given to the following factors: (1) job satisfaction, (2) satisfaction with retirement residence, (3) maintenance of an accustomed standard of living, and (4) happiness of the family with the father's retirement. Job satisfaction implies success in changing from a military career to a civilian career. Work itself is an important ingredient in the life of every adult male, and a retiree who is not engaged in constructive employment can be suspected of maladjustment. Satisfaction with retirement residence indicates whether the individual is happy with his choice of a place to settle. Unhappiness with one's retirement residence may tend to magnify other dissatisfactions. Maintenance of an accustomed standard of living has far-reaching implications. If the retired individual finds it necessary radically to reduce his standard of living, a lowering of his self-esteem could result. It may imply to him and to others inadequacy or inability to compete sucessfully in the civilian labor market. Failure to compete would probably suggest that the individual is a misfit who can function only in the military setting. This feeling of inadequacy may lead to maladjustive behavior, causing an increase of symptoms which, in turn, further hinder productivity. In addition, familial happiness is also an important index of the retiree's adjustment. It can be assumed that family members unhappy with the father's retirement will create or intensify difficulty for the retiree (McNeil and Giffen, 1965b).

THE MILITARY FAMILY

The military community is a relatively distinct social system that, prior to World War II, traditionally dictated its own patterns of behavior. As is true in other social systems, career military personnel and their families internalized the codes and values of this community, incorporating them as a way of life (Janowitz, 1960). Few professional or occupational groups have work and nonwork roles so intermingled as is found in the military service. There is a loss of demarcation between work and home, and this tends to be more so if the family occupies a residence on the military installation. Social relationships may be weighted heavily toward activities with other military families, almost to the exclusion of nonmilitary families. Many social and welfare services are provided on the military installation that decrease the need to seek outlets in the civilian community. Examples of these resources are "Officers" and "Noncommissioned Officers" clubs, with their wives' activities that center around swimming pools, riding stables, bowling alleys, and even aeroclubs. Nurseries, kindergartens, schools, and "teen clubs" may also be provided. There are other basic facilities, such as hospitals, chapels, and commissaries. Within this type of quasi-total community, wives and children soon become aware of the military adage, RHIP, or "rank has its privileges." Each individual learns his or her position on the hierarchical ladder.

In recent years there has been some breakdown in the extent of social cohesiveness within the military community. Several factors have contributed to this breakdown, but a major one is that of a general increase in the number of people within the community. It has been necessary to maintain a relatively large military force since World War II and it has been manned largely by short-term service individuals who remain primarily civilian-oriented. A hard-core professional force is in the minority. Sufficient family housing on the military installation is not available to provide a residence for each family. Large numbers of families live in the civilian community, thus increasing the demarcation between work and social roles. Actually, though, many of these civilian communities cater to military personnel and individuals who are employed by the military. In spite of these counterforces, the family of the career military person still tends to incorporate the values of the system. As retirement approaches, its impact may be felt as strongly by family members as by the serviceman himself.

In our culture, there is usually a direct relationship between a person's earnings and his social status. After retirement many individuals are compelled to accept a lower status position than the one previously held in the military service. Status mobility, in either an upward or a downward direction, may precipitate stress not only for the individual but for his family as well. The man may lose face with his wife and children. They may cease to respect him or, even worse, come to pity or condemn him.

Some insight into family members' perception of the retiree's plight may be gained by the following excerpts from interviews with retired personnel and their families. Interestingly, when the retiree himself was asked to what extent his family seemed affected, he often replied that they were not affected. Without being asked, one wife volunteered, "It hurts me to see my husband start at the bottom again; I also hate to see other people get credit for what he does and that's what his present boss is doing." Still another wife related an incident in which a neighbor asked their ten-year-old son what he liked most about the military service and he responded that "I liked the fact that my father was an officer and I was somebody." The father at that time was employed as an assembly line worker. A retiree's eighteen-year-old daughter remarked pitifully that her father was "smart enough to do more than he is doing now."

As the husband becomes concerned about retirement, the family group may reflect this distress. The loss of security that a military career supposedly provides may trigger anxiety among the family members. Shifting from a relatively closed social system to one in which there is less specificity of roles may also pose a problem. At the time of retirement, the wife may be in a more vulnerable position with the onset of menopause and the resultant change of self-concept to which she must also adjust. The intensity of the anxiety experienced by family members may range from expressions of concern about the adjustment required, to rather severe disabling symptoms. The approach or the actuality of the husband's retirement from the military service may overwhelm family members' previously tried and proved coping mechanisms.

SUMMARY NOTE

A major thrust of this study has been to describe the elusive and nebulous quality of the concept, retirement, as it relates to the career military person. Retirement is a descriptive term that suggests a point in time during the life cycle of the individual and/or his family. Theory development has been painfully slow in the entire area of retirement and, even more so, regarding an understanding of the dynamics of retirement from the military service. Explanatory efforts have been made utilizing diverse approaches such as psychoanalytic role and crisis theories. Each approach is found lacking. Predictive quality, which is the sine qua non of any theory, simply suggests that every military retiree or potential retiree is vulnerable to emotional stress at the time of retirement and that some persons are affected more than others. There is no means of determining who will be affected to a significant degree. Complicating such predictions is that one's adequacy or masculinity may be questioned if problems are admitted, so affected persons may decide to suffer in silence. Knowledge that everyone is affected to some extent by the retirement syndrome, however, does indicate the need for organized programs that would be designed to facilitate the transition from a military career to a career in the civilian marketplace.

Earlier it was pointed out that the military services tend to see their responsibility to the retiree as quite limited. As the cost of military retirement increases, the services and benefits to retirees and their families decrease. Retirees are often powerless to influence policy in an important way that will be beneficial to them. One of the reasons for this situation was discussed before, that is, the lack of voice benefit recipients have in noncontributory retirement programs. Another reason for the retirees' powerlessness in this area is the prohibition against career military personnel being actively involved in the political arena. Upon retirement, this pattern of behavior does not change radically. Two factors, lack of political sophistication and that of being beneficiaries of retirement benefits to which the retiree did not directly contribute, work to his detriment. Two arguments against change will underscore these factors. Traditionally, Americans have demanded subservence of the military to civilian control. Involvement of military personnel in the political institution would alter this vital tenet of democracy. A contributory retirement system would amount to a massive short-term savings program in that relatively few persons who serve in the military service continue on to attain retirement eligibility. Prior to World War II, most persons remained on active duty until they were of an age that retirement to leisure was acceptable. Services and fringe benefits tended to meet most of their needs. Today other services are needed.

Budgetary policies to contain the costs of military retirement seemingly have been aimed exclusively at Department of Defense fiscal management. Since military retired pay and benefits are funded from the general tax revenue, a broader perspective of monetary control probably should be considered. For example, programs such as Project Referral and Project Transition have been discontinued. While their discontinuation is a saving for the Department of Defense budget, it increases the likelihood of retirees' applying for benefits and services through other programs. An unemployed retiree will receive unemployment benefits or enroll as a student and receive education benefits through the Veterans' Administration. Adequate preretirement services may minimize the need for other services following retirement. Money to aid the retiree is now spent after he leaves the military service, rather than before. Although the funds are channeled through another administrative structure, the source is the same general tax revenue. By denying the retiree adequate preretirement preparatory services, the probability that he and his family will be more severely affected by the retirement syndrome increases. Should this situation occur, it may delay his success in finding a job and, therefore, prolong the period of time that he is a nonproductive citizen. As a result, the individual and the national economy are negatively affected.

Families, as well as the retiree, need to know what to expect during the pre- and postretirement periods. The more information an individual has about experiences, the better he or she can cope with them. Individuals who have severe problems usually come to the attention, eventually, of medical personnel and receive at least symptomatic treatment. A preventive approach, however, could work to the benefit of all of the 60,000 career military personnel and their families who retire annually. When attention is given to the reality that retirement is a misnomer, that it is rather a change of career at middle age, then the need for retirement assistance programs becomes obvious.

Chapter 10

THE SECOND CAREER: PERCEIVED SOCIAL MOBILITY AND

ADJUSTMENT AMONG RECENT ARMY RETIREES AND

WIVES OF ARMY RETIREES

RONALD JOHN PLATTE

INTRODUCTION

One of the emerging developments in life cycle research which is currently of much interest to scholars of several disciplines is the *second career.* The possibility of middle-aged men or women pursuing second careers, after having spent a major segment of their adult lives in one occupation, can, at least in part, be attributed to the increased length of life. Increased life expectancy, as well as midlife career change, are fundamentally an outgrowth of sociocultural change, a complex set of technological, medical, scientific, and socioeconomic political advances.

The military profession is a particularly apt illustration of an occupational group in which individuals had a "first career." Retirement from the Uniformed Services generally occurs between forty and fifty years of age, when most individuals are relatively healthy and productive. Psychologically, socially, and economically, full retirement at this age is not feasible for the majority. Movement into second careers is a life cycle transition that can profitably be conceptualized at a higher level of abstraction as an instance of social mobility.

Since the first systematic sociological treatment of the subject (Sorokin, 1927), it has been hypothesized that social mobility may be disruptive to individuals and groups. This chapter explores the assumption that patterns of social mobility associated with midlife career change are related to personal and marital adjustment and attempts to find answers to the following questions: (a) Does the direction of social mobility make a difference in psychological well-

AUTHOR'S NOTE: This chapter is an adaptation of Platte, R.J. "The Second Career: Perceived Social Mobility and Adjustment Among Recent Army Retirees and Wives of Army Retirees," an unpublished doctoral dissertation prepared for Florida State University, 1974.

being? (b) Does the direction of social mobility make a difference in marital adjustment? and (c) If the direction of social mobility does make a difference in psychological well-being and/or marital adjustment, can the location and nature of the differences be identified?

REVIEW OF THE LITERATURE

The retired military population in the United States has steadily increased in size from an estimated three thousand individuals in the year 1900 (Giffen and McNeil, 1967) to nearly nine hundred thousand in November of 1972 (Glenn, n.d.). The rate of increase climbed to sixty-five thousand new retirees in 1968. Annual increments of comparable magnitude are anticipated throughout the 1970s (Biderman, 1971). Generally, the lower age limit of retired populations studied is around sixty-five years, the traditional retirement age in the United States. However, variants of this pattern have been emerging, and military careerists have been singled out by Carp (1966) as a special group which merits attention as a data source for much needed information on early retirement and second careers. The military retirement system operates primarily on the basis of years of service and health status, rather than age. According to one of the principal investigators in the substantive area (Biderman, 1971), nondisability retirement after thirty years of military service became permissible in the year 1870. Then, through changing customs and finally legislation passed in 1949, all military personnel became eligible for retirement after twenty years of service.

There seems to be a consensus about the manifest institutional functions of the early retirement system in the military (Biderman and Sharp, 1968; Janowitz, 1960; McNeil and Giffen, 1965b). These include maintaining a rank distribution which is approximately pyramidal in shape, keeping the opportunity system open for upward mobility within the organization, and providing a relatively young and healthy pool of human resources for carrying out national defense activities. Most careerists choose to retire shortly after twenty years, rather than pursuing full thirty-year military careers. Consequently, from an individual standpoint, the vast majority of military personnel are eligible to, and do, retire during what are generally seen as years of peak productivity.

In general terms, retirement benefits after twenty years of service include a minimum monthly retirement income equivalent to 50 percent of "basic pay" at the time of separation. In computing retirement pay, other active-duty financial allowances such as subsistence pay, quarters allowance, and special duty allowances are excluded. It must be remembered that a majority of the enlisted men and officers retiring from active duty are married and have children who are still living at home. This reality is rarely given more than cursory attention in the literature (Giffen and McNeil, 1967). The retiree and his dependents also retain the privilege of utilizing many of the military support facilities. However, in some matters, such as medical and dental care, active-duty personnel and their families frequently have priority over retirees. Given the limitations of retirement pay as the sole source of income, the relative youth of the retiree, and the normatively prescribed value of work in our society, it is not surprising that a second career in the civilian labor market has become the "preferred pattern" (Janowitz, 1960) over the years. Attention has been drawn to potentially problematic second career efforts and outcomes (Biderman, 1972; Biderman and Sharp, 1968). However, it seems unnecessarily limiting to restrict scientific inquiry to this level when transactions with the world of work and the larger economic sphere have implications for personal identities (Gross, 1971), conjugal relations (Scanzoni, 1970), and the psychological well-being of the individual military retiree (Garber, 1971).

Several mental health professionals have been interested in the more pervasive ramifications of military retirement. For example, McNeil and Giffen (1967) discuss the "retirement syndrome," an ill-defined but popularized term used to describe a variety of reactive disorders observed among some individuals who have retired or are preparing to retire from active-duty military service. The basic difficulty of the transition from military to civilian life appears to revolve around the radical change in life style, of which occupational change is one facet. From this perspective, outcomes are evaluated in terms of the presence or absence of clinical symptoms, the resolution of time-limited role confusion, and levels of satisfaction with the new situation overall. However, these data derived from clinical populations fall short of representing the general military retiree population because of sampling bias; the inferences made offer hypotheses to be tested rather than empirically supported theoretical assertions.

Adjustment to Military Retirement: Sample Survey Results

A large-scale survey of military retirees was conducted by the Bureau of Social Science Research (BSSR) of Washington, D.C., in the early 1960s. Jointly supported by the Department of Labor and the Department of Defense, the BSSR study focused on second career attempts among retirees from all branches of the Armed Forces. The position taken was that the "phenomenon of 'retirement,' in the new sense of midlife career change in occupational role, institution, or both, is not peculiar to the military"; it is a reflection of the more general trend toward early retirement (Biderman and Sharp, 1968: 383). They found that prior to retirement the majority of the respondents were optimistic about their chances for a smooth transition from military to civilian careers. Most (83%) planned to enter the civilian labor market immediately after retirement. A few (13%) planned to seek out a job after a period of relaxation. Over half of the officers and one-fourth of the enlisted men felt they would not experience a decline in economic well-being, even during the first year after retirement. In fact, nearly 50 percent of the officers expected to be "much better off" in the long run. Very few (3%) anticipated long-range reductions in income.

Six months after retirement, however, second career outcomes (Biderman and Sharp, 1968) indicated that initial expectations were overly optimistic. Although most were able to find civilian employment, lower incomes and lower levels of skill utilization were the rule rather than the exception. Among the unemployed minority, officers were likely to be enrolled in school or fully retired on a voluntary basis. Unemployed enlisted men were most likely to be actively seeking work. Retired army enlisted men were having the most serious reemployment problems, in that 25 percent of this subgroup were unemployed but actively seeking work six months after retirement. Closer inspection revealed that most of these unemployed enlisted retirees were former ground-combat specialists. The more highly educated officers tended to have a distinct advantage in job hunting (Biderman and Sharp, 1968).

Garber (1971) also focused on military retirement as a midlife career change. He extended the research problem to predict a relationship between direction of self-assessed occupational prestige change and psychological well-being. He hypothesized that identification with salient reference groups (military and/or civilian) would buffer the psychological impact of losses or gains in occupational prestige associated with the transition to a second career. His primary study group consisted of fully employed army retirees, residing in the Los Angeles, California, area, who, as a group, indicated a relatively high level of psychological well-being. There were variations in positive affect level associated with the direction of change in occupational prestige, however. The horizontally mobile reported the highest level of psychological well-being. Among the vertically mobile, those who had experienced prestige losses reported the lowest levels of psychological well-being. The upwardly mobile tended to be less satisfied than the horizontally mobile but more positive than the downwardly mobile.

Garber found no relationship between identification with civilian reference groups and the well-being of the horizontally mobile. Among those who experienced prestige gains, an identification with civilian reference groups modified but did not significantly diminish the negative impact of second career discontinuity. Those who reported losses in prestige *and* did not identify with civilian reference groups tended to score lower on the psychological well-being scale than the downwardly mobile who did identify with civilian groups. Identification with the military, or its absence, did not seem to be an intervening factor with regard to the psychological well-being of the horizontally and upwardly mobile. However, the downwardly mobile once again seemed to be the least well adjusted, particularly if they did not identify with either military or civilian reference groups (Garber, 1971).

Adjustment to Military Retirement: Case Study Observations

Several clinicians have speculated about the possible impact of military retirement on the individual retiree and his family. Although observations on clinical samples cannot be generalized to the larger nonclinical population of military retirees, nevertheless, like all other data collection methods, case study has its advantages as well as disadvantages. Furthermore, relevant aspects of phenomena can be more fully explicated through the use of, or findings from, studies employing different methodologies (Webb, Campbell, Swartz, and Sechrest, 1966). Therefore, it is felt that the inferences growing out of case observations are relevant in this study for generating testable hypotheses and for exploring meaningful questions.

Bellino (1969), a civilian psychiatrist interested in both the prevention and treatment of reactive disorders among military retirees and their families, suggested that a constellation of "situational dilemmas" confront the retiree. Among the attitudinally and behaviorally demanding situations are: (1) a need for civilian employment and new financial arrangements, (2) adjustment to the loss of military occupational role and social position, (3) adapting to a civilian way of life, (4) integration into a permanent community after a life of transiency, and (5) adjustment to a new and perhaps more intense pattern of family interaction. Bellino contended that the transition places parallel demands on the family of the military retiree. Because the family's social status is likely to be associated with the occupation of the husband/father, the outcome of the job hunt also has a great deal to do with family status placement and the family members' sense of well-being in the civilian community. The family's movement away from the military life style is considered demanding in and of itself.

McNeil and Giffen (1965a) conceived of a "three-phase transition model" of the retirement process which rests on the assumption that reactions to military retirement vary in relation to the specific situational forces impinging upon the individual and his basic personality characteristics. The first phase begins in preretirement. By actively preparing for anticipated changes, the prospective retiree can reduce his level of anxiety. Next, irrespective of previous actions, the period immediately following retirement constitutes a phase of "role confusion" which lasts approximately one year. Third, the period of "role confusion" is followed by a leveling-off phase characteristically dominated by reequilibrium or disequilibrium; the retiree ultimately establishes either a pattern indicative of positive adjustment or one of chronic maladjustment. Within the family, wives, in particular, seem susceptible to role confusion and identity conflict comparable to that experienced by their husbands (McNeil and Giffen, 1965a).

RELATED LITERATURE ON CIVILIAN RETIREES

Midlife Career Change

Sheppard (1969) considers displacement of middle-aged workers and their subsequent reemployment efforts as a problem in "applied industrial gerontology." He found that, among skilled workers who are displaced, those thirty-nine years of age and older had more difficulty finding new jobs than younger displaced workers. In addition, once unemployed, the "older worker" runs a greater risk of long-term joblessness. Even when reemployed, most older workers experience a reduction in wages while younger workers experience increases.

Moving beyond the dynamics of the job hunt and its outcomes, Aiken and Ferman (1966) explored the social psychological impact of technological displacement on middle-aged automobile workers. Their theoretical expectation was that different patterns of mobility (upward, downward, horizontal) following job loss would lead to different outcomes. They found that those who had multiple mobility experiences (i.e., were reemployed and then left the second job) had the strongest negative feelings and were the most likely to withdraw from intimate social relationships with relatives and friends. The upwardly mobile reemployed men who were still in their second jobs made the most positive psychological adjustment. A serendipitous finding was that men who did not go back to work at all were not significantly less well adjusted than the upwardly mobile. Aiken and Ferman (1966: 56) conclude that "more and more industrial workers are experiencing disruptions in their work careers as a result of the changing skill mix of different industries, the rationalization of work, and automation." In turn, these disruptions are of consequence to the individual's mental health and patterns of social interaction. Their observation is consistent with Gross' (1971) contention that a man's occupation is related to his sense of well-being.

Intragenerational Social Mobility and Individual Adjustment

The body of literature on social mobility is quite extensive. Wilensky (1966) was critical of the relative inattention to intragenerational social mobility; he argued that mobility associated with the work life cycle may have more of an impact on the individual. Kessin (1971), who was interested in testing Sorokin's (1927) hypothesis that vertical mobility produces interpersonal and psychic stress, found that both the upwardly and downwardly mobile were less well adjusted emotionally than the stable or horizontally mobile group. The vertically mobile also tended to interact less with extended family, friends, and other informal groups characterized by intimate patterns of interaction. The upwardly mobile tended to report high levels of anxiety and psychosomatic symptoms, while the downwardly mobile reported the lowest levels of overall emotional adjustment.

Although primarily concerned with the effects of intergenerational occupational mobility, Kessin recognized Wilensky's (Wilensky, 1966) argument that intragenerational mobility may be at least as useful an explanatory variable as intergenerational mobility. Thus, intragenerational occupational mobility can be a threat to mental health and interpersonal relations. In the light of the prevailing success ideology, the theoretical expectation and empirical observations are that the most extreme negative responses are found among the downwardly mobile, according to Blau (1956). The upwardly mobile are susceptible to similar, but less intense, reactions. Janowitz (1956) was writing in the same period as Blau, when empirical studies of intragenerational mobility were relatively scarce, and he suggested that vertical mobility is most likely to disrupt an individual's relationships with primary groups, whereas secondary group relationships may remain relatively intact.

Intragenerational Social Mobility and Marital Adjustment

Speculation about the possible effects of different patterns of career mobility on the family is found in the descriptive literature (Strauss, 1971). Except for case studies conducted during the atypical Depression years (Angell, 1936; Cavan and Ranck, 1938; Komarovsky, 1940), the effects of intragenerational mobility on the nuclear family and marital interaction are not well documented. In fact, Hollingshead and Redlich (1955) felt it was unfortunate that research has usually described social mobility effects in individual and not familial terms, particularly since available evidence suggests that other primary group relations are disrupted. Usually, the male head of the household is studied apart from his family, even though he is functionally related to and interdependent with his wife and children. As Cavan observed, mobility is "a function either of the family or of an individual. In either case, the immediate results for the family may be disruptive" (1964: 569).

THE PURPOSE

The primary effort of this study was directed toward determining whether or not there are significant differences in levels of psychological well-being and/or marital adjustment among the three social mobility groups (upward, horizontal, downward). Theoretically, relevant independent variables were also considered: (1) status concern, (2) geographical mobility, and (3) time since retirement.

Hypotheses

There were one main hypothesis and two subhypotheses put forth by this study, which were as follows:

> Main Hypothesis: The direction of perceived social mobility will make a difference in observed levels of psychological well-being and marital adjustment.
> Subhypothesis #1: Individuals who perceive horizontal social mobility will report higher levels of psychological well-being and marital adjustment than individuals who perceive vertical social mobility.
> Subhypothesis #2: Individuals who perceive upward social mobility will report higher levels of psychological well-being and marital adjustment than individuals who perceive downward social mobility.

DESIGN OF THE STUDY

Population

The population consisted of all nondisability retirees who retired from active-duty service in the United States Army between January 1, 1972 and February 28, 1973. All were retired army careerists or the wives of retired army careerists who had experienced retirement from active duty during the past twenty-four months. The following categories of retirees were excluded: (1) female retirees; (2) individuals without validated mailing addresses or with addresses indicating overseas residence; (3) Title III retirees (reservists who retired at the age of 62 without serving for an extended period on active duty); and (4) all individuals who were misclassified on the population list.

METHODOLOGY

Sampling Procedures

A relatively large sample was needed in order to have interpretable data available for testing the hypotheses on the four independent subsamples: (a) retired officers; (b) wives of retired officers; (c) retired enlisted men; and (d) wives of retired enlisted men. Oversampling through a procedure recommended by Blalock (1972) was employed to compensate for attrition rate within each subsample and to ensure adequate representation of minority groups. Controls for stratum of origin and sex were introduced at the outset. The total sample then consisted of four subsamples[1] which were approximately equal in size: (a) retired officers (319); (b) wives of retired officers (318); (c) retired enlisted men (368); and (d) wives of retired enlisted men (368).

The Questionnaire

A fifteen-page self-administered mailed questionnaire was used for the purpose of data collection and was designed primarily to measure the main variables: perceived social mobility, psychological well-being, and marital adjustment. Also included were: (a) single items to measure time since retirement and postretirement geographical mobility, (b) a composite index of status concern, and (c) other items for collecting pertinent demographic and biographical data. The reliability and validity of the scales developed for use in this study were estimated.

Measurement of Variables

Psychological Well-Being. Psychological well-being was measured by using an index constructed from Bradburn's (1969) *The Structure of Psychological Well-Being.* Modifications found viable in a pretest were included in the final measurement instrument. A difference score between positive and negative affect scores was used as the indicator of an individual's level of psychological well-being.

Marital Adjustment. In its broadest sense, marital adjustment encompasses the total range of positive and negative aspects of the marital relationship at any given point in time. Independent investigators (Bradburn, 1969; Hawkins, 1968) emphasize the need to study both aspects of marital adjustment in order to understand more fully degrees of marital satisfaction or dissatisfaction. Theoretically and operationally comparable to the scale used to measure psychological well-being, the Marital Adjustment Balance Scale (Orden and Bradburn, 1969) was used for this study.

The contention of this research project was that the perceived direction of social mobility associated with the transition from military to civilian life was central enough to the individuals concerned that variations would be observed among those who were upwardly, downwardly, or horizontally mobile.

Perceived Social Mobility. The measurement of this variable was grounded in the assumption that when a person defines a situation as real, it is real in its consequences. It has been brought out (Strauss, 1971; Svalastoga, 1964) that most of the empirical literature on social mobility is concerned with the measurement of status changes between fathers and sons (the intergenerational mobility of males). More often than not, "objective" indices, such as occupational prestige score changes, shifts from manual to nonmanual occupations, etc., are used. Consequently, there were few previously tested summated rating scales or single-item indexes available to measure self-defined intragenerational mobility. Therefore, a measurement of subjectively perceived status change (or lack thereof, in the case of horizontal mobility) between two points in the work life cycle (i.e., between first and second career) was constructed for use in this study. The use of occupational variables alone has been sharply criticized (Jackson and Curtis, 1972; Kessin, 1971; Miller, 1956) because it reduces a very complex phenomenon to an oversimple construct. Wilensky (1966) argued that, in order to understand more fully the effects of an individual's social mobility experiences, we need to consider the multidimensional aspects of continuity and discontinuity. He suggests that measures might include indicators of status change, such as occupational prestige, education, income, authority, residence, standard of living, and life style (Wilensky, 1966: 129). While this list is not intended to be exhaustive, it does convey the multidimensional measurement perspective adopted in this study.

Twelve social mobility items were constructed into an index, from which a total score was obtained for each individual. The distribution of social mobility scores was partitioned into three subclasses to represent the upwardly mobile, the horizontally mobile, and the downwardly mobile. Upwardly Mobile (UM) individuals were those whose total scores on the social mobility index were more than one-half standard deviation above the sample mean; the Horizontally Mobile (HM) were those individuals whose total scores on the social mobility index are equal to or less than one-half standard deviation above or below the sample mean, and Downwardly Mobile (DM) individuals those whose total scores on the social mobility index are more than one-half standard deviation below the sample mean. Factor analysis supported the hypothesis that the social mobility items formed a scale measuring one phenomenon.

Status Concern. Status concern was measured by a modified version of Kaufman's (1956) *Status Concern Scale.* This Likert-type scale attempts to directly measure attitudes toward status and social mobility.

Respondents and Nonrespondents. Out of the original sample of 1,373, 47.2 percent of the subjects' questionnaires were returned, and 583 returns were usable. Table 1 reveals that within the higher status group 195 (61.1%) of the retired officers' questionnaires and *186 (58.4%) of the retired officers' wives'* questionnaires were accounted for. Within the lower status group, 166 (45.1%) of the retired enlisted mens' questionnaires and *173 (47.0%) of the question-naires sent to wives of enlisted men* were accounted for. Thus, it became apparent that the response rates for men and women within each stratum were nearly identical. Respondents and nonrespondents were compared on three salient characteristics for possible sample selection bias: (a) military rank, (b) number of months retired, and (c) age. No significant differences were noted among the independent subsamples of men and women.

Description of Subjects

The resulting 583 subjects (178 retired officers, 135 wives of retired officers, 157 retired enlisted men, and 113 wives of retired enlisted men) in this study were predominantly white, married, healthy, middle-aged individuals with at least a high school education and one or more children still living at home. Table 2 shows the biographical and demographic characteristics of the total sample and the four subsamples.

With respect to ethnic background, there were far more whites (77%) than nonwhites (15%). Some individuals (9%) did not report. Relatively few officers (5%) or wives of officers (7%) were nonwhite. A larger proportion of enlisted men (25%) and wives of enlisted men (26%) did not have Caucasian ethnic backgrounds. The majority of the sample (75%) were between 40 and 54 years of age. However, some of the wives of officers (25%) and wives of enlisted men (42%) were under 40 years of age. A small percentage (7%) of the total sample was 55 years of age or older. Over half of the total sample (52%) had a high school education or less. The wives of enlisted men tended to have the least amount of formal education. Eight out of ten in this subsample had either less than a high school education (41%) or a high school diploma (41%) with no further formal education. Most of the enlisted retirees (88%) and the wives of

TABLE 1

DISTRIBUTION OF STUDY SUBSAMPLES BY DISPOSITION OF QUESTIONNAIRE WITH TEN PERCENT
ADJUSTMENT FOR NATURAL ATTRITION RATE AMONG WIVES' SUBSAMPLES

| | | | | | Subsample | | | | | | |
Questionnaire Disposition	Total No.	%	Officer No.	%	Officer Wife No.	%	Enlisted No.	%	Enlisted Wife No.	%
Accounted for	720	52.4	195	61.1	186	58.4	166	45.1	173	47.0
Not accounted for	653	47.6	124	38.9	132	41.6	202	54.9	195	53.0
Total	1373	100.0	319	100.0	318	100.0	368	100.0	368	100.0

TABLE 2
CHARACTERISTICS OF THE TOTAL SAMPLE AND SUBSAMPLES

| | Total Sample | | Subsample | | | | | | | |
| | | | Officer | | Officer's Wife | | Enlisted | | Enlisted Man's Wife | |
Variable	No.	%	No.	%	No.	%	No.	%	No.	%
Ethnic Background										
White	448	76.8	162	91.0	119	88.1	95	60.5	72	63.7
Nonwhite	85	14.6	8	4.5	9	6.7	39	24.8	29	25.7
Not Reported	50	8.6	8	4.5	7	5.2	23	14.6	12	10.6
Total	583	100.0	178	100.0	135	100.0	157	100.0	113	100.0
Age										
Under 35	17	2.9	--	--	6	4.4	--	--	11	9.7
35-39	86	14.8	6	3.4	28	20.7	15	9.5	37	32.7
40-44	229	39.3	81	45.5	40	29.6	77	49.0	31	27.4
45-49	120	20.6	34	19.1	21	15.6	42	26.8	23	20.4
50-54	89	15.3	41	23.0	30	22.2	13	8.3	5	4.4
55-59	37	6.3	14	7.9	7	5.2	10	6.4	6	5.3
60-64	4	.6	2	1.1	2	1.5	--	--	--	--
Not Reported	1	.2	--	--	1	.7	--	--	--	--
Total	583	100.0	178	100.0	135	100.0	157	100.0	113	100.0
Education										
Did not graduate from high school	74	12.7	1	.6	12	8.9	15	9.6	46	40.7
High school diploma	226	38.8	23	12.9	57	42.2	100	63.7	46	40.7
Some college	163	28.0	63	35.4	49	36.3	38	24.2	13	11.5
College degree	47	8.1	30	16.9	10	7.4	2	1.3	5	4.4
Some post graduate work	31	5.3	26	14.6	4	3.0	--	--	1	.9
Graduate degree	39	6.7	35	19.7	3	3.2	--	--	1	.9
Not Reported	3	.5	--	--	--	--	2	1.3	1	.9
Total	583	100.0	178	100.0	135	100.0	157	100.0	113	100.0

Table cont'd

| | Total Sample | | Subsample | | | | | | | |
| | | | Officers | | Officer's Wife | | Enlisted Men | | Enlisted Man's Wife | |
Variable	No.	%	No.	%	No.	%	No.	%	No.	%
Health										
Excellent	242	41.5	89	50.0	62	45.9	63	40.1	28	24.8
Good	279	47.9	82	46.1	63	46.7	75	47.8	59	52.2
Fair	49	8.4	5	2.8	8	5.9	17	10.8	19	16.8
Poor	9	1.5	1	.6	2	1.5	1	.6	5	4.4
Very poor	3	.5	1	.6	--	--	1	.6	1	.9
Not Reported	1	.2	--	--	--	--	--	--	1	.9
Total	583	100.0	178	100.0	135	100.0	157	100.0	113	100.0
Marital Status										
Presently married	555	95.2	169	94.9	134	99.3	140	89.2	112	99.1
Separated	2	.3	--	--	1	.7	--	--	1	.9
Divorced	9	1.4	3	1.7	--	--	6	3.8	--	--
Widowed	3	.5	--	--	--	--	3	1.9	--	--
Never married	14	2.4	6	3.4	--	--	8	5.1	--	--
Total	583	100.0	178	100.0	135	100.0	157	100.0	113	100.0
Number of Children Living at Home										
None	134	23.0	46	25.8	43	31.9	26	16.6	19	16.8
One	120	20.6	43	24.2	27	20.0	32	20.4	18	15.9
Two	115	19.7	27	15.2	29	21.5	31	19.7	28	24.8
Three	98	16.8	32	18.0	19	14.1	23	14.6	24	21.2
Four	42	7.2	11	6.2	9	6.7	13	8.3	9	8.0
Five or more	45	7.6	10	5.6	8	5.9	12	7.6	15	13.3
Not applicable	26	4.5	9	5.1	--	--	17	10.8	--	--
Not Reported	3	.5	--	--	--	--	3	1.9	--	--
Total	583	100.0	178	100.0	135	100.0	157	100.0	113	100.0

officer retirees (79%) had a high school diploma or a high school education with some college. The majority of the officers had either some college (36%) or a college degree (51%).

Nearly nine out of ten (89%) in the total sample reported good to excellent health. Enlisted retirees (12%) and wives of enlisted retirees (22%) were somewhat more likely than officers (4%) or wives of officers (7%) to report fair to very poor health. Nearly three-fourths (72%) of the total sample had one or more children still living at home, with very slight differences among the four subsamples in this regard.

Military Rank Distribution. The subjects in the study included the entire spectrum of the military rank structure, with the exception of the lowest four enlisted grades (E1 to E4) and the two lowest commissioned officer ranks (2LT and 1LT). Individuals at these lower levels are unlikely to be eligible for retirement unless disabled at a relatively young age before serving twenty years on active duty. Reference to Table 3 shows that the majority of the officers (52%) and spouses of officer wives (59%) were lieutenant colonels or colonels. In both enlisted subsamples, the modal grade was sergeant E7.

Years Active Duty. The majority (66%) of the total sample was credited with twenty to twenty-four years of active-duty military service. The enlisted men (61%) and spouses of enlisted wives (62%) were apparently more likely to retire with twenty to twenty-two years of active duty than were officers (48%) or spouses of officer wives (40%). The latter subsamples tended to spend longer periods of time on active duty after becoming eligible for retirement.

Months Retired. With respect to number of months retired, 234 (40%) of the total sample had been in a civilian status for thirteen to sixteen months, 159 (27%) for a year or less, and the remainder (33%) for over seventeen months. This general pattern held for all subgroups, with the thirteen- to sixteen-month retiree somewhat overrepresented among the spouses of enlisted wives.

Employment Status. Overall, the vast majority of the retirees and spouses of retirees in the sample (80%) were employed. The minority were either attending school (7%), fully retired (5%), or unemployed but still interested in a civilian job (9%). The ratio of employed officers (81%) to enlisted men (80%) was quite comparable. Spouses of officer wives (73%) were somewhat less likely to be employed than spouses of enlisted wives (85%).

RESULTS

The present study hypothesizes that the direction of social mobility will influence individual and marital adjustment. Data were analyzed and results

TABLE 3

DISTRIBUTION OF TOTAL STUDY SAMPLE AND SUBSAMPLES BY MILITARY RANK OF THE RETIREE*

Rank	Total		Subsample							
			Officer		Officer Wife		Enlisted		Enlisted Wife	
	No.	%	No.	%	No.	%	No.	%	No.	%
General Officer	3	.5	2	1.1	1	.7				
Colonel	89	15.3	48	27.0	41	30.4				
Lieutenant Colonel	83	14.2	45	25.3	38	28.1				
Captain or Major	25	3.9	18	10.2	7	5.2				
Warrant Officer 3 & 4	52	8.9	27	15.1	25	18.5				
Warrant Officer 1 & 2	61	10.3	38	21.4	23	17.0				
E9	16	2.7					12	7.6	4	3.5
E8	70	12.0					49	31.2	21	18.6
E7	124	21.3					65	41.4	59	52.2
E6	47	8.1					25	15.9	22	19.5
E5	13	2.2					6	3.8	7	6.2
Total	583	99.4	178	100.1	135	99.9	157	99.9	113	100.0

*In the case of wives' subsamples, military rank denotes the retired Army rank of their husbands.

presented separately for each of the four subsamples. In view of serendipitous findings from previous research on midlife career change, the unemployed were included in the analysis on an exploratory basis. Within each of the four subsamples, the main hypothesis that direction of perceived social mobility will make a difference in psychological well-being and marital adjustment was tested among four subgroups: (a) the downwardly mobile, (b) the horizontally mobile, (c) the upwardly mobile, and (d) those not employed. The main research hypothesis was tested utilizing one-way analysis of variance. Duncan's "new multiple range test" was employed to test the two subhypotheses when the F test results supported the main hypothesis. Product-moment correlation coefficients between three theoretically relevant variables and adjustment were computed for descriptive purposes.

Retired Officers

The pattern of social mobility within this subsample is illustrated in Table 4. Of the 178 retired officers, 53 (30%) were downwardly mobile, 41 (23%) horizontally mobile, 50 (28%) upwardly mobile, and 34 (19%) unemployed.

Perceived Social Mobility and Psychological Well-Being. Direction of social mobility did make a difference in psychological well-being among retired Army officers. The F ratio of 7.37 was statistically significant beyond the .001 level (see Table 5). The level of psychological well-being among the downwardly mobile officer retirees was significantly lower ($p < .01$) than levels of well-being

TABLE 4

PERCEIVED SOCIAL MOBILITY AMONG RETIRED OFFICERS

Social Mobility	Number	Percent
Downward	53	29.8
Horizontal	41	23.0
Upward	50	28.1
Not Employed	34	19.1
Total	178	100.0

TABLE 5

ANALYSIS OF VARIANCE: PSYCHOLOGICAL WELL-BEING
FOR RETIRED OFFICER SOCIAL MOBILITY GROUPS

Source of Variation	Degrees of Freedom	Sum of Squares	Mean Square	F Ratio	p
Between Groups	3	703.31	234.44		
				7.37	<.001
Within Groups	172	5472.48	31.82		
Total	175	6175.80			

DUNCAN MULTIPLE RANGE TEST: OFFICER RETIREES BY DIRECTION OF
SOCIAL MOBILITY AND LEVEL OF PSYCHOLOGICAL WELL-BEING*

Psychological Well-Being	Direction of Social Mobility			
	DM	NE	HM	UM
$\overline{X}$	5.40	9.03	9.33	10.42

*A line is drawn under all subsets of adjacent means that are not significantly different. Social mobility groups are arranged in ascending order of psychological well-being, from left to right.

among the three other groups. This finding supported the hypothesis that the downwardly mobile would be the least well adjusted psychologically. On the other hand, there was no reason to believe there were any significant differences between or among the upwardly mobile, the horizontally mobile, and the unemployed with respect to psychological well-being.

Perceived Social Mobility and Marital Adjustment. The main hypothesis was also supported with regard to marital adjustment among retired officers. Table 6 shows an F ratio of 3.72 with an associated probability of .01. There were no statistically significant differences in marital adjustment between the horizontally and vertically mobile or between the upwardly and downwardly mobile. However, it was found that the downwardly mobile reported significantly lower levels of marital adjustment than the retired officers who were not engaged in second careers.

Theoretically Relevant Variables and Adjustment

Strauss (1971) suggested that the dynamics of "mobility effects" are as yet inadequately understood. Therefore, in order to provide a more detailed profile of each mobility group, zero order product-moment correlation coefficients between theoretically relevant variables and adjustment were computed. The three salient variables were: (a) months retired, (b) distance of geographical mobility after retirement, and (c) status concern.

Table 7 reveals a weak relationship between the number of months retired and adjustment. This held true for each of the four retired officer mobility groups. Generally speaking, the distance of geographical mobility after retirement was also weakly related to adjustment with the social mobility groups. One exception was observed among the upwardly mobile retired officers. In this case, a positive relationship between geographical mobility and marital adjustment was statistically significant at the .01 level. It cannot be discounted as mere sampling error. The fact that the strength of the relationship ($r = .39$) was moderately low suggested other factors, in combination with social and geographical mobility, were operating.

The zero order correlation coefficients between status concern and adjustment within each social mobility group are shown in Table 8. The only statistically significant relationships were found among the vertically mobile groups. Within the downwardly mobile group, the inverse relationship between status concern and psychological well-being was statistically significant at the .01 level. It was also noteworthy that the association between status concern and marital adjustment within the upwardly mobile was statistically significant at the .05 level.

TABLE 6

ANALYSIS OF VARIANCE: MARITAL ADJUSTMENT
FOR OFFICER SOCIAL MOBILITY GROUPS

Source of Variation	Degrees of Freedom	Sum of Squares	Mean Square	F Ratio	p
Between Groups	3	903.28	301.09	3.72	.01
Within Groups	163	13182.06	80.87		
Total	166	14085.34			

DUNCAN MULTIPLE RANGE TEST: RETIRED OFFICERS BY DIRECTION
OF SOCIAL MOBILITY AND LEVEL OF MARITAL ADJUSTMENT*

Marital Adustment	Direction of Social Mobility			
	DM	UM	HM	NE
$\overline{X}$	18.56	20.17	20.90	25.3

*A line is drawn under all subjects of adjacent means that are not significantly different. Social mobility groups are arranged in ascending order of marital adjustment, from left to right.

TABLE 7

RELATIONSHIP BETWEEN MONTHS RETIRED AND ADJUSTMENT AMONG
RETIRED OFFICERS BY DIRECTION OF SOCIAL MOBILITY

Direction of Social Mobility	Adjustment	
	Psychological Well-Being *r =*	*Marital Adjustment* *r =*
Downward	.21	.11
Horizontal	-.09	-.10
Upward	-.26	-.03
Not Employed	-.14	-.13

TABLE 8

RELATIONSHIP BETWEEN STATUS CONCERN AND ADJUSTMENT AMONG
RETIRED OFFICERS BY DIRECTION OF SOCIAL MOBILITY

Direction Social Mobility	Adjustment	
	Psychological Well-Being	*Marital Adjustment*
Downward	-.40**	-.13
Horizontal	-.12	.23
Upward	-.05	.33*
Not Employed	-.25	.09

*Statistically significant at or below the .05 level.
**Statistically significant at or below the .01 level.

Wives of Retired Officers

Among the 135 wives of retired officers, there were 42 (31%) who were downwardly mobile, 32 (24%) who were horizontally mobile, 22 (16%) who were upwardly mobile, and 39 (29%) whose husbands were not employed.

Social Mobility, Psychological Well-Being, and Marital Adjustment. Direction of social mobility did not appear to make a difference in psychological well-being among wives of retired Army officers. Nor did the direction of social mobility seem to have an effect on marital adjustment among wives of retired Army officers.

Theoretically Relevant Variables and Adjustment. Examination of Table 9 reveals statistically significant zero order correlations between months retired and adjustment within both vertical mobility groups of the retired officers' wives subsample. First, there was a low to moderate positive relationship ($r = .31$) between months retired and psychological well-being among the downwardly mobile wives. Second, among the upwardly mobile wives, there was a low to moderate negative correlation ($r = -.35$) between months retired and marital adjustment.

There were no statistically significant correlations between geographical

TABLE 9

RELATIONSHIP BETWEEN MONTHS RETIRED AND ADJUSTMENT AMONG WIVES
OF RETIRED OFFICERS BY DIRECTION OF SOCIAL MOBILITY

| | Adjustment | |
Direction of Social Mobility	Psychological Well-Being	Marital Adjustment
Downward	.31*	.29
Horizontal	.19	.17
Upward	.08	-.35*
Not Employed	-.02	.20

*Statistically significant at or below the .05 level.

mobility and adjustment among the wives of retired officers. Status concern and adjustment were also basically unrelated within the mobility groups of this subsample.

Retired Enlisted Men

Within the subsample of 157 retired enlisted men, 50 (32%) were downwardly mobile, 32 (20%) horizontally mobile, 45 (29%) upwardly mobile, and 30 (19%) were not employed.

Perceived Social Mobility and Psychological Well-Being. The main hypothesis was supported in that perceived social mobility did make a difference in psychological well-being among retired Army enlisted men in the sample. The F ratio of 6.64 was statistically significant beyond the .001 level.

One subhypothesis of this study predicted that the vertically mobile would be less well adjusted than the horizontally mobile. This was not supported, in that the horizontally mobile were observed to be intermediate between the upwardly and downwardly mobile in terms of psychological well-being, and not significantly higher or lower than either. However, a second subhypothesis, that individuals who perceived upward social mobility would show higher levels of psychological well-being than individuals who perceived downward social mobility, was supported by the Duncan Multiple Range Test.

Perceived Social Mobility and Marital Adjustment. Also supported was the prediction that perceived social mobility would make a difference in marital adjustment. The F ratio of 4.65 was statistically significant at the .01 level. Although the main hypothesis was supported, it was not possible to determine whether or not the data supported the two subhypotheses. It did seem apparent, however, that the results tended to support subhypothesis #2, which predicted higher levels of marital adjustment among the upwardly mobile when compared to the downwardly mobile. The first subhypothesis did not appear to be supported in that the horizontally mobile were intermediate to the vertically mobile groups with respect to marital adjustment. It was also noteworthy that the upwardly mobile and the unemployed enlisted retirees tended to have the highest levels of marital adjustment.

Theoretically Relevant Variables and Adjustment. There was a weak negative relationship between months retired and adjustment within each enlisted retiree social mobility group. Zero order correlation coefficients between geographical mobility and adjustment were somewhat higher overall, but remained statistically and substantively insignificant.

Among otherwise negligible patterns of association, Table 11 reveals that status concern and psychological well-being co-vary to a statistically significant degree among upwardly mobile enlisted retirees.

TABLE 10

ANALYSIS OF VARIANCE: PSYCHOLOGICAL WELL-BEING
FOR ENLISTED SOCIAL MOBILITY GROUPS

Source of Variation	Degrees of Freedom	Sum of Squares	Mean Square	F Ratio	p
Between Groups	3	641.05	213.68		
				6.64	> .001
Within Groups	147	4729.67	32.18		
Total	150	5370.72			

DUNCAN MULTIPLE RANGE TEST: ENLISTED RETIREES BY DIRECTION OF
SOCIAL MOBILITY AND LEVEL OF PSYCHOLOGICAL WELL-BEING*

Psychological Well-Being	Direction of Social Mobility			
	DM	NE	HM	UM
X	3.38	5.13	6.80	8.52

*A line is drawn under all subjects of adjacent means that are not significantly different. Social mobility groups are arranged in ascending order of psychological well-being from left to right.

Wives of Retired Enlisted Men

Of the 113 wives of retired enlisted men, 30 (26%) were downwardly mobile, 25 (22%) horizontally mobile, 40 (35%) upwardly mobile, and 18 (16%) were married to retirees not engaged in second careers.

Perceived Social Mobility and Psychological Well-Being. Direction of social mobility did make a difference in psychological well-being among the wives of enlisted retirees. Table 12 reveals an F ratio of 3.48 which was statistically significant at the .01 level. The subhypothesis that levels of psychological

TABLE 11

RELATIONSHIP BETWEEN STATUS CONCERN AND ADJUSTMENT AMONG
RETIRED ENLISTED MEN BY DIRECTION OF SOCIAL MOBILITY

Direction of Social Mobility	Adjustment	
	Psychological Well-Being	Marital Adjustment
Downward	-.08	.12
Horizontal	.12	.01
Upward	.36**	.12
Not Employed	.01	.19

**Statistically significant at or below the .01 level.

well-being among the vertically mobile were not significantly lower than levels observed among the horizontally mobile was not supported. For that matter, the wives of unemployed retirees were no less personally happy than wives in other social mobility groups. On the other hand, the second subhypothesis, that the downwardly mobile wives were psychologically less well adjusted than the upwardly mobile wives of enlisted retirees, was supported by the Duncan Multiple Range Test.

Perceived Social Mobility and Marital Adjustment. Perceived social mobility did not make a difference in level of marital adjustment between or among any of the mobility groups within the subsample of retired enlisted men's wives.

Theoretically Relevant Variables and Adjustment. Analyses showed there were no statistically significant correlations either between months retired, geographical mobility, and status concern and psychological well-being or between those three variables and marital adjustment within the four enlisted wives' social mobility groups.

DISCUSSION AND CONCLUSIONS

Midlife career change, after working primarily in one occupational role and/or setting, is fundamentally an outgrowth of sociocultural change. This change is

TABLE 12

ANALYSIS OF VARIANCE: PSYCHOLOGICAL WELL-BEING
FOR ENLISTED WIFE SOCIAL MOBILITY GROUPS

Source of Variation	Degrees of Freedom	Sum of Squares	Mean Square	F Ratio	p
Between Groups	3	490.30	163.43		
				3.48	.01
Within Groups	103	4840.25	46.99		
Total	106	5330.55			

DUNCAN MULTIPLE RANGE TEST: WIVES OF ENLISTED
RETIREES BY DIRECTION OF SOCIAL MOBILITY
AND LEVEL OF PSYCHOLOGICAL WELL-BEING*

Psychological Well-Being	Direction of Social Mobility			
	DM	HM	NE	UM
$\overline{X}$	0.75	4.88	5.60	5.92

*A line is drawn under all subjects of adjacent means that are not significantly different. Social mobility groups are arranged in ascending order of psychological well-being, from left to right.

manifested in a complex set of technological, medical, scientific, socioeconomic, and political advances. Two implications for the individual are a longer life expectancy and the possibility of a second career. A phenomenon such as the advent of the second career involves status changes which are of consequence to individuals and families. The military profession provides an apt illustration of second careers among individuals who have completed one career and enter another when they are between forty and fifty years of age. The military offers a classic example of the early retirement concept and the participants provide an unusually large and accessible source of data on second career outcomes.

Since the first edition of Sorokin's *Social Mobility* was published in 1927, sociologists have hypothesized that social mobility is disruptive to individual adjustment and group relations. In addition, one common thread running through the speculative, sample survey, and case study approaches to describing and/or analyzing the impact of military retirement is the prediction that the direction of social mobility experienced by retirees who enter second careers will have psychological and social-psychological meaning to both the individual and "significant others" in his environment.

Research by Biderman and Sharp (1968) represented an early attempt to utilize systematic social survey techniques to examine factors associated with the relative success or failure of second career attempts among military retirees. Garber (1971) broadened the substantive topic by directly relating psychological well-being to self-assessed losses or gains in occupational prestige among Army retirees engaged in second careers. Observers such as Bellino (1969, 1970) and the clinical team of McNeil and Giffen (1965a, 1965b, 1967) also suggested that the direction of social mobility in second careers was related to individual adjustment after military retirement. In addition, they speculated that the retiree's family was similarly affected. Relevant research and theory related to midlife career change and intragenerational social mobility tended to support the findings based on samples of military retirees. Thus, the independent variable in this study was social mobility. The focus was on the individual's definition of the situation—his perception of downward, horizontal, or upward mobility.

The main gaps in military retirement and social mobility research up to this time have centered around the familial context of adjustment. There were no systematically collected data available to confirm or refute the assumption that family members were affected by the husband/father's second career status placement. Second, the absence of reliable data on family-related phenomena within this population prompted the selection of marital adjustment, in addition to psychological well-being, as a dependent variable.

The main hypothesis of the present study was the general prediction that perceived direction of social mobility would make a difference in both psychological well-being and marital adjustment. Furthermore, it was predicted that individuals who perceived vertical social mobility would report lower levels of adjustment than individuals who perceived themselves to be horizontally mobile. Finally, it was hypothesized that the downwardly mobile would be less well adjusted than the upwardly mobile. The unemployed were included in the study on an exploratory basis.

The broad hypothesis that the direction of perceived social mobility would make a difference in levels of psychological well-being was supported by the data from three of the four independent subsamples: (1) retired officers, (2) retired enlisted men, and (3) wives of retired enlisted men. However, perceptions of social mobility did not seem to have an effect on the psychological well-being of the wives of retired officers.

Follow-up tests on the three subsamples enumerated above provided minimal support for the first subhypothesis, which predicted higher levels of psychological well-being among the horizontally mobile when compared with the upwardly and downwardly mobile. Only the downwardly mobile officers reported lower levels of psychological well-being than horizontally mobile officers. Upwardly and horizontally mobile retired officers were not different to any meaningful extent with respect to psychological adjustment. Within the subsamples of enlisted retirees and wives of enlisted retirees, there were virtually no differences in levels of psychological well-being between the vertically and horizontally mobile. The second subhypothesis was supported in each of the three subsamples. Those who perceived downward mobility were lower in levels of psychological well-being than those who perceived upward mobility.

Turning to social mobility and marital adjustment: the independent variable did not seem to affect the marriages of wives of officers or wives of enlisted men. However, when the hypothesis was tested on retired officers and retired enlisted men, there were differences found in marital adjustment by direction of perceived social mobility. With the retired officer subsample, both subhypotheses were unsupported. The horizontally mobile did not report significantly higher levels of marital adjustment than the vertically mobile. Nor did the upwardly mobile report significantly higher levels of marital adjustment than the downwardly mobile retired officers. The noteworthy difference was between the unemployed officers and the downwardly mobile officers; unemployed officers are better adjusted in their marriages than downwardly mobile officers. The findings also indicated that perceived social mobility makes a difference in the marital adjustment of retired enlisted men, but the exact location of these differences could not be specified.

An overall interpretation of the data would suggest that direction of perceived social mobility does make a difference in psychological adjustment following military retirement. Repeated, separate tests of this general hypothesis on independent subsamples in the study led to the conclusion that this relationship is more likely to be true for retired men than the wives of retired men, although the psychological well-being of lower status wives also seemed to be affected. The primary threat to psychological well-being is downward mobility.

Comparable conditional statements might be made about perceived social mobility and marital adjustment. It would appear that perceived social mobility makes no difference in marital adjustment among wives of officer or enlisted retirees. On the other hand, social mobility does seem to affect the marriages of men, at least from their point of view. Within the subsample of retired officers, it could be said that it matters most, in terms of social mobility and marital adjustment, whether a man is fully retired on a voluntary basis or employed but downwardly mobile. The first group of individuals report the highest levels of marital adjustment, while the latter report the lowest. Definitive statements with regard to the impact of social mobility on the marital adjustment of retired enlisted men are more difficult to make, but they appear to be along the same lines as found for officer retirees.

The only difference in levels of marital adjustment that was meaningful was between the unemployed officer retirees and the downwardly mobile retired officers. The unemployed had the highest levels of marital adjustment within the subsample, whereas the downwardly mobile had the lowest. In the absence of relevant social mobility and/or military retirement research utilizing marital adjustment as a dependent variable, interpretations of this finding were tentative. The higher levels of marital adjustment among officers who were unemployed was a novel finding apparently not investigated or reported in the existing military retirement literature. Strauss (1971) makes the point that voluntary unemployment or downward mobility may have vastly different interactional consequences than involuntary unemployment or downward mobility. One of the most striking characteristics of the unemployed officers in this study was that nearly all were voluntarily unemployed. That is, they were fully retired and not interested in second careers.

Thus, if we consider the unemployed retired officers voluntarily downwardly mobile individuals, an important question would be, "How legitimate is the new status claimed by the downwardly mobile person as seen by him and others?" (Strauss, 1971: 178). Based on their higher levels of marital adjustment, it could be deduced that there was some degree of consensus, within the family at least, about the legitimacy of full retirement for officers after a military career. A fully retired colonel made a poignant observation: "Retirement goals should be agreed upon by both man and wife. After retirement, the individual should be active and maintain a regular schedule."

Possibly the status of unemployed officer retirees who are involuntarily without civilian jobs is less legitimate in the eyes of the retiree or his wife. It would have been interesting to compare the voluntarily and involuntarily unemployed with respect to levels of marital adjustment. These comparisons were not possible in this study because there were very few involuntarily unemployed officer retirees.

Basically, the findings of this study indicated that the direction of perceived social mobility can make a difference in adjustment. However, two additional questions needed to be answered: (a) for whom does it make a difference, and (b) in what way(s) does it make a difference?

It could be said that the psychological well-being and marital adjustment of retirees, irrespective of their military stratum of origin, is influenced by status changes associated with movement into second careers. The downwardly mobile are the most likely to be adversely affected. On the other hand, adjustment among wives of Army retirees is generally less influenced by social mobility.

Deleterious psychological consequences did seem to accompany downward mobility among the wives of retired enlisted men, although marital relationships were not affected. Perceived social mobility had little or no effect on either the psychological well-being or the marital adjustment of wives of retired officers. It was concluded that it is advantageous in social mobility research to include women and to control for stratum of origin and sex.

This study has examined only the effects of social mobility associated with movement into second careers on psychological well-being and marital adjustment; other factors may be important determinants of adjustment. Finally, it should be remembered that adopting a second career in middle age, after a full career in the military, constitutes but one case of a broader subject; namely, adopting a second career on the part of *any* person after completing *any* first career.

NOTES

1. The men and women in this study are *not* couples. *Either* the sampled retiree *or* his wife was sent a research packet. This approach was adopted for two reasons: (1) to minimize the possibility of spurious results owing to husband-wife collaboration when completing the questionnaire; and (2) to maximize the probability of statistical independence and therefore bolster confidence in the empirical findings as they relate to these four groups of individuals.

V

OVERVIEW OF RESEARCH

Chapter 11

RESEARCH ON THE MILITARY FAMILY: A REVIEW

HAMILTON I. McCUBBIN
BARBARA B. DAHL
EDNA J. HUNTER

THE LEGACY OF FAMILY RESEARCH IN THE MILITARY

In any review of family research in the Armed Forces, it is essential to keep in mind the political and social context in which such developments or lack of developments occurred. The history of the military, its mission, its perception of the role of the family within the military, and the Zeitgeist of the behavioral sciences in the military provide the perspectives required to appreciate the evolution of research on the family in the military system.

Although the Family Studies Branch of the Center for Prisoner of War Studies (an Army-Navy-Marine Corps activity within the Naval Health Research Center) was established as late as 1972, many of the myths, assumptions, and prejudices which had previously shaped the course of research on the military family were inherited. It is a frustrating legacy of intermittent research activity in the face of a myriad of obstacles and overt resistance by a military system unsure of the value of such scientific inquiries. The basis for such a legacy is complex and woven into the fabric of the military as an institution. Historically, the military has been concerned with the single man (Bennett, Chandler, Duffy, Hickman, Johnson, Lally, Nicholson, Norbo, Omps, Pospisil, Seebert, and Wubbena, 1974; Janowitz, 1960; Little, 1971; Moskos, 1970). As recently as 1952, the marriage rate for enlisted personnel was as low as 29.7 percent (U.S. Department of the Army, 1973). In the "old" military the saying, "if Uncle Sam wanted you to have a wife, he would have issued you one," had special meaning and served as a warning against family interference with the demands of military

AUTHORS' NOTE: This chapter is an expanded version of McCubbin, H., Dahl, B., and Hunter E. "Research on the Military Family: An Assessment," in Goldman, N., and Segal, D. *Proceedings: Research Conference on the Social Psychology of Military Service,* Inter-University Seminar on Armed Forces and Society, 1975, pp. 117-144. Military family research publications completed during the period from 1940 to May 1975 were reviewed in this chapter.

[291]

life. It also served as a reminder of the importance of unit solidarity and the priority of the military mission. Janowitz (1960: 178) pointed out that in the single man's army, "the problem of choosing between work and family life did not exist." A military organization and a community evolved emphasizing esprit de corps. The military family was viewed as an integral part of this total system which defined the role of the family in terms of the husband's rank and social status in the system. The predominant attitude which prevailed was that the family, and in particular the serviceman's wife, played an important but subordinate role in the husband's career. Satisfied with the status of the military family, the military community was not particularly concerned with the search for knowledge about family development and functioning. Social and psychological problems were absorbed by the military community: "The military took care of its own."

Despite the ever changing profile of the military toward a "married man's army" (Bennett et al., 1974; Little, 1971) and the changing patterns of military community life away from its Gemeinschaft-like qualities and away from solidarity (Coates and Pellegrin, 1965; Janowitz, 1960), the military system has been slow to recognize the need for a reexamination of the assumptions and prevailing philosophy regarding the military family. Policy makers have tried to maintain a delicate balance between meeting family needs through medical and community services and establishing the "priority" of preparing men for combat.

Since the late 1940s, the growth of behavioral science research, represented by the emergence of large civilian and military laboratories to investigate various aspects of performance, behavior under stress, and human effectiveness, has been reinforced by the military's mission to create and maintain a combat-ready military institution. Therefore, research emphasis has constantly been placed upon selection procedures, troop morale, combat effectiveness, and socialization of the soldier into military life. It was not until recently that family research was even considered as a possible approach to understanding the development and functioning of military personnel.

FOCI OF RESEARCH ON THE MILITARY FAMILY

It was primarily during and immediately following World War II that the importance and feasibility of conducting scientific investigations with military families became generally recognized and accepted (Boulding, 1950; Eliot, 1946;

Hill, 1949). This period was characterized by significant strides toward the goal of identifying relevant factors which are associated with the effects of war on family life (Freud and Burlingham, 1943; Waller, 1940, 1944). Two purposes were served by the literature of this era: (1) to illustrate the extreme importance of understanding the military family, and (2) to demonstrate the significant value of studying families under stress. One need only review the findings of a few of these and more recent studies to recognize that the "military family" is influenced by a host of acute and chronic stresses related to, if not unique to, life in the military. No other large group is exposed so uniformly to the pressures of father absence and geographical mobility (Gonzalez, 1970).

From the available literature on military families, all identifiable and obtainable research articles, along with the most scholarly clinical and descriptive papers, were selected for review in the present chapter. Although this review is not exhaustive, care was taken to include as many of the studies as possible in order to reflect the full range of research or clinical investigations undertaken on the military family. Attempts to classify these research and clinical articles into existing classification schemes of families under stress (Hill, 1949; Hill and Hansen, 1964; Parad and Caplan, 1960) presented difficulty, since no single system appeared adequate. Final categorization of the studies was accomplished by adhering to the topics to which the students of family research are most likely to refer: Mobility, Child Adjustment and Development, Adjustment to Separation, Family Reunion and Reintegration, Adjustment to Loss, Families in Transition, and Services to Families under Stress.

I. GEOGRAPHICAL MOBILITY

The few studies dealing with how the military family system is affected by geographical mobility have emphasized the uniform exposure of the family to the pressures of frequent moves within the United States and foreign countries. Several studies have focused upon the negative effects of living experiences fashioned out of a series of transiencies which can produce a segmented, discontinuous, and uninvolved existence. Bower (1967: 790), in his survey study of army families in overseas communities, found that although many families find overseas duty an exhilarating and highly educative experience, "the phenomenon of 'culture shock' is a real and significant fact to many families living in Europe. For many, the familiar cues of living are gone." Bower contends that problems associated with relocation can be attributed to the loneliness felt by the wife, who finds it difficult to accept the change in life style and is unable or unwilling to become involved within the host country. McKain (1969, 1973) came to a similar conclusion in his study of 80 enlisted army families interviewed just after having made a move. His findings indicated that the army family likely to experience the greatest incidence of family problems associated with geographical relocation is the family in which the wife/mother feels alienated from society and from the community. Furthermore, McKain found that the greatest incidence of family problems are associated with moving when the family resides off the military post.

Marsh (1970) focused on the economic instability of the military family, in particular the enlisted family, engendered by frequent moves. After viewing the frequency and type of disruption families experience during moving in his study, involving 205 army enlisted families, Marsh concluded that the military requires them to move but fails to subsidize the move fully and, therefore, forces the family into a financial crisis which further complicates the family's already overtaxed emotional and social stability.

Family mobility, an inherent aspect of military life, may have detrimental effects upon the children's emotional and social development. Coates and Pellegrin (1965), in their extensive volume devoted to the study of American military institutions and military life, focus on the social-psychological costs of frequent geographical relocation to the children in a military family. These authors stress the fact that not only must the children become accustomed to giving up old friends and establishing new ones when each move occurs but are also faced with the problem of changing from one school to another, which considerably complicates their educational experiences. The child has to adapt to several school programs, teachers, and classmates and attempt at each locale to take up where the thread of life has left off. Kurlander, Leukel, Palevsky, and Kohn (1961) reported a median of six geographical moves for military children referred to a child guidance clinic. Although Pepin (1966), in his study of three groups of high school students (a military mobile group, a nonmilitary mobile group, and a nonmobile group) in the same community, found no significant differences among the three groups with regard to the number of residential and school changes and the number of personal adjustment problems on eight of eleven categories of the Mooney Problem Cheklist, there were significant differences in three problem areas: (1) finances, living conditions, and employment; (2) curriculum and teaching procedures, and (3) adjustment to schoolwork.

Gonzalez (1970), in his case studies of military "brats" referred for psychological help, emphasized that children, particularly adolescents, have to discontinue their immediate, familiar life pattern, and depend primarily on the type of ties that exist within the family. He also found that younger children primarily react not to geographic change but to the emotional changes in the parents, and that generally the children's reactions to moves depend on the emotional relationships in the family prior to moving. Pedersen and Sullivan (1964) corroborated this observation that parental attitudes toward mobility were important in determining the child's ability to adjust to the move. In their study of 27 emotionally disturbed military children and 30 matched normal military children, although the incidence of geographical mobility in the histories of the children did not differentiate the groups, parental attitudes did. Mothers of normal children appeared significantly more accepting of frequent relocation, and both parents of the normal group showed significantly stronger identification with the military community.

II. CHILD ADJUSTMENT AND DEVELOPMENT

A number of studies have emphasized the thesis that children growing up in the military are unique because of positive aspects of life in the military system. Lyon and Oldaker (1967), in their descriptive study of military dependents in an elementary school system, pointed out the unique sense of security afforded this population, such as the fact that each has a working father (or stepfather) presently living with the child's mother. In addition, these authors indicate that there is relative homogeneity among these children, since among military men there is little income differential, except for the officer-enlisted dichotomy; there is free medical care available to the families; and all the fathers tend to be at least average in intelligence. When Kenny (1967), in his study of American children living in a military community in Germany, found that the military children were significantly higher in IQ and had better school adjustment and less juvenile delinquency than the United States child population as a whole, he, too, explained these differences by the fact that the military is a "select community."

Several investigators have taken the opposite point of view, stressing the nonapplicability of this "uniqueness" phenomenon. Blochberger (1970) studied 30 families of military men in an effort to assess the potential influences of the military on the family's life style. The focus of this investigation was whether military families were more alike than different and whether the location of family residence, on or off post, was important in differentiating military life styles. From his observations he concluded that it was a fallacy to consider only one "type" of military family, but went on to state that the on-base families were more easily described by the characteristic of similarity in their attitudes and their sources for activities than off-base families where diversity was the theme. Darnauer (1970), in his investigation of adolescents and their parents in 60 career army families, suggested that teen-age development in the Army may not be unique. In fact, his data indicated that, in general, neither the adolescents nor their parents appeared to view adolescent life in the army family as dissimilar to adolescent life in civilian communities. The major difference or unique aspect of military life was the adolescents' vulnerability to relocations.

Children, by virtue of their youth, proximity to a war, or because of a family member's involvement in a war, are extremely vulnerable to the direct as well as the indirect stresses of war. A number of studies during World War II and more recently, during the Yom Kippur War in Israel, have pointed up the traumatic effects of war upon children's emotional and social development. Freud and Burlingham (1943), in their clinical study of children in three nurseries in England during World War II, observed children's reactions to bombing, destruction, and early separation from families. They concluded that war has a direct effect upon the children in that it disrupts homes and causes enforced separations and also causes anxiety in parents "which is almost without exception reflected in the child." In a clinical-descriptive report of children whose fathers or brothers enlisted in the Armed Services during World War II, Gardner and Spencer (1944) found that among the "delinquent group" (children referred to the juvenile court), in more than half the cases the first offense occurred following the enlistment. Milgram and Milgram (1975) compared pre- and postwar anxiety levels in Israeli children (85 fourth- and fifth-graders) and discovered that the general anxiety level of the children nearly doubled, with the children who reported the lowest prewar anxiety levels reporting the highest postwar levels. Contrary to expectation, however, the rise in the anxiety level was not related to war-related stress or personality parameters, but to socioeconomic status, sex, and intelligence. Ziv (1975) also investigated manifest anxiety levels of children from different socioeconomic backgrounds before and after the Yom Kippur War and found that only among children from lower socioeconomic backgrounds did level of anxiety increase significantly. Kedem, Gelman, and Blum (1975), in their study conducted shortly after the Yom Kippur War, attempted to evaluate the effects of the war on the attitudes and values of young adolescents. In their responses to a questionnaire, subjects, who were junior high school students, indicated that the war had a strong effect on their political-social attitudes but the amount of active participation of members in the war did not affect the students' attitudes.

Additional studies carried out recently during the Arab-Israeli conflicts have investigated children's responses to family deaths owing to wartime casualties. Smilansky (1975) and Lifshitz (1975) investigated the perception of death by Israeli children and the environment's influence on this perception to assess the need for professional intervention in helping children with the bereavement process. Weider and Nashim (1975) noted parallel reactions among young children and their mothers during the missing in action and notification of death periods. The children evidenced such behaviors as regression and sleep disturbances which appeared to be in response to the loss of their mothers, who went into varying stages of psychological suspension, depression, regression, and rage.

But what about the long-term effects of war-related stress? Studies concerning second generational effects of the concentration camp experience, i.e., its effects upon the children of survivors, have emphasized the value and need for longitudinal studies to address this question. Dor-Shav (1975), who compared concentration camp survivors and their children to control groups on a battery of clinical tests, found differences between the groups with regard both to personality factors and to aspects of perceptual-cognitive functioning. Evidence of impoverishment of the personality, and particularly their inner life, was found on the Rorschach, and there were indications of problems in affectivity.

Rakoff (1966), in his description of three adolescent children of concentration camp survivors displaying severe psychiatric symptomatology, indicates that it would almost be easier to believe that they, rather than their parents, had suffered. Rakoff, Sigal, and Epstein (1967), in their clinical studies of families of concentration camp survivors, describe numerous features which these families have in common. They observed a deterioration in the organization of the family and found limit setting by the parents as either rigid or chaotically ineffectual, but rarely related to the needs of the child. In addition, they reported that the children lacked appropriate involvement in the world. While in some cases, apathy, depression, and emptiness often appear, in other cases they discovered an agitated hyperactivity reflecting great dissatisfaction with parents and society at large. They conclude that, after a relatively brief clinical inquiry, what usually emerges is that there is not one disturbed member but that the family itself is a collection of severely disturbed and traumatized individuals.

In a more sophisticated clinical study, Sigal and Rakoff (1971) observed 32 families of concentration camp victims as well as 24 clinical controls. Their findings indicated that, when compared to control families, concentration camp families showed significantly more complaints of excessive sibling rivalry, overvaluation of the children, and difficulties in self-control or control of the behavior of the children. The authors postulated a causal link between the preoccupation of the parents and the problems in the family. In a later study involving 25 adolescent children of concentration camp survivors and 20 controls, Sigal, Silver, Rakoff and Ellin (1973) found that the children of the concentration camp victims had more behavioral and other disturbances and less adequate coping behavior than the controls. Once again the authors suggested parental preoccupation as a contributing factor—the parents were viewed as seeing their children's needs as an interference in the mourning process or as an extra burden. As a further test and confirmation of Sigal et al.'s (1973) thesis of a relationship between the stresses of captivity and the father-child relationship following father's return, McCubbin, Dahl, Lester, and Ross (1975b) found that among the numerous background, family adjustment to separation, psychiatric, and stress of captivity variables collected on 48 returned American PWs from Vietnam and their families, the stresses (psychological and physical) of captivity were isolated as the critical predictors (negatively related) of the father-child relationship one year after the family reunion.

III. ADJUSTMENT TO SEPARATION

Family separations owing to wartime assignments, unaccompanied tours, and repeated temporary duty assignments have a profound impact upon the family system and the emotional health of its individual members. Fagen et al. (1967), in their investigation designed to examine the pattern of factors, both predispositional and mediational, which relate to differential adjustment to father absence in 23 army families, stressed the importance of recognizing the possible differential impacts of the father absence "crisis situation" and its potential for facilitating more adaptive or less adaptive modes of behavior. In Hill's (1949) classic study of families who experienced separation because the husband/father served in the military during World War II, the degree of adjustment was judged by effectiveness of role reorganization, by degree of accompanying nervous strain and emotional maladjustment, and, in general, by whether the family continued to satisfy the needs of its members. Hill (1949) concluded that the family's adjustment to separation was a function of (1) the wife's perception of the separation; (2) the resources the family brings to the situation; and (3) the hardships of the separation.

Numerous studies have emphasized the emotional and social problems associated with the wives' adjustment to separation. Lindquist (1952), in her study of 52 Air Force (SAC) families, reported the deleterious effects of frequent separation on family life. Findings of this survey study indicated that family stability was endangered by wives' fear of philandering, assumption of the matriarchal role, and/or reliance on relatives for emotional support and protective functions. MacIntosh (1968) found that a significant number of military wives who were referred to a psychiatrist had symptoms directly related to separation. In his comparative study of 63 military wives experiencing psychiatric disturbances while separated from their husbands for military reasons, MacIntosh, like Belt and Sweney (1973) in their study of Air Force wives, suggested that separations for a military wife may be a developmental task which is more difficult early in life and becomes easier with practice. Furthermore, both studies emphasize Hill's (1949) thesis that the wife's perception of the husband's absence is a critical factor in determining her response to the separation.

Frances and Gale (1973: 172) also indicate that periodic separations tax the resourcefulness of the military and its families. They point out that the most dramatic separation is the assignment of the husband/father overseas, perhaps under threat of death or injury, where wives' fantasies take various forms—"of abandonment, incapacitation, or, on the other hand, hope that his safe return will lead to a higher level of harmony. A particularly common hope is that sexual appetite and performance will be improved, denying that the causes of deficits in sexual relatedness prior to separation will still exist." Bey and Lange (1974), in their study of 40 noncareer army wives whose husbands were serving in Vietnam, concluded that waiting wives experience many demands and frustrations and might benefit from preventive psychiatry programs during husband/father absence.

The extreme situation of a husband missing in action or a prisoner of war brings into focus the complexity of prolonged separations. In this situation the normal emotional and social adjustment processes are thwarted and complex adjustments in the family's life style are required. In a study of 40 Navy PW/MIA wives, Hunter and Plag (1973) indicated that these families had experienced a variety of adjustmental problems, paramount among these being emotional and legal difficulties. Nelson (1974) stressed that the legal complications were, in part, a function of the length of absence; for these women, even simple legal transactions, e.g., sale of homes, stocks, and other belongings, were often complicated by the fact that powers of attorney had expired. McCubbin, Hunter, and Metres (1974) and McCubbin, Hunter, and Dahl (1975), in their study of 215 PW/MIA families, emphasized the extreme complexity of prolonged separations and their effect upon the family; 31.3 percent of the wives were either receiving therapy or had been in treatment at some time during husbands' absence. An additional 51.4 percent appeared to be in need of psychological assistance. In a clinical, treatment setting with eleven wives of men who were listed as prisoners in Vietnam, Hall and Simmons (1973) also found that these wives' major concerns centered around problems caused by the husbands' leaving the family structure: problems of role definition, problems of sexual adjustment, and problems caused by isolation. Furthermore, these investigators reported that the single most important issue for these wives was their ambivalence concerning their husbands' return and subsequent guilt that these feelings engendered. Their observations are reminiscent of Isay's (1968) "submariners' wives syndrome," in which the wife experiences sleep disturbances, depression, irritability, etc., shortly before or after the return of her husband from sea duty. Isay postulated that the primary etiologic factor of this "syndrome" appeared to be an unacceptable rage over desertion and suggested that a contributing cause of the depression may be the loss, when the spouse returns, of one or more of the gratifications that the separation provides—e.g., resumed dependency upon parents, opportunity to assume masculine or shared responsibilities, avoidance of physical or emotional intimacy with the marital partner.

Brown and Huycke (1974) described the burden placed upon the mother to raise the family single-handedly and pointed out that, in spite of the PW/MIA wives' efforts to perform their roles well, the wives received little satisfactory feedback and had to deal with the realization that there were few if any socially acceptable outlets to enhance their self-esteem. In group discussions with PW/MIA wives, Hunter, McCubbin, and Metres (1974) and Benson, McCubbin, Dahl, and Hunter (1974) also indicated that socializing appeared to be a very difficult area of adjustment for these women. One of the problems voiced by the women was that they were handicapped by not finding a proper social outlet, and dating often resulted in both guilt feelings and feelings of frustration. Price-Bonham (1970), in a study of 32 wives of men missing in action in Vietnam, corroborated this finding; social life was the most unanimous problem of the women interviewed—wives reported feeling out of place, unable to fit in with any social group.

Although the majority of studies which touch on the subject of coping with separation, i.e., how families and wives, in particular, respond to and endure the hardships engendered by short-term and prolonged separation, have tended to emphasize the dysfunctional responses to separation, Fagen, Janda, Baker, Fischer, and Cove (1967), on the basis of a battery of psychological tests and clinical interviews, attempted to define functional as well as dysfunctional patterns of wives' adjustment.

They described four groups of wives: (1) anxious but adaptive wives were realistic, sought support, and exhibited self awareness; (2) anxious but maladaptive wives denied problems, emphasized loneliness, and indirectly sought help; (3) nonanxious but maladaptive wives indulged themselves in sadness and discouragement; and (4) stable and adaptive wives met problems head on and were efficient in problem solving. McCubbin, Dahl, Lester, Benson, and Robertson (1975) also stressed the need for more definitive and objective measures of the family's coping responses to separation; they attempted to delineate a broader range of responses to separation, one which would emphasize the positive aspects of adjustment, not just the idiosyncratic and pathological behaviors. On the basis of data obtained from wives adjusting to prolonged war-induced separations, these investigators were able to isolate six coping patterns: Seeking Resolution and Expressing Feelings (I); Maintaining Family Integrity (II); Establishing Autonomy and Maintaining Family Ties (III); Reducing Anxiety (IV); Establishing Independence through Self-Development (V); and Maintaining the Past and Dependence on Religion (VI). These patterns appeared to be a function not only of the wives' background, education, and occupation, the husbands' education and career commitment, and the families' development (quality of the marriage) but also of the stresses that the families were forced to face during the prolonged separation. Boss (1975) in studying these same families identified "maintenance of psychological father presence" as an additional coping mechanism, but found it to be dysfunctional.

Although Duvall (1945) indicated that the wife experiencing the loneliness of husband absence may find that children restrict her outside participation, the wife may also view the children as a source of support and comfort. Yet, the children are also subject to direct and indirect stresses resulting from father's absence and/or mother's adjustment to the stresses of separation. Gonzalez (1970), in his clinical case studies of children experiencing father absence, indicated that the loss of father's valued presence may precipitate symptoms of grief, depression, and anxiety, and the child may feel deprived of a source of comfort, pleasure, and security.

Murphy and Zoobuck (1951) reported on 50 consecutive case referrals of school adjustment problems to a military child guidance clinic. In rank-ordering those factors in military life which appeared most stressful in the cases studied, the investigators found that the most important was absence of the father from the home—64 percent of the cases had a family history of father absence for over six months. The study of father absence by Baker, Cove, et al. (1968) emphasized the mother's difficulty in maintaining family controls as a factor in the children's behavior problems. Social introversion and associated feelings of loneliness by the children were common in their particular study group. Igel (1945), in his clinical study of father absence owing to wartime military duty, observed children referred for treatment because of parental reports of undesirable behavior occurring after the father's enlistment. He postulated that when the father-child relationship was sound, absence might be felt more in the beginning but recovery would take place faster. Gonzalez (1970) and Trunnell (1968a, b) also stressed the fact that the child's reaction depends on numerous variables, including the father-child relationship and the role of father in the family.

Baker, Fagen, et al. (1967) compared a group of boys from military families whose fathers were absent with a group whose fathers were present and found increased masculine striving and poorer peer adjustment among the father-absent group. Gabower (1960) compared a group of 15 military children referred for psychological treatment and a control group of military children and found that although no marked differences appeared between the two groups in relation to the length of separations from the father, each child in the behavior problem group had had more separations than the controls. The greatest difference between Gabower's two groups was that while many in the control group expressed their need to have Dad at home, none of the children in the behavior group expressed such a need. In a similar study, Pedersen (1966) compared 27 disturbed male military dependents with 30 controls and found that within the disturbed group the extent of father absence in the child's history was highly predictive of an independent index of emotional disturbance.

McCubbin, Hunter, and Metres (1974) observed, in group discussions with children whose fathers were missing in Vietnam, that, unlike their mothers, the children's reactions did not appear to be attributable to the grieving process, but rather to the emergence of various struggles with identity formation and interpersonal relationships which may be unique to children at different ages. Several other studies have mentioned the "age" factor as crucial in understanding the adjustment of a child to his father's absence. Dickerson and Arthur (1965) and Brown and Huycke (1974) have emphasized the harmful nature of separation during critical stages of development in both boys and girls—stages that require a father figure in order to proceed satisfactorily. Seplin (1952) compared 43 children who had experienced father absence during the "early years" to their 43 siblings who had not experienced father absence in the early years to discern the effects on the child's later development of the father's absence from the home for military service. When the children in the study group gave evidence of being more deeply disturbed than the control group, Seplin concluded that the disturbances were directly attributable to the father's period of military service during the child's "formative years." However, in the Pedersen (1966) study, cited earlier, the data did not support an effect specific to a particular age period. In investigations with children of returned prisoners of war (Dahl and McCubbin, 1974, 1975) and children of servicemen missing in action (Dahl, McCubbin, and Ross, 1975), findings indicated that these children, who had experienced extended periods of father absence (a mean of 5 years), revealed significantly lower personal and social adjustment scores than the norms on the *California Test of Personality*. To explain the contradictory findings that age was not a critical factor, investigations like Hillenbrand's (1970) study of 126 Marine children, postulated that the detrimental effects of separation upon the older child may have been offset by the added responsibilities of new role assignments—the older child, who occupies the position of "responsible one" among his siblings, may have been reinforced for this role and consequently benefited from the total experience.

One aspect of family separation often overlooked is the adjustment of parents of sons who are serving military duty during wartime, more specifically, those of sons who do not return. In group discussions held with 79 parents of MIAs,

McCubbin and Metres (1974) found that grieving was a major facet of the parents' total adjustment process; as a whole, mothers especially needed to talk about their experience, grief, frustrations, and aspirations, whereas fathers needed help in expressing their feelings and getting in touch with their hidden anger and frustrations. Hunter, McCubbin, and Benson (1974) also found that mothers of sons missing in action approached the stresses of separation by making unique demands upon themselves and upon others. For most mothers there was a never-ending search for answers and a constant struggle with their feelings about their sons' loss. For them answers could only be found by the "full accounting" of their sons' whereabouts and through reference to religion. Religious retreats offered parents a chance to express their feelings and renew their trust in others.

FAMILY REUNION AND REINTEGRATION

Reuben Hill (1949), in his study of 135 families who experienced separation and reunion in World War II, concluded that family reunion was an extremely complex process and could not be understood without taking into consideration the family's history, characteristics of family members, the family's adjustment during the separation, as well as family interactions at the time of the reunion. He emphasized that the process of reunion involves the reestablishment of bonds of coherence and family unity, of which the husband-wife relationship, the division of labor within the home, the reallocation of roles, the revitalization of the father-child relationship, and the stabilization of husband-wife, mother-child, and father-child relationships are paramount.

Numerous other investigators (Brown, 1944; Cuber, 1945; Griffith, 1944; Hill, 1945) have also consistently indicated that reintegration into the family system is a major stress requiring an extensive effort on the part of the family as well as of the returning serviceman. Schuetz (1945), in a descriptive study of returning World War II veterans, pointed out that men away from their families tended to idealize persons, places, and past events, and they returned to their families with a distorted view of how things really had been when they left. While a returning serviceman may recognize changes in himself resulting from the stresses of war, he is often apt to forget that those who remained at home may also have changed (Cuber, 1945).

Certainly, separation has a profound and disturbing effect upon the family unit during the serviceman's absence, and this may, in turn, have an effect upon the reunion. Hill (1949) emphasized the wives' difficulties in coping with their husbands' absence, particularly in the areas of role adjustment and emotional adjustments. For most families, adjustment to separation involved the process of "closing ranks" (closing out of the husband's role) in order for the family to develop a more efficient and functional pattern of operation. Although closing ranks was an essential feature of coping with separation, among Hill's families it was found to precipitate difficulties at the time of reunion. For the wives who experienced prolonged separations, reunion posed a threat to one or more of the gratifications that separations provide, i.e., the opportunity to assume greater freedom, the latitude to determine the use of their income, and the avoidance of any confrontation with the manner in which they had conducted themselves during their husbands' absences (McCubbin, Hunter, and Dahl, 1975; Metres, McCubbin, and Hunter, 1974).

With the exception of recent research on families of servicemen missing in action (MIA), returned prisoners of war (RPW), and families of servicemen listed as prisoners of war (PW), only one major research investigation on family reunion has appeared since the classic studies following World War II. Baker, Cove, Fagen, Fischer, and Janda (1968) studied the effects of father absence and reunion upon the family system and its individual members. In a comparative study of 12 separated and 6 nonseparated families, the investigators revealed that the returning servicemen did not realize the changes in the family system which had evolved in their absence and expected to resume the position of power in the family after they returned. Emotional struggles, particularly feelings of rejection, emerged, making the reestablishment of affectional bonds between husband and wife and father and child extremely complex and difficult.

Investigators at the Center for Prisoner of War studies, through their longitudinal research efforts, have attempted to replicate and expand upon the studies carried out following World War II by placing particular emphasis upon the long-term effects of dismemberment and subsequent reunion upon the family system. Segal (1973) discussed the fact that the returned prisoner of war carries to all his interpersonal relationships, particularly to those with his family, the remorse, anger, and frustrations engendered by his unique and stressful experiences during captivity. Hall and Malone (1974), on the basis of in-depth and continuing interviews with six families of returned prisoners, emphasized the potentially disturbing effects of the psychiatric residuals of the stresses of captivity upon family reunions. The returning man, having experienced the extremes of physical and psychological abuse, is also vulnerable to feeling rejected and overwhelmed by the changes in the family system and his children. Reunion, for some men, was characterized by withdrawal, isolation, and feelings of not being wanted or being estranged from their families.

The problems and stresses encountered by the wives of returned prisoners of war during the separation period have been causally linked to the initial conflicts surrounding family reunions. On the basis of a study of 215 PW/MIA families, McCubbin, Hunter, and Dahl (1975) noted that the social and psychological stresses of prolonged separation encouraged families to develop behaviors and styles of life which lessened the probability of successful reunions. Wives' independence and personal growth as well as their movement toward total autonomy during their husbands' absences, in part fostered by women's liberation, contributed to conflicts and confrontations between husband and wife at the time of the reunion—the returning serviceman was confronted with changes in the family for which he was not totally prepared (McCubbin, Hunter, and Dahl (1975); Metres, McCubbin, and Hunter, 1974). In following the families of prisoners of war returned from Southeast Asia in 1973, McCubbin and Dahl (1974b) found that 26.9 percent of the families who had been married before the separation had since received divorces or were in the process of obtaining a divorce one year following their family reunion. Certainly, these observations are in contrast with Boulding's (1950) conclusions following World War II; she emphasized that following the initial "honeymoon euphoria" at time of reunion, families generally returned to more or less their prewar patterns of family interaction.

The research on families of returned prisoners of war has permitted the careful study of relationships between longitudinally collected data and criterion indices of families' adjustment. In an initial study of 54 families of returned PWs, McCubbin and Dahl (1974a) isolated three factors which explained the dynamics of family reunions: (a) length of marriage, (b) the husband's plans for the future which he had thought about during captivity, and (c) the degree to which the family was prepared for the separation. To determine the factors involved in family reintegration or disintegration, McCubbin, Dahl, Lester, and Ross (1975) examined data on the psychiatric functioning of the returning serviceman (determined at the time of his release from captivity), data on family adjustment to separation (obtained before the man's release from captivity), and data regarding background and demographic information on the man and his family, and related these data to family adjustment one year following family reunion. The variability in family reintegration could be explained by three variables (out of 42 considered in the analyses): (a) the length of the marriage before the separation, (b) the wife's retrospective assessment of the quality of the marriage before the separation, and (c) a negatively related variable, the wife's emotional dysfunction during the separation period. The investigators concluded that for these families it appeared that a relationship strong enough to endure the stresses of separation, reunion, and reintegration was established early in the marriage.

Because of deep concern for the children who experience prolonged separations, particular attention has been devoted to the father-child relationship at the time of the family's reunion. In an early controlled study of father relations of children born during World War II, Stolz (1954) showed that the returning father had difficulties in adjusting to his first-born child, and that his consequent attitude and behavior toward this child adversely affected the child's normal development.

In a predictive study of father-child reintegration one year following father's return from captivity in Southeast Asia, McCubbin, Dahl, Lester, and Ross (1975) isolated two variables which explained the variability in the father-child relationship: (a) a residual of captivity—the degree to which father felt he experienced physical abuse in captivity, and (b) the family's preparation for separation. In an initial study of children of prisoners of war returned from Southeast Asia, Dahl and McCubbin (1975) revealed that children exhibited significantly lower scores on indices of social and personal adjustment when compared with norms established for the *California Test of Personality*. To examine further the impact of father's return, these investigators (Dahl, McCubbin, and Ross, 1975) compared the earlier results with scores obtained by children of servicemen missing in action (children whose fathers did not return). Findings revealed that family reunion (father's return) appeared to have only a slight effect upon the children's personal and social development. Both groups of children, those from reunited and those from nonreunited families, were below the norm in most areas of personal and social adjustment. Children of reunited families indicated significantly higher scores in the areas of community relations and freedom from nervous symptoms. Thus, the importance of father's return to the family was only partially supported, leaving the issue of the effects of father's reunion open to further investigation.

ADJUSTMENT TO LOSS

Family adjustment to death of a serviceman has been studied as a cultural and psychological process of bereavement and mourning. The majority of the studies focus on bereavement precipitated by a war-induced tragedy with emphasis upon the wife's adjustment to the crisis. Several reports (Golan, 1975; Lieberman, 1971a, b; Palgi, 1970, 1973, 1975; Spolyar, 1974; Zunin, 1974) discuss the existence of several phases which the wife must go through in her slow process of coming to grips with her loss and the criteria for her adjustment. Spolyar (1974) described a grief cycle which includes periods of shock, anxiety, depression, heightened preoccupation with the departed, and feelings of guilt and hostility. He stressed the point that although there is no common or universal grief experience, since each person undergoes the grief cycle differently owing to individual circumstances and personality characteristics, the final phase should eventually result in a readjustment to reality and a future life of social normality. Golan (1975), in a study of Israeli war widows, discussed a two-stage transitional process that may take months or even years to encompass: moving from being a wife to being a widow, and then from being a widow to being a woman ready to engage in future personal investment with others, including another man. Bereavement was emphasized as a transition situation rather than a crisis. Palgi (1970, 1973, 1975), through her work with Israeli war widows, observed variation in mourning behaviors which appeared to be a function of the wife's age, the community, and the culture in which these women lived. Among some of the Jewish women, Palgi (1973) observed the existence of death rites consisting of definite phases that she felt may correspond to the discrete intrapsychic stages of the mourning process. Zunin (1974), in his group work with wives of men killed in the Vietnam conflict, noted the normal stages of the grieving process but also observed and emphasized the importance of the final stages of this process. There appeared to be two special indices of adjustment which reflected when these women had reorganized their lives and were ready to begin anew. First, there was a primary identification readjustment associated with the feeling that "I am a single woman"; second, there was the time they chose to remove their wedding rings.

A number of recent studies have focused on adjustment of wives to a more enigmatic loss; i.e., the situation of having a husband classified as missing in action (MIA) or as an unconfirmed prisoner of war (PW). Investigators of the Family Studies Branch of the Center for Prisoner of War Studies (McCubbin, Hunter, and Metres, 1974; McCubbin, Hunter, and Dahl, 1975), on the basis of in-depth interviews with 215 PW/MIA wives, stressed the findings that for these women the future remained uncertain and any attempt to resolve the situation was fraught with feelings of guilt and ambivalence. Spolyar (1974), on the basis of his work with MIA families, emphasized that the indeterminate absence created a certain amount of anxiety and unknown fear; the wives were suspended in limbo until more definite facts were known. Spolyar pointed out that of particular significance in the MIA situation was the problem of "anticipatory grief" which usually developed, not as a result of definite death, but as an unconfirmed loss under the threat of death. He cautioned that two problems appeared to be related to anticipatory grief. First, if the wife worked through the grieving process prior to the actualization of her husband's death, there may be emotional complications when her husband's death is confirmed, such as a sense of guilt or feeling of shame brought about by the cultural directive to mourn, a process she had already completed. Second, in the case where the husband returns and the wife has emancipated herself through anticipatory grief, the emotional readjustments which follow present a major crisis for the family.

Eliot (1946) observed that adjustment to loss appears to be a function of the wife's age; when a young woman loses her husband, it is easier for her than for the older woman to go on with her life. In contrast, Benson, McCubbin, Dahl, and Hunter (1974: 159) pointed out that youth and age are not significant in the case of the MIA wife whose loss is uncertain; for this group of women, "anxieties and depression have fluctuated month after month and year after year in a cyclical rhythm which has defied resetting into an on-going pattern of adjustment."

Although the process of grieving is a difficult one for the MIA wife held in limbo, several studies suggest that for the parents of the missing men the adjustment to the loss of a son may be even more difficult. Shortly after the return of American prisoners of war from Vietnam in the spring of 1973, Hunter, McCubbin, and Benson (1974) interviewed mothers and wives of American servicemen missing in action in Southeast Asia; in general, mothers were struggling to come to terms with their feelings about the loss of their sons; the wives, on the other hand, appeared to be more concerned with the practical issues of raising a family, pursuing a career, or establishing a new life style—i.e., coming to terms with themselves and projecting themselves into the future. McCubbin and Metres (1974), in a series of group discussions with 79 parents of sons missing in action, observed that for these men and women grieving was just one facet of their total adjustment process—grieving appeared to fluctuate with other life stresses. The normal work of mourning appeared to be modified by many factors, including the personality of the parent, the nature of the relationship between the parents and their son, the social and communication climate in which the loss occurred, and the ambiguity of the situation which left these parents in a state of limbo as to the finality of their loss. The investigators concluded that, as a whole, mothers talked about their grief, whereas fathers showed difficulty in expressing their feelings.

The basic question as to how children react to the loss of a father or to a situation in which father's fate is unknown is, at best, controversial. While grieving is the most accessible concept available to describe children's reaction to loss, the literature is neither clear nor uniformly consistent on the subject. Research on children's reactions to loss has tended to emphasize the children's sensitivity to their mother's reaction to the loss, rather than the children's involvement in a personal grief (McCubbin, Hunter, and Metres, 1974a). On the basis of group interviews with a total of 124 children of men missing in action or listed as prisoners of war in Southeast Asia, McCubbin, Hunter, and Metres (1974a) concluded that the children's reactions did not appear to be attributable to the grieving process but rather to the emergence of various struggles with identity formation, interpersonal relationships, and peer relations. The investigators also emphasized the fact that there may be limited value in making comparisons between the mourning of adults and the mourning of children. Although adult-child comparisons may show similarities, the authors cautioned against misconstruing them as identical and assuming the existence of identical metaphysical processes. Smilansky (1975), Lifshitz (1975), and Teichman (1975), in their studies of bereaved families in Israel, attempted to evaluate the children's levels of adjustment in order to assess the need for professional intervention. Teichman (1975) pointed out that the children, especially the young ones, reacted to the general stress atmosphere at home rather than to the specific loss. She also observed that a potential source of conflict between adults and children was the fact that the children did not express grief continuously. Parental resentment and even hostility emerged and were directed toward the "unfeeling" children. Sanua (1975) found that often the bereaved mother would isolate herself, not sharing her grief with her children; and in such instances the children lost not one but both parents.

FAMILIES IN TRANSITION

Life's changes, such as marriage, divorce, or retirement, are family stresses which may have a profound impact upon the individual members of the family. How the family system adapts to these life stresses has been a subject of great interest to the military community, but has received little attention in the research literature.

Research on marriage in the military has been, for the most part, limited to the complex problems associated with the marriage of servicemen to wives of foreign origin. Druss (1965), in his study of 56 foreign-born wives, noted the common symptoms and problems presented by these wives in their adjustment to their marriages. Although the marriages may have been functional overseas, upon coming to America, these wives became depressed, homesick, and overwhelmed by the problems of adjustment to the customs of a new culture. The wives often found themselves isolated, if not rejected, by the husbands' parents, friends, or neighbors. In addition, support from their own families was unavailable. Montalvo (1968), in his study of families experiencing separation, also noted the significantly greater amount of difficulties exhibited by wives of foreign origin and their general isolation from the mainstream of life in the community. Although these wives were found to be more dependent upon the military community for assistance, they were relatively unknowledgeable of services in the community to assist them in time of need. Kimura (1957) compared 324 war brides of Japanese husbands with three other mixed cultural groups: Japanese brides of non-Japanese husbands, European brides of Japanese

husbands, and European brides of non-Japanese husbands. This study emphasized the importance of the husband's cultural background and his family's
background in determining the outcome of the marriage. A significant relationship was found between good in-law relationships and satisfactory marital
adjustment; an unexpected finding was the larger proportion of the European
wives of Japanese husbands with positive in-law relationships compared with
those of Japanese brides of Japanese men.

Divorce in the military has also been a subject of considerable concern to the
military but has received only one reference in the literature. Williams (1971)
compared divorce statistics of one segment of the Armed Services, officers in the
United States Air Force, with divorce trends in the United States in general. He
used his findings to support or explain a number of factors which have been
associated with lower or higher divorce rates in the literature. In general, he
found the divorce rates for the military sample to be substantially lower than
rates for the general population. The investigator attributed the lower divorce
rates to the style of life in the military community, a style of life which
emphasizes commitment to the military, offers extensive services to the families,
and stigmatizes divorce in the military setting.

A life change receiving greater emphasis in the literature has been retirement
from the military. In 1969 Bellino pointed out that only recently have military
physicians recognized that many of the somatic complaints presented to them
by servicemen shortly prior to or subsequent to leaving the military are closely
associated with the patient's social and interpersonal adjustment to retirement.
He found that free-floating anxiety and depression are often the first signs of the
military retiree's predischarge emotional conflict, and emphasized that if these
problems are recognized early they can usually be handled effectively through
brief counseling. However, if neglected, the initial demands of retirement can
lead to prolonged anxiety.

The symptoms of adjustment to retirement follow a predictable pattern,
according to McNeil and Giffen (1965a), which allows it to be described as a
syndrome. The most common symptoms of the retirement syndrome are anxiety
and/or depression, and manifestations of these symptoms include irritability,
loss of interest, lack of energy, increased alcoholic intake, and reduced efficiency
(McNeil and Giffen, 1967). The retirement syndrome is likely to be evident at
three rather distinct points in time: (1) the two- or three-year period prior to
actual retirement, (2) the period of "role confusion" immediately subsequent to
retirement, and (3) the period when the retiree has difficulty negotiating and
clarifying his role following retirement.

Garber's 1971 survey of 666 recently retired military personnel showed that
those men who perceived no change in occupational prestige following retirement reported higher levels of well-being than those who experienced a loss or

gain in prestige. This finding was corroborated by Platte (1974) in his study of 583 retirees and their patterns of adjustment in moving from first careers (military) to second careers (civilian). Platte (1974), in his comparison of four subsamples of retirees (retired officers, wives of retired officers, retired enlisted men, wives of retired enlisted men), found that those who perceived retirement as a step down in mobility were lowest in levels of psychological well-being. Moreover, the transition from military status to retired status may have a differential effect upon the marital relationship. Platte (1974) reported that unemployed officers fully retired and not interested in second careers reported significantly higher levels of marital adjustment than the employed officers who perceived themselves downwardly mobile following retirement. In essence, families of retirees experience difficulties similar to those of the servicemen in adjusting to the pre- and postretirement periods (McNeil, 1964). As retirement approaches, the family feels the impending loss of a way of life which has proved secure and satisfying (Giffen and McNeil, 1967). As added complications to the normal stresses of transition, it is highly probable that at about the same time as the man's retirement, the wife may face menopause and there may be intra-family conflicts resulting from the children's reaching adolescence (Greenberg, 1973). Milowe (1964) also approached retirement as a crucial stress which could affect family stability, cautioning that the return of the military man to normal society may trigger off tenuously compensated husband-wife or parent-child relationships, as well as conflicting, unresolved developmental problems of the family members.

Factors which contribute to adjustment problems of retirees and their families have been examined to some degree as comparisons between military and civilian retirees. Bellino (1970) compared military and civilian retirement populations and found some similarities, as well as substantial differences, between the groups. For example, community acceptance, social status, and residences are areas of conflict for the military retiree immediately upon retirement, whereas his civilian counterpart, who has roots in the community and retains the same friends and social ties, does not experience such a disruptive change. In a series of studies, Biderman (1959, 1964, 1971, 1972) has examined the characteristics and adjustments of military retirees and has emphasized the impact of military retirement upon the community and stressed the importance of job competition and group identification to the retiree. In another recent paper, Biderman and Sharp (1968) pointed out the remarkable similarity between civilian and military retirees. The overwhelming majority (83%) of military retirees plan to enter the labor market immediately upon retirement; the large-scale Michigan survey (1960-61) indicated that slightly over half of the officers on the retired list at the time had an easy transition to civilian employment (Biderman and Sharp, 1968).

SERVICES TO FAMILIES UNDER STRESS

The vulnerability of families to the exigencies of life in the military during routine or wartime assignment has been partially offset by the availability of medical, legal, social, psychological, and outreach services and the support of the military community in which the family is situated. Frances and Gale (1973: 172), in their examination of the special stresses that families undergo as part of military life, i.e., periodic separation, rigid social hierarchy, and frequent moves, indicated that the military is aware of these stresses and attempts to provide a total environment and "to take care of its own." "There are few subcultures that so dramatically influence the course of its members' lives as does the military in which families are called upon to meet many unique stresses and, in return, are offered supports that are not generally available to others." Hartog (1966) was also concerned with the military's ability to assist families in their adjustment to the stresses of military life. In his study of 29 psychotic and borderline psychotic military wives, he observed that the relatively closed military community was compelled to provide some form of help for these women.

Yet, to what extent are families living on a military base aware of these resources located in the military community, and what is their perception of the social cost of using such facilities? Spellman (1965) addressed these questions in his study of 655 career army families and found a definite relationship between rank and knowledge of available resources as well as perception of social cost—as rank status increased, so did knowledge of what was available in the community for resolving family conflict, and the perceived social cost attributed to the use of military community resources tended to decrease. In general, however, Spellman observed considerable anxiety, particularly among the lower-ranking enlisted group, attending the use of help resources within the military community. He concluded that this anxiety apparently related to a rather widespread belief that family conflict, either marital or parent-child, which comes to official attention will be dealt with in a punitive way by the commanding officer and by lack of interest by the professional consulted. Allen (1972), in his survey of 430 father-absent army families living at Schilling Manor, a single-parent military community, also described residents, responding to perceived crisis situations affecting the family or community, most consistently and frequently selecting a close neighbor or chaplain to assist in the situation—generally, the residents used the informal community structure before contacting representatives of the formal community services. Bevilacqua (1967), in his survey of 1,706 army families, was concerned with the question of whether health and welfare resource participation could be predicted on the basis of commitment to the military. He found that demographic factors such as age, education, length of service, and rank were predictive—increased age, education level, length of service, and rank were associated with increased participation. Contrary to these findings, Myles (1970), in his program evaluation survey of 50 Army Community Services (ACS) centers, found that of four ACS client types, active-duty army enlisted men and their dependents most often experienced each of 21 social welfare problems, and their dependents most often utilized the services provided by the centers. Furthermore, he found that professional service deliverers were generally selected as first choice to provide services encompassing conflict resolution and system reconstitution.

Other investigators, like Saunders (1969) in his study of poverty among army families, stress the importance of going beyond the military community to provide the range of services now necessary to cope with all the social welfare problems of families in the military. Another proponent of better utilization of civilian welfare resources by the overtaxed military services was Marsh (1970) who, in his study of 205 army enlisted families undergoing the strains of the moving process, described the insufficiency of existing resources such as the ACS, the Red Cross, and the Army Emergency Relief to provide such resources. Montalvo's (1968) study focused on problem-solving experiences of career military families experiencing husband absence owing to unaccompanied 12-month military assignments overseas. He observed the importance of the informal problem-solving resources (friends, relatives) and found that families who were able to make fuller use of civilian resources encountered fewer problems and adapted better to the separation experience.

Studies dealing with the prolonged separation undergone by families of PWs and MIAs of the Vietnam War have also emphasized issues such as a lack of availability of services designed specifically to assist with this unique situation, as well as a reluctance on the part of the military family members to use existing services. Powers (1974) described the evolution of a strong and determined National League of Families of American Prisoners and Missing in Southeast Asia as a key group in the awakening of the public conscience to the unique needs of these families and in spurring the eventual development of improved and essential family services to them. Hunter and Plag (1973), on the basis of a study of a select group of Navy PW/MIA families, suggested the need for an aggressive program and proposed the development of a more flexible, coordinated, and professionally based "Family Assistance Program" for PW/MIA families. McCubbin and Dahl (1974a, 1974b), in their discussion of a program to provide comprehensive services with a preventative aim to families of returned prisoners of war (RPW) and families of the missing in action, emphasized the applicability and potential of outreach services, since, in spite of availability of mental health services in the military, there remains a discrepancy between the numbers who could benefit from professional counseling and those who step forward to obtain it. In studying the impact of outreach services, McCubbin and Dahl (1974c) found that 42.4 percent of the RPW families took advantage of outreach services. Hall and Malone (1974), in their clinical assessments of six PW families, found that unsatisfactory experiences with uninformed civilian and military professionals, together with a natural reluctance to seek counseling, were critical factors mitigating the families' involvement in mental health services. McCubbin, Hunter, and Metres (1974) and McCubbin, Hunter, and Dahl (1975) also observed, in their interviews with 215 PW/MIA families, that families tended to avoid seeking help for reasons ranging from denial to abortive and unsatisfactory experiences with health professionals. Westling (1973), in a manual designed to provide concrete assistance to Navy chaplains in their ministry to the PW returnee and his family, emphasizes the need for counseling procedures within the pastoral role because of the reluctance on the part of the family to seek professional assistance.

A number of investigators have pointed out the beneficial aspects of self-help and volunteer programs with families of men experiencing wartime disasters. Duncan (1969), Zunin (1974), and Zunin and Barr (1969) described a program, "Operation Second Life," that was set up in an effort to help Vietnam War widows and uses their common tragedy to turn them toward the future; the program was launched with the idea that the best help for widows can come from other widows. Eloul (1975) and Kirschner (1975), in their work with Israeli widows of the Six-Day and Yom Kippur Wars, also found that self-help groups were efficient in helping these women to overcome their grief and start on the road to rehabilitation. Halpern (1975), Levy (1975), Teichman, Spiegel, and Teichman (1975), Sternberg (1975), and Caplan (1975) encouraged the use of volunteers to help bereaved families. Halpern (1975: 243), in her work with MIA families during the Yom Kippur War, viewed volunteering as a way in which communities hit by a disaster could successfully cope with the crisis situation; furthermore, volunteering was seen as indigenous and as having that "human ingredient that tries to alleviate the pain which is experienced by both helper and helped in times of disaster." Halpern, Levy, Teichman et al., and Sternberg noted that the volunteers who worked with bereaved MIA families in Israel identified with their charges' life difficulties—they did not treat them as patients and, foremost, did not maintain a professional distance. Caplan encouraged the use of volunteers as intermediaries between the professionals and the families.

CRITIQUE OF RESEARCH

In contrast to the long crescive histories of family research, particularly in the realm of theory building (Burr, 1973; Hill and Rodgers, 1964; Pitts, 1964; Sirjamaki, 1964; Stryker, 1964), measurement (Straus, 1964, 1969), and prediction (Bowerman, 1964), research on the military family has been somewhat sporadic, beginning with Hill's (1949) classic study of family separation and reunion. The result has been a theoretical eclecticism leading toward research in breadth rather than depth: an index of its conceptual adolescence.

Most of the studies dealing with families in the military system are subject to the same general criticisms. First, not only are the studies that set out to test specific hypotheses few in number, but also many start and end as broad clinical observations, studies with untested, common-sense assumptions. Second, for most studies, researchers employed samples from available local populations, samples that were not necessarily representative. Readers have thus been forced to establish generalizations based on conclusions drawn from varying types of samples. Third, many of the studies were ex post facto and, therefore, dependent upon data collected retrospectively.

Despite these general criticisms, however, the studies of the family in the military system unquestionably contribute to our understanding of the military families under stress by offering general data upon which hypotheses can be formulated for more rigorous research and for a more differentiated approach to the study of the military family. The most provocative sources for hypotheses appear to be post facto explorations of discussions which are mixed in with the findings of both clinical and survey reports.

One significant aspect of many of the existing studies is that the behavioral scientists who interested themselves in services to families viewed family research in terms of its influence upon policy. Our concern with narrowly focused and policy-oriented research is that it may often set aside well-defined and theory-based variables for more unobtrusive or obvious variables which policy makers define as acceptable and influential. Appropriately, Coates and Pellegrin (1965) have suggested this shortcoming in their critique of research in the military; they stress the inability of researchers to build upon past research and therefore contribute to a body of knowledge. Although the degree to which family research is designed and implemented to influence policies regarding families is self-evident, this does not appear to have been a futile exercise, since the accumulated topics such as separation, father absence, child abuse, and mobility have sensitized the policy makers to the immediate and long-term implications of their decisions affecting the military family.

THE POTENTIAL FOR FAMILY RESEARCH IN THE MILITARY

The state of research on the military family, based on work completed, would appear to be indeterminate, with more issues raised than answered. It has been concluded here that the climate for family research in the military has, over the years, been less than optimum, that research on the military family has not been accretive, with minimum evidence of cumulating generalizations and theory, and that existing research has revealed little about the dynamic, interactional, and developmental aspects of the family in the military community. Only touched upon, and as yet unresolved, are such questions as follow:

A. SOCIALIZATION IN THE MILITARY COMMUNITY
   1. How are families socialized into the military community?
   2. What are the effects of socialization in the military community upon the family, its stability, and its development?
   3. With the increase in females entering the military system, what will be the socialization process for the husband/spouse and the family in the military community?
B. FAMILY DEVELOPMENT AND FUNCTIONING IN THE MILITARY COMMUNITY
   1. What types of family patterns are necessary to function within the military community?
   2. What effect does life in the military have upon the family development cycle, and developmentally, how do military families differ from their civilian counterparts?
C. FAMILIES UNDER STRESS IN THE MILITARY COMMUNITY
   1. What types of families are better able to endure and develop within the military community?
   2. Why are some families more vulnerable to the stresses of life in the military and under what conditions?
   3. In what ways has life in the military community positively influenced or, possibly, undermined the stability of married military personnel and their families?
D. THE FAMILY AND ITS EFFECT UPON THE MILITARY SYSTEM
   1. What are the roles and potential influences of the military family in the career patterns of military personnel?
   2. What are the major family factors which weigh heavily upon retention of the military member, and under what conditions are these factors critical in determining the outcome?
   3. How much of the variance in the performance of military personnel can be explained by the family and its functioning?

Although this chapter can only begin to deal with and respond to these critical illuminating questions, it is hoped that, at the very least, some of the more important and pertinent areas have been identified and introduced. The question, however, still remains as to what the future holds for family research in the military.

At first glance, there is reason to believe that the prevailing attitude toward the family and family research has not changed. An index of the importance of the family in the military should be evident in the reports on the Volunteer Army [VOLAR] and the factors policy makers see as critical to recruitment, development, and retention of career soldiers. However, in reviewing recent documents related to VOLAR, a special study group of the Army War College concluded:

> It is interesting to note that, in the report, *The Volunteer Army—One Year Later,* dated February, 1974 little attention is paid to reporting improvements in the quality of family life . . . in the body of the document little more than a paragraph is devoted to Army families (Bennett et al., 1974: 6).

Even in those areas of military life in which the family should be considered, policy makers have chosen to give less priority to family considerations. The same special study group of the Army War College concluded:

> Policy, born of operational necessity, concentrates on the movement and assignment of the member. There is little, if any, focus on the impact of the separation upon the family (Bennett et al., 1974: 119).

In spite of the absence of more obvious indices of changing attitudes towards the military family and family research, there are developments within the military community which suggest that the Armed Services realize the need for something more than the allocation of funds to support new housing construction, commissary and exchange services, and medical services if its requirements for a motivated volunteer program are to be met (Doodeman, 1974; Finlayson, 1969; Ryan and Bevilacqua, 1964). The necessity for a greater understanding of the role and influence of the military family has been fostered by the developments in the field of family research which document the impact of the family upon individual behavior and health (Grolnick, 1972; Jackson, 1965; Lewis, Beavers, Gossett, and Phillips, 1974; Livsey, 1972; Schmale, 1958). Furthermore, the development of a Family Studies Branch within the Center for POW Studies and the research being conducted by this branch with families of prisoners of war and families of servicemen missing in action strongly indicate the value of such research and the importance of longitudinal studies of the military family (Plag, 1974).

The emergence of the National League of Families of American Prisoners and Missing in Southeast Asia as a politically powerful and influential organization, supported by parallel developments in the women's liberation movement, signaled an increasingly active role for military families (Powers, 1974). This organization not only brought into focus the critical issue of family needs but also exposed the classic struggle between two social institutions: the military and the family. Out of frustration families sought answers to their questions: what was the status of their men? They sought help and understanding of the dilemma they faced after the many years of waiting. The military's traditional modes of handling routine disputes with families were inept in calming the discontent. The

families were unwilling to accept the military's usual approach to family problems—the "classified information" approach, the "we are checking into it"
approach, or the subtle but ever present "buck-passing" tactics which the
families felt were so characteristic of the military system. Even placement of key
family members into strategic advisory positions to assist the military in planning for family needs was not viewed as sufficient. Families inadvertently used
these invitations to obtain more information about the mechanics and functioning of the military system and sometimes proceeded to expose the tenuous and
often inconsistent logic and assumptions upon which many family-related decisions were based.

The methodical approach of the military and the complicated network of
various governmental procedures were judged by many of the families as ineffi-
cient and ineffective. Through the National League of Families these military
families had come of age as a politically viable social institution capable of
demanding information, exposing inconsistencies and bureaucratic apathy, and
pushing their way into the international sphere demanding what seemed to be
impossible. They questioned the constitutionality of laws governing servicemen
missing in action and prisoners of war—laws which had gone unquestioned in
previous wars (Nelson, 1974). Brash but influential, this collective group of
families contributed significantly to the welfare of all military families by
bringing to the surface the feelings, attitudes, sensitivities, and needs of families
who experience the hardships of life in the military and the tragedies of war.
They brought to the forefront the frustrations, the fears, doubts, and angry
feelings which had raged from time to time but were seldom articulated to the
point of demanding attention and action. More important, these families
exposed a relative lack of knowledge of families in the military and made the
public aware of the importance of family stability in the military system (Hunter
and Plag, 1973; McCubbin, Dahl, Metres, Hunter, and Plag, 1974).

Obviously, the changing profile of the military community toward a "married
man's" military (Bennett et al., 1974; Coates and Pellegrin, 1965; Janowitz,
1960; Little, 1971) has and will continue to have a profound impact upon
policies regarding the military family. Coates and Pellegrin (1965) pointed out
that the family is important because: first, it is very likely that a large percentage
of men who leave the service do so because of an inability to arrive at a
satisfactory family adjustment within the context of the military milieu—which,
of course, results in the loss of extremely valuable manpower, wasted training,
and lowered military efficiency; and second, it is also likely that men who are
experiencing family problems are unable to operate at their most effective level.
The evolution of human relations, community services, medical programs
(CHAMPUS), and social work services in the Navy are indices of this growth in
sensitivity to family needs (Hunter and Plag, 1973; Little, 1971; McCubbin and

Dahl, 1974a, 1974d). Hill (1974) touched upon a critical point: two social institutions, the military and the family, compete for the same resource, the serviceman. In the long run the family wins. Certainly, the family has a profound impact upon the serviceman and his behavior, but to what degree this hypothesis is true and under what conditions remains to be investigated.

CONCLUSIONS

As family research moves through several stages of development, from observation and speculation to exploratory fact-finding research and hypothesis testing, so the study of the military family will probably have to undergo its own disquietudes of growth and maturity. We hope we shall witness a plethora of research inquiries with techniques, methods, and theories appropriated from the vast and ever increasing literature already available to assess the unique aspects of the family life in the military system. Out of parochialism, family research in the military should not go its own way; it is, however, expected that we will not witness the independent amassing of simplistic data and that we will avoid family research that does not take into account the wisdom of what has already been done.

The field of family research in the military must be divided into areas which have been more meaningfully and logically developed through intimate knowledge of the family rather than on the basis of administratively defined concepts or variables, e.g., "families of servicemen killed in action" or other definitions borrowed from the military community. As we move closer and closer to the mainstream of family research, we hope we will acknowledge the extreme complexity of family life and seek to understand not only the deviant but also the normal. Investigations dealing with the normal crises of life in the military and in symptom-free families are sorely needed.

It is important to point out, however, that our emphasis upon the urgency for greater knowledge of the military family is not without recognition of the fact that support of the military family is not the major mission of the Armed Forces. Yet, any mission which tends to view these families as "invisible" people cannot realistically assess their impact on the total military system. Our review of the literature has led us to appreciate the wisdom of Hill's (1949: 361) conclusion that what is needed is a policy designed to "help all families, not as a sentimental movement, but as a basic need for national stability and social order."

Chapter 12

RESEARCH ON THE MILITARY FAMILY:

AN ANNOTATED BIBLIOGRAPHY

SUSAN FARISH
FRANÇOISE BAKER
MARILYN ROBERTSON

Only recently has the military family been perceived as an appropriate, meaningful, and fruitful area of research and investigation. This change in perception has arisen largely because of a growing concern and interest by the military community both in the United States and abroad as to the effect of the military on the family, and likewise, the effect of the family on the military. Owing to the relative novelty of the topic, research on the military family has suffered from nonprofileration of reports, difficulty in locating existing reports, and the subsequent isolation of existing reports from the general public. As an aid in correcting these deficiencies, this chapter has for its intent the identification and summarization of both published and unpublished studies to date on the military family to provide a comprehensive reference source for all present and future researchers of the military family. The bibliography is not exhaustive, however, as some original articles were unobtainable, and the very recent and rapidly accelerated research presently under way in countries such as Israel precludes the possibility at this writing of presenting a completely up-to-date bibliography on the subject of the military family. The references are presented in the form of an annotated bibliography, alphabetically arranged by author. The annotations themselves vary in length and emphasis, yet they have a common focus on a general presentation of hypotheses and findings rather than on specific methodology. Since all research studies, articles, and books available on the subject of the military family are included, the reader is made aware of the breadth, scope, and diversity in orientation of literature in this area. Psychological, psychiatric, and social work research studies, doctoral dissertations, and descriptive articles of a theoretical nature together constitute this bibliography and attest to the diversity of the studies. It is noteworthy, yet only open to conjecture, why certain aspects of military family research such as family development and child development in the military setting appear to be largely ignored, while other areas such as military retirement and family adjustment to separation have been given more attention by researchers. The answer to this and other crucial questions will, we hope, be found through ongoing and future comprehensive research on the military family.

ALLEN, H. (1972) "Schilling Manor: A survey of a military community of father absent families." Unpublished doctoral dissertation. Catholic University of America.

Schilling Manor, a military community for wives and children of military servicemen assigned to unaccompanied tours of duty overseas, was systematically investigated as to residents' community participation, military identification, perceptions of the community, role played by the neighborhood chairman, and utilization of available caretaking resources. Family participation in community activities was found to be positively correlated with higher rank, number of months residing at Schilling, years of active service, and residents' level of education. Wives of foreign birth were less socialized and identified less with the military. The dysfunctional aspects of community leadership and the total community system were emphasized.

BAKER, S., L. COVE, S. FAGEN, E. FISCHER, and E. JANDA (1968) "Impact of father absence: III. Problems of family reintegration following prolonged father absence." American Journal of Orthopsychiatry 38: 347 (Abstract).

A three-phase investigation was carried out to determine the effects of prolonged father absence on family reintegration. Data were collected prior to separation (Phase I), during (Phase II), and after separation (Phase III) on families of regular Army middle-rank enlisted men who were experiencing an unaccompanied-by-family tour of duty, as well as on a control group. In all three phases families were administered the identical battery of tests. Reunion data (Phase III), which are emphasized in this report, identified personality changes in the husbands of the father-absent group, the specific role shifts in the family after reunion, and significant increases in hostile envy of siblings during the separation and at reunion. Suggestions of a primary prevention, secondary prevention, and tertiary prevention nature for community support programs for families during father separation periods were made.

BAKER, S, S. FAGEN, E. FISCHER, E. JANDA, and L. COVE (1967) "Impact of father absence on personality factors of children." American Journal of Orthopsychiatry 37: 269 (Abstract).

The effect of father absence on the children of military personnel, specifically in terms of parent and child personality variables and various dimensions of parent-child relationships, was studied. Data were obtained from the wife, husband, and their five-to-eight-year-old son both before and after the father's departure on an overseas duty tour. Family adjustment to father absence was found to be multidetermined. The effects were exaggerated in male children, who showed increased masculine identification and activities. Feelings of guilt and abandonment were alleviated in the child by community and maternal acceptance of hardship tours as being appropriate.

BAROCAS, H. (1970) "Children of purgatory: reflections on the concentration camp survival syndrome." Corrective Psychiatry and Journal of Social Therapy 16: 51-58.

This study reviews the literature on the "Concentration Camp Survival Syndrome," an idiosyncratic syndrome manifested by symptoms of chronic anxiety, nightmares, sleeplessness, inability to concentrate, and continual depression. Concentration camp survivors are unable to establish interpersonal contacts, display marked reactions to any additional stress, convey feelings of mistrust and hostility bordering on the paranoid, and exhibit a shallowness in emotional reaction. Children of survivors have been reported to display either explosive, aggressive behavior or severe depressed reactions. Explanations for the long-term effects on both the survivors and their children are given and a plea for further research is made.

BELLINO, R. (1969) "Psychosomatic problems of military retirement." Psychosomatics 10: 318-321.

This report presents a discussion and review of the literature of psychosomatic problems, ranging from somatic complaints of headaches and peptic ulcers to such depressive symptoms as insomnia and impotence, occurring because of military retirement. The specific adjustments facing the military retiree are also identified. Psychosomatic problems which occur in dependents of retirees are noted. A multidirectional treatment approach with total family involvement is suggested.

BELLINO, R. (1970) "Perspectives of military and civilian retirement." Mental Hygiene 54: 580-583.

This descriptive study contrasts areas of conflict for civilian and military retirees, highlighting difficulties with the interpersonal, social, and financial stresses of retirement. Military retirees are usually much younger and somewhat better off financially than civilian retirees. Both groups, however, suffer from labor market prejudices when seeking new employment. Additional stresses unique to the military retiree include nontransferability of his skills to the civilian labor market, disruption of social ties and finding a new social position in the civilian community, potential conflict within the family, and lack of available counseling resources.

BELT, J. and A. SWENEY (1973) "The Air Force wife: her knowledge of, and attitudes toward, the Air Force." Paper presented at Military Testing Association Conference on Human Resources, San Antonio, Texas (October).

Wives of men assigned to a strategic missile wing were interviewed concerning their attitudes and opinions about the military. Data indicated that the Air Force wife was not well informed as to the facilities and services that are available. Formal military briefings regarding services available were looked upon by the wives with skepticism and were not well attended. The only alternate source of information, their husbands, also proved to be insufficient. A desire to find more accessible information channels and to participate more in the system were indicated. Comparisons made between various groups within the wing were also discussed, and it was concluded that, generally, the Air Force wife holds a favorable attitude toward her role as a military dependent.

BENNETT, W., H. CHANDLER, J. DUFFY, J. HICKMAN, C. JOHNSON, M. LALLY, A. NICHOLSON; G. NORBO, A. OMPS, V. POSPISIL, R. SEE-BERG, and W. WUBBENA (1974) "Army families." U.S. Army War College, Carlisle Barracks, Pennsylvania.

The structural relationship between the army family and the military installation is examined with respect to issues of housing, health, economic factors, education, and recreation. In addition, the social psychological community of army personnel and their families is described in relation to factors of career advancement, privacy, sense of community, mobility, separation, and marital status. Current statistics on the military family, mobility, and housing are presented. While psychosocial and stressful aspects of life in the military are touched upon, they are not examined in any depth. Additional research on the complex relationship between the army family and the military is recommended.

BENSON, D., H. McCUBBIN, B. DAHL, and E. HUNTER (1974) "Waiting: the dilemma of the MIA wife," pp. 157-168 in H. McCubbin, B. Dahl, P. Metres, Jr., E. Hunter, and J. Plag (eds.) Family Separation and Reunion. Washington, D.C.: U.S. Government Printing Office.

The reaction of wives to prolonged absence of a husband still classified as missing in action was investigated. In group discussions, the wives examined their feelings about their husbands' absence, personal and emotional adjustment, and perceptions of their children's adjustment. Although most of the women had concerns for their children's welfare and experienced difficulties with their own identities, all were acutely aware that life must go on and many had made tremendous strides in adapting to a new life style.

BEVILACQUA, J. (1967) "Civilianization and health-welfare resource participation on an Army post." Unpublished doctoral dissertation. Brandeis University.

The phenomenon of social change represented by the diminishing separation of military and civilian communities has commonly been referred to as a "civilianization" of the military. In this study, civilianization was operationalized in terms of commitment to the military and examined in relation to the family's use of civilian and military health and welfare resources. Findings indicated that civilianization, for certain groups, i.e., certain age groups, educational levels, etc., was not related to the use of health and welfare services. With the increasing breakdown of military and civilian boundaries, the author questions the efficacy of the military's goal of providing health and welfare services to foster cohesion within the system.

BEY, D. and J. LANGE (1974) "Waiting wives: women under stress." American Journal of Psychiatry 131: 283-286.

A three-part discussion of the various stresses experienced by 40 wives whose husbands were serving in Vietnam is presented. Predeparture time was characterized by depressive symptoms of guilt, anger, and concern for husband's career. Loneliness, anxiety, frustration, and awkward social position were features of the separation period. At the time of the husband's return, tension, apprehension at possible changes, irritation at loss of independence and authority, impaired communication, and children's discipline problems were the major concerns. The unfilled need of preventive psychiatric help for these women was noted.

BIDERMAN, A. (1959) "The prospective impact of large scale military retirement." Social Problems 7: 84-90.

This study is concerned with the effect of large-scale military retirement and focuses on the potential social problems which might occur. A major distinguishing characteristic of the military retiree is that he is much younger upon retirement than a civilian retiree. Other unique features of military retirees are their choice of a second career and their settlement together in large concentrations in selected localities. The impact of the retirees on the community is predicted to be increased job competition, participation in certain voluntary associations, social stereotyping by the community, and retiree group identification.

BIDERMAN, A. (1964) "Sequels to a military career: the retired military professional." pp. 287-336 in M. Janowitz (ed.) The New Military: Changing Patterns of Organization. New York: Russell Sage Foundation.

This paper deals largely with the problems of second careers, which the majority of military retirees are forced to enter in order to maintain their economic and social status. Financial, economic, psychological, job-related, and environmental aspects of the second career pursuits are considered. Specialized careers pursued in the military provide a transferability of skills to high-paying civilian jobs. For the retiree who has no specialized skill, preretirement counseling and access to placement services are provided. The problem of establishing a second career is complicated by federal statutes, which restrict many officers from taking second career jobs related to their particular training and by overconcentration of retirees in favorable locations. Government, public service-oriented federal jobs, and managerial positions seem to attract retired military officers.

BIDERMAN, A. (1971) "The retired military." pp. 123-163 in R. Little (ed.) Handbook of Military Institutions. Beverly Hills, California; Sage Publications.

This study examines the characteristics, adjustments, and impact on American society of former professional military men pursuing careers in civilian society after retirement. Owing to a number of factors, a large group of middle-aged ex-military men are competing directly with civilians for well-paying jobs. The retiree's success in obtaining a second career depends on how transferable his skills and credentials are to the civilian labor market. Environmental explanations are given for why the retirees tend to cluster together in certain areas.

BIDERMAN, A. and L. SHARP (1968) "The convergence of military and civilian occupational structures: evidence from studies of military retired employment." American Journal of Sociology 73: 381-399.

Data from several studies on second career employment of retired military men show a pattern of actual convergence between military and civilian institutions. Four particular aspects of this convergence were discussed: structural similarities, dynamic similarities, interpenetrability, and attitudinal and ideological similarities. Most military retirees obtained comparable civilian employment, concentrated largely in governmental and institutional employment areas. Civilian job success was related more to educational level and rank than to specific skills or abilities. It was hypothesized that civilian institutions are becoming more militarized, and military institutions more civilianized.

BLOCHBERGER, JR., C. (1970) "Military families: differential lifestyles." Unpublished doctoral dissertation, University of California, Berkeley, School of Social Work.

Thirty families were compared on the basis of questionnaires and clinical records with respect to the variables of military culture affecting the career military family. Specifically, location of residence, either on or off base, was examined as a possible discriminating factor between the families. Although families had a number of common bonds, off-base families preferred a life style in which there are minimal restrictions, privacy, open atmosphere, and no constraints on their choice of housing. On-base families preferred to reside on the military installation for reasons of safety, convenience, and financial savings.

BOULDING, E. (1950) "Family adjustments to war separations and reunions." The Annals of the American Academy of Political and Social Science 272: 59-67.

This article examines the effects of wartime husband/father absence. Successful coping was found to depend on many factors: preinduction family situation, children's attitude toward the new situation, presence or absence of in-laws, housing problems, health problems, economic problems, and mother's employment. Good adjustment at reunion was a function of good prewar marital adjustment and "open ranks" families. Although this work is primarily concerned with aspects of separation, a variety of reunion adjustments are mentioned.

BOWER, E. (1967) "American children and families in overseas communities." American Journal of Orthopsychiatry 37: 787-796.

This paper presents a discussion of the various problems experienced by American military families based in Europe. Problems included difficulty in making friends, a feeling of uninvolvement, segmentation and loss of stability as a result of the transient living situation, and insufficient and cramped military housing. Major difficulties were the restricted availability of school facilities and teaching aids, of limited school and community resources for dealing with children's behavioral problems, and of mental health services.

BROWN, D. and E. HUYCKE (1974) "Problems of Vietnam prisoners of war and their families." Social Psychiatry 1: 91-98.

A list of the medical and psychiatric problems of 1,591 Vietnam prisoners of war and missing in action and their families are presented. Problems of captives from World War II and the Korean conflict are also discussed. Responses to the conditions of captivity are examined, including fear of the unknown and hardships and indignities inflicted on the men. Problems of repatriation and readjustment are given consideration, while repercussions of the men's return on the families are also examined.

BROWN, M. (1944) "When our servicemen come home." Journal of Home Economics: 626-628.

This article is a presentation of a list of twenty-five dos and don'ts, a series of suggestions by the Homemaking Education Service of the U.S. Office of Education, dealing with ways to ease the stress of reentry into civilian life for the World War II serviceman. The suggestions, listed under such headings as "Have Respect for the Serviceman's Maturity, Be Fair about His Gripes," recommend that the veteran, following his war experiences, be dealt with in a supportive and sympathetic fashion in order to make his reentry into American society a nonstressful occasion.

CAPLAN, G. (1975) "Organization of support systems for civilian populations." Paper presented at the International Conference on Psychological Stress and Adjustment in Time of War and Peace, Tel Aviv, Israel (January).

This study focuses on the means by which community intervenors (i.e., mental health specialists, social scientists, and community organizers) organize support systems for civilian populations in the event of war or disaster. Supportive organizational efforts are differentiated according to subpopulation categories of (1) families of casualties; (2) families of potential casualties; and (3) dependent and needy individuals. General principles of intervention, such as linking directly involved family members with significant others, avoiding diagnostic labeling of the individuals, and organizing mutual help groups and networks was discussed. Specific intervention principles are described for dealing with the various families.

COATES, C. and R. PELLEGRIN (1965) Military Sociology: A Study of American Military Institutions and Military Life. Maryland: Social Science Press.

A sociological perspective of American military institutions is presented through examination of (I) concepts of military sociology; (II) the traditional role of American military institutions; (III) military bureaucracy and systems of formal and informal organization; (IV) development of military professionalism; and (V) military society and life. Within the last section, some problems arising as a result of crucial role changes involving military men and their families are described. Because of the increasing size and impersonal nature of the military base, more families choose to reside in the civilian community. Being geographically isolated, the wife has lost familiarity with traditional base functioning, participates less in her husband's career, and, consequently, has become less accepting of the inconveniences of military life. The authors emphasize the movement away from the unique military community which "took care of its own" and the need to examine the stresses of the new military upon the family.

COVE, L., S. FAGEN, and S. BAKER (1967) "Military families in crisis: father goes to war." Unpublished manuscript.

This study examines the effects of father absence and family dislocation resulting from the husband/father's assignment to unaccompanied military duty. It focuses on two issues: (1) the impact of father absence on personality development in the male child, and (2) the total family adjustment to the separation and reintegration experience. A general surface "father absence syndrome" was observed among the family members. Male children exhibited symptomatic behavior in their failure to resolve developmental crises and in a hostile rejection of objects. On closer examination, the families were found to differ markedly in their characteristic responses to the crisis. Two general classes of coping behaviors are discussed.

CUBER, J. (1945) "Family readjustment of veterans." Marriage and Family Living 7: 28-30.

This article provides glimpses into the emotional readjustment to civilian life of a group of 200 college veterans over a three-year period. There appears to be general agreement that the majority of veterans are preoccupied with their economic situation, that they tend to idealize what they have left behind, and that they tend to forget that civilians at home are also in the process of changing. Beyond these common factors, the author discusses seven additional changes affecting domestic reassimilation, including feelings of social, material, and emotional insecurity or inadequacy, familial responsibilities and obligations, lack of needed skills, and loss of morale.

DAHL, B. and H. McCUBBIN (1974) "The adjustment of children of returned prisoners of war: a preliminary report." Paper presented at the Second Joint

Medical Meeting on Prisoners of War, Department of Defense, San Antonio, Texas (November).

The personal and social adjustments of 57 children of returned prisoners of the Vietnam War who had experienced prolonged father separation were investigated. The California Test of Personality was administered according to appropriate ages and grade levels, and a number of specific hypotheses related to the children's adjustment were made. Results indicated that the children of returned prisoners of war were below the norm on overall adjustment, but intergroup differences owing to age and sex of the children were not supported by the findings. Length of father absence significantly affected the children's school adjustment.

DAHL, B. and H. McCUBBIN (1975) *"Children of returned prisoners of war: the effects of long-term father absence." Paper presented at the Annual Meeting of the American Psychological Association, Chicago, Illinois (August).*

An investigation to determine the effects of long-term father absence owing to wartime separation was undertaken with 99 children of men who had been taken prisoners during the Vietnam War. Subjects were administered the California Test of Personality approximately 1 to 2 years after their fathers' return. Findings indicated that the children of returned prisoners of war revealed poorer personal and social adjustment than the norm. Numerous intergroup findings are discussed.

DAHL, B., H. McCUBBIN, and K. ROSS (1975) *"Second generational effects of war-induced separations: comparing the adjustment of children in reunited and non-reunited families." Paper presented at the National Council on Family Relations Meeting, Salt Lake City (August) and published in the Journal of Military Medicine, in press.*

This study was designed to compare the second generational effects of long-term father absence on children who have been reunited with their fathers and children who have not been reunited with their fathers. The study focused on three major variables: (a) sex of the children, (b) age of the children, and (c) length of father absence. All subjects were administered the California Test of Personality approximately 12 to 24 months after the return of American prisoners of war from Vietnam. Findings indicated differences between the two groups in the areas of nervous symptoms and community relations. The impact of father's return following the prolonged separation is discussed.

DARNAUER, P. (1970) "The adolescent experience in career army families."
Unpublished doctoral dissertation. University of Southern California.

This report assessed the influence of the Army on the adolescent experience of youth in career army families, specifically in terms of their friendship patterns, school experience, and social advantages/disadvantages, as perceived by the adolescents and their parents. Adolescents and parents generally responded similarly and felt that being an adolescent in the Army was not unique. It was concluded that the "army brat" is obsolete, since the adolescents showed little sense of group solidarity.

DICKERSON, W. and R. ARTHUR (1965) "Navy families in distress." Military
Medicine 130: 894-898.

Children of Navy families brought to a Naval Child Guidance Clinic were studied. Evaluation showed that the children, ranging in age from 3 to 19 years, were either experiencing school difficulties or behavioral problems, or were suffering from neurotic complaints. Parents blamed their child's difficulty on institutional pressure (Navy or school), on themselves, or on an unknown cause. Testing revealed a profile of the mothers as depressed, ambivalent, and anergic. Discrepancies existed in the mother's and father's reports concerning the nature of child rearing, perceptions of the marriage, and feelings toward each other.

DOODEMAN, L. (ed.) (1974) "Mili-wife questionnaire results: the comment
page wives speak out on—the military, pro and con, moving, children, rank
consciousness, housing, benefits, women's liberation." Ladycom 6: 22-52.

This paper reports on a survey dealing with the reactions of 4,500 *Ladycom* readers to their status as military wives. The 85 item multichoice questionnaire covered various personal and psychological aspects of the military wife's life. Military wives' assessment and comments on the military, pro and con, with respect to moving, children, housing, benefits, and women's liberation are presented.

DOR-SHAV, N. (1975) "On the long-range effects of concentration camp
internment on Nazi victims and their children." Paper presented at the
International Conference on Psychological Stress and Adjustment in Time of
War and Peace, Tel Aviv, Israel (January).

This study represents an attempt to assess the long-term effects of extreme psychological stresses suffered by Nazi victims in concentration camps (CC) on their personality functioning and that of their children. The hypothesis that primitivation and impoverishment of personality and a deficiency in perceptual and cognitive functioning would be found in the CC groups was supported by the findings. The author concluded that the victims manifested predictable deficits in functioning and had not yet recovered from their traumatic experience.

DRUSS, R. (1965a) "Foreign marriages in the military." Psychiatrics Quarterly 39: 220-226.

Military couples with foreign-born wives were studied. Most men had married their wives while on a tour of duty overseas and were attracted to their wives because they were not as "pushy and aggressive" as American women. The richness of American men and the glamour of America appealed to the wives. Adjustment for the couples was often difficult, e.g., wife's difficulties with the language, culture shock, rejection, and children's problems were sometimes aggravated by the stricter rules and cultural characteristics of the mother.

DRUSS, R. (1965b) "Problems associated with retirement from military service." Military Medicine 130: 383-385

The author presents a discussion of the problems associated with retirement from the military. On the basis of extensive work with potential retirees at a military base, the author identified marital problems, psychosomatic problems, or poor work performance as the major symptoms of adjustment reactions to impending retirement. New social changes include assuming a novice status within a civilian work situation, and the sudden loss of security and prestige. Therapeutic intervention aimed at prevention is recommended.

DUNCAN, A. (1969) "Vietnam War widows learn to live and love again." Family Weekly (November): 6-7.

Anecdotal experiences of Vietnam War widows as they learn to work out their feelings of grief, helplessness, and insecurity within a program called Operation Second Life are described. Through group workshops, the wives search for a new identity and self-awareness and share their feelings on such topics as problems with child rearing, parents, in-laws, and giving solace to new members. Prevention-oriented counseling programs of this nature are recommended.

DUVALL, E. (1945) "Loneliness and the serviceman's wife." Marriage and Family Living 7: 77-81.

A loneliness scale was developed using the exact phrases given by 77 wives and fiancées of servicemen, separated from their servicemen/husbands during wartime. The scale differentiated five groups on the basis of degree of loneliness.

Forty-seven percent of the wives felt considerable to extreme loneliness, while 41 percent felt moderate or little loneliness. It was found that the length of marriage, length of separation, and wife's work experience were not significantly related to the wife's loneliness score. However, it was determined that the extent of the wife's social participation was closely related to her degree of loneliness; thus more active wives felt less lonely than less active wives.

ELIOT, T. (1946) "War bereavements and their recovery." Marriage and Family Living 8: 1-5, 8.

This paper explores the unique nature of war bereavements. War bereavements are often more difficult owing to inaccessibility of details which may lead to imagined horrors concerning the death, accepting the news through the bluntness of a telegram, and often being prevented from having any funeral ritual which would confirm the death to the survivors. The author discusses principles by which a person can aid the bereaved, such as learning about the grief process itself, and offers suggestions that may help the bereaved to focus his attention outside himself.

ELOUL, J. (1975) "Basic issues in group work with war widows." Paper presented at the International Conference on Psychological Stress and Adjustment in Time of War and Peace, Tel Aviv, Israel (January).

This paper deals with some of the basic issues concerning war widows in Israel. Groups of war widows were formed in order that they might examine expressions of feelings, attitudes, and reactions concerning the past (in relation to the dead husband) and the future. Special problems, such as posthumous children, additional deaths in the family, and delayed burials, as well as personal conflicts were discussed. Suggestions for assistance, including public services, mental health clinics, and community health programs, were presented.

FAGEN, S., E. JANDA, S. BAKER, E. FISCHER, and L. COVE (1967) "Impact of father absence in military families: II. factors relating to success of coping with crisis." Technical Report. Washington, D.C.: Walter Reed Medical Center.

This paper examines the pattern of factors, both predispositional and mediational, which relate to differential family adjustment to the crisis of a father's absence. Data obtained prior to husband's departure and 6 to 9 months after his departure revealed several findings, emphasizing that the varieties of behavior of persons in crisis can be classified into a relatively small number of patterns, and that father's absence can have totally different impacts on different families and may facilitate either adaptive or maladaptive behavior.

FINLAYSON, E. (1969) "A study of the wife of the army officer: her academic and career preparation, her current employment and volunteer services." Unpublished doctoral dissertation. George Washington University.

The participation of Army officer wives in the areas of education, employment, and volunteer work and the peculiar aspects of military life which affect this participation were examined in this study. Findings indicated that 40 percent of the wives held a Bachelor's degree, almost half engaged in volunteer services, and 80 percent were working either full or part time for financial reasons. Owing to the frequent transfers characteristic of military life, wives experienced a number of employment disadvantages and interferences with their educational goals. Education, nursing, and clerical work were the most common occupational fields of these wives.

FRANCES, A. and L. GALE (1973) "Family structure and treatment in the military." Family Process 12: 171-178.

This article examines the special stresses—uprooting, periodic separation, frequent moves, rigid social hierarchy, necessity to conform, dependency within the nuclear family—experienced by military families and the effects of these stresses on the personalities of family members. The interactions of the various family members are described and examples given. The authors suggest that the family be treated as a unit in therapy, rather than treating only one family member.

FREUD, A. and D. BURLINGHAM (1943) War and Children. New York: International University Press.

At wartime nurseries in England, the authors studied the effects of war on children. Part I presents case histories concerning children's reactions to war experiences and to separation from their family: reactions to destruction, air raid anxiety, reactions to evacuation and separation from the mother. Part II describes day-to-day events in the nurseries during the year 1941-42, including case reports of children and their parental relationships. The importance of the parental relationships for the young child in the war nurseries and the creation of proper emotional relationships between the child and the outside world are emphasized.

GABOWER, G. (1960) "Behavior problems of children in Navy officers' families." Social Casework 41: 177-184.

This study investigated the social conditions and interactions of Navy families in relation to the behavior of their children. Behaviors of a group of 15 children found to be manifesting emotional difficulties and 15 children in a matched control group were examined in relation to several variables: e.g., a family move, changing roles of the parents owing to father absence, and parents' ways of dealing with the child. Parents whose children were in the behavior problem group were found to be less involved with their children, exhibited more physical problems, showed ineffective use of finances, and expressed discrepant attitudes toward their children.

GARBER, D. (1971) "Retired soldiers in second careers: self-assessed change, reference group salience, and psychological well-being." Unpublished doctoral dissertation. University of Southern California.

The impact of midlife career change on retired soldiers is examined. Those men who were able to transfer their military skills to the civilian labor market had a number of advantages—prestige, finance, and psychological well-being—as compared with those who had to embark upon a totally new career. Social discontinuity created by a geographic move was a problem in some cases where identification with the new environment was difficult to achieve.

GARDNER, G. and H. SPENCER (1944) "Reactions of children with fathers and brothers in the Armed Forces." American Journal of Orthopsychiatry 14: 36-43.

The reactions of boys and girls to enlistment of a brother or father in the Armed Services during World War II were described. Two groups were observed: those referred for treatment by child guidance clinics for behavioral problems or personality disorders, and delinquent boys referred to Juvenile Court. In general, some children exhibited an immediate reaction of fear, anxiety, or grief toward their family member's enlistment and, in a few cases, the referral problem became more severe after the family member's departure. Unique characteristics of the delinquent group were noted.

GIFFEN, M. and J. McNEIL (1967) "Effect of military retirement on dependents." Archives of General Psychiatry 17: 717-722.

The problems related to retirement from the military and their effects on dependents are discussed. In addition to the psychosomatic and psychiatric symptoms experienced by retirees, retirement comes at a time when the wife, because of her age, may suffer from gynecological problems, and children approaching adolescence may indulge in acting-out behavior. Retirement is discussed within the framework of crisis theory, and several case histories are presented.

*GLICK, P. (1943) "Family status of men of military age." American Socio-
logical Review 8: 157-163.*

The family status of men eligible for military duty at the close of 1943 is
analyzed according to characteristics of age distribution, marital status, number
of dependents, education, and occupational backgrounds. In order to increase
the number of men in the Armed Forces from 7 to 12 million, it was estimated
that 4 million married couples would be separated, including one-third of those
under the age of 38, and one-sixth of all men under the age of 38 who have
children. The author emphasizes the significance of such an enormous dislocation of the country's manpower as an important area for future research.

*GOLAN, N. (in press) "From wife to widow to woman: a process of role
transition." Social Work.*

A role transition model is presented as a paradigm for the handling of the
bereaved military wife, and the processes by which she moves from being wife to
widow and then to woman again are explored. In the initial phase, practical
decisions must be made as the widow continues in the routine activities as
mother and housekeeper. The next phase is that of taking on the role of
"widow" and experiencing the role of single parent and the reality of physical
aloneness. Then she begins to consider her future and exhibits interests in
outside activities.

GONZALEZ, V. (1970) Psychiatry and the Army Brat. Illinois: C.C. Thomas.

This book is a series of clinical case studies of military children who were seen
for brief psychiatric therapy. Its intent is to delineate the distinctive common
stresses of children in the military setting, and, in so doing, to clarify the
relationship between stress and reaction, for the benefit of military children as
well as for the field of child psychiatry. Each chapter discusses the impact of a
specific stress situation on the military child, e.g., extended father absence,
frequent family moves, and culturally mixed marriages. In addition, an overview
of the medical and psychiatric help available to military families is discussed.

*GREENBERG, H. (1973) "Psychiatric symptomatology in wives of military
retirees." American Journal of Psychiatry 123: 487-490.*

This study presents four case histories of army wives experiencing emotional
upheavals as a result of their husbands' retirement from the service. The
diagnoses included such psychological problems as an acute situational reaction
to fear of loss of financial stability, depression in response to anticipated loss of
self-esteem, hysteria, and a schizo-affective disorder. A program utilizing both

military and civilian community support, in which mental hygiene plays a definite, but not definitive role, is recommended.

GRIFFITH, C. (1944) "The psychological adjustments of returned servicemen and their families." Marriage and Family Living 6: 65-67, 87.

This paper presents a discussion of the various conflicts that may impede the psychological adjustment of the returning World War II serviceman. The author stresses that it is the serviceman's family that must grow in maturity and learn to adjust to the moral, ethical, and social problems that may occur. Suggestions include treating the serviceman with understanding and respect, acknowledging him as a person, and avoiding excesses of concern and pity. The family must become an informed source of vocational counseling and more humanistic in its basic approach to living.

HALL, R. and P. MALONE (1974) "Psychiatric residuals of prolonged captivity," pp. 127-146 in H. McCubbin, B. Dahl, P. Metres, Jr., E. Hunter, and J. Plag (eds.) Family Separation and Reunion, Washington, D.C.: U.S. Government Printing Office.

Clinical assessment of a small group of PW returnees suggests that the stresses of prolonged captivity are specific and can be viewed in the framework of general knowledge concerning man's reaction to stress. Applying the Gross Stress Model, the authors discuss four phases of stress reaction: (1) the anticipatory phase, (2) the impact phase, (3) the recoil phase, and (4) the posttraumatic phase. The authors emphasized: (1) the importance of contacting the wife and family prior to the prisoner's reentry; (2) a slowdown in the return and the reunion process; (3) creation of a climate of trust with the therapist; and (4) preparation for the PW's work situation and job performance.

HALL, R. and P. MALONE (1975) "Psychiatric effect of prolonged Asian Captivity: a two year follow-up." Paper presented at the American Psychiatric Association Meeting, Anaheim, California (May).

This paper describes the effects of captivity on the social reintegration of six returned prisoners of war and discusses previously unreported problems faced by these men and their families. The findings suggest that not only were cognitive, social, professional, emotional, and family difficulties present in most of the men but also that the difficulties were quite specific, each following an identical, if not synchronized, course of onset, impact, and resolution. Recommendations for handling the reentry of future PWs are given.

HALL, R. and W. SIMMONS (1973) "The POW wife—a psychiatric appraisal." Archives of General Psychiatry 29: 690-694.

Clinical data gathered on two groups of PW wives undergoing group therapy before their husbands' returns are described. Feelings expressed in therapy centered on themes of repressed anger, feelings of perceived desertion, concerns for the children, a redefinition of role as a result of change from dependent wife to independent family provider, difficulties of sexual adjustment and social isolation, and ambivalence and guilt felt toward the prospect of the husband's return. Children's difficulties were also described. Specific recommendations for treatment of PW wives are given.

HALPERN, E. (1975) "Volunteering as a 'natural phenomenon': an integration within Caplan's theory of support systems." Paper presented at the International Conference on Psychological Stress and Adjustment in Time of War and Peace, Tel Aviv, Israel (January).

This paper discusses the phenomenon of volunteering in times of community crisis within the framework of Caplan's (1974) theory of support systems. Based on volunteer work with families of men missing in action in the October 1973 war in Israel, it was observed that "targeting" of volunteer efforts was an effective means of coping with the type of crisis in which there exist no cultural patterns. The author proposes that the natural phenomenon of volunteering can be "mimicked" by targeting helping efforts during specific phases of a crisis. Volunteering is viewed as a reciprocal venture in which both the helper and those being helped receive mental health benefits.

HARTOG, J. (1966) "Group therapy with psychotic and borderline military wives." American Journal of Psychiatry 122: 1125-1131.

Two heterogeneous groups of military wives with psychotic and borderline problems, who were participating in outpatient group psychotherapy, are described. Some of the problems unique to the military wife and factors which had profound effect upon success or failure of treatment were: forced absences of the soldier from his family, producing a period of physical and social isolation for the wife and children; potential disruption of the marriage relationship when the military authorities were forced to coerce the husband into not obstructing the wife's treatment; and the stress placed on the husband's career by the wife's illness.

HILL, R. (1945) "The returning father and his family." Marriage and Family Living 7: 31-34.

Viewed as an essential figure for the emotional, social security, and development of his family, the repercussions of father's removal from the family unit are described. The deleterious effects can be minimized and the preseparation relationship sustained by establishing meaningful correspondence. Reunion difficulties, usually marked by a period of emotional intoxication followed by anxieties, can be alleviated by seeking prompt and effective professional counseling.

HILL, R. (1949) *Families Under Stress: Adjustment to the Crises of War Separation and Reunion. New York: Harper and Brothers.*

The characteristics and processes which differentiate successful from unsuccessful families in the face of adjustment to two war-born crises, war separation and reunion, were investigated. In Part I, the effect on research gathering and family adaptation to the fact that the family is a closed system were discussed. In Part II, a description of the experience of father absence owing to military commitments showed that crisis was a function of (1) the hardships of the event, (2) the resources of the family, and (3) the family's definition of the event. Proposals for national and state policies concerning the family were suggested.

HILLENBRAND, E. (1970) *"Father absence in military families." Unpublished doctoral dissertation. George Washington University.*

The relationship of father absence to variables of IQ, verbal and quantitative ability, teacher ratings of classroom behavior, maternal dominance, parental identification, birth order, and number of older male or female siblings was examined in sixth-grade pupils attending a school for Marine Corps dependents. Results indicated that there were several differences between first- and later-born boys with regard to the variables measured. Theories surrounding the behavior of first- and later-borns in relation to different coping reactions during father absence are discussed.

HOFFER, C. (1945) *"The impact of war on the farm family." Rural Sociology 10: 151-156.*

A study of farming families in rural Michigan showed that a high percentage were actively involved in war-related activities. A greater number of families accustomed to prewar participation in community affairs tended to join in war-oriented activities than the more self-centered families. Internal family relationships were disrupted only by the removal of a member to military duty. Increase in family cooperation was noted, as well as strengthening of community and neighborhood relationships.

HUNTER, E., H. McCUBBIN, and D. BENSON (1974) *"Differential viewpoints: the MIA wife vs. the MIA mother," pp. 179-190 in H. McCubbin, B. Dahl, P.*

Metres, Jr., E. Hunter and J. Plag (eds.) Family Separation and Reunion. Washington, D.C.: U.S. Government Printing Office.

The role of religion was examined at a religious retreat attended by families of servicemen missing in action (MIA). How they come to terms with inner beliefs and feelings about their husbands'/sons' absence was also examined. Responses by MIA wives and mothers showed significant differences between the two groups in their reasons for attendance at the retreat. The MIA mothers had previously been more socially isolated since their son's casualty, so that the retreat provided a unique opportunity to talk about feelings with others in the same situation. MIA wives, however, viewed the retreat as a vacation and opportunity to be alone with their children. In addition, the wives sought guidance in coping with daily stresses, while the mothers sought religious solace for the loss of their sons.

HUNTER, E., H. McCUBBIN, and P. METRES, JR. (1974) "Religion and the PW/MIA wife," pp. 85-94 in H. McCubbin, B. Dahl, P. Metres, Jr., E. Hunter, and J. Plag (eds.) Family Separation and Reunion. Washington, D.C.: Government Printing Office.

One hundred and seven PW/MIA wives who had indicated religion to be a substantial source of help during prolonged husband/father absence were compared with a group of PW/MIA wives who reported receiving no help from religion. Between-group differences were examined for age and background factors, choice of leisure activities, manifestation of emotional symptoms, present feelings about the marriage, and the frequency of adjustment and behavior problems reported for their children. Results indicated a different pattern of coping behaviors and demographic characteristics for the two groups.

HUNTER, E. and J. PLAG (1973) "An assessment of the needs of POW/MIA wives residing in the San Diego metropolitan area: a proposal for the establishment of family services." Report No. 73-39. San Diego, California: Navy Medical Neuropsychiatric Research Unit.

Forty Navy PW/MIA wives, interviewed as to their adjustment during the period subsequent to their husbands' report of casualty, indicated they had experienced a variety of adjustmental problems, especially in the area of emotional and legal difficulties. Emotional problems for a majority of the wives were severe enough to warrant treatment or for treatment to be recommended. Not only were legal problems encountered during the absence of their husbands, but many wives indicated that they foresaw complex legal issues arising in the future.

IGEL, A. (1945) "The effect of war separation on father-child relations." The
Family Journal of Social Case Work 26: 3-9.

The effect of war separation on father-child relations was reported in five
cases of children referred to the New York Bureau of Child Welfare at the time
of World War II, following the father's enlistment in the service. The author
indicates the undesirable behavior, in three of the cases cited, as the child's
emotional response to the breakdown in family relationships. Cases are also
reported in which the mother exhibited a reaction to the father's absence,
precipitating a breakdown in family organization and subsequent need for
removal of the children from the home.

ISAY, R. (1968) "The submariners' wives syndrome." Psychiatric Quarterly 42:
647-652.

A reactive depression, termed the Submariners' Wives Syndrome, characterized 262 of 432 submariners' wives seen in a Naval hospital outpatient clinic
shortly before or after their husbands' return from patrol. The etiology of the
depression appeared to be unacceptable rage over the desertion, a frustrated
need to be cared for, and sudden loss of certain gratifications, gained during the
separation, when the husband returns.

JANOWITZ, M. (1960) The Professional Soldier: A Social and Political Portrait.
New York: The Free Press of Glencoe.

The leadership, organizational properties, and the nature of professional life
within the American military structure are described. The author places emphasis upon the role of the family in the professional military. While noting the
traditions connected with being a military wife, the importance of the supportive family, the author also emphasizes the disruptive nature of family life in
the military and the movement away from community support through voluntary self-help. The author also describes the style of life, etiquette, and
ceremony of the military community, and traces the organizational realities of
the military; the social origins, motivations, and avenues of ascent in career
patterns; identity, ideology, political behaviors, and techniques in order to assess
the professional soldier's position of power in contemporary American society.

KEDEM, P., R. GELMAN, and L. BLUM (1975) "The effect of the Yom Kippur
War on the attitudes, values and locus of control of young adolescents."
Paper presented at the International Conference on Psychological Stress and
Adjustment in Time of War and Peace, Tel Aviv, Israel (January).

The effects of the Israeli Yom Kippur War upon the attitudes and values of
adolescents were examined with respect to: (1) what attitudes, in particular,

were affected by the war; (2) were attitudes and values affected by the amount of fighting by a family member; and (3) were the war's effects different among adolescents as a result of internal versus external locus of control? Data from questionnaires indicated that students' political and social attitudes were affected by the war, while relatives' participation in the war had no effect on attitudes. Differences in attitudes were also found among the students with respect to internal versus external locus of control.

KENNY, J. (1967) "The child in the military community." Journal of the American Academy of Child Psychiatry 6: 51-63.

Variables affecting children in a military community were examined. Comparisons were made between officer and enlisted families in relation to child adjustment and broken homes, and between military and civilian children in relation to intellectual functioning, emotional adjustment, and juvenile delinquency. Military children surpassed their civilian counterparts in intellectual functioning, had fewer emotional disturbances, and displayed less incidence of juvenile delinquency. Selection and education among military fathers are proposed as reasons for the higher scores exhibited among military children.

KIMURA, Y. (1957) "War brides in Hawaii and their in-laws." American Journal of Sociology 63: 70-76.

This study investigates the concept of acculturation, hypothesizing that people of similar cultures will establish relationships quickly and easily. In-law relations of 324 war brides in Hawaii were examined. The data suggest that having the same cultural background restricts relationships and spontaneous interaction with in-laws because of unfulfilled role expectations. In cases where the cultural background is dissimilar, relations are improved because of a lack of defined roles and the perceived need of adjusting to each other.

KIRSCHNER, E. (1975) "Pilot study on bereavement and rehabilitation of war widows of the Six-Day and Yom Kippur Wars." Paper presented at the International Conference on Psychological Stress and Adjustment in Time of War and Peace, Tel Aviv, Israel (January).

The purpose of this pilot study was: (1) to observe the grief pattern of widows, the onset and duration and effect of bereavement, and the comparison of the grief patterns of two groups of widows; (2) to observe the rehabilitation process of widows; (3) to determine the effect of the mutual help groups and individual therapy on widows. With wives' self-developed criteria for good and bad adjustment and Lindeman's "grief syndrome," a questionnaire was devised and answered by the widows during interviews.

KRISTAL, L. (1975) "The effects of a wartime environment upon the psychological development of children in border settlements." Paper presented at the International Conference on Psychological Stress and Adjustment in Time of War and Peace, Tel Aviv, Israel (January).

A control group of 69 children living in inland Israel, not exposed to wartime stress, were compared to an experimental group of 66 children, living less than one kilometer from the Israel-Jordan cease-fire line, who were exposed to shelling, bombardment, death, and other wartime stresses. Degree of manifest anxiety, autonomy patterns, and various symptoms of physical stress were measured. Results were discussed in terms of the developmental impact of extended stress, the credibility of the latent anxiety theory, the validity of laboratory-derived statements of psychological stress, and implications for field studies.

KUHLEN, R. (1951) "Nervous symptoms among military personnel as related to age, combat experience, and marital status," Journal of Consulting Psychology 15: 320-324.

This study examined the possible manifestation of nervous symptoms in 8,700 enlisted naval personnel passing through a preembarkation center during a six-month period between 1944 and 1945. Results indicated that married men, whether or not they had children, expressed more nervous symptoms on the questionnaire than did unmarried men. It appears that, owing to the existence of marital and family responsibilities, a greater reaction to the stress of war experiences does occur in these men.

KURLANDER, L., D. LEUKEL, L. PALEVSKY, and F. KOHN (1961) "Migration: some psychological effects on children—a pilot study." Paper presented at the American Orthopsychiatric Association Annual Meeting, New York (March).

This paper investigates the psychological effects of frequent "migrations" on a group of 138 children referred to a Child Guidance Clinic. The disorders observed fell into groups of behavior problems and neurotic problems, affecting military children more than nonmilitary children. Special characteristics of the military family, such as frequent moves, absence of father, disruption of social and emotional continuity, are credited for the high incidence of problems.

LEVY, D. (1944) "The war and family life." Report for the War Emergency Committee.

Based on general observations and case histories from various social agencies, the effects of war on 50 families were described. General changes in family life included increased protectiveness, responsibility within the home, and family solidarity as a result of the threat of danger and privation; increased personal self-esteem from participation in voluntary activities; a reduction in family tensions by induction of male members into the service or employment of a family member; and financial benefits occurring from openings becoming available in the labor force. The demoralizing influences were described, the most frequent being the absent mother who uses voluntary activities as a means of avoiding family responsibilities.

LEVY, S. (1975) "Social work self-involvement in a disaster situation." Paper presented at the International Conference of Psychological Stress and Adjustment in Time of War and Peace, Tel Aviv, Israel (January).

This study describes the volunteer efforts of Haifa University social work faculty members and practitioners from various family social agencies in helping bereaved families of the Israeli Yom Kippur War. Relationships of the volunteer workers to their clients were characterized by an element of self-identification with the bereaved families, while the professional role transcended a therapeutic relationship and took on the qualities of social interaction. Feedback sessions, attended by volunteers and professionals, provided exchange of ideas from various disciplines.

LIEBERMAN, E. (1971a) "War and the family: the psychology of antigrief." Modern Medicine (April): 179-183, 191.

Disturbing statistics and personal impressions of the Vietnam War reported in this essay reveal a contemporary American psychology of "antigrief." In order to deal with the realities of modern warfare, the stoic ideal of detachment prevails as the nation's mode of defense. Grief, the author says, is a necessary process by which ambivalence must be "faced, worked through, and integrated." The war widow and disabled veteran must "first mourn that missing part of their lives, in order to reconstitute their lives on a meaningful basis." Neglect of healthy grief, on a public level, it is inferred will inhibit growth and change for society as well.

LIEBERMAN, E. (1971b) "American families and the Vietnam War." Journal of Marriage and the Family 33: 709-721.

The impact of war upon the family is described through demographic information and awesome statistics of previous American wars (particularly the Vietnam War) with regard to casualties, ethnic selection, special problems of military families, bereavement, and resocialization of veterans. An overview of the Vietnam conflict emerges, characterized by socioracial discrimination within the draft, poverty amongst lower-echelon servicemen, an increasing caseload of disabled veterans, and competition between the returning serviceman and his wife for family roles. A need for more family participation in the policies of war and peace is suggested.

LIFSHITZ, M. (1975) "Social differentiation and organization of the Rorschach in fatherless and two-parented children." Journal of Clinical Psychology 31: 126-130.

How family structure affects a child's cognitive structure (his level of differentiation and integration) and the degree of relationship between the social perceptual differentiation and cognitive interaction was investigated. The study of 136 Israeli middle-class children, one-fourth of whom had lost their fathers in the war, showed no significant differences between orphans and nonorphans in their degree of perceptual differentiation of their basic family unit. Nonorphans did show a direct relationship between the amount of social differentiation and their degree of perceptual organization.

LIFSHITZ, M., D. BERMAN, A. GALILI, and D. GILAD (1975) "Bereaved children: The effect of mother's perception and social system organization on their adjustment." Paper presented at the International Conference on Psychological Stress and Adjustment in Time of War and Peace, Tel Aviv, Israel (January).

The short-term effects of father loss on 48 bereaved children of the Israeli Yom Kippur War were examined with regard to the mother's approach to the child, the unique system of family organization, and the child's degree of adjustment to life without his father. Interview and test results indicated that (1) moshav and city boys showed more disorganization of behavior as a result of their fathers' deaths than kibbutz children; (2) boys appeared to be more affected by the loss than girls; and (3) children who, according to a concrete-affective criterion, were perceived, and perceived themselves, to be like one of their parents, displayed less problem behaviors. Differences in social systems, kibbutz or moshav and city, are described.

LINDQUIST, R. (1952) "Marriage and family life of officers and airmen in a Strategic Air Command Wing." Technical Report No. 5. Institute for Research in Social Science, University of North Carolina.

The effects of a husband's duty with the Strategic Air Command (SAC) upon his family life were examined. Most wives indicated that SAC requirements negatively affected their family life. They reported that the SAC routine fostered a stressful and demanding environment with regard to family organization and roles, husband-wife relationships, housing/living arrangements, financial planning, home management and child care, social and civic activities, planning for the children's future, and planning for retirement.

LITTLE, R. (1971) "The military family," pp. 247-270 in R. W. Little (ed.) Handbook of Military Institutions. Beverly Hills, California: Sage.

The historical development of the changing status of the military family is examined, from World War I to the present. Its current status is discussed and supporting evidence is given for the thesis that the military family is now considered an essential component in personnel policy and management. Common features of family life in the military were noted and their effects on family life evaluated. It was predicted that the military family will have an increasing impact on the civilian community, largely through the development of CHAMPUS and the influx of retired military personnel into the civilian community and labor force.

LYON W. and L. OLDAKER (1967) "The child, the school, and the military family." American Journal of Orthopsychiatry 37: 269-270.

Based on efforts to supply psychological services to children in a military elementary school, the authors provide a description of military dependents as a stable population. The notion that frequent father absences and family moves are detrimental to military children is qualified by observations that frequent father absenteeism is often compensated for by the father's authoritarian role, and the child is conditioned to accept mobility as commonplace. Military children are also relatively homogeneous as a group because of such influences as little income differential among servicemen and similar average intelligence levels.

MAC INTOSH, H. (1968) "Separation problems in military wives." American Journal of Psychiatry 125: 260-265.

Sixty-three military wives experiencing psychiatric symptoms precipitated by separation from their husbands because of military duties, when compared to a control group, were found to be significantly younger, less educated, more apt to be Army rather than Air Force wives, and enlisted rather than officer's wives. Neurotic reactions were found to be more common than psychotic symptoms. Psychoanalytic interpretations are offered to account for the findings.

MARSH, R. (1970) "Family disruption during the moving process." Unpublished doctoral dissertation. Brandeis University.

Hardships endured by families while leaving one community and settling into another were studied. Two hundred and five men, whose families had recently moved to an Army post, were interviewed to determine the nature of family disruption and to isolate those factors which could account for the disruption. Causes of family disruption were: moving costs being greater than the Army's payable allowances for moving, families' need to borrow money for additional moving costs, delay in monthly pay owing to loss of finance records during transferral, and separation of family during moving.

McCUBBIN, H. and B. DAHL (1974a) "Social and mental health services to families of returned prisoners of war." Paper presented at American Psychiatric Association Meeting, Detroit, Michigan (May).

The need for provision of social and mental health services to families of servicemen missing in action (MIA) or returned prisoners of war (RPW) is discussed within a community mental health framework. Comprehensive services (i.e., medical, psychological, legal, and administrative) with a preventative aim— in particular, provision of outreach services, coordination of collaborative services with other agencies from a multiplicity of disciplines, provision of mental health consultation, and establishment of research emphasizing long-range follow-up studies, are the essential components of the mental health program. Statistics regarding the use of outreach services are presented.

McCUBBIN, H. and B. DAHL (1974b) "An overview of the initial stages of longitudinal study of families of servicemen missing in action and returned prisoners of war." Paper presented at Prisoner of War Research Conference, Naval Health Research Center, San Diego, California (April).

This presentation identified the importance of a longitudinal study of returned prisoners of war families; described and discussed findings from data previously collected; examined family adjustment, specifically divorce and separation; and enumerated the lessons learned concerning services to PW/MIA and RPW families. Covering adjustment at time of reunion, divorce, and separation, and family adjustment 10 months following repatriation, it discussed the major factors predictive of successful adjustment to reunion and those predictive of divorce. It concluded that family preparation for reunion, family services, and preparation of the husband for his return may be important factors for successful family adjustment.

McCUBBIN, H. and B. DAHL (1974c) "Families of returned prisoners of war: a review." Paper presented at Second Joint Medical Meeting on Returned Prisoners of War, Department of Defense, San Antonio, Texas (November).

Focusing on the adjustment of families of returned prisoners of war, this paper reports on the findings and plans of the Center for Prisoner of War Studies in San Diego, California. Statistics regarding divorce/separation rates and follow-up services to families are presented. The authors emphasized: (1) the importance of the total follow-up programs and services; (2) the importance of assessing the family's adaptation; (3) the role of the family in the adjustment of the returned prisoner of war; and (4) the importance of a longitudinal assessment of the children's adjustment within the family unit.

McCUBBIN, H. and B. DAHL (1974d) "Social and mental health services to families of servicemen missing in action or returned prisoners of war," pp. 191-198 in H. McCubbin, B. Dahl, P. Metres, Jr., E. Hunter, and J. Plag (eds.), Family Separation and Reunion. Washington, D.C.: U.S. Government Printing Office.

Social and mental health services to families of servicemen missing in action (MIA) or returned prisoners of war (RPW) are discussed within a community mental health framework. Expanding on an earlier paper, the authors emphasize the community mental health approach for these men and their families in order to ensure provision of comprehensive services (i.e., medical, psychological, legal, and administrative) with a preventive aim. The essential components of the mental health program are described: (1) provision of outreach services; (2) the coordination of collaborative services with other agencies from a multiplicity of disciplines; (3) provision of mental health consultation; and (4) establishment of research in order to increase knowledge of the various aspects of father absence, and the effects of captivity on the RPW as well as his future adjustment.

McCUBBIN, H., B. DAHL, and E. HUNTER (1975) "Research on the military family: an assessment," in N. Goldman and D. Segal (eds.) Proceedings of the Inter-University Seminar on the Armed Forces and Society: Social Psychology of Military Services (in press).

Social and psychological studies conducted on military families during the past four decades were categorized and reviewed in relationship to: mobility, child adjustment and development, adjustment to separation, family reunion and reintegration, adjustment to loss, families in transition, and services to families under stress. The limitation but importance of family research in the military is emphasized, while the historical antecedents of family research in the military were critiqued.

McCUBBIN, H., B. DAHL, G. LESTER, D. BENSON, and M. ROBERTSON (1975) "Coping repertoires of families adapting to prolonged war-induced separations." Technical Report No. 75-56. Naval Health Research Center, San Diego, California.

The adjustment of 47 families of servicemen missing in action in the Vietnam conflict was studied to dilineate specific coping patterns wives employ in response to prolonged separations. Six coping behavior patterns were isolated: I—Seeking Resolution and Expressing Feelings; II—Maintaining Family Integrity; III—Establishing Autonomy and Maintaining Family Ties; IV—Reducing Anxiety; V—Establishing Independence through Self-Development; and VI—Maintaining the Past and Dependence on Religion. Independent predictors—background, attitudinal and situational variables—were analyzed in relation to each of the coping patterns. Findings are explained in terms of both psychological and sociological theories of coping.

McCUBBIN, H., B. DAHL, G. LESTER, and B. ROSS (1975) "The returned prisoner of war: factors in family adjustment." Paper presented at the International Conference on Psychological Stress and Adjustment in Time of War and Peace, Tel Aviv, Israel (January).

In this investigation, which concentrates on data longitudinally collected on 48 families of returned prisoners of war, an attempt was made to identify the best combination of factors which may be used to explain the degree of reintegration of the returned prisoner of war into his family system. Four sets of data—(1) backbround characteristics of both the husband and wife; (2) indices of family preparedness for separation and reunion; (3) reports by the returnees on their prison experience and reports of their psychiatric status at the time of repatriation; and (4) measures of family adjustment during the separation period—were considered. Results and implications were discussed.

McCUBBIN, H., B. DAHL, G. LESTER, and B. ROSS (1975) "The returned prisoner of war: factors in family reintegration." Journal of Marriage and the Family 37: 471-478.

This expanded version of an earlier paper concentrates on data longitudinally collected on 48 families of returned prisoners of war. An attempt was made to identify the best combination of factors which may be used to explain the degree of reintegration of the returned prisoner of war into his family system. Linear multiple regression procedures were utilized for the purpose of analyzing the unique contributions of each of the predictor variables in accounting for the variance in the criterion and for deriving an equation in which the variables could be optimally weighted. Results indicated the importance of the quality of the marriage, length of the marriage, and the wife's emotional adjustment during the separation period. The importance of follow-up services is emphasized.

McCUBBIN, H., B. DAHL, G. LESTER and B. ROSS (1975) "The returned prisoner of war and his children; evidence for the origin of second generational effects of captivity." Paper presented at the Third Annual Joint Medical Meeting Concerning POW/MIA Matters. Naval Health Research Center. San Diego, California.

The authors initiated a study of the theory that the stresses of internment affect the parent-child relationship, which, over the years, may have a detrimental effect upon the children's social and emotional development. From data longitudinally collected on 42 families of returned prisoners of the Vietnam War, an attempt was made to identify the combination of factors that could explain the variability in the quality of the father-child relationship subsequent to the father's release from prison. Data considered were: (1) background characteristics of parents; (2) measures of family adjustment; (3) stresses of the returned prisoner's captivity; (4) psychiatric status of the returned prisoner at repatriation; and (5) an index of the father-child relationship one year following the family's reunion. The stresses of captivity and the subsequent father-child relationship were found to be significantly related.

McCUBBIN, H., B. DAHL, P. METRES, E. HUNTER, and J. PLAG (eds.) (1974) Family Separation and Reunion: Families of Prisoners of War and Servicemen Missing in Action. Washington, D.C.: Superintendent of Documents, U.S. Government Printing Office.

This volume is concerned with the process of adapting—the ways in which men responded to the stresses of war and captivity; the ways in which the family unit adapted itself to the prolonged and seemingly indeterminate absence of a father; how the returnee and his wife and children reintegrate their family unit after the long separation; and how a family copes with and prepares itself for a future without the father and husband.

McCUBBIN, H., E. HUNTER, and B. DAHL (1975) "Residuals of war: families of prisoners of war and servicemen missing in action." Journal of Social Issues 31(4).

The adjustment problems experienced by 215 families of servicemen missing in action or prisoners of war were examined one year prior to the release of the prisoners. Results indicated: (a) the normal patterns of coping with father/ husband absence were disturbed by the indeterminate length of his absence, and (b) that much of the social acceptance, stability, and continuity which are taken for granted in the intact family were lacking or severely taxed in the PW/MIA family. Health care service to these families is discussed.

McCUBBIN, H., E. HUNTER, and P. METRES, JR. (1974) "Adaptation of the family to the prisoner of war and missing in action experience," pp. 21-48 in H. McCubbin, B. Dahl, P. Metres, Jr., E. Hunter, and J. Plag (eds.), Family Separation and Reunion. Washington, D.C.: U.S. Government Printing Office.

The families of servicemen missing in action or prisoners of war in the Southeast Asian conflict have experienced stresses resulting in social and emotional adjustments within the family unit. This proposition was specified and examined in terms of the adaptive behaviors and emotional adjustments which emerged during the serviceman's absence, as reported by 215 families. Adaptation of the family to the PW/MIA situation through modification in family roles, physical and emotional adjustment of wives and children, and the utilization of services were examined.

McCUBBIN, H. and P. METRES, JR. (1974) "Maintaining hope: the dilemma of parents of sons missing in action," pp. 169-178 in H. McCubbin, B. Dahl, P. Metres, Jr., E. Hunter, and J. Plag (eds.), Family Separation and Reunion. Washington, D.C.: U.S. Government Printing Office.

Observations of parents of sons missing in action or prisoners of war, and reactions to their issues, were described. Some techniques utilized by the parents ranged from understanding the loss of their son by looking at the situation through their son's eyes, i.e., his love for the military; obtaining additional information from foreign governments and the press; to involving themselves in PW/MIA activities both locally and nationally. Most parents would have preferred some definite resolution to their son's situation rather than none at all. Mothers generally freely discussed their feelings and grief concerning their sons, while fathers remained silently angry and grieved.

McCUBBIN, H., E. HUNTER, and P. METRES, JR. (1974) "Children in limbo," pp. 65-76 in H. McCubbin, B. Dahl, P. Metres, Jr., E. Hunter and J. Plag (eds.), Family Separation and Reunion. Washington, D.C.: U.S. Government Printing Office.

The reaction of children to the prolonged absence of a father missing in action or a prisoner of war was investigated. Group discussions with the children were conducted and feelings about their fathers' absence or recent return, their personal and emotional adjustment, and their perceptions of mothers' adjustment were examined. The children whose fathers had not returned indicated several difficult areas of adjustment owing to social as well as family responsibilities, conflicts with other children in the school setting, and frustrations over coping with fathers' prolonged absence. Advanced maturity and greater sensitivity to other people were perceived by all the children as benefits of their situation. The nature of their reactions and the implications for the long-term adjustment of the children are discussed.

McKAIN, J. (1969) "Feelings of alienation, geographical mobility, and Army family problems: an extension of theory." Unpublished doctoral dissertation: Catholic University of America.

The relationship between feelings of alienation and family problems associated with moving in Army families was assessed. A significant correlation was found between feelings of alienation and family problems associated with moving. Family problems were found to occur more in families where the mother feels alienated from both society and the Army community. For off-post resident families, when compared with on-post residents there was a significantly higher correlation between alienation and family problems associated with moving.

McKAIN, J. (1973) "Relocation in the military: alienation and family problems." Journal of Marriage and the Family 35: 205-209.

The effects of geographical mobility were examined in relation to alienation and intra- and interpersonal family problems within the Army. Using lack of identification with the military as a measure of alienation, the author found that the alienated wife experienced many personal, marital, and child-related problems, and viewed moving as a negative situation for the family, while the low-alienated wife was able to integrate herself in the new community more easily and perceived moving more positively.

McNEIL, J. (1964) "Adjustment of retired Air Force officers." Unpublished doctoral dissertation. University of Southern California.

This study investigates the degree of preparation and successful adjustment of former military officers to retirement. The majority of the 46 officers interviewed were relatively young, had completed college, had two or more dependent children, had retired voluntarily, and had chosen a second career. Most officers felt some anxiety associated with retiring, had delayed actively preparing for retirement, and had experienced role confusion for the first few months following retirement. The need for services to aid in preparation for retirement was emphasized.

McNEIL, J. and M. GIFFEN (1965a) "Military retirement: some basic observations and concepts." Aerospace Medicine 36: 25-29.

The impact of military retirement is described in terms of phases, from retirement preparation to eventual adjustment or maladjustment to civilian life. Preparation for retirement is suggested in the areas of retirement activity, residence, finances, appraisal of health, and constructive channeling of the anxiety naturally aroused in being confronted with a new situation. Problems confronted by the retiree in adjusting to a civilian career include working up a hierarchal ladder all over again, encountering civilian prejudice against military retirees, dealing with the handicap of lack of transferability of skills, and a lower pay scale.

McNEIL, J. and M. GIFFEN (1965b) "The social impact of military retirement." Social Casework 46: 203-207.

Various social issues related to large-scale military retirement, its immediate impact on the man and his family and on an already shrinking labor market, and eventual cost to the public are described. Although retirees, in seeking civilian employment, may accept salaries below the prevailing wage scale, and inadvertently affect labor markets in those areas in which retirees tend to cluster, the author argues against the notion that military retirees, more than any other citizens, influence to any degree the political patterns and social institutions in those areas in which they retire.

McNEIL, J. and M. GIFFEN (1967) "Military retirement: the retirement syndrome." American Journal of Psychiatry 123: 848-854.

The problems unique to retirement from the military service are described, along with several case examples. The retirement syndrome is described as three stages, beginning with preretirement anxiety, depression, and somatic complaints, moving into a period of role confusion soon after retirement, and culmination in failure to assimilate the transitional role confusion period successfully. A preventative treatment approach to the retirement problem is suggested through realistic preretirement planning and emphasizing the transitional quality of the role confusion period in order to bolster the retiree's confidence and self-esteem.

McNEIL, J. and R. ZONDERVAN (1971) "The family in cultural isolation." Military Medicine 136: 451-454.

Some of the factors contributing to breakdown in military families living overseas are examined within a conceptual framework of general systems theory. Causative factors of disruption in the family system include culture shock, an altered dependency-independency ratio between spouses, disturbed perceptions relating to distance from America, boredom, and a temporary suspension of life style. Therapeutic intervention is directed towards reestablishing homeostasis and a balance between input and output within the family system.

METRES, JR., P., H. McCUBBIN, and E. HUNTER (1974) "Families of returned prisoners of war: some impressions on their initial reintegration," pp. 147-156 in H. McCubbin, B. Dahl, P. Metres, Jr., E. Hunter, and J. Plag (eds.), Family Separation and Reunion. Washington, D.C.: U.S. Government Printing Office.

Informal interviews with 26 recently returned prisoners of war (RPWs) and 21 of their wives who were participating in a religious retreat yielded impressions concerning initial reintegration experiences and plans for the future. Admitting to extensive adjustment problems, the returnees' group discussions centered on themes of ambivalence toward public versus family commitments, difficulties with role readjustments, concerns for their children's adjustment as a result of their lengthy absence, and feelings of "survivor guilt." The beneficial effects of the group process afforded these men and their families are emphasized.

MILGRAM, R. and N. MILGRAM (1975) "The effects of the Yom Kippur War on anxiety level in Israeli children." Paper presented at the International Conference on Psychological Stress and Adjustment in Time of War and Peace, Tel Aviv, Israel (January).

This report presents a comparative study of the level of anxiety in peacetime and wartime in fifth- and sixth-grade children before and after the Yom Kippur War. Results indicated that the wartime anxiety level nearly doubled and that children with the lowest prewar level of anxiety were the ones with the highest level of postwar anxiety. Moreover, this high anxiety level seemed related more to sex and to socioeconomic status than to war stress or personality parameters.

MILOWE, I. (1964) "A study in role diffusion: the chief and sergeant face retirement." Mental Hygiene 48: 101-107.

Emotional maladjustments in Coast Guard Chief Petty Officers facing retirement from the service are described. The case examples revealed individual and family disorganization and neurotic problems precipitated by the stress of retirement. The choice of the military service as a career is interpreted as a "pseudo-moratorium" providing a sense of personal identification and temporary escape from "unconsciously determined individual conflicts." Retirement is seen as a crisis situation which robs the Chief of his "stable self-concepts engendered by service roles."

MONTALVO, F. (1968) "Family separation in the Army: A study of the problems encountered and the caretaking resources used by career Army families undergoing military separation." Unpublished doctoral dissertation, University of Southern California.

The problems faced by families during the father's 12-month overseas duty tour are investigated with regard to the nature of caretaking resources used for problem-solving, the degree to which problems can be attributed to the father's absence or to the family's relocation into a new community, the wives' emotional responses to the separation, and the extent of family involvement in the community subculture. Over half of the families' problems were found to be related to the families' forced relocation into a new community rather than to the actual absence of the fathers. Since family relocation, generally away from the military community, appears to be more stressful than separation from the father/husband, the author suggests that family adjustment to separation would be improved by allowing the family to remain in the military community during the father's absences.

MOSKOS, JR., C. (1970) *The American Enlisted Man: The Rank and File in Today's Military*. New York: Russell Sage Foundation.

Through personal observations and interviews of American servicemen stationed abroad, the author presents an overview of enlisted culture. The soldier is seen as he is portrayed in the mass media, film, and literature through four war periods: World War II, the Korean War, the Cold War, and the Vietnam War. Strains between single-term and career soldiers, differences in levels of education, the juxtaposition of both authoritarian and egalitarian standards, and military family life characterized by the inconvenience of family moves and separations are described as common elements underlying enlisted culture. In addition, the serviceman overseas, racial relations, and the behavior of combat soldiers are examined.

MYLES, D. (1970) *"A survey of Army community services centers: welfare problems, services, personnel and resources."* Unpublished doctoral dissertation. Catholic University of America.

The organization and operations of fifty Army Community Service Program (ACS) centers which are designed to support and assist military families were examined in relation to such factors as type and frequency of social welfare problems, social welfare services, the manner in which specific tasks are assigned to social welfare personnel, and the competence and skills of those assigned to deal with them. In addition, various community resources were identified and the nature of their interaction with ACS described.

NELSON, R. (1974) *"The legal plight of the PW/MIA family,"* pp. 49-64 in H. McCubbin, B. Dahl, P. Metres, Jr., E. Hunter, and J. Plag (eds.), *Family Separation and Reunion*. Washington, D.C.: U.S. Government Printing Office.

Some of the various legal problems encountered by families of servicemen missing in action (MIA) or prisoners of war (PW) during the course of the Vietnam War are described. The problems highlighted included: determination of the husband's status and declarations of death; the purchase, sale, and disposition of property; divorce proceedings in the husband's absence; propriety of remarriage; adoption attempts; availability of federal benefits; disposition of the serviceman's pay; and estate administration problems. The shortcomings of obsolete federal provisions are discussed.

NIELSON, L. (1971) "Impact of permanent father loss on the intellectual level, vocational interests, personal adjustment and career plans of male war orphans." Unpublished doctoral dissertation. University of Utah.

This study examined the differences in intellectual level, vocational interests, personal adjustment, and career plans of 200 male war orphans in relation to the onset and duration of the fathers' absence from the family. Significant differences were found between the groups as to their occupational interest and personal adjustment. Orphans experiencing early father absence without step-father replacement were less inclined to express any occupational interest and were more likely to encounter problems in pursuing their educational objectives.

PALGI, P. (1973) Socio-Cultural Expressions and Implications of Death, Mourning and Bereavement in Israel Arising out of the War Situation. Israel: Jerusalem Academic Press.

A theoretical and research approach dealing with the functions and relativity of mourning customs in Israel is described. The effect of acculturation on mourning customs is examined in terms of the form and display of grief, the status of the young widow, the role and function of the ceremonial meal during the mourning period, visits to the grave, and activation of magical beliefs. Differential reactions to war deaths by various family types, the isolated family among the postwar Holocaust survivors, the traditional Muslim family, and the Ashkenazi old established families, are presented.

PALGI, P. (1975) "Culture and mourning: expressions of bereavement arising out of the war situation in Israel." Paper presented at the International Conference on Psychological Stress and Adjustment in Time of War and Peace, Tel Aviv, Israel (January).

Bereavement in modern-day war-torn Israel is systematically analyzed. Variations in certain features of the mourning process which can become areas of personal conflict are presented. An analysis was given of three family types in terms of their strengths and weaknesses in dealing with crises: old established Ashkenazi families, the isolated family among postwar Holocaust survivors, and the traditional Muslim immigrant family.

PATTERSON, R. (1945) "Neurotic reactions in wives of servicemen." Diseases of the Nervous System 6: 50-52.

The neurotic reactions of three servicemen's wives were clinically described. Two cases depicted women whose anxiety reactions were manifestations of repressed feelings of guilt and depression directly related to their husbands' induction. The third case described a dependent, immature wife whose level of adjustment grossly decompensated when the security and support her husband normally gave her were withdrawn owing to his induction.

PEDERSEN, F. (1966) "Relationships between father-absence and emotional disturbance in male military dependents." Merrill-Palmer Quarterly 12: 321-331.

The effects of father absence in the military in relation to emotional disturbance in two groups of male children are examined. Specifically, the study included emotionally disturbed as well as normal children and focused upon the amount of father absence occurring during three developmental stages of the child: early childhood (birth-3 years), Oedipal period (3-5 years), and middle childhood (5-9 years). The degree of father absence was not significantly different between the two groups. The author hypothesizes that children's disturbance was related to the interaction between father absence and maternal pathology.

PEDERSEN, F. and E. SULLIVAN (1964) "Relationships among geographical mobility, parental attitudes, and emotional disturbances in children." American Journal of Orthopsychiatry 34: 575-580.

The effects of geographical mobility on military children are examined with the prediction that emotionally disturbed children would show a greater number of moves accompanied by the ensuing difficult period of adaptation. Contrary to predictions, the histories of disturbed children and normal children did not show any significant differences. In general, parental attitudes toward mobility were found to be more important than the moves themselves in affecting the adjustment of the children.

PEPIN, R. (1966) "A study of scholastic achievements and personal adjustments of military and non-military transitory high school students." Unpublished doctoral dissertation. University of Connecticut.

This study investigates the impact of residential and school changes upon the school and personal adjustment of ninth- and tenth-grade children. Measures including selected standardized achievements tests, grade point average, and reports of personal adjustment problems were obtained. In general, findings did not reveal significant differences between military mobile, nonmilitary mobile, and civilian nonmobile children, with the exception of results of standardized mathematics achievement, in which the nonmobile scored higher.

PLAG, J. (1974) "Proposal for the long-term follow-up of returned prisoners of war, their families, and the families of servicemen missing in action: a basis for the delivery of health care services." Paper presented at the PW Research Consultants' Conference, San Diego, California (April).

The Director of the Center for Prisoner of War Studies (CPWS) in San Diego, California, outlines the mission and study plans of the long-term follow-up and medical evaluation of returned prisoners of war (RPW) and the families of returned prisoners of war and men missing in action (MIA). The aims of the Center include a follow-up program extending over a period of several decades in which health care services are rendered to the families, in conjunction with the systematic collection of standardized health and adjustment research data, and the designation of a comparable control group of military men and their families.

PLATTE, R. (1974) "The second career: perceived social mobility and adjustment among recent army retirees and wives of army retirees." Unpublished doctoral dissertation. Florida State University.

This study investigates the retired serviceman's psychological and marital adjustment as a function of his perception of social mobility in changing careers in middle age. Specifically, it was proposed that the horizontally mobile would be more adjusted than the vertically mobile, and that less adjustment would be reported by the downwardly mobile than the upwardly mobile. Hypotheses were confirmed. Perceived social mobility was found to affect the retiree's adjustment.

POWERS, I. (1974) "National League of Families and the development of family services," pp. 1-10 in H. McCubbin, B. Dahl, P. Metres, Jr., E. Hunter, and J. Plag (eds.), Family Separation and Reunion. Washington, D.C.: U.S. Government Printing Office.

The author presents a brief historical background of the development of the National League of Families of American Prisoners and Missing in Southeast Asia. The purpose of the League was to obtain humanitarian treatment for prisoners, stimulate concern about the men's families, improve communication and information, and obtain release of the prisoners. In tracing the growth of the League, the author points out the political potency and impact of its organization and its emphasis upon the provision of counseling services to families.

PRICE-BONHAM, S. (1972) "Missing in action men: a study of their wives." International Journal of Sociology of the Family 2: (September).

Thirty-two wives of men missing in action in Vietnam were interviewed as to their attitudes toward their husbands' being either alive or dead, in relation to eleven selected variables. Variables found to be significantly related to the wife's attitude included length of time the husband had been missing, number and age of children, her education and employment, her plans for the future, and her attitudes toward the marriage. In general, wives who believed their husbands to be dead seemed to be better adapted to their present life but indicated greater anxiety at the prospect of reunion with the husband.

RAKOFF, V. (1966) "Long-term effects of the concentration camp experience." Viewpoints 1: 17-21.

Investigating the thesis that children of concentration camp (CC) survivors experience severe psychiatric problems, the author examined the case histories of three adolescents. The children were aware of their parents' ordeal. After a normal childhood, they exhibited problems of rebellion, anger, phobia, and depression in adolescence and suffered from a heavy parental expectation that they psychologically replace the murdered relatives. The article concludes with the implication that there may be no real "survivors" of the concentration camps.

RAKOFF, V., J. SIGAL, and N. EPSTEIN (1967) "Children and families of concentration camp survivors." Canadian Mental Health 14: 24-26.

The long-term consequences of concentration camp (CC) experience were examined in 26 postwar families of CC survivors. The social adjustment of CC survivors was observed to have been easier than their emotional adjustment to parenthood. Parents reacted to their children by being too strict or totally lacking in disciplinary measures, and showed an absence of affect. Unreasonable expectations of having the children reincarnate murdered family members was an additional heavy burden which resulted in apathy, depressive feelings of emptiness, hyperactivity, and/or lack of involvement in normal youth activities by the children.

ROGERS, C. (1944) "Wartime issues in family counseling." Journal of Marriage and the Family 68-69, 84.

This paper presents a discussion of the validity of client-centered therapy, as opposed to directive counseling, in dealing with family adjustments and problems expected to occur in the postwar period following World War II. The author supports the aims of client-centered therapy because it "respects the integrity and personal autonomy of the individual, his enormous capacity for readjustment, and his drive toward maturity and positive health," and discusses its advantages in relation to marital and family relationships, in terms of safety, and in being consistent with democratic ideals.

ROGERS, C. (1945) "Counseling with the returned serviceman and his wife." Marriage and Family Living 7: 82-84.

Client-centered counseling is discussed as a viable means for aiding readjustment in marriages disrupted by wartime separation. Examples of families who have experienced wartime separation are presented. The effectiveness of the counselor's conveying a nondirective, nonjudgmental attitude towards his client, establishing a warm, permissive atmosphere in which any thoughts and feelings can be expressed, and accepting and mirroring sentiments conveyed to him are emphasized with this population.

SANUA, V. (1974) "The psychological effects of the Yom Kippur War." Unpublished manuscript, City College–The City University of New York.

The author relates his experience and findings as a research psychologist in Israel during the Yom Kippur War. The process by which a select team is chosen to inform a family of a soldier's death and the reactions of grieving family members are described. The unique manner in which Israeli parents perpetuate their son's memory through displays, pictures, and commemorative books was examined and theorized as a possible innovative research avenue.

SATTIN, D. and J. MILLER (1971) "The ecology of child abuse within a military community." American Journal of Orthopsychiatry 41: 675-678.

Studies of mental disorders using an ecological approach reveal a greater prevalence of mental disorder among poor, disorganized communities with either transient populations or socially isolated populations. This study tested two hypotheses: (a) abusive parents reside in specific types of areas of the city i.e., poor, transient neighborhoods; and (b) abusive parents for the most part live in different residential areas than nonabusing parents. Financial and other environmental stresses, in combination with certain personality types, are factors offered to explain the incidence of child abuse found in 29 military families residing in such neighborhoods.

SAUNDERS, D. (1969) "Poverty in the Army." Social Service Review 43: 396-405.

This study reveals that poverty does exist within the Army, and that poverty is more a function of Army inadequacies than of personal negligence on the part of families or soldiers. Poverty affects mostly soldiers with large families, those convicted of disciplinary offenses, and those from low-income or minority backgrounds. Major factors responsible for an increase in poverty are considered, and a variety of recommendations are made to ameliorate the problem.

SCHUETZ, A. (1945) "The homecomer." American Journal of Sociology 50: 369-376.

This paper analyzes the word "home" in terms of its physical, philosophical, and sociological connotations for the returning veteran. For the man away from home, new experiences influence his perception of home; he tends to pseudo-type his home and its members. People at home remember him as he was in the past, and engage in a similar pseudo-typification of him, and these pseudo-typifications are significant obstacles to an adaptive homecoming. Preparation for homecoming (e.g., through realistic portrayals by the media) is suggested for the sake of the returning veteran as well as for that of the home group to which he will be returning.

SEGAL, J. (1973) "Therapeutic considerations in planning the return of American POWs to continental United States." Military Medicine 138: 73-77.

This article provides recommendations concerning the speed and manner in which American PWs should return from Vietnam. It is suggested that the return process should provide a period during which physical and psychological rehabilitation procedures could be started in a sheltered environment—such a protective buffer against rapid immersion in a changed world appears as an important therapeutic tool for successful personal and family adjustment. The author suggests that such a buffer would be more beneficial if maintained outside the Continental U.S. and that a return voyage by ship might prove helpful for the PWs.

SEGAL, J. (1974) "The family adjustment of men returning from captivity: some theoretical and research issues." Unpublished manuscript.

Various theoretical and research issues concerning the effects of paternal absence are described, specifically in reference to the family adjustment of men returning from captivity. Many theoretical interpretations are surveyed which may explain the high incidence of delinquency within father-absent homes. The effects of father absence unique to a military setting are described, emphasizing factors of intermittent father separations based on a cycle of absence and return, the unique aspects of a "military" father and his absences, and problems related to developmental stages and age of the child.

SEPLIN, C. (1952) "A study of the influence of father's absence for military service." Smith College Studies in Social Work 22: 123-124.

Children in the military setting were studied to determine the effect of father's absence from the home as a result of military duties. Children whose fathers were absent during their formative years were found to be more disturbed, showed signs of Oedipal upheaval, displayed behavior problems, and had a closer relationship with the mother than did control group children.

SIGAL, J. (1974) "Effects of parental exposure to prolonged stress on the mental health of the spouse and children: families of Canadian army survivors of the Japanese World War II camps." Paper presented at the Annual Meeting of the Canadian Psychiatric Association, Ottawa.

This study yields clinical impressions acquired during interviews of families who were second-or-more generation Canadians, largely not Jewish, where the father only was a survivor of the Japanese concentration camps. Clinical data revealed that the oldest female child was most likely to be affected; she tended to be depressed, withdrawn, dependent, and unassertive, owing to identification with a depressed mother. The mother, in turn, appeared depressed by the effects of the camp experience on her husband.

SIGAL, J. (1971) "Second generation effects of massive psychiatric trauma." International Psychiatry Clinics 8: 55-65.

The dynamics within families of survivors of wartime persecution are described. The effects of the concentration camp experience linger on and manifest themselves in various symptoms in the survivor, while the inability to gain control over the "precipitating stress" serves as a continual source of difficulty in family interaction and development. Children of concentration camp survivors may either lose control, exhibiting sibling rivalry or aggressive behavior, or withdraw into fantasy or an affectless state similar to that of their parents. In identifying with depressed and depleted people, the author suggests that the child becomes like them, so that the negative effects may continue on and be felt past the second generation.

SIGAL, J., and V. RAKOFF (1971) "Concentration camp survival: a pilot study of effects on the second generation." Canadian Psychiatric Association Journal 16: 393-397.

The extent to which children of survivors of the concentration camp experience are adversely affected by their parents' trauma was examined in 32 Jewish families. Parents were found to exhibit problems in self-control, marked overevaluation and lack of control of their children; while the children displayed a greater degree of sibling rivalry and aggressive behavior. The significant results obtained from parents who had not themselves been in a concentration camp, but had experienced the loss indirectly (i.e., family member), suggest that affective consequences of the loss are the root of problems within the family.

SIGAL, J., D. SILVER, V. RAKOFF, and B. ELLIN (1973) "Some second-generation effects of survival of the Nazi persecution." American Journal of Orthopsychiatry 43: 320-327.

Based on previous observations that survivors of Nazi persecution (SNP) experience a dysfunction in their capacity for human relations which, in turn, affects the normal development of their children, it was hypothesized that children of SNP would exhibit problems in impulse control while experiencing a sense of anomia and alienation. Children did report a greater sense of anomia and feelings of alienation in relation to their community and family, while parents were found to perceive their children as having more personality problems and less adequate coping behaviors, and as exhibiting excessive dependency and immaturity. "Preoccupation" of the parents was suggested as the critical factor determining the nature of parental life events' influencing the behavior of the children.

SMILANSKY, S. (1975) "Development of the conceptualization of death in children, ages 4-10." Paper presented at the International Conference on Psychological Stress and Adjustment in Time of War and Peace, Tel Aviv, Israel (January).

The way in which Israeli children perceive death and how this perception is influenced by the environment is the focus of this study. Children's conceptualizations of death were examined in relation to variables of age, sex, intelligence, personal experience, socioeconomic background, exposure to death in the family or neighborhood, and life in military camps and religious families. The aspects of death scrutinized were finality, causality, irreversibility, and unavoidability. The report discusses the results and their utility in helping children through the bereavement process.

SPELLMAN, S. (1965) "Orientations toward problem-solving among career military families: a study of the knowledge of available resources in a military community and perception of the social cost of using them for the resolution of family conflict." Unpublished doctoral dissertation. Columbia University.

Five hundred and twelve occupants of a military family housing community were interviewed as to their knowledge of available resources for coping with interpersonal conflict and the perceived social cost of using them. Women and higher-ranking military men were found to have more knowledge of resources available to them for the resolution of family conflict, and women were less fearful about actually using the resources. The least educated respondents were more likely to believe that their status in the military community would be hampered by exposing serious family difficulties.

SPOLYAR, L. (1974) "The grieving process in MIA wives," pp. 77-84 in H. McCubbin, B. Dahl, P. Metres, Jr., E. Hunter, and J. Plag (eds.), Family Separation and Reunion. Washington, D.C.: U.S. Government Printing Office

This descriptive paper portrays the grieving process and its components faced by wives of servicemen missing in action. The predictable cycle involving shock, emotional release, states of anxiety and depression, and physical symptoms of distress, as well as guilt feelings, identification with the husband, and substitution of another image, is described. Special attention is focused on problems resulting from the process of anticipatory grief, whereby the wife has worked through most of the grief cycle prior to any finalization of her husband's death.

STANTON, M. (1975) "The military family: Its future in the all volunteer context," in N. Goldman and D. Segal (eds.), Proceedings of the Inter-University Seminar on the Armed Forces and Society: Social Psychology of Military Services.

Trends occurring within the military family are discussed in relation to emerging societal family trends and an all-volunteer force. Emergence of the nuclear family unit, greater participation by women in family decision-making policies and activities outside the home, less acceptance of relocations and family mobility, and an increase in tolerance and flexibility in values fostered by the communications media are societal trends that have implications for including the family in military policy and decision making. Specific recommendations and changes in policy toward the military family are suggested.

STERNBERG, T. (1975) "Work of volunteers with bereaved families of the Yom Kippur War." Paper presented at the International Conference on Psychological Stress and Adjustment in Time of War and Peace, Tel Aviv, Israel (January).

The work of 50 volunteer psychologists and social workers aiding families in Israel to cope with the loss of a missing in action or deceased family member was examined to determine the effects of their work on themselves as well as on the families being helped. Unlike professional volunteers, untrained volunteers tended to identify with the guilt feelings of family members and thus ignored the needs of the family. The need for reliable professionals to help such families under stress is emphasized.

STOLZ, L. (1954) Father Relations of War-Born Children: The Effect of Postwar Adjustment of Fathers on the Behavior and Personality of First Children Born While Fathers were at War. Palo Alto: Stanford University Press.

The purpose of this study was to assess the developmental effects on the personalities of first-born children of father's war-induced separation during the first year of the child's life. Findings indicated that war-separated fathers were concerned about many aspects of their first-born's behavior, had a high self-rejection score, and perceived both himself and his first-born as predominantly passive. Both parents perceived the mother to be closer to the first-born child. The first-born war-separated child had poorer relations with peers, had more behavioral and psychological problems, and was more demanding of adults and teachers.

TEICHMAN, Y. (1975) "The stress of coping with the unknown regarding a significant family member." Paper presented at the International Conference on Dimensions of Anxiety and Stress, Oslo (June).

This paper reports on observations made by nonprofessional helpers assigned to MIA families of the October 1973 Middle East War as they aided the families in coping with the crisis and its consequences. Because of the diversity of the soldiers' ages, parents, wives, and children were encountered and both unique and cross-generation reaction patterns were observed. General coping patterns of the families and specific reactions of parents and wives are identified. The children's wide range of observed reactions were seen as manifestations of the general stress atmosphere rather than as results of their specific loss.

TEICHMAN, Y., Y. SPIEGEL, and M. TEICHMAN (1975) "Volunteers report about their work with families of servicemen missing in action." Paper presented at the International Conference on Psychological Stress and Adjustment in Time of War and Peace, Tel Aviv, Israel (January).

Thirty-two volunteers reported on their work with families of servicemen missing in action after the October 1973 Middle East War. After meetings and interactions with the families, volunteers answered a questionnaire concerning the family's reaction to and their own reaction to their volunteer work. Families of Oriental descent seemed most accepting of help. The more socially involved the family, the more ready it was to accept help and to talk on emotional themes. Common volunteer reactions included ambivalence, distress, and conflict. Volunteers successfully offered help to the majority of families, largely in terms of help with formalities and of psychological support.

TROSSMAN, B. (1968) "Adolescent children of concentration camp survivors." Canadian Psychiatric Association Journal 13: 121-123.

Stress reactions of adolescent children of concentration camp survivors are described. Problems observed ranged from academic difficulties to behavioral problems, and they were diagnosed as exhibiting from mild adolescent adjustment reactions to tenuous borderline states. As a result of excessive parental overprotection, and parental mistrust of the Gentile world, the children tended to become moderately phobic or hostile toward the parent's smothering behavior, and learned to distrust the outside world and become paranoid themselves. Because many of the parents are antagonistic and mistrustful toward psychiatric intervention, treatment for these children is often directed toward encouraging activities and contacts with peers outside the home as a means to correct distorted attitudes learned within the family.

TRUNNELL, T. (1968) "A review of studies of the psychosocial significance of the absent father." Paper presented at the Western American Psychiatric Association Meeting, Seattle, Washington (August).

The effects of father absence on the development of the child are reviewed through selected studies. Results of studies with select groups indicate that even transient father absence—e.g., the alcoholic, the "out of town" businessman—can seriously affect the normal psychological development of the child. Psycho-analytic case studies are cited relating father absence to the psychological difficulties in the child or adult. Father absence is found to be related to a decrease in masculinity and an increase in immaturity and aggressiveness in the child.

WENDT, J. (1971) "The unmaking of the 'military brat'." Family 7-14 (December).

Various counselors describe their experiences of dealing with the special problems of emotionally disturbed military children. According to one counselor, the primary difficulty for the military child, living a mobile style of life, is difficulty making friendships and risking making ties that will eventually have to be severed. Another counselor attributes the children's problems to a lack of communication within the home, i.e., patterns set by the parents rather than the military way of life. Group sessions, in which the children gain confidence in asserting themselves, develop simple social skills, and practice talking about their feelings and fears, are described and recommended as providing an opportunity for social growth.

WESTLING, JR., L. (1973) "Ministry to prisoner of war returnees and their families in the long-term readjustment period: a manual for Navy chaplains." Unpublished doctoral dissertation, San Francisco Theological Seminary.

This manual was developed to assist the U.S. Navy chaplain in his ministry to the returned prisoner of war and his family. The reactions and interactions of the chaplain, returnee, and the family are discussed, and emphasis is placed on the chaplain's evaluation of himself in such a context. A number of family counseling techniques are suggested for use by the chaplain or other qualified professionals. The chaplain must be receptive and sensitive to the individual PW returnee, his experiences, feelings, frustrations, and fears, his need for open discussion, and his hopes and plans for the future.

WIEDER, S. and E. NASHIM (1975) "Parallel reactions of widows and young children following the death of their fathers in the Yom Kippur War." Paper presented at the International Conference on Psychological Stress and Adjustment in Time of War and Peace, Tel Aviv, Israel (January).

Mental health professionals studied the reactions of families of soldiers missing in action in the Yom Kippur War and found parallel reactions in mothers and children. The children, though outwardly acknowledging death, denied its reality by not grieving and/or by developing fantasies of the father's return. They had symptoms of regression, somatization, and sleep disturbance. Mothers reacted to the loss in the form of denial, depression, repression, rage, and inability to care for themselves or the home. The major and immediate function of professionals was to aid mothers in understanding how their children's responses to the situation paralleled their own responses.

WILLIAMS, J. (1971) "Divorce in the population of the United States and in a homogeneous subset of that population (United States Air Force Officers) 1958-1970." Unpublished doctoral dissertation. Mississippi State University.

A comparison was made between divorce rates of United States Air Force officers and the United States population as a whole during 1958-70. Divorce rates in the United States are high and increasing rapidly, compared to only a 1 percent divorce rate among Air Force officers. Various explanations for the low divorce rate among officers were proposed and discussed. Strong group cohesiveness, group attractiveness, marriage visibility, good income and security, sharing of reference groups by the couple, separation from in-laws, high education of officers, internal supports by the Air Force, and the couple's involvement in external networks and interests were emphasized.

ZIV, A. (1975) "Empirical findings on children's reactions to war stress." Paper presented at the International Conference on Psychological Stress and Adjustment in Time of War and Peace, Tel Aviv, Israel (January).

This report integrates six separate studies involving children of kibbutzim and of urban areas. Children's cognitive, emotional, and social reactions to war were investigated. Anxiety levels did not differ significantly between bombarded kibbutz children and nonbombarded kibbutz children. Children in bombardment conditions did not have greater negative attitudes toward the Arabs, contrary to the frustration-aggression hypothesis. Group cohesion and local patriotism were stronger in bombarded groups than in control groups.

ZUNIN, L. (1974) "A program for the Vietnam widow: Operation Second Life," pp. 218-224 in H. McCubbin, B. Dahl, P. Metres, Jr., E. Hunter, and J. Plag (eds.) Family Separation and Reunion. Washington, D.C.: U.S. Government Printing Office.

This paper describes the establishment and implementation of the program "Operation Second Life," a discussion group designed to assist the wives of servicemen killed in action in Vietnam. This group was mainly composed of officer's wives between 25 and 35 years of age. Issues pertaining to grief, adjustment to the loss, as well as issues concerning plans for the children and for the future, were discussed. The author found that most women of the group were very patriotic, had strong religious feelings, idealized their marriages, and did not indulge in self-pity.

COMPILED REFERENCES

AICHHORN, A. (1938) Wayward Youth. New York: Viking Press.

AIKEN, M. and L.A. FERMAN (1966) "Job mobility and the social integration of displaced workers." Social Problems 14 (Summer), 48-56.

ALLEN, H. (1972) "Schilling Manor: A survey of a military community of father absent families." Unpublished doctoral dissertation, Catholic University of America.

ANDERSON, R.E. (1968) "Where's dad? Paternal deprivation and delinquency." Archives of General Psychiatry, 18:641-649.

ANDERSON, R.G. (1966) "Greenwoods' youth: A study of the problematical, social circumstances of adolescents in a suburban high school." Unpublished D.S.W. dissertation. University of California.

ANGELL, R.C. (1936) The Family Encounters the Depression. New York: Charles Scribner's and Sons.

ARENSBERG, C.M. and S.T. KIMBALL (1965) Culture and Community. New York: Harcourt, Brace & World, Inc.

Armed Forces Directory Service (1967) Unofficial Guide, Fort [...], [...]. San Francisco: Armed Forces Directory Service.

BAILEY, M. (1958) "Community orientations toward social casework and other professional resources: a study of attitudes toward professional help for interpersonal problems and knowledge of resources in an urban community." Doctoral dissertation. Columbia University.

BAKER, S., S. FAGEN, E. FISCHER, E. JANDA, and L. COVE (1967) "Impact of father absence on personality factors of boys: I. An evaluation of the military family's adjustment." Paper presented at the 44th Annual Meeting of the American Orthopsychiatric Association, Washington, D.C. (March).

BAKER, S., L. COVE, S. FAGEN, E. FISCHER and E. JANDA (1968) "Impact of father absence: III. Problems of family reintegration following prolonged father absence." American Journal of Orthopsychiatry, 38: 347 (Abstract).

BALLARD, P.A. (1973) Psychological aspects of captivity and repatriation. In C. Peck (ed.), Medical care for repatriated prisoners of war: a manual for physicians. San Diego, Ca.: Navy Medical Neuropsychiatric Research Unit.

BANDURA, A. and R.H. WALTERS (1959) "Adolescent aggression." New York: Ronald Press.

Bank of America National Trust & Savings Association (1967) Focus on [. . .] County. [. . .]: Bank of America NT&SA.

BECK, B.B. (1958) "The adolescent's challenge to casework." Social Work. 3 (April): 89-95.

BELL, D. (1967) "Toward a communal society." Life (May 12): 110-124.

BELL, J.E. (1963) "A theoretical position for family group therapy." Family Process II: 1-14.

BELL, N.W. and E.F. VOGEL (1960) "Toward a framework for the functional analysis of family behavior," pp. 1-36 in N.W. Bell and E.F. Vogel (eds.). A Modern Introduction into the Family. Glencoe, Illinois: The Free Press.

BELL, W. (1957) "Antomie, social isolation and class structure." Sociometry XX: 105-116.

BELLINO, R. (1969) "Psychosomatic problems of military retirement." Psychosomatics, 10: 318-321.

––– (1970) "Perspectives of military and civilian retirement." Mental Hygiene, 54: 580-583.

BELT, J. and A. SWENEY (1973) "The Air Force wife: her knowledge of, and attitudes toward, the Air Force." Paper presented at Military Testing Association Conference on Human Resources, San Antonio, Texas (October).

BENNETT, W., H. CHANDLER, J. DUFFY, J. HICKMAN, C. JOHNSON, M. LALLY, A. NICHOLSON, G. NORBO, A. OMPS, V. POSPISIL, R. SEEBERG, W. WUBBENA (1974) "Army Families." U.S. Army War College, Carlisle Barracks, Pa.

BENSON, D., H. McCUBBIN, B. DAHL, and E. HUNTER (1974) "Waiting: the dilemma of the MIA wife," pp. 157-168 in H. McCubbin, B. Dahl, P. Metres Jr., E. Hunter, and J. Plag (eds.), Family Separation and Reunion, Washington, D.C.: U.S. Government Printing Office.

BETTELHEIM, B. (1953) "Individual and mass behavior in extreme situations." Journal of Abnormal and Social Psychology, 38: 417-452.

––– (1969) The Children of the Dream. Toronto: The Macmillan Company.

––– and E. SYLVESTER (1950) "Notes on the impact of parental occupations: some cultural determinants of symptom choice in emotionally disturbed children." American Journal of Orthopsychiatry. (Oct): 785-795.

BEVILACQUA, J. (1967) "Civilization and health-welfare resource participation on an Army post." Unpublished doctoral dissertation, Brandeis University.

BEY, D. and J. LANGE (1974) "Waiting wives: women under stress." American Journal of Psychiatry, 131: 283-286.

BIDERMAN, A. (1959) "The prospective impact of large scale military retirement." Social Problems 7 1: 84-90.

––– (1964) "Sequels to a military career: the retired military professional." Pp 287-336 in M. Janowitz (ed.) The New Military: Changing Patterns of Organization. New York: Russell Sage Foundation.

––– (1967) "Life and death in extreme captivity situations." In M.H. Apply and R. Trumbull (Eds.), Psychological stress. New York: Appleton Century Crofts.

––– (1971) "The retired military." Pp. 123-163 in R. Little (ed.) Handbook of Military Institutions. California: Sage Publications.

––– (1972) "Retired soldiers within and without the military-industrial complex." Pp. 95-126 in S. Sarkesian, and C. Moskos (eds.), The Military-Industrial Complex, II. A Reassessment. California: Sage Publications.

BIDERMAN, A. and L. SHARP (1968) "The convergence of military and civilian occupational structures: evidence from studies of military retired employment." American Journal of Sociology, 73: 381-399.

BILLER, H.B. (1968) "A multiaspect investigation of masculine development in kindergarten age boys." Genetic Psychology Monographs, 76: 89-139.

BLALOCK, H.M., Jr. (1972) Social Statistics (second edition). New York: McGraw-Hill Book Company.

BLAU, P. (1956) "Social mobility and interpersonal relations." American Sociological Review 21 (June), 290-294.

BLOCHBERGER, C. JR. (1970) "Military families: differential lifestyles." Unpublished doctoral dissertation, University of California, Berkeley.

BLUM, A.F. (1966) "Social structure, social class, and participation in primary relationships." Pp. 77-86 in W.F. Goode (ed.) Dynamics of Modern Society. New York: Atherton Press.

BORGATTA, E.F. (1960) "Role and reference group theory," pp. 16-27 in L.S. Kogan (ed.) Social Work Theory and Social Work Research. New York: National Association of Social Workers.

BOSS, P.G. (1975) "Psychological father absence and presence: A theoretical formulation for an investigation into family systems pathology." Unpublished doctoral dissertation, University of Wisconsin-Madison.

BOTT, E. (1957) Family and Social Network. London: Tavistock Publications, Ltd.

BOULDING, E. (1950) "Family adjustments to war separations and reunions." The Annals of the American Academy of Political and Social Science, 272: 59-67.

BOWER, E. (1967) "American children and families in overseas communities." American Journal of Orthopsychiatry, 37: 787-796.

BOWERMAN, C. (1964) "Prediction studies." Pp. 215-246 in H. Christensen (ed.) Handbook of Marriage and the Family. Chicago: Rand McNally.

BOWLBY, J. (1952) "Maternal care and mental health." Monograph Series, No. 2, Geneva, World Health Organization.

BRADBURN, N.M. (1969) The Structure of Psychological Well-Being. Chicago: Aldine Publishing Company.

BROWN, D.E. (1972) "Dark and lonely is the silent night." U.S. Navy Medicine, 58: 4-7.

BROWN, D., and E. HUYCKE (1974) "Problems of Vietnam prisoners of war and their families." Social Psychiatry, 1, 91-98.

BROWN, M. (1944) "When our servicemen come home." Journal of Home Economics, 626-628.

BUCKLEY, W. (1967) Sociology and Modern Systems Theory. Englewood Cliffs, New Jersey: Prentice-Hall, Inc.

BURCHINAL, L.G., and W.W. BAUDER (1965) "Adjustment to the New Institutional Environment," in p. 201 Family Mobility in Our Dynamic Society. Ames, Iowa: Iowa State University.

BURGESS, E.W. and L.S. COTTRELL (1939) Predicting Success or Failure in Marriage. New York: Prentice-Hall, Inc.

BURGESS, E.W. and H.J. LOCKE (1953) The Family. New York: American Book Co.

BUROS, O.K. (Ed.) (1965) Sixth Mental Measurements Handbook. Highland Park, New Jersey: Grypon Press.

——— (Ed.) (1970) Personality Tests and Reviews. New Jersey: The Gryphon Press.

BURR, W. (1973) Theory Construction and the Sociology of the Family. New York: John Wiley & Sons, Inc.

BUTLER, R.M. (1956a) "Mothers' attitudes towards the social development of their adolescents." Social Casework: 219-226.

――― (1956b) "Mothers' attitudes toward the social development of their adolescents." Social Casework: 37:280-288.

CAPLAN, G. (1975) "Organization of support systems for civilian populations." Paper presented at the International Conference on Psychological Stress and Adjustment in Time of War and Peace, Tel Aviv, Israel (January).

CAPLAN, G. and S. LEBOVICI [eds.] (1969) Adolescence: Psychosocial Perspectives. New York: Basic Books, Inc.

CARP, F.M. (ed.) (1966) The Retirement Process. Public Health Service Publication No. 1778. Washington, D.C.: U.S. Government Printing Office.

CARTWRIGHT, D. and A. ZANDER, eds. (1953) Group Dynamics, Research and Theory. Evanston, Ill.: Row, Peterson and Co.

CAVAN, R.S. (1964) Subcultural Variations and Mobility," pp. 535-581 in H.T. Christensen (ed.), Handbook of Marriage and the Family. Chicago: Rand McNally.

――― and K.H. RANCK (1938) The Family and the Depression: A Study of One Hundred Chicago Families. Chicago: The University of Chicago Press.

CHASKEL, R. (1964) "Effects of mobility on family life." Social Work. 9 (October): 83-91.

CHESLEY, L. (1973) Seven Years in Hanoi. Salt Lake City: Bookcrest, Inc.

CLEMENTS, A. (1968) Marital Problem Checklist. Department of Sociology, The Catholic University of America.

CLINARD, M.B. (1957) Sociology of Deviant Behavior. New York: Holt, Rinehart, and Winston, Inc.

――― (Ed.) (1964) Anomie and Deviant Behavior. Glencoe: The Free Press.

COATES, C. and R. PELLEGRIN (1965) Military Sociology: A Study of American Military Institutions and Military Life. Maryland: Social Science Press.

COHEN, A.K. and H.M. HODGES, Jr. (1963) "Characteristics of the Lower Blue-Collar Class," Social Problems, X (Spring).

COLEMAN, J.S. (1961) The Adolescent Society. New York: The Free Press of Glencoe.

Committee on Adolescence, Group for the Advancement of Psychiatry (1968) Normal Adolescence. New York: Charles Scribner's Sons.

CUBER, J. (1945) "Family readjustment of veterans." Marriage and Family Living 7: 28-30.

CUMMING, E. (1968) "Unsolved problems of prevention," Canada's Mental Health Supplement Number 56 (January-April).

CUSTER, E.B. (1961) Boots and Saddles. Norman, Oklahoma: University of Oklahoma Press.

DAHL, B. and H. McCUBBIN (1974) "The adjustment of children of returned prisoners of war; a preliminary report." Paper presented at the Second Joint Medical Meeting on Prisoners of War, Department of Defense, San Antonio, Texas (November).

――― (1975) "Children of returned prisoners of war: the effects of long-term father absence." Paper presented at the Annual Meeting of the American Psychological Association, Chicago, Illinois, (August).

DAHL, B., H. McCUBBIN and K. ROSS (1975) "Second generational effects of war-induced separations: comparing the adjustment of children in reunited and non-reunited families." Paper presented at the National Council of Family Relations Meeting, Salt Lake City, Utah (August).

DARNAUER, P.F. (1969) "Army brats―growing up in an army family." Paper presented at the 96th Annual Forum of the National Conference on Social Welfare, New York, (May).

——— (1970) "Adolescent experience in career Army families." Unpublished doctoral dissertation, University of Southern California.

DAVIS, J.A. (1960) "Emotional problems of service families in Japan." Social Work V (Jan): 100-105.

Demographic Yearbook (New York: UN, department of Economics and Social Affairs. Statistical Office of the United Nations, 1970).

Department of the Army (1968a) Sample survey of military personnel as of 29 February 1968: permanent changes of station of male military personnel during period 1 March 1967 through 29 February 1968. OPOPM Report No. 25-68-E, Washington, D.C.: Office of Personnel Operations.

——— (1968b) Sample survey of military personnel as of 29 February 1968: survey estimate of marital status and dependents of Army male personnel. OPOPM Report No. 26-68-E, Washington, D.C.: Office of Personnel Operations.

DICKERSON, W. and R. ARTHUR (1965) "Navy families in distress." Military Medicine, 130: 894-898.

DOODEMAN, L. (Ed.) (1974) Mili-Wife questionnaire results: the comment page wives speak out on the military, pro and con, moving, children, rank consciousness, housing, benefits, women's liberation." Ladycom 6: 22-52.

DOR-SHAV, N. (1975) "On the long-range effects of concentration camp internment on NAZI victims and their children." Paper presented at the International Conference on Psychological Stress and Adjustment in Time of War and Peace, Tel Aviv, Israel, (January).

DOUVAN, E. and J. ADELSON (1966) The Adolescent Experience. New York: John Wiley & Sons, Inc.

DRUSS, R. (1965) "Problems associated with retirement from military service." Military Medicine, 130: 383-385.

DUNCAN, A. (1969) "Vietnam War widows learn to live and love again." Family Weekly (November): 6-7.

DURKHEIM, E. (1947) The Division of Labor in Society. New York: The Free Press of Glencoe.

DUVALL, E. (1945) "Loneliness and the serviceman's wife." Marriage and Family Living, 7: 77-81.

DYER, W. (1962) "Work and the family," in S. Noson and W. Form (eds.) Man, Work and Society. New York: Basic Books, Inc.

EITINGER, L. (1964) "Concentration camp survivors in Norway and Israel." London: Allen and Unwin.

ELIOT, T. (1946) "War bereavements and their recovery." Marriage and Family Living, 8: 1-5, 8.

ELOUL, J. (1975) "Basic issues in group work with war widows." Paper presented at the International Conference on Psychological Stress and Adjustment in Time of War and Peace, Tel Aviv, Israel (January).

ERIKSON, E.H. (1950) Childhood and Society. New York: W.W. Norton & Co., Inc.

——— (1968) Identity: Youth and Crisis. New York: W.W. Norton & Co., Inc.

——— (1969) Identity and the Life Cycle: Selected Papers. Monograph 1, Psychological Issues, Vol. 1, No. 1. New York: International Universities Press, Inc.

FABER, B. and L. BLACKMAN (1960) "Marital role tension and number and sex of children." American Sociological Review: 596-600.

FAGEN, S., E. JANDA, S. BAKER, E. FISCHER and L. COVE (1967) "Impact of father absence in military families: II. factors relating to success of coping with crisis." Technical Report, Walter Reed Medical Center, Washington, D.C.

FELLIN, P. (1964) "A reappraisal of changes in American family patterns," Social Casework, XLV (May) 263-267.

FESTINGER, L., S. SCHACTER and K. BACK (1953) "The operation of group standards," in D. Cartwright and A. Zander (eds.) Group Dynamics, Research and Theory. Evanston, Ill.: Row, Peterson and Co.

FINLAYSON, E. (1969) "A Study of the wife of an Army officer: her academic and career preparation, her current employment and volunteer services." Unpublished doctoral dissertation, George Washington University, Washington, D.C.

FRANCES, A. and L. GALE (1973) "Family structure and treatment in the military." Family Process, 12: 171-178.

FRANKL, V.E. (1968) "Man's search for meaning." New York: Washington Square Press.

FREUD, A. and D. BURLINGHAM (1943) War and Children. New York: International University Press.

FRIED, M. (1963) "Grieving For a Lost Home," in pp. 151-171 Leonard J. Duhl (ed.) The Urban Condition. New York: Basic Books, Inc.

––– (1964) "Social Problems and Psycho-pathology," in pp. 405-446, Group for the Advancement of Psychiatry. Urban America and the Planning of Mental Health Services.

––– (1965) "Transitional Functions of Working Class Communities: Implications for Forced Relocation," in pp. 123-165, M.R. Kautor (ed.) Mobility and Mental Health. Springfield, Illinois: Charles C Thomas.

––– and J. LEVIN (1968) "Some Social Functions of the Urban Slum," in pp. 60-83, B.J. Frieden and R. Morris (eds.). Urban Planning and Social Policy. New York: Basic Books, Inc.

FRIEDENBERG, E.Z. (1959) The Vanishing Adolescent. Laurel Edition. New York: Dell Publishing Co., Inc.

––– (1968) "Adolescence as a social problem," in H.S. Becker (ed.) Social Problems: A Modern Approach. New York: John Wiley & Sons, Inc.

FRIENDS, J. and E. HAGGARD (1948) "Work adjustment in relation to family background." Applied Psychology Monographs 16.

GABOWER, G. (1959) Behavior Problems in Children in Navy Officers' Families. Washington, D.C.: The Catholic University Press.

––– (1960) "Behavior problems of children in Navy officers' families." Social Casework, 41: 177-184.

GAITHER, R. (1973) With God in a POW Camp. Nashville: Broadman Press.

GANS, H.J. (1962) The Urban Villagers. Glencoe, Ill.: The Free Press.

GARBER, D. (1971) "Retired soldiers in second careers: self-assessed change, reference group salience, and psychological well-being." Unpublished doctoral dissertation, University of Southern California.

GARDNER, G. and H. SPENCER (1944) "Reactions of children with fathers and brothers in the Armed Forces." American Journal of Orthopsychiatry, 14: 36-43.

GESELL, A., F.L. ILG and L.B. AMES (1956) Youth: The Years from 10 to 16. New York: Harper and Brothers.

GIFFEN, M. and J. MCNEIL (1967) "Effect of military retirement on dependents." Archives of General Psychiatry, 17: 717-722.

GILLILAND, C.H. (1959) "The relationship of pupil mobility to achievement in the elementary school." Abstract of Research Study No. 1-1958, University Microfilms, Inc., Ann Arbor, Michigan.

GINGRAS, A. and M. DEIBLER (1969) What Every Military Kid Should Know. Harrisburg, Pa.: Stackpole Books.

GLENN, J.B. (n.d.) Unpublished data prepared for the Office of the Assistant Secretary of Defense, Manpower and Reserve Affairs.

GLICK, P.C. (1975) "A Demographer Looks at American Families," Journal of Marriage and the Family, XXXVII (Feb): 15-26.

GOFFMAN, E. (1958) "The characteristics of total institutions," in Symposium on Preventive and Social Psychiatry. Washington, D.C.: Walter Reed Institute of Research.

GOLAN, N. (in press) "From wife to widow to woman: a process of role transition." Social Work.

GONZALEZ, V. (1970) Psychiatry and the Army Brat. Illinois: C.C Thomas.

GOODE, W.J. (1956) After Divorce. New York: The Free Press.

——— (1970) "Marital Satisfaction and Instability: A Cross-Cultural Analysis of Divorce Rates." Eds. P.H. Glasser and L.N. Glasser, Families in Crisis. New York: Harper and Row.

GOODMAN, P. (1960) Growing up Absurd. New York: Random House, Inc.

GREENBERG, H. (1973) "Psychiatric symptomatology in wives of military retirees." American Journal of Psychiatry, 123: 487-490.

GRIFFITH, C. (1944) "The psychological adjustments of returned servicemen and their families." Marriage and Family Living, 6:65-67, 87.

GROLNICK, L. (1972) "A family perspective of psychosomatic factors in illness: a review of the literature." Family Process 11:457-486.

GROSS, E. (1971) "Industrial problems." Pp. 254-290 in Erwin O. Smigel (ed.) Handbook on the Study of Social Problems. Chicago: Rand McNally and Company.

GURIN, G., J. VEROFF, and FELD, S. (1960) Americans View Their Mental Health: A Nationwide Interview Survey. New York: Basic Books, Inc.

HALL, C.S. and G. LINDZEY (1957) Theories of Personality. New York: John Wiley & Sons, Inc.

HALL, R. and P. MALONE (1974) "Psychiatric residuals of prolonged captivity." Pp. 127-146 in H. McCubbin, B. Dahl, P. Metres, Jr., E. Hunter, and J. Plag (eds.), Family Separation and Reunion. Washington, D.C. U.S. Government Printing Office.

HALL, R. and W. SIMMONS (1973) "The POW wife–a psychiatric appraisal." Archives of General Psychiatry, 29: 690-694.

HALPERN, E. (1975) "Volunteering as a 'natural phenomena': an integration within Caplan's theory of support systems." Paper presented at the International Conference on Psychological Stress and Adjustment in Time of War and Peace, Tel Aviv, Israel, (January).

HARRIS, T. (1964) Counseling the Serviceman and His Family. New Jersey: Prentice Hall.

HARTOG, J. (1966) "Group therapy with psychotic and borderline military wives." American Journal of Psychiatry, 122: 1125-1131.

HAVIGHURST, R.J. et al. (1962) Growing up in River City. New York: John Wiley & Sons, Inc.

HAWKINS, J.L. (1968) "Associations between companionship, hostility, and marital satisfactions." Journal of Marriage and the Family 30 (November), 647-650.

HEARN, G. (ed.) (1969) The General Systems Approach: Contributions Towards an Holistic Conception of Social Work. New York: Council on Social Work Education.

HERBST, P.G. (1960) "Task differentiation of husband and wife in family activities." Pp. 339-346 in N.W. Bell and E.F. Vogel (eds.), The Family. Glencoe, Ill.: The Free Press.

HERNTON, C.C. (1965) Sex and Racism in America. New York: Grove Press, Inc.

HETHERINGTON, E.M. (1966) "Effects of paternal absence on sex-typed behaviors in negro and white pre-adolescent males." Journal of Personality and Social Psychology, 4: 87-91.

––– (1972) "Effects of father absence on personality development in adolescent daughters." Developmental Psychology, 7, 313-326.

HILL, R. (1945) "The returning father and his family." Marriage and Family Living, 7: 31-34.

––– (1949) Families Under Stress: Adjustment to the Crisis of War Separation and Reunion. New York, Harper & Bros.

––– (1958) "Generic features of families under stress," Social Casework, XXXXIX (February-March) 139-150.

––– (1974) "Consultant's Comments." Presented at the Prisoner of War Research Conference, Naval Health Research Center, San Diego, California (April).

HILL, R. and D. HANSEN (1964) "Families under stress." Pp. in H. Christensen (ed.), Handbook of Marriage and the Family. Chicago: Rand McNally.

HILL, R. and R. RODGERS (1964) "The developmental approach." Pp. 171-211 in H. Christensen (ed.), Handbook of Marriage and the Family. Chicago: Rand McNally.

HILLENBRAND, E. (1970) "Father absence in military families." Unpublished doctoral dissertation, George Washington University.

HILLER, E.T. (1947) Social Relations and Structures. New York: Harper and Brothers.

HOLLINGSHEAD, A.B. (1950) "Social Class and Family," The Annals of the American Academy of Political and Social Science, 252:39-46.

HOLLINGSHEAD, A.B. and F.C. REDLICH (1955) "Social mobility and mental illness." American Journal of Psychiatry 112 (September), 179-185.

––– and ––– (1958) Social Class and Mental Illness. New York: John Wiley & Sons, Inc.

HUNTER, E., H. McCUBBIN, and D. BENSON (1974) "Differential viewpoints: The MIA wife vs. the MIA mother." Pp. 179-190 in H. McCubbin, B. Dahl, P. Metres, Jr., E. Hunter, and J. Plag (eds.), Family Separation and Reunion. Washington, D.C., U.S. Government Printing Office.

HUNTER, E., H. McCUBBIN, and P. METRES, JR. (1974) "Religion and the PW/MIA wife." Pp. 85-94 in H. McCubbin, B. Dahl, P. Metres, Jr., E. Hunter, and J. Plag (eds.), Family Separation and Reunion. Washington, D.C., U.S. Government Printing Office.

HUNTER, E. and J. PLAG (1973) "An assessment of the needs of POW/MIA wives residing in the San Diego metropolitan area: a proposal for the establishment of family services." Report No. 73-39, San Diego, Navy Medical Neuropsychiatric Research Unit.

IGEL, A. (1945) "The effect of war separation on father-child relations." The Family Journal of Social Case Work, 26: 3-9.

ISAY, R. (1968) "The submariners' wives syndrome." Psychiatric Quarterly, 42: 647-652.

JACKSON, D. (1965) Family homeostasis and the physician. California Medicine 103:239-242.

JACKSON, E.F. and R.F. CURTIS (1972) "Effects of vertical mobility and status inconsistency: a body of negative evidence." American Sociological Review 37 (December), 701-713.

JANOWITZ, M. (1956) "Some consequences of social mobility in the United States." Transactions of the 3rd World Congress of Sociology, Volume III. Pp. 191-201. London: International Sociological Association.

––– (1959) Sociology and the Military Establishment. New York: Russell Sage Foundation.

––– (1960) The Professional Soldier: A Social and Political Portrait. New York: The Free Press of Glencoe.

––– (1965) Sociology and the Military Establishment. Revised ed. New York: Russell Sage Foundation.

JANOWITZ, M. and W. DELANY (1957) "The bureaucrat and the public: A Study of Informational Perspectives." Adm. Sc. Quarterly 2: 141-162.

KAISER, H.F. (1958) "The varimax criterion for analytic rotation in factor analysis." Psychometrika, 23: 187-200.

KANTOR, M.B. (1965) Mobility and Mental Health. Springfield: Charles Thomas.

KATZ, D. and R.L. KAHN (1966) The Social Psychology of Organizations. New York: John Wiley & Sons, Inc.

KAUFMAN, W.C. (1956) "Status, Authoritarianism, and Anti-Semitism," in American Journal of Sociology, 62 (November), pp. 379-382.

KEDEM, P., R. GELMAN, and L. BLUM (1975) "The effect of the Yom Kippur War on the attitudes, values and locus of control of young adolescents." Paper presented at the International Conference on Psychological Stress and Adjustment in Time of War and Peace, Tel Aviv, Israel, (January).

KELLY, R.K. (1969) Courtship, Marriage, and the Family. New York: Harcourt, Brace and World, Inc.

KENNY, J. (1967) "The child in the military community." Journal of the American Academy of Child Psychiatry, 6: 51-63.

KEPHART, W.M. and T.P. MONAHAN (1954) "Divorce and desertion by religious and mixed religious groups." American Journal of Sociology, IX: 454-465.

KESSIN, K. (1971) "Social and psychological consequences of intergenerational occupational mobility." American Journal of Sociology 77 (July), 1-18.

KEY, W.H. (1967) When People Are Forced to Move. Topeka: Menninger Foundation.

KIMURA, Y. (1957) "War brides in Hawaii and their in-laws." American Journal of Sociology, 63: 70-76.

KINZER, B. and M. LEACH (1966) What Every Army Wife Should Know. Harrisburg, Pa.: Stackpole Press.

KIRKPATRICK, C. (1963) The Family as Process and Institution. New York: The Ronald Press Company.

KIRSCHNER, E. (1975) "Pilot study on bereavement and rehabilitation of war widows of the Six-day and Yom Kippur Wars." Paper presented at the International Conference on Psychological Stress and Adjustment in Time of War and Peace, Tel Aviv, Israel, (January).

KOMAROVSKY, M. (1940) The Unemployed Man and His Family: The Effect of Unemployment Upon the Status of the Man in Fifty-Nine Families. New York: Dryden Press, Inc.

KURLANDER, L., D. LEUKEL, L. PALEVSKY and F. KOHN (1961) "Migration: some psychological effects on children–a pilot study." Paper presented at the American Orthopsychiatric Association Annual Meeting, New York (March).

LAND, E. and C.V. GLINES, JR. (1956) The Complete Guide for the Serviceman's Wife. Boston: Houghton Mifflin Co.

LANG, K. (1964) "Technology and career management in the military establishment," pp. 39-82 in M. Janowitz (ed.) The New Military: Changing Patterns of Organization. New York: Russell Sage Foundation.

LANSING, J.B. and E. MUELLER (1967) The Geographic Mobility of Labor. Ann Arbor: Institute for Social Research, The University of Michigan.

LEVINGER, G. (1970) "Marital Cohesiveness and Dissolution: An integrative review," Eds. P.G. Glasser and L.N. Glasser, Families in Crisis. New York: Harper and Row.

LEVY, S. (1975) "Social work self-involvement in a disaster situation." Paper presented at the International Conference on Psychological Stress and Adjustment in Time of War and Peace, Tel Aviv, Israel, (January).

LEWIS, J.W., J. BEAVERS, J. GOSSETT, V. PHILLIPS (1974) "Family systems and physical illness." Paper presented at the American Psychiatric Association, Mtg., Detroit, Michigan (May).

LIDDLE, G.P. (1955) "An analysis of the sociometric scores of newcomers." Quincy Youth Development Project, Quincy, Ill. Unpublished manuscript.

LIEBERMAN, E. (1971a) "War and the family: the psychology of antigrief." Modern Medicine, (April) 179-183, 191.

――― (1971b) "American families and the Vietnam War." Journal of Marriage and the Family, 33: 709-721.

LIFSHITZ, M., D. BERMAN, A. GALILI, and D. GILAD (1975) "Bereaved children: The effect of mother's perception and social system organization on their adjustment." Paper presented at the International Conference on Psychological Stress and Adjustment in Time of War and Peace, Tel Aviv, Israel (January).

LINDQUIST, R. (1952) "Marriage and family life of officers and airmen in a Strategic Air Command Wing." Technical Report No. 5, Institute for Research in Social Science, University of North Carolina.

LINDZEY, G. (ed.) (1954) Handbook of Social Psychology, Vol. 1, Theory and Method. Reading, Mass.: Addison-Wesley.

LITTLE, R.W. (1971) "The military family." Pp. 247-270 in R.W. Little (ed.), Handbook of Military Institutions. California: Sage.

LITWAK, E. (1960) "Geographical mobility and extended family cohesion." American Sociological Review XXV (March): 385-394.

LIVSEY, C. (1972) "Physical illness and family dynamics." Advances in Psychosomatic Medicine 8:237-251.

LOCKE, H.J. (1951) Predicting Adjustments in Marriage: A Comparison of a Divorced and a Happily Married Group. New York: Henry Holt and Co., Inc.

LYNN, D.B. (1974) The father, his role in child development. Belmont, Ca.: Brooks/Cole Publishing Co.

LYNN, D.B. and W.L. SAWREY (1959) "The effects of father-absence on Norwegian boys and girls." Journal of Abnormal and Social Psychology, 258-262.

LYON W. and L. OLDAKER (1967) "The child, the school, and the military family." American Journal of Orthopsychiatry, 37: 269-270.

MacINTOSH, H. (1968) "Separation problems in military wives." American Journal of Psychiatry, 125: 260-265.

MALZBERG, B. and E. LEE (1956) Migration & Mental Diseases: A Study of First Admission to Hospital for Mental Disease, New York 1939-1941. N.Y. Social Science Research Council.

MANNHEIM, K. (1940) Man and Society in an Age of Reconstruction. New York: Harcourt, Brace and Co.

MARCOIN, M. (1972) Assistantes Sociales Service Controle de l'Action Sociale des Armees, Paris, France. Personal Communication (September).

――― (1975) Assistantes Sociales Service Controle de l'Action Sociale des Armees, Paris, France. Personal Communication (January).

MARSH, R. (1970) "Family disruption during the moving process." Unpublished doctoral dissertation Brandeis University.

MASTERSON, J.F., Jr. (1967) The Psychiatric Dilemma of Adolescence. Boston: Little, Brown & Co.

McBROOM, E. (1962) "Social work practice theory relating to problems of adolescence." Unpublished manuscript.

McCLOSKY, H. and J.H. SCHARR (1957) "Psychological dimension of anomie." American Sociology Review XXX (July): 14-40.

McCUBBIN, H. and B. DAHL (1974a) "Social and mental health services to families of returned prisoners of war." Paper presented at American Psychiatric Association Meeting, Detroit, Michigan. (May).

––– (1974b) "An overview of the initial stages of longitudinal study of families of servicemen missing in action and returned prisoners of war." Paper presented at Prisoner of War Research Conference, Naval Health Research Center, San Diego, California (April).

––– (1974c) "Families of returned prisoners of war: a follow-up assessment." Paper presented at Second Joint Medical Meeting on Returned Prisoners of War, Department of Defense, San Antonio, Texas, (November).

––– (1974d) "Social and Mental Health Services to Families of Missing in Action or Returned Prisoners of War," in Family Separation and Reunion, pp. 191-197.

McCUBBIN, H., B. DAHL, and E. HUNTER (1975) "Research on the military family: an assessment." In N. Goldman and D. Segal (Eds.), Proceedings of the Inter-University Seminar on the Armed Forces and Society: Social Psychology of Military Services.

McCUBBIN, H., B. DAHL, G. LESTER, D. BENSON and M. ROBERTSON (1975) "Coping repertoires of families adapting to prolonged war-induced separation." Naval Health Research Center, Report No. 75-56, San Diego, California.

McCUBBIN, H., B. DAHL, G. LESTER and B. ROSS (1975a) "The returned prisoner of war: factors in family reintegration." Journal of Marriage and the Family. 37 (3): 471-478.

–––, –––, ––– and ––– (1975b) "The returned prisoner of war and his children: evidence for the origin of second generational effects of captivity." Paper presented at the Third Annual Joint Medical Meeting Concerning POW/MIA Matters. Naval Health Research Center, San Diego, Ca.

McCUBBIN, H., B. DAHL, P. METRES, JR., E. HUNTER, and J. PLAG [eds.] (1974) Family Separation and Reunion: Families of Prisoners of War and Servicemen Missing in Action. Washington, D.C.: Superintendent of Documents, U.S. Government Printing Office.

McCUBBIN, H., E. HUNTER and B. DAHL (1975) Residuals of war: families of prisoners of war and servicemen missing in action. Journal of Social Issues, 31 (4).

McCUBBIN, H.I., E.J. HUNTER and P.J. METRES, JR. (1974a) "Children in limbo." Pp. 65-76 in H. McCubbin, B. Dahl, P. Metres, E. Hunter and J. Plag (Eds.), Family separation and reunion. Washington, D.C.: U.S. Government Printing Office.

McCUBBIN, H., E. HUNTER, and P. METRES, JR. (1974b) Adaptation of the family to the prisoner of war and missing in action experience. Pp. 21-48 in H. McCubbin, B. Dahl, P. Metres, Jr., E. Hunter, and J. Plag (eds.), Family Separation and Reunion. Washington, D.C.: U.S. Government Printing Office.

McCUBBIN, H. and P. METRES, JR. (1974) Maintaining hope: the dilemma of parents of sons missing in action. Pp. 169-178 in H. McCubbin, B. Dahl, P. Metres, Jr., E. Hunter, and J. Plag (eds.), Family Separation and Reunion. Washington, D.C.: U.S. Government Printing Office.

McKAIN, J.L. (1965) "Needs of the military family." Medical Bulletin U.S. Army Europe, 22: 294-297.

McKAIN, J. (1969) "Feelings of alienation, geographical mobility, and Army family problems: an extension of theory." Unpublished doctoral dissertation: Catholic University of America.

––– (1973) "Relocation in the military: alienation and family problems." Journal of Marriage and the Family, 35:205-209.

McKINLEY, D.G. (1964) Social Class and the Family Life. New York: The Free Press.

MCNEIL, J.S. (1964) "Adjustment of retired Air Force officers." Unpublished doctoral dissertation, University of Southern California.

MCNEIL, J. and M. GIFFEN (1965a) Military retirement: some basic observations and concepts. Aerospace Medicine, 36: 25-29.

——— (1965b) "The social impact of military retirement." Social Casework 46: 203-207.

——— (1967) "Military retirement: the retirement syndrome." American Journal of Psychiatry 123: 848-854.

MEIR, D.L. and W. BELL (1959) "Anomie and differential access to life goals." American Sociology Review XXIV (July): 189-202.

MERTON, R.K. (1957) Social Theory and Social Structure. New York: The Free Press of Glencoe.

METRES, P. Jr., H. McCUBBIN and E. HUNTER. (1974) "Families of returned prisoners of war: some impressions on their initial reintegration." Pp. 147-156 in H. McCubbin, B. Dahl, P. Metres, Jr., E. Hunter, and J. Plag (eds.), Family Separation and Reunion. Washington, D.C.: U.S. Government Printing Office.

MILGRAM, R. and N. MILGRAM (1975) "The effects of the Yom Kippur War on anxiety level in Israeli children." Paper presented at the International Conference on Psychological Stress and Adjustment in Time of War and Peace, Tel Aviv, Israel (January).

MILLER, S.M. (1956) "The concept and measurement of mobility." Pp. 144-154 in Transactions of the 3rd World Congress of Sociology, Volume III. London: International Sociological Association.

MILOWE, I. (1964) "A study in role diffusion: the chief and sergeant face retirement." Mental Hygiene, 48: 101-107.

MOLES, O., R. LIPPIT and S. WITHEY (1959) A Selective Review of Research and Theory on Delinquency. Ann Arbor, Mich.: Institute for Social Research.

MONAHAN, T.P. (1955) "Is Childlessness Related to Family Stability?" American Sociological Review, XX (August): 446-456.

——— (1961) "Educational Achievement and Family Stability," The Journal of Social Psychology, LV: 253-263.

MONTALVO, F. (1968) "Family separation in the Army: A study of the problems encountered and the caretaking resources used by career Army families undergoing military separation." Unpublished doctoral dissertation, University of Southern California.

——— (1970) "Services to families with handicapped children." (In press).

MOSKOS, C.C., JR. (1969) "The changing relationship of the military and American society." pp. 198-208 in Leadership in the Post-70s: A Leadership Workshop Conference. West Point, N.Y.: United States Military Academy.

——— (1970) The American Enlisted Man: The Rank and File in Today's Military. New York: Russell Sage Foundation.

MOWRER, O.H. (1950) "Identification: a link between learning theory and psychotherapy." In Learning theory and personality dynamics. New York: Ronald Press.

MURPHY, E.B. and A.G. ZOOBUCK (1951) "School Adjustment Problems of Military Dependents as seen in 50 cases presented in the Child Guidance Clinic of Brooke Army Hospital." Unpublished Masters thesis, Worden School of Social Service, Our Lady of the Lake College.

MURPHY, M.K. and C.B. PARKER (1966) Fitting in as a New Service Wife. Harrisburg, Pa.: Stackpole Press.

MUUSS, R.E. (1962) Theories of Adolescence. New York: Random House, Inc.

MYLES, D. (1970) "A survey of Army community services centers: welfare problems, services, personnel and resources." Unpublished doctoral dissertation, Catholic University of America.

NELSON, R. (1974) "The legal plight of the PW/MIA family." Pp. 49-64 in H. McCubbin, B. Dahl, P. Metres, Jr., E. Hunter, and J. Plag (eds.), Family Separation and Reunion. Washington, D.C.: U.S. Government Printing Office.

NETTLER, G. (1957) "A measure of alienation." American Sociological Review XXII (December): 670-677.

OGBURN, W.F. and M.F. NIMKOFF (1964) Sociology, 4th Ed. Boston: Houghton Mifflin Co.

OPOPM Report 25-68-E (1968) Sample Survey of Military Personnel: Permanent Changes of Station of Male Military Personnel During Period 1 March 1967 through 29 February 1968. Washington: Office of Personnel Operation, Department of the Army.

ORDEN, S.R. and N.M. BRADBURN (1969) "Working wives and marriage happiness. American Journal of Sociology 74 (January), 392-407.

PALGI, P. (1970) "The adaptability and vulnerability of family types in the changing Israeli society." In A. Jarus, and J. Marcus, Children and Families in Israel. New York: Gordon and Breach.

——— (1973) Socio-Cultural Expressions and Implications of Death, Mourning and Bereavement in Israel Arising out of the War Situation. Israel: Jerusalem Academic Press.

——— (1975) "Culture and mourning: expressions of bereavement arising out of the war situation in Israel." Paper presented at the International Conference on Psychological Stress and Adjustment in Time of War and Peace, Tel Aviv, Israel, (January).

PARAD, H. and G. CAPLAN (1960) "A framework for studying families in crises" Social Work 5:3-15.

PARSONS, T. (1951) The Social System. New York: The Free Press.

PARSONS, T. and R.F. BALES (1955) Family Socialization and Interaction Process. Glencoe, Ill.: The Free Press.

PARTIN, G.R. (1967) "A survey of the effect of mobility on dependent military children." Unpublished Ed.D. dissertation. American University.

PEARLMAN, C.A., Jr. (1970) "Separation reactions of married women." American Journal of Psychiatry, 126 946-950.

PECK, H.B. and V. BELLSMITH (1954) Treatment of the Delinquent Adolescent. New York: Family Service Association of America.

PEDERSEN, F. (1966) "Relationships between father-absence and emotional disturbance in male military dependents." Merrill-Palmer Quarterly, 12: 321-331.

PEDERSEN, F. & E. SULLIVAN (1964) "Relationships among geographical mobility, parental attitudes, and emotional disturbances in children." American Journal of Orthopsychiatry, 34: 575-580.

PEPIN, R. (1966) "A study of scholastic achievements and personal adjustments of military and non-military transitory high school students." Unpublished doctoral dissertation, University of Connecticut.

PITTS, J. (1964) "The structural-functional approach." Pp. 51-124 in H. Christensen (ed.) Handbook of Marriage and the Family. Chicago: Rand McNally.

PLAG, J. (1974) "A Proposal for the Long-term Follow-up of Returned Prisoners of War, Their Families, and Families of Servicemen Missing in Action: A Basis for the Delivery of Health Care Services. Paper presented at the Prisoner of War Research Conference, Naval Health Research Center, San Diego, Ca. (April).

PLATTE, R. (1974) "The second career: perceived social mobility and adjustment among recent army retirees and wives of army retirees." Unpublished doctoral dissertation,

Florida State University.

PLUMB, C. (1973) I'm No Hero. Missouri: Independence Press.

POWERS, I. (1974) "National League of Families and the Development of family services." Pp. 1-10 in H. McCubbin, B. Dahl, P. Metres, Jr., E. Hunter, and J. Plag (eds.), Family Separation and Reunion. Washington, D.C.: U.S. Government Printing Office.

PRICE-BONHAM, S. (1972) "Missing in action men: a study of their wives." International Journal of Sociology of the Family 2: (September).

RAINWATER, L. (1966) "Crucible of identity: the negro lower-class family," Daedalus, XCV (Winter) 172-216.

RAKOFF, V. (1966) "Long-term effects of the concentration camp experience." Viewpoints, 1: 17-21.

RAKOFF, V., J. SIGAL and N. EPSTEIN (1967) "Children and families of concentration camp survivors." Canadian Mental Health, 14: 24-26.

REDL, F. (1969) "Adolescents—Just how do they react?" in G. Caplan and S. Lebovici (eds.) Adolescence: Psychosocial Perspectives. New York: Basic Books, Inc.

REYNOLDS, R.B. (1966) The Officer's Guide. 31st ed., Harrisburg, Pa.: Stackpole Press.

ROBERTS, A.H. and M. ROKEACH (1956) "Anomie, authoritarianism and prejudice: A replication." American Journal of Sociology, LXI (June): 355-358.

ROGERS, C. (1944) "Wartime issues in family counseling." Journal of Marriage and the Family, 68-69, 84.

ROSSI, P.H. (1955) Why Families Move. New York: The Free Press of Glencoe.

RUTLEDGE, H. and P. RUTLEDGE (1973) In the Presence of Mine Enemy. New Jersey: Fleming H. Revell Co.

RYAN, F. and J. BEVILACQUA (1964) "The military family: an asset or a liability." Military Medicine 129:956-959.

SANTROCK, J.W. (1972) "The relation of type and onset of father absence to cognitive development." Child Development, 43: 455-469.

SANUA, V. (1974) "The psychological effects of the Yom Kippur War." Unpublished manuscript, City'College—The City University of New York.

SATIR, V. (1964) Conjoint Family Therapy. Palo Alto, California: Science and Behavior Books.

SATTIN, D. and J. MILLER (1971) "The ecology of child abuse within a military community." American Journal of Orthopsychiatry, 41:675-678.

SAUNDERS, D. (1969) "Poverty in the Army." Social Service Review, 43: 396-405.

SCANZONI, J. (1965) "A Reinquiry Into Marital Disorganization," American Sociological Review, XXIX (August).

——— (1970) Opportunity and the Family. New York: The Free Press.

SCHEIN, E. H. (1957) "Reaction patterns to severe, chronic stress in American Army prisoners of war of the Chinese." Journal of Social Issues, 13: 21-30.

SCHEIN, E.H., W.E. COOLEY and M.T. SINGER (1960) A psychological follow-up of former prisoners of war of the Chinese communists. (Contract No. DA-49-007-MD-754) Cambridge: Massachusetts Institute of Technology.

SCHEIN, E.H., I. SCHNEIR and C.H. BARKER (1961) Coercive persuasion: a socio-psychological analysis of the 'brainwashing' of American civilian prisoners by the Chinese communists. New York: Norton.

SCHMALE, A. (1958) "Relationship of separation and depression to disease." Psychosomatic Medicine 20: 259-277.

SCHROEDER, C.W. (1939) Divorce in a City of 10,000 Population. Peoria, Illinois: Bradley Polytechnic Institute Library.

SCHUETZ, A. (1945) "The homecomer." American Journal of Sociology, 50: 369-376.

SEARS, R.R., L. RAU and R. ALPERT (1965) Identification and child rearing. Stanford: Stanford University Press.

SEGAL, J. (1973) "Therapeutic considerations in planning the return of American POWs to continental United States." Military Medicine, 138: 73-77.

SELLTIZ, C. et al. (1959) Research Methods in Social Relations. Revised ed. New York: Holt, Rinehart and Winston.

SEPLIN, C. (1952) "A study of the influence of father's absence for military service." Smith College Studies in Social Work, 22: 123-124.

SHEA, N. (1954) The Army Wife. 3rd ed. rev., New York: Harper and Bros.

——— (1966) The Army Wife. 4th ed., New York: Harper and Row, Inc.

SHEETS, J.R. (1969) "Times exchange: opinions invited on 'Army brats' . . ." Army Times (March).

SHEPPARD, H.L. (1969) "Aging and manpower development." Pp. 161-200 in Matilda W. Riley, et al. (eds.). Aging and Society, Volume II: Aging and the Professions. New York: Russell Sage Foundation.

——— (1970) "The potential role of social science in the solution of the older worker problem," American Behavioral Scientist, 14: 71-80.

SHERIF, M. and C.W. SHERIF (1964) Reference Groups. New York: Harper and Row.

SIEGEL, S. (1956) Nonparametric Statistics for the Behavioral Sciences. New York: McGraw-Hill Book Company, Inc.

SIGAL, J., and V. RAKOFF (1971) "Concentration camp survival: a pilot study of effects on the second generation." Canadian Psychiatric Association Journal, 16: 393-397.

SIGAL, J., D. SILVER, V. RAKOFF and B. ELLIN (1973) "Some second-generation effects of survival of the Nazi persecution." American Journal of Orthopsychiatry, 43: 320-327.

SIRJAMAKI, J. (1964) "The institutional approach." Pp. 33-50 in H. Christensen, (ed.) Handbook of Marriage and the Family. Chicago: Rand McNally.

SMILANSKY, S. (1975) "Development of the conceptualization of death in children, ages 4-10." Paper presented at the International Conference on Psychological Stress and Adjustment in Time of War and Peace, Tel Aviv, Israel, (January).

SMITH, W.D. (1959) Late School Entrance, Social Acceptance, and Children's School Achievement. Tallahassee, Florida, Florida State University Dept. of Psychology and Institute of Human Development. Unpublished manuscript.

——— and J.S. DEMMING (1958) Pupil Mobility and Adjustment. Tallahassee, Florida, Florida State University Dept. of Psychology and Institute of Human Development. Unpublished manuscript.

SNYDER, J.M. (1967) "Student mobility and achievement." Unpublished Ed.D. dissertation. American University.

→ SOROKIN, P.A. (1927) Social Mobility. New York: Harper and Brothers.

——— (1959) Social and Cultural Mobility. New York: The Free Press of Glencoe.

SPELLMAN, S. (1965) "Orientations toward problem-solving among career military families: a study of the knowledge of available resources in a military community and perception of the social cost of using them for the resolution of family conflict." Unpublished doctoral dissertation, Columbia University.

SPIEGEL, J. (1957) "The resolution of role conflict within the family," in M. Greenblatt, D. Levinson and R. Williams (eds.), The Patient and the Mental Hospital. Glencoe: The Free Press.

SPOLYAR, L. (1973) "The dynamics of grief of wives and families of military personnel missing in action." Medical Service Digest, 24: 20-24.

——— (1974) "The grieving process in MIA wives." Pp. 77-84 in H. McCubbin, B. Dahl, P.

Metres, Jr., E. Hunter, and J. Plag (eds.), Family Separation and Reunion. Washington, D.C.: U.S. Government Printing Office.

SROLE, L.J. (1956) "Anomie, authoritarianism and prejudice." American Journal of Sociology 60 (July): 63-67.

——— (1962) Mental Health in Metropolis. New York: McGraw-Hill.

STANFORD, E.P. (1970) "Retirement anticipation in the military." The Gerontologist 11 (Spring), 37-42.

STEPHENS, W.N. (1961) "Judgments by social workers on boys and mothers in fatherless families." Journal of Genetic Psychology, 99: 59-64.

STERNBERG, T. (1975) "Work of volunteers with bereaved families of the Yom Kippur War." Paper presented at the International Conference on Psychological Stress and Adjustment in Time of War and Peace, Tel Aviv, Israel, (January).

STOLZ, L. (1954) Father Relations of War-Born Children: The Effect of Post-war Adjustment of Fathers on the Behavior and Personality of First Children Born while Fathers were at War. Palo Alto: Stanford University Press.

STRANG, R. (1957) The Adolescent Views Himself. New York: McGraw-Hill Book Co.

STRAUS, M. (1964) "Measuring families." Pp. 335-400 in H. Christensen (ed.), Handbook of Marriage and the Family. Chicago: Rand McNally.

——— (1969) Family Measurement Techniques, 1935-1965. Minneapolis: University of Minnesota Press.

STRAUSS, A.L. (1971) The Contexts of Social Mobility: Ideology and Theory. Chicago: Aldine Publishing Company.

STRYKER, S. (1964) "The interactional and situational approaches." Pp. 125-170 in H. Christensen (ed.), Handbook of Marriage and the Family. Chicago: Rand McNally.

SULLIVAN, H.S. (1953) The Interpersonal Theory of Psychiatry. New York: W.W. Norton & Co., Inc.

SUMMERHAYES, M. (1908) Vanished Arizona, Recollections of My Army Life. J.B. Lippincott.

SUSSMAN, M.B. (1959) "The isolated nuclear family: fact or fiction," Social Problems, VI (Spring) 333-340.

SUSSMAN, M.B. and L. BURCHINAL (1962) "Kin family network: unheralded structure in current conceptualizations of family functioning," Marriage and Family Living, XXIV (August) 231-240.

SVALASTOGA, K. (1964) "Social differentiation." Pp. 530-575 in Robert E. L. Faris (ed.), Handbook of Modern Sociology. Chicago: Rand McNally and Company.

TEICHMAN, Y. (1975) "The stress of coping with the unknown regarding a significant family member." Paper presented at the International Conference on Dimensions of Anxiety and Stress, Oslo (June).

TEICHMAN, Y., SPIEGEL, Y. and TEICHMAN, M. (1975) "Volunteers report about their work with families of servicemen missing in action." Paper presented at the International Conference on Psychological Stress and Adjustment in Time of War and Peace, Tel Aviv, Israel, (January).

TEITZE, C.P. (1942) "Personality disorder and spatial mobility." American Journal of Sociology XLXIII (Jan): 29-40.

TERMAN, L.M. (1938) Psychological Factors in Marital Happiness. New York: McGraw-Hill Book Company, Inc.

The Officer's Guide, 8th ed. (1942) Harrisburg, Pa.: The Military Service Publishing Co.

THOMAS, J.L. (1956) The American Catholic Family. New Jersey: Prentice Hall.

THOMAS, W.I. and D.S. THOMAS (1928) The Child in America. New York: Alfred A. Knopf.

TILLER, P.O. (1961) Father separation and adolescence. Oslo: Institute for Social Research.

TOFFLER, A. (1970) Future Shock. New York: Random House.

TRUNNELL, T.L. (1968a) "The absent father's children's emotional disturbances." Archives of General Psychiatry, 19: 180-188.

––– (1968b) "A review of studies of the psychosocial significance of the absent father." Paper presented at the Western American Psychiatric Association Meeting, Seattle, Washington (August).

TYHURST, J.S. (1957) "The role of transitional states–including disasters–in mental illness," Symposium on Preventive and Social Psychiatry. Washington, D.C.: Walter Reed Army Institute of Research, 149-167.

UDRY, J.R. (1966) "Marital Instability by Race, Sex, Education, Occupation and Income Using 1960 Census Data," American Journal of Sociology, LXXII (September): 203-209.

U.S. Army (1968) "Permanent Changes of Station of Male Military Personnel During the Period March 1, 1967 through February 29, 1968," no. 2568E Office of Personnel Operations, Department of the Army, Washington, D.C.

U.S. Army (1963) Career Attitudes of Wives of Junior Officers. Standards and Systems Office, Washington, D.C.: Office Personnel Operations.

U.S. Army Regulation 608-1 (1965) Army Community Services. Washington, D.C.: Department of the Army (November).

U.S. Bureau of the Census (1966) Current Population Reports, Series P-28, No. 1417, "Special census of [. . .] County, [. . .]: Feb. 7, 1966." Washington, D.C.: Government Printing Office.

––– (1968) Current Population Reports, Series P-25, No. 416, "Estimate of the population by age, race, and sex: July 1, 1968." Washington, D.C.: Government Printing Office.

––– (1969) Current Population Reports, Series P-20, No. 193, "Mobility of the population of the United States: March 1968 to March 1969." Washington, D.C.: Government Printing Office.

––– (1969) Statistical Abstract of the United States. 90th ed. Washington, D.C.: Government Printing Office.

––– (1963) U.S. Census of Population: 1960. Detailed Characteristics. United States Summary, PC(1)-D. Washington, D.C.: Government Printing Office.

U.S. Department of the Army (1973) Selected Demographic Trends, 1952-1972. DAPC-PMP Report No. 50-73-E.

U.S. Department of Labor (1973) Women Workers Today. Employment Standards Administration, Washington, D.C.: Women's Bureau.

U.S. Public Law 89-614 (re medicare provisions for servicemen and their families).

VIDICH, A.J. and STEIN, M.R. (1960) "The dissolved identity in military life," in M. Stein, A. Vidich, and D. White (eds.), Identity and Crisis. Glencoe, Ill.: The Free Press.

VINCENT, C.E. (1967) "Mental Health and the Family," Journal of Marriage and the Family, Vol. 24: 18-39.

Vital and Health Statistics Reports, Final Divorce Statistics, HEW, 1958-1974.

WALLER, W. (ed.) (1940) War and the Family. New York: Dryden Press.

––– (1944) The Veteran Comes Back. New York: Dryden Press.

WALTER, P. (1958) "Military sociology," in J. Roucek (ed.), Contemporary Sociology. New York: Philosophical Library, Inc.

WEBB, E., D.T. CAMPBELL, R.D. SWARTZ, and L. SECHREST (1966) Unobtrusive Measures: Nonreactive Research in the Social Sciences. Chicago: Rand McNally and Company.

WEINBERG, A. (1961) Migration and Belongings. Hague, Netherlands: Martinus Nizhoff.

WESTLING, L. JR. (1973) "Ministry to prisoner of war returnees and their families in the long-term readjustment period: a manual for Navy chaplains." Unpublished doctoral dissertation, San Francisco Theological Seminary.

WHEELER, S. (1961) "Socialization in correctional communities." American Sociological Review 26 (Oct): 697-712.

WHYTE, W. (1956) The Organization Man. New York: Simon and Schuster, Inc.

WIEDER, S. and E. NASHIM (1975) "Parallel reactions of widows and young children following the death of their fathers in the Yom Kippur War." Paper presented at the International Conference on Psychological Stress and Adjustment in Time of War and Peace, Tel Aviv, Israel, (January).

WILENSKY, H.L. (1966) "Measures and effects of mobility." Pp. 98-140 in Neil Smelser and Seymour Lipset (eds.), Social Structure and Mobility in Economic Development. Chicago: Aldine Publishing Company.

WILLIAMS, J. (1971) "Divorce in the population of the United States and in a homogeneous subset of that population (United States Air Force Officers) 1958-1970." Unpublished doctoral dissertation, State College, Mississippi.

WILLIAMS, R. (1960) American Society (2nd ed.) New York: Knopf.

WILLIAMSON, R.C. (1966) Marriage and Family Relations. New York: John Wiley and Sons, Inc.

WILNER, D.M. (1962) The Housing Environment and Family Life. Baltimore: John Hopkins Press.

WOLINS, M. (1954) "Welfare Problems and Services in Berkeley, California," Berkeley Council of Social Welfare and University of California, Berkeley School of Social Welfare. Berkeley, Ca.: (November).

YOUNG, L.L. and D.H. COOPER (1944) "Some factors associated with popularity." Journal of Educational Psychology XXXV: 513-535.

ZELDITCH, M. JR. (1955) "Role differentiation in the nuclear family: a comparative study." In T. Parsons and R.F. Bales (eds.), Family, socialization and interaction processes. Glencoe: Free Press.

ZIMMERMAN, C. and L. CERVANTES (1960) Successful American Families. New York: Pageant Press.

ZIV, A. (1975) "Empirical findings on children's reactions to war stress." Paper presented at the International Conference on Psychological Stress and Adjustment in Time of War and Peace, Tel Aviv, Israel (January).

ZUNIN, L. (1974) "A program for the Vietnam widow: Operation Second Life." Pp. 218-224 in H. McCubbin, B. Dahl, P. Metres, Jr., E. Hunter, and J. Plag (eds.), Family Separation and Reunion. Washington, D.C.: U.S. Government Printing Office.

ZUNIN, L. (1974) "A program for the Vietnam widow: Operation Second Life." Pp. 218-224 in McCubbin, H., Dahl, B., Metres, P. Jr., Hunter, E., and Plag, J. (eds.) Family Separation and Reunion. Washington, D.C.: U.S. Government Printing Office.

ZUNIN, L. and N. BARR (1969) "Therapy program aids servicemen's widows." U.S. Medicine, 5: 12.

ABOUT THE CONTRIBUTORS

Françoise D. Baker is currently employed as a research assistant in the Family Studies Branch of the Center for Prisoner of War Studies, where her primary work includes translations of research conducted by foreign countries on the military family.

Barbara B. Dahl has worked as an editorial assistant for the *Journal of Applied Psychology*. She is presently a research psychologist who has served as Publications Editor and a member of the Family Studies Branch of the Center for Prisoner of War Studies, Naval Health Research Center, since 1973, and is presently Assistant Head of the Family Studies Branch.

Paul F. Darnauer is Social Service Consultant to The Surgeon General, Department of the Army. In addition to his clinical social work experience, he has extensive staff experience in the personnel administration and research areas. He had a significant role in the development of the military Survivor Benefit Plan.

Susan J. Farish is a research assistant for the Family Studies Branch of the Center for Prisoner of War Studies. She is presently in charge of an ongoing project to compile and update bibliographic sources on the subject of veterans and the military family.

Elizabeth M. Finlayson, an associate professor at Madison College, Harrisonburg, Virginia, is the Dean of Summer School, Orientation and Academic Advising. The wife of a career army officer for over twenty years, she completed the requirements of her doctoral program while on an overseas tour. Thus she has had firsthand experience with the special problems of the military wife who attempts to combine her own personal educational and career aspirations with the military's expectations of her as an officer's wife.

Edna J. Hunter is a clinical psychologist who has been affiliated with the Naval Health Research Center since 1967. She devoted five years to research in the areas of the psychophysiology of sleep and the physiological aspects of developmental dyslexia prior to her current efforts in family studies at the Center for PW Studies, where she serves as the Assistant Director for Administration.

Raymond M. Marsh has had extensive experience in planning and implementing social welfare services for military families. His military assignments have included service with the Army General Staff, Headquarters, Department of the Army, and he is currently the Director of the Alcohol and Abuse Prevention Policy in the Office of the Assistant Secretary of Defense for Health and Environment.

Hamilton I. McCubbin is a Captain in the Medical Service Corps of the U.S. Army and is presently Head of the Family Studies Branch and the U.S. Army Liaison to the Center for Prisoner of War Studies of the Naval Health Research Center. In his previous capacities as Chief of Research in a correctional program and Director of a military drug and alcohol program, he has published various articles on military deviance and drug abuse.

Jerry L. McKain is the Social Work Consultant to the United States Army Health Services Command. He is the author of eight articles and two books dealing with the military system and has had extensive clinical, consultative, training, and program development responsibilities during his 15 separate assignments in the military service.

John S. McNeil is Chief Social Worker, U.S. Air Force, and Assistant Chairman, Department of Mental Health, David Grant Medical Center, Travis AFB, California. He has several years of experience as a social worker, and his publications include four articles dealing with the social and emotional impact of military retirement.

Frank F. Montalvo, consultant, has extensive clinical, research, planning and teaching experience in child guidance, family welfare, ethnic studies and mental health information systems and was formerly the Director of the Army's Community Service Program and the Minority Studies curriculum for the Defense Race Relations Institute.

Ronald J. Platte is a Major in the United States Army and is presently Chief, Social Work Service, 2nd General Hospital, Landstuhl, Germany. In addition to post-masters training and experience in the child guidance setting, he specialized in marriage and family relations in his doctoral work. He is a member of the National Association of Social Workers, the Academy of Certified Social Workers, the National Council on Family Relations, and the Society for Hospital Social Work Directors.

Marilyn L. Robertson is presently a research assistant at the Center for Prisoner of War Studies of the Naval Health Research Center. Her present interests and work lie in the areas of coping responses of families to father separation and communication patterns characteristic of family interactions.

Seth W. Spellman is Dean at the Allen Collegiate Center and Professor of Social Welfare, State University of New York at Albany. He is the author of a number of studies dealing with the structure of human service delivery systems, including social work services, education, and the family as a system. He served for many years in the U.S. Army where he was primarily involved in the prevention and treatment of inter-personal and family dysfunction.

John W. Williams, Jr., is a Colonel in the U.S. Air Force and head of the Department of Behavioral Sciences and Leadership at the Air Force Academy. His current research efforts center around the integration of women into previously all-male institutions.

SUBJECT INDEX

Adjustment
emotional 91, 116, 120-123, 264, 324,
335, 339, 348-350, 358
marital 120, 259, 264-267, 272, 274,
276-280, 284-287, 309-311, 326,
357
role see Roles
school, see School Adjustment
social 116, 349-350, 358
to loss 296-297, 306-309, 344, 347, 350,
355, 359, 361, 363, 366-367
to reintegration following separation 117,
321, 328, 336, 347-348 see also, Reintegration
to reunion 117, 321, 326, 338, 346-347,
349, 360, see also, Reunion
to separation 46, 114, 120-122, 321,
326, 328-329, 338, 340, 345-349, see
also, Separation
Adolescent
acting out behavior among 334
formal group involvement of 43, 49,
57-58
friendship patterns of 43, 49, 57-58, 63,
294, 330, 365
peer associations 58-59, 65, 365
school experience of 43, 49, 57, 330
school performance of 49, 54, 56-57, 59,
63
social behavior of 63, 330
values of 64, 340-341, see also California
Test of Personality
Aerospace Defense Command, 224
Age; it's influence upon
participation in volunteer activities, 32
use of help resources 179, 189-194, 198,
201-203, 324
wives' employment patterns 37-38
Alcoholism 121, 218
Alienation 69-71, 75-78, 80-81, 89, 91, 96,
141, 151, 155, 294, 350-352, 362, see
also Anomie; Geographical Mobility
All Volunteer Force 219
Anomie 72-73, 78, 81, 88, 90-91, 362, see
also Srole Anomie Scale
Anxiety

in response to separation 119, 120-123,
324, 355, 358
child 334, 342, 353, 366
wife 119, 123, 324, 358, 363
see also, retirement
Army Community Services 28, 30, 64, 71,
108, 156-157, 312, 354
Army Emergency Relief 181, 313
Army War College 317
Attitude toward Relocation Scale 98-100
Benefits
general military 152-153
retirement 240, 245, 256-257, 259
Bereavement 306-309, 332, 335, 343, 355,
362-363, 366, see also Children, Grief,
Israel
Blackman's Index of Marital Role Tension
79
Broken families 61, 341
California Test of Personality 133-137, 302,
306, 329
Captivity
conditions of 127, 327
coping in 124
hardships of 114, 126, 306, 327
isolation during 127
stresses of 127, 306, 336, 349
Casualty 118-119, 121, 327, 339, see also
Missing in Action, Prisoner of War
Center for Prisoner of War Studies 113-114,
116-117, 126, 133, 138, 291, 304, 317,
346, 357
Champus 245, 318, 345
Child Abuse 359
Child Care 345
Child Rearing 45, 330, 331
Children
adjustment to geographical mobility 45,
61-63, 74, 294, 335, 342, 345, 351,
356
adjustment to separation 115-117, 119,
123-124, 298, 301-302, 329, 333,
347
adjustment to war 296, 333 see also Separations, war-induced; Israel, studies
of behavioral problems 95, 123-124,